# MARXISM AND THE AGRARIAN QUESTION

*Also by Athar Hussain*

MARX'S 'CAPITAL' AND CAPITALISM TODAY
RECENT ECONOMIC REFORMS IN CHINA

*Also by Keith Tribe*

LAND, LABOUR AND ECONOMIC DISCOURSE
GENEALOGIES OF CAPITALISM

# MARXISM AND THE AGRARIAN QUESTION

Second Edition

Athar Hussain
Keith Tribe

© Athar Hussain, Keith Tribe 1981, 1983

All rights reserved. No part of this publication may be reproduced or transmitted, in any form or by any means, without permission

First edition (2-volume hardcover) 1981
Second edition (1-volume paperback) 1983

*Published by*
THE MACMILLAN PRESS LTD
*London and Basingstoke*
*Companies and representatives*
*throughout the world*

ISBN 978-0-333-34994-6      ISBN 978-1-349-06752-7 (eBook)
DOI 10.1007/978-1-349-06752-7

The paperback edition of this book is sold subject to the condition that it shall not, by way of trade or otherwise, be lent, resold, hired out, or otherwise circulated without the publisher's prior consent, in any form of binding or cover other than that in which it is published and without a similar condition including this condition being imposed on the subsequent purchaser

# Contents

*Preface to the Second Edition* vii
*Preface to the First Edition* viii
*Acknowledgements* x

Part 1: German Social Democracy and the Peasantry 1890–1907
1 The Agrarian Question 1
2 Some Aspects of German Agriculture 20
   International Competition in Agriculture 20
   Tariffs 29
   The Prussian Road 40
   Rural Labourers and the Flight from the Land 51
   Rural Indebtedness 58
   Differentiation in the Countryside 60
3 *Landagitation* 72
4 Theoretical Writings on the Agrarian Question 102
5 Social Democracy and the Agrarian Question 133

*Notes to Part 1* 139
*Bibliography* 146

Part 2: Russian Marxism and the Peasantry 1861–1930
Introduction 153
6 Russian Agriculture 1860–1900: Some Effects of the Emancipation Settlement 156
7 Russian Marxism and the Agrarian Question 171
8 The Russian Social Democratic Labour Party and the Development of an Agrarian Programme 206
9 The Russian Peasantry as Object of State Policy, 1906–1929 235
   The 'Wager on the Strong' 238
   The Peasantry 'Take the Land' 247
   NEP and the Conditions for a Worker-Peasant Alliance 256

|     | The 'Agrarian Question' as a Problem of Soviet Administration | 268 |
| --- | --- | --- |
| 10  | Conclusion | 287 |
|     | *Notes to Part 2* | 305 |
|     | *Bibliography* | 314 |
|     | *Index* | 320 |

# Preface to the Second Edition

Written as a single text in 1978–79, this book was split into two volumes according to the principal subject-matter and issued as a hardback in 1981. For this one-volume paperback edition we have restored the original form and taken the opportunity of correcting some errors, but have left the text itself unaltered. While we both might wish to change certain emphases in the concluding chapter, neither felt that these were of a significance to demand a redrafting. Naturally enough if the book were to be written now it might turn out very different; the arguments advanced in the body of the book, however, are we believe valid and defensible, and we do not wish to alter them.

*Keele, September 1982*　　　　　　　　　　　　　　ATHAR HUSSAIN
　　　　　　　　　　　　　　　　　　　　　　　KEITH TRIBE

# Preface to the First Edition

The cases of German and Russian Social Democracy as exemplars of Marxism's treatment of agrarian issues have been selected for study here primarily because the problems that arose gave rise to writings which have today become classical sources of Marxist analysis. Reference to the work of Kautsky and Lenin has become obligatory in discussion of Marxist approaches to agrarian politics; but paradoxically, despite their status as monuments of Classical Marxism, *Die Agrarfrage* and *Development of Capitalism in Russia* are more often referred to in passing than studied in any depth. Furthermore, the habitual treatment of Marxism as a developing system of ideas, rather than a series of discourses developing around specific political and economic issues, obscures the particular value of such textual monuments. Serious study of the Sozialdemokratische Partei Deutschlands (SPD) and the peasantry in the 1890s only began in the 1960s, and there is as yet no work in English dealing with such issues that supersedes Bertrand Russell's *German Social Democracy*. A similar situation exists in the case of Russia, despite the extent of the studies of Bolshevism and Russian Social Democracy. Lenin's agrarian writings, which Harding has recently shown to be seminal, meet with almost universal neglect in such studies.

As a result of this situation the two [now parts] that make up this book are devoted to an exposition and discussion of the manner in which German and Russian Social Democracy confronted a diversity of issues that became known generically as 'the agrarian question'. However, just as the 'Marxism' of German and Russian Social Democrats developed in different ways, so the issues constituting this 'question' were distinct for each movement. The 'agrarian question' that we are to discuss below is not the timeworn problem of the neglect of the peasantry by Marxists, a mythical conception fostered by Mitrany among others. Our examination of the debates and forms of organisation current among German and Russian socialists at the turn of the century will show that on the contrary a number of problems related to the state of agriculture and the condition of the peasantry were a major concern of Marxists.

Indeed, there is so much material available that this book can in no way be treated as an adequate or comprehensive historical analysis of the movements which we examine. Such is in any case not the object: we propose not to write a history of aspects of German and Russian Marxism, but rather select a limited number of problems which either illuminate features of Classical Marxism or raise important issues for agrarian politics and economic organisation.

This book was written as a single text, in which Athar Hussain wrote up the material on the SPD and Keith Tribe the chapters dealing with Russia. The bulk of the manuscript dictated that either serious alterations be made, or it be divided in two; and so, following the latter course, the book appears as two volumes, the first on Germany and the second on Russia, Athar Hussain taking responsibility for the first volume, and Keith Tribe for the second. In each volume, four chapters deal substantively with the issues raised; but as the reader will notice, there is no uniformity between the two volumes in terms of the manner in which the issues have been isolated. This is not the outcome of an authorial division of labour, however, for it should be apparent that the arguments advanced through the two volumes are by and large consistent. The differences in organisation of the material of the two volumes are the result of the difference in the political and economic conditions under which the two movements operated, combined with a consideration of the English language sources available to the reader. In volume 1 therefore the first chapter deals with aspects of the political development of the SPD before in the second chapter providing a lengthy account of the structure of German agriculture in this period. Only in the third chapter is the agrarian policy of the SPD directly considered, dealing with the years 1891–5. Chapter 4 deals with Kautsky's *Agrarfrage*, and this is followed by a brief conclusion to the first volume. In volume 2 the treatment of the structure of the Tsarist agrarian economy in the first chapter is relatively brief, more space being given in chapter 2 to the development of Russian Social Democracy to 1899, the date of publication of Lenin's *Development of Capitalism in Russia*. Chapter 3 considers the role of agrarian politics in the drafting and revision of the programme of the Russian Social Democratic Labour Party (RSDLP) up to 1907, while chapter 4 outlines some aspects of state policy from the Stolypin Reform of 1906 to collectivisation. The continuity of the arguments presented through the two volumes is then emphasised in the conclusion. In addition, there is a reader in preparation by the authors in which translations related to the material of volume 1 will be presented, and it is hoped that this will in some measure compensate for the relatively cursory treatment that some points receive in the present texts.

Finally, in volume 2 some readers might notice that no effort has been made to standardise Russian orthography; in particular, German versions of Russian names are retained. The reason for this is that it was felt that only confusion would result if the names of authors were altered from the form in which they appeared originally to a more acceptable modern form. On the other hand, while one form is consistently used for individual authors, there is no uniformity across persons.

All translation from foreign-language sources found below is the work of the authors.

*Keele, April 1979*                                               ATHAR HUSSAIN
                                                                                      KEITH TRIBE

# Acknowledgements

We would like to thank the following individuals for the help and advice they have offered while we have been working on this book: Dave Blackbourn, Liz Brown, Tony Cutler, Geoff Eley, Les Fishman, Barry Hindess, Paul Hirst, Jill Hodges, Caroline Humphrey, Peter Lawrence.

We would like gratefully to acknowledge the assistance received from the Research Fund of the University of Keele, and also a grant from the SSRC which enabled us to visit the Bayerische Staatsbibliothek in Munich.

# Part 1
# German Social Democracy and the Peasantry 1890–1907

# 1 The Agrarian Question

> The bourgeois and reactionary parties wonder why everywhere among socialists the peasant question has suddenly been placed upon the order of the day. What they should be wondering at, by rights, is that this has not been done long ago. From Ireland to Sicily, from Andalusia to Russia and Bulgaria the peasant is a very essential factor of population, production and political power. (From an article by Engels, *The Peasant Question in France and Germany*.[1])

Engels wrote this article in 1894 shortly before his death. Despite its title, however, the article has very little by way of analysis of the peasantry or agriculture. There, as indeed elsewhere, the peasantry is merely used as a generic term to cover all those rural inhabitants who are neither capitalists nor workers. In fact, the article is a set of directions and protocols about the contents of the agrarian programme of the Social Democratic Party. Most of it is a criticism of the Nantes programme of the *Parti Ouvrier Français* (Guesdists) – the Marxist fraction in the fissured socialist movement in the France of that time – although it was primarily addressed to German socialists. The article was initially published in *Die Neue Zeit*, the theoretical journal of the German Social Democratic Party (SPD); it had the status of a definitive intervention by the theoretical mentor in the debates within the party over the agrarian programme to be appended to the main programme (the Erfurt Programme) and agitational work in rural areas.

The question of agriculture and the peasantry had become an object of discussion and political programme not only in France and Germany but also in Belgium, Italy, Denmark and, of course, Russia. The two main Marxist works written in the 1890s – Kautsky's *Die Agrarfrage* and Lenin's *Development of Capitalism in Russia* – were both concerned with the question of agriculture and the peasantry. So it is in relation to this question that the first additions to the analyses of Marx and Engels were made.

In essence the agrarian question was a political question and it acquired importance with the rise and growth of the parties of the Second International. However, economic and political conditions were not the same in all the countries where the agrarian question was discussed. The Germany of the 1890s was already among the most developed industrial economies and only a third of its population then lived in rural areas, a proportion much lower than one is likely to find in the Third World countries of today. By contrast the majority of the French population at that time lived in rural areas.[2] Moreover, the political conditions were not the same. The countries of Western Europe in which the agrarian question was raised and discussed were all parliamentary democracies of one kind or the other. In those countries, in fact, the rise of parliamentary democracy, of which the formation and growth of the parties of the Second International was a necessary component, and the posing of the agrarian question were closely related. Conditions in Russia were different. Though there was no parliamentary democracy in Russia the interest in agriculture and the peasantry was, none the less, political. That the political discussion in Russia was centred around the question of peasantry and political change presupposed a change in economic and political conditions in the countryside. We leave aside the case of Russia for later discussion and turn to the relation between parliamentary democracy and the agrarian question with reference to Germany.

If the unification of Germany in 1871 was an important political event in European history, so too was the spectacular growth of the SPD from the middle 1880s onwards. Like the Unification, its effects were not limited to the German frontiers. The Second International was anchored in the SPD, owed its prestige and political effectivity to German Social Democracy and, unlike its predecessor, the International Working Man's Association (the First International), it had political stature, which it owed to its constituent political parties. As a matter of fact, the First International never went beyond the stage of being an assemblage of socialist factions and sects of different varieties.[3] Indeed it could not go beyond that stage for mass socialist parties had yet to come into existence.

Socialist parties of the Second International were the first mass political parties and they played a central role in the development and extension of parliamentary democracy in European countries. At the turn of the century the SPD was a model mass party – a party committed to securing the widest possible membership on the basis of its political programme. In its functioning the party pioneered devices which have since become common: the holding of annual conferences to discuss the programme and the tactics of the party, the regular election of party leaders by the rank and file, the financing of the party through contributions from its members. In contrast to the SPD other political parties in Germany duplicated established hierarchies: the leadership of those parties was automatically assumed to be a privilege of notables from appropriate walks of life.[4]

In terms of its organisation the SPD represented a social innovation in Germany, for it departed from existing social divisions, ranks and hierarchies when it grouped together individuals under the banner of the party programme. It did establish its own hierarchy however; not only in German history but also in the history of Marxism the SPD occupies a nodal position, since it is through this party that Marxism came to be an important political force. This is the main reason why we have chosen Germany – in particular the SPD – as one of the two cases for studying the relationship between Marxism and the agrarian question.

But Marxism was not always a dominant ideology within the SPD. The party itself was founded in 1875 in Gotha in the form of the union of the two socialist factions in Germany at that time; one founded by Lassalle and the other allied to the First International and in touch with Marx and Engels, but both with fairly similar programmes.[5] The union was based on the Gotha programme which has achieved notoriety due to its severe critique by Marx.

Marx's critique, which questions thematic statements as well as specific demands of the programme, was addressed to the leaders of the Marxist faction (Bebel, Liebknecht), but it was not made public until 1891 when the SPD had formally decided to replace the programme.[6] Marx and Engels objected to Lassalle for his laws: the *iron law of wages* (left to themselves wages cannot rise beyond the absolute minimum), for his sweeping generalisations (all classes except the working class are reactionary), his collaboration with Bismarck and his belief that substantial social and economic changes can be accomplished by converting the personnel in positions of power to the cause, e.g. the emperor.[7] The Lassallean influence pervades the Gotha programme and Marx's critique of it is essentially a critique of Lassalle.

Though the programme does not call for collaboration with the Government, it is based on the assumption which was common (and not just among bourgeois reformers in Germany of that time) that substantial reforms can be accomplished through the agency of the existing institutions of the state. One of the things which Marx strongly objects to in the Gotha programme is the set of demands addressed to the state to help establish cooperatives and to provide equal elementary education etc. For Marx and Engels believed that a change in the form of government was the necessary precondition of significant economic and social change in Germany. To what extent reform and social change could be accomplished within the existing structure of the government remained a central question within the SPD. It is the differences in the answers to this question which divided the party later at the time the revisionist controversy broke out in the late 1890s, when Bernstein as well as others set out to question the basic premises of the Erfurt programme.

The party did not, however, enjoy the period of legal existence for long after its foundation. Bismarck, with the approval of the Reichstag, banned all Social Democratic organisations and publications on the excuse that social democrats engineered the attempt on the life of the Emperor in 1878. But the real reason was the growing popularity of the Social Democrats. Social Democratic organisations were constantly harassed by the authorities before, during, and after the period of illegality, so the banning of the party was part of the wider strategy to hinder the work of the party.[8] Nevertheless, the ban left an important loophole: it did not disqualify known Social Democrats from contesting federal elections. Thus the SPD, despite being an illegal organisation, contested federal elections and it was the number of votes cast for Social Democrats in the elections which provided the index of the popularity of the party during the 1880s. After the initial setback the SPD quickly adapted itself to illegality; it built an elaborate organisation to distribute Social Democratic literature and devised ingenious ways to conduct agitation and propaganda. From the middle of the 1880s onwards the party steadily increased its share of the votes in the Reichstag elections. The Anti-Socialist Law did not stop the growth of Social Democracy, therefore, but it did restrict the incidence of Social Democratic propaganda and limit the scope of the party's work.[9]

The banning of the party did not change its political strategy and orientation. Socialist propaganda, education and the building of a mass base remained as before the main tasks. Soon after being outlawed, however, the SPD did shorten the stipulation from the Gotha programme that it would struggle for socialism through 'all legal means' to 'all means'. But the illegal work of the party – which included practically everything except contesting elections and the participation of the SPD members of the Reichstag in parliamentary proceedings – never took the form of insurrectionary tactics. In fact, during the period of the Anti-Socialist law those who favoured insurrectionary tactics left the party to form a separate anarchist organisation. So far as the general policy of the party was concerned the main opposition was not between legal and illegal work but between the building of a mass party, on the one hand, and the formation of a tightly knit group committed to insurrectionary tactics, on the other. But the second option was never a serious alternative within the party. Parliamentary democracy in Bismarckian Germany was feeble and the Reichstag had very limited powers; despite all this the SPD had no alternative but to be a parliamentary party, for the election campaigns were the most effective means of mass propaganda. As a matter of fact, the banning of the party increased the importance of election campaigns and participation in parliamentary proceedings as a means of disseminating the Social Democratic programme. Illegality had put severe limitations on the distribution of printed material and the organisation of meetings.[10]

The SPD always remained a parliamentary party in the sense that parliamentary elections and proceedings remained central to its strategy, if not as a means of bringing about change and reforms then as a means of extending the network of the party. In fact, this has not been peculiar to the SPD but has been in general true for socialist and communist parties of Western Europe. Contrary to popular belief, therefore, the controversy surrounding Bernstein's revision of the basic doctrines of the party was not one about whether the party should take a parliamentary or non-parliamentary road. Rather it revolved around a number of different issues: economic tendencies of capitalism, the likelihood of the breakdown of capitalism, the proletarianisation of the middle strata and coalition with other parties to bring about reforms. In fact some of the issues (such as the first two), had by themselves no discernible immediate implications for the policy of the party. Others, like coalition with other political parties and the likelihood of bringing about economic and social reforms, presupposed that the party would remain a parliamentary party as it had been in the past. The controversy in these cases was about the tactics of a parliamentary party. For the purposes of the argument in this book, however, our primary concern is not that the revisionist questioning presupposed the importance of parliamentary work to the party rather than argued for it, but that the discussion of the agrarian question and work in the countryside took place in the context of parliamentary politics.

The Anti-Socialist Law did not change the nature of the party but it did have two important effects: it strengthened the urban and industrial bias of the party and, secondly, it led to the eclipse of Lassallean ideology within the party. The Lassallean influence, however, lingered on in the person of individuals like Vollmar.[11]

In its composition and orientation the SPD, since its foundation, remained a party of town dwellers as well as of industrial workers. The bias was clear at the level of ideology and programme. For the Gotha programme proclaimed that 'The emancipation of labour must be the work of the working class, in contrast to which all other classes are but one reactionary mass'. The first part of the proclamation is effectively the same as the opening sentence of the General Rules of the First International, which Marx helped to draft, while the second part was a Lassallean addition and was violently attacked by Marx. The urban and industrial bias of the party was, however, not exclusively due to Lassalle's influence, nor was it premised on the treatment of all classes other than the working class as one reactionary mass. The bias is there in the Erfurt programme too. For the preamble of this programme, which charted the trajectory of capitalism from crises to the breakdown, is based on the assumption that of all the classes only the working class is consistently revolutionary. In addition the specific demands of the programme were addressed to either the democratisation of state apparatuses, electoral reforms, extension of the domain of representative government and so on or merely to the economic interests of the working class.

The Erfurt programme was a Marxist programme and it therefore took the working class to be revolutionary on the grounds that it did not own the means of production, and in addition had no interest in owning them, employed as it was in the processes where the means of production were used collectively rather than individually by each worker. Thus in the fight for socialism or the collective ownership of the means of production, the underlying assumption was that the working class is pre-eminent by very virtue of its social position. It should be emphasised, however, that the organisation and practical work of the party was not completely mapped out by its programme and ideology. In those domains the bias was as much towards urban inhabitants in general as it was towards the industrial workers. The party recruited its militants among industrial workers as well as other urban citizens; and it was towards these two sections of the population that its propaganda was directed. The essential point is that in the conditions which existed in Bismarckian Germany a socialist party had to be an urban as well as a proletarian party – and that not just for ideological reasons, for the factory and the city were the places which brought together a large number of individuals, thereby providing the possibility for the formation and continuation of a mass political organisation. The rural areas with the spatial dispersion of their population and their lack of a complete separation between the household and the place of work – hence the absence of individual freedom which goes with it – did not provide a fertile ground for the establishment of political organisations that did not duplicate the existing social differences and hierarchies.

The Anti-Socialist Law reinforced the urban bias of the party. Initially after the passing of the Law the SPD had to restrict its activities to the areas where it had already built up support, and such areas were invariably urban. Even later, during the period of illegality, when the support for the party had started growing, it still remained easier in urban rather than rural areas to get away with distributing Social Democratic literature and organising meetings under the façade of cultural and political organisations. In fact, the staging of social and cultural events under the Social Democratic umbrella remained an important feature of the SPD's work even after the expiry of the Law. However, according to police reports of the mid and late 1880s the SPD workers had started to venture out into rural areas adjacent to towns. But the proportion of rural votes for the party even in the elections of 1890 remained either small or negligible.[12]

As we said above, the other feature of the period of illegality was the rapid disappearance of the Lassallean influence on the ideological plane. This took a number of different forms: the decision to replace the Lassallean Gotha programme, although first taken in 1887, was not carried out till 1891 when the party had become legal.[13] Besides that, Marxism became dominant in party publications like *Sozialdemokrat* (edited by Bernstein) and *Die Neue Zeit* (edited by Kautsky).

Though Marx and Engels together with Lassalle were regarded among its founding fathers their respective relations to the socialist movement in Germany were not the same. Marx and Engels were never more than theoretical mentors to the movement and their relations to it never went beyond correspondence with some of its leaders. Lassalle, on the other hand, was never much of a theorist but he was an influential publicist and organiser. In fact, it was Lassalle who popularised Marx and Engels in the Germany of the 1860s and it was he who helped organise the first labour organisation in 1863, a constituent organisation of the SPD. Lassalle died in 1864, well before the foundation of the party, but throughout the 1870s and even later he was popularly remembered in Social Democratic circles and his works were widely read.[14] It was because of Lassalle's popularity that Marx's critique of the Gotha programme was not made public later.[15]

What did Lassalleanism consist of and what did its disappearance actually signify? There were, as we indicated earlier, certain general laws, propositions and types of demand associated with Lassalle and Lassalleanism; but of these only two are directly relevant for our purpose: first, the importance accorded to the establishment of the 'ideal' social and economic organisation (producers, cooperatives, for Lassalle) and, second, the implicit belief that substantial social and economic reforms could be accomplished within the confines of existing apparatuses of the state.

Marx poured scorn on the very project of building the institutions of socialism under the existing state. The establishment of cooperatives, Marx argued, may be a worthy objective but it has nothing to do with the struggle for socialism, especially when done with the help of state aid. The idea of forming cooperatives or other such 'ideal' organisations was not peculiar to Lassalle; it was widespread among the large variety of associations which came to constitute the socialist movement. Schulze–Delitsch in the Germany of the 1850s had founded a large number of workingmen's friendly societies and these societies had a considerable following among the higher class of artisans and hand craftsmen. These societies prospered but they soon lost the political significance that they had as organisations of social reform and they drifted away from the socialist movement.[16] What Marxism did was to shift the attention away from all projects of the construction of 'ideal' social structures. In general Marxists regarded the cooperative movement either as an example of well-meaning but misguided utopianism or with suspicion. For instance, Kautsky in *Die Agrarfrage* dismissed agricultural cooperatives on the grounds that they are not associations of equal producers, but rather a mechanism for perpetuating existing inequalities in the countryside. A consequence of the Marxist position is that whatever movements of cooperation in agriculture have developed, they have done so as non-Marxist strands in the socialist movement.[17]

Marxist attitude towards cooperatives was premised on the general political postulate that a change in the form of government and the capture of political power by socialists is necessary before any economic change in the direction of socialism could be affected. The priority placed on political change was what distinguished Marxists from Lassalleans and from the followers of Proudhon in the First International, about which we shall have something to say later.

The triumph of Marxism over Lassalleanism within the SPD had two important effects: first, it stopped basing the demands in its programmes on the future economic organisation of socialism. Second, the party became hostile to the measures which led to an increase in the power of the Government. These included measures like nationalisation – even the nationalisation of land – subsidies and so on.

During the 1880s, the period of banishment of the SPD, reforms through extension of the power of the Government came to be classified as State Socialism and were clearly separated from socialism. The call for such reforms came to be exclusively associated with *Kathedersozialisten* (socialists of the chair) – a group of university professors who argued that it was the Government which should take the lead in solving social problems and drew up a menu of reforms for the Government to carry out. In the 1870s some of the *Kathedersozialisten*, like Wagner, had considerable influence among Social Democrats, but later on orthodox opinion in the SPD became very hostile to any increase in economic intervention by the Government. For that reason orthodox theorists of the party, especially Kautsky, were referred to as *Manchestermänner* (Men of Manchester).[18] This hostility had important effects both on the Erfurt programme and the discussions of the agrarian question in the 1890s, as we shall see in chapter three.

For our purposes what the triumph of Marxism during the period of illegality meant was that the agrarian question and the party's work in the countryside – among the first issues to be discussed after the expiry of the Anti-Socialist Law – had to be discussed within the parameters of Marxism. But Marxism had little to say about peasantry or agriculture, and the article by Engels (quoted at the beginning of this chapter), which appeared at the height of controversy around the proposed agrarian programme of the SPD, was meant to fill the gap.

It is not that the socialist movement noticed the peasantry and agriculture and began to talk about them for the first time in the 1890s. The question of the ownership of agricultural land was more or less a constant subject of discussion in the First International during its short and precarious existence in the 1860s. The divisions were clear cut. In general, Proudhonists or Mutuellistes, as they were called, supported peasant property while Marxists or collectivists, in contrast, supported the nationalisation of land on the ground that it is no different from any other means of production. The nationalisation of land was first discussed in the Lausanne congress of 1867 and again a year later in the Brussels congress when the International, despite the protests of the Proudhonists, passed a resolution in favour of the nationalisation and leasing of land to cooperatives rather than individual cultivators. And then, finally, the principle of the nationalisation of land and its collective control was reaffirmed in the Basle congress of 1869, when the International adopted the collectivist position as its own.[19]

But the opposition between the ideals of self-subsistent peasantry and collective control of all means of production, including land, had nothing to do with either practical work in the countryside or immediate political struggles. In fact it was part of a general discussion about the forms and strategy of the International. The opposition between Mutuellistes and Collectivists over the nationalisation of land did not so much concern the organisation of political struggles as it did the importance of political activity. The Proudhonists wanted the International to concentrate on building self-help societies in the cities and peasant cooperatives in the countryside. The Collectivists, on the other hand, did not have an alternative form of organisation to counterpose to self-help societies and cooperatives.

It is true that they would have argued in favour of large scale production controlled by the workers but that is not essential. The essential point about the Collectivist position was that it accorded primacy to political struggles rather than to building ideal forms of organisation. For Collectivists political struggles meant primarily the building of political parties, the struggle to change the form of government and to improve the economic conditions of workers. All these requirements and the emphasis on political struggles may seem fairly obvious now, but only because all these things have happened since then. But to Proudhonists at that time these were not only unnecessary but diversionary. In fact, Proudhonists were against meddling in any kind of political activity.

From what is said here Proudhonism may just seem like a variant of Lassalleanism. There is indeed an overlap between the two in that both gave central importance to the building of cooperatives and self-help societies. The overlap was not accidental for initially the cooperative movement was a major component of the socialist movement, and it was only later when the socialist movement came to be embodied in political parties that the cooperative movement either became separated from it or turned into its appendage. There are also important differences between Lassalle and Proudhon, for Lassalle did regard political struggles, especially struggles for universal suffrage, as being crucial and he had no love or admiration for the peasantry.

Its denigration of political activities led to the defeat of Proudhonism in the First International and its eclipse in the socialist movement later. The converse is true for Marxism. It is not the theoretical sophistication of Marxism nor the fact that Marxism, as its followers have always claimed, is anchored to a science rather than to an ideology or a utopia, but rather the priority that Marxism gave to political struggles, which was responsible for the dominating position it came to occupy within European socialist parties. The political struggles to which Marx and Marxists gave pre-eminence were of a particular form and they had to be conducted through specific institutions. The dispute between Bakunin and his followers, on the one hand, and Marxists, on the other, makes it clear that the emphasis on political struggle did not mean any support for insurrectionary activities intended to overturn the state. The emphasis instead was on the formation of socialist political parties and the conduct of political struggles through them rather than by factions or groups of politically motivated individuals.

This claim, though seemingly uncontroversial, is in fact paradoxical. It is well known that for Marx and for Marxists political struggles are in fact class struggles and therefore it is classes, rather than political parties, parliaments, governments, etc that are the real subjects of political activity. This is obvious for instance in the opening sentence of the General Rules of the First International which Marx drafted, i.e.: 'That the emancipation of the working class must be conquered by the working class itself.' We cannot go into the assessment of the Marxist analysis of classes here for it has been done elsewhere.[20] The point is that proclamations like the one above do not have any direct implications for political activity. For strictly speaking classes do not do anything; they do not have political programmes, they do not have a strategy nor do they fight battles, even in their own interest or for their own emancipation. So what is pertinent to the claim here is not general statements concerning classes and class struggles but positions on the kind of organisation which should be formed. Marx and Marxists came to emphasise the importance of the formation of a political party at a time when the field of political activity in European countries was being reconstituted around parliamentary democracy. An important component of that reconstitution was the appearance of a new category of political agents, namely political parties.

This appears to have taken us far away from our general discussion of the peasantry and agriculture in the First International. The point which needs emphasising is that the principle of the nationalisation of land which Marx and Marxists favoured and which the First International accepted did not have any immediate political bearing, and it could not furnish an adequate basis for the formulation of agrarian programmes. In fact, the demand for the nationalisation of land did not occupy an important place in the Marxist agrarian programmes formulated at the turn of century. In most cases the demand was left out altogether, not because the Marxist parties finally came round to recognising the 'human weakness' for property in land (as Mitrany in his *Marx Against The Peasant* suggests), but because the political questions concerning the demand were not answered in the first place.

Though the issue of the nationalisation of land was discussed in relation to the question of whether or not private property in land is consistent with socialism, Marx did not regard the demand as socialist. On the contrary he regarded the nationalisation of land as an economic necessity under capitalism and as something which could well be demanded by a bourgeois liberal party. The argument runs as follows: given the fact that the total cultivable area is fixed by natural factors, an increase in demand for agricultural goods arising out of an increase in population can only be satisfied through a more rational and intensive cultivation of the existing land. But according to the main premise of the argument rational cultivation is inconsistent with private property in land. Underlying the alleged inconsistency is the assumption that rational cultivation requires large units of production as well as qualified personnel. When land is owned privately, the argument is, distribution of the cultivated area into units of cultivation is less affected by the requirements of rational cultivation than by factors such as the forms of inheritance, the pressure of population, etc. The result is that in a number of cases farms are smaller than those which are required for efficient cultivation. Similarly, the cultivators may be those who happen to own the land and who know little about the methods of cultivation.[21]

In general terms the case against private property in land is that the existing distribution of land, either among individuals or among farms is not what is required for efficient cultivation, and that private property helps to perpetuate that distribution. Nationalisation of the land would allow the technical requirements of efficient cultivation to determine the distribution of land among farms and persons. The nature of these arguments is important. The case against private property in land is technical and as such it is no different from the arguments of agronomists when they point out why certain forms of property, for example communal property, are a barrier to the efficient use of land,[22] but the case in favour of nationalisation is not positive; it rests on the shortcomings of private property. National ownership is not defined therefore by its positive features, but as the complement of private ownership.

The technical argument is not the only one which Marx uses to explain why the nationalisation of land is possible under capitalism. The other type of argument is distributive. Rent on land is part of surplus value and it arises because the quantity of land is fixed and is owned by a specific group of individuals (absolute rent) and, in addition, because land is not of homogeneous quality (differential rent). The possibility of the nationalisation of land under capitalism rests on the fact that the condition of existence of absolute rent is private property in land, and that, moreover, rent is deduction from profit and it is thus paid by capitalists. So in the context of this argument nationalisation simply means the abolition of a particular category of income.[23] The two arguments are not mutually exclusive; in fact, they complement each other.

Both the arguments about why the nationalisation of land is possible and may even be necessary under capitalism leave the political questions unanswered. For whom is the nationalisation of land a functional necessity? Which political force fights for nationalisation? What is the pertinence of the nationalisation of land to different sections of the rural population? Is there any reason to suppose that the nationalisation of land will lead to the rational cultivation of land? These questions are important for the nationalisation of land is an eminently political measure. As a matter of fact both the arguments rest on particular assumptions which are not always valid.

The first argument, for instance, rests on the assumption that land, once nationalised, will be distributed among farms and persons by, for example, a directorate of agronomists. But one cannot attribute any particular distribution to the nationalised land; its distribution will crucially depend on the nature of the state. The national ownership of land in the legal sense has not been a rarity nor is it something utopian. There is national ownership of land in socialist countries and apart from that, at the time when the SPD was discussing the agrarian question, a fair proportion of land in Wilhelmine Germany was nationally owned, in the sense of belonging to the Crown. The national ownership of land does not necessarily imply large units of cultivation, as it does in the Soviet Union or in China; it has also existed in peasant economies where land is parcelled out in small lots to peasants. Under the system of land tenure known as the Ryotwari system, which has existed in parts of India, the land belongs to the Government while peasants – most of them either small or middle peasants – have inheritable possession of the land. Now it is clear that one cannot associate either a particular form of organisation of farms, or the distribution of land among farms, with nationally-owned land. The delegates to the congresses of the First International were indeed aware of this, since they recommended not only the nationalisation but also the leasing of the nationalised land to cooperatives rather than to individual cultivators. But the fact is that if one cannot associate a particular form of farm organisation and land tenure with national ownership of land, then neither can one associate a particular economic effect like rational cultivation with it. But then Marx's argument that the nationalisation of land becomes a functional necessity under capitalism at a certain stage is not valid.

The second argument – the distributive argument – also rests on a special assumption, i.e. landlords are separate from those who use land.[24] For the existence of pure rentiers is necessary if one is to talk of rent as being a burden on capitalists and of a resulting contradiction between capitalists and landowners, as Marx does. In fact, in his discussion of rent Marx relies heavily on the English case, the case where the leasing of land is common and thus rent is a distinct category of income which accrues to a group of agents who do not play any direct part in the cultivation of the soil. The important feature of the English case is that there exists then a section in the countryside who may well be in favour of the nationalisation of land, namely the cultivators. But by the same reasoning when land is owner- rather than lessee-cultivated it is not at all clear who in the countryside might favour the measure. Really the argument in general terms is that the nationalisation of land is a political measure, and thus it has to have some political force behind it if it is to be put in practice.

It is clear that there is no reason to assume, as Marx seems to, that the demand for the nationalisation of land is economically and politically relevant to all capitalist societies. In fact Engels does acknowledge this in a preface to *The Peasant War in Germany* when he talks about the decision of the First International which we referred to earlier:

> Here we come to the famous decision of International Working Men's Association in Basle that it is in the interest of society to transform landed property into common national property. This resolution was adopted mainly for countries where there is big landed property, and where, consequently, these big estates are operated by one master and many labourers. This state of affairs is still largely predominant in Germany, and, therefore, next to England, the decision was most timely precisely for Germany. (Marks and Engels *Selected Works*, vol. II pp. 164–5)

The implication is clear that the demand for nationalisation of land is not relevant to the economies where small to medium peasantry dominates; and for Engels the demand is more political than economic because he sees the nationalisation of land as a means of undermining the power of landlords and estate owners.

There are indeed, as is obvious by now, important inconsistencies and lacunae in the discussion of the nationalisation of land in Marx and Engels.

The point, however, is not simply to register these but also to use them to indicate why Marxist parties did not frame their agrarian programmes around the demand for the nationalisation of land. To start with the Guesdistes, the Marxist fraction in the French socialist movement, did include the nationalisation of land as a major demand in their Le Havre programme of 1880, but the demand took no account of the differences in the countryside; it simply called for the expropriation of private property in land and the collective use of land. Moreover, it did not indicate what institutional form the collective use of land would take. However, in successive congresses the demand for expropriation was watered down out of recognition for concrete conditions in the countryside and the hostility which the demand gave rise to. In fact, the Nantes programme of the Guesdistes, passed in 1894, did not even mention the nationalisation of peasant property and its collective use.[25] By the 1890s it became established that the demand for nationalisation did not apply to peasant property and Engels reaffirmed this in his *Peasant Question in France and Germany*.

The demand for land nationalisation did not figure in the programme of the SPD at all. Those who favoured the peasantry were naturally against the nationalisation of land but the orthodox, such as Kautsky, were opposed to it too. Kautsky, the guardian of the orthodoxy within the SPD, even opposed the nationalisation of the big estates to the east of the Elbe – a measure which Engels earlier had regarded necessary in order to break the power of the estate owners. But Kautsky had good Marxist reasons to be opposed to the measure. For the argument was that estate owners, or Junkers, already had considerable influence on the functioning of the state apparatuses, so the nationalisation of land and the consequent leasing of land by a state agency would not undermine their political power and might even consolidate it and work to the Junkers' advantage.[26] So the demand for the nationalisation of land was regarded as inappropriate even in Germany – a country for which the demand was meant to be timely.

The result was that the demand for the nationalisation of land under capitalism just dropped out of the socialist agrarian programmes of the 1890s. Bolsheviks did include it in their programme of 1906 but the demand was premised on political revolution and a complete overhaul of the state apparatuses. But the leaving out of the demand did not mean any support for private property in land; for the orthodox opinion, as Engels reiterated in his *Peasant Question*, still remained that private property in land, which included both large private estates and peasant property, was inconsistent with socialism.

This principle did not have any direct bearing on the agrarian programmes, however, for they were specifically meant to be programmes to be implemented under capitalist conditions; but it did affect what was central, namely the discussion concerning the attitude socialist parties should adopt *vis à vis* the peasantry. For Engels and for the orthodoxy within the SPD, not only was peasant property inconsistent with socialism but also doomed to disappear soon.

> It is the duty of our party to make clear to the peasants again and again that their position is absolutely hopeless so long as capitalism holds sway, that it is absolutely impossible to

preserve their holdings as such, and that capitalist large scale production is absolutely sure to run over their impotent and antiquated system of small scale production as a train runs over a pushcart. (*Peasant Question in France and Germany*, p. 472)

The imminence of the disappearance of the peasantry was taken to imply that there is no point in a socialist party trying to support or prop up the peasant property which is meant to be inconsistent with socialism in the first place.

The assumption of the imminent disappearance of the peasantry was not peculiar to those who wanted the socialist programme to remain neutral to the peasantry – contrary to what Mitrany's *Marx Against The Peasant* may suggest, neither Marx nor Engels nor any Marxist in the 1890s ever suggested a programme directed against the peasantry. For example the Nantes programme of the Guesdistes which Engels criticised also assumed that the peasantry was about to disappear but, on the contrary, it took that as a ground for making demands to 'rescue' the peasantry, e.g. by writing off debts, decreasing the rate of interest, etc. Whether or not the peasantry is disappearing and whether or not Social Democracy should support peasant property were the issues which divided the SPD in its discussion of the agrarian question in the 1890s. The revisionist position was that the peasantry was not only managing to survive but even prospering under capitalism and there were good reasons for supporting the peasantry. But we leave this for further discussion in chapter three.

Apart from Engels' *Peasant Question* and Marx's comments on nationalisation there were precious few analyses to guide the Marxist discussion of the agrarian question in the 1890s. There are occasional comments about the nature of the peasantry as class in *The Eighteenth Brumaire* and besides that a substantial portion of *Capital* vol. III, first published in 1894, is devoted to the discussion of rent – occasionally in that connection it talks of the different forms of organisation of production in agriculture. But these writings were not of much use. For it was neither the peasantry as class nor rent as category of income which was at issue in the agrarian question. The agrarian question was composed of a set of questions which the Social Democratic parties faced: how to win the electoral support of the peasantry, which section of the rural population should the party try to appeal to and on what basis?

Within the SPD a number of events coincided which gave a particular significance to the discussion of the agrarian question within the party. These events, which we mentioned earlier, were: the substitution of a Marxist for a non-Marxist programme, the start of the political work in the countryside (or *Landagitation* as it was called) and later the discussion of the political strategy of the party as part of the post-mortem on the *Landagitation* and the formulation of an agrarian programme which in fact never materialised. 'Reformism' and 'revisionism' first broke out in the party in relation to the discussion of agriculture and the peasantry. It was not Bernstein who invented revisionism; it could be said that he systematised the discussions which had already taken place in the party. But before going into the details of these discussions we first turn to the structure of German agriculture in the last quarter of the nineteenth century.

# 2 Some Aspects of German Agriculture

The aim of this chapter is not so much to provide an even coverage of German agriculture as to focus on some of its particular aspects. The features which we have chosen to discuss in this chapter are either directly relevant to the issues, policies and discussion which together constitute the agrarian question, or those which occupy a central place in Marxist analyses of the development of capitalist agriculture. The discussion of the Prussian reforms of the beginning of the nineteenth century is an example of the latter. In our analyses we have not restricted ourselves to any particular category of literature; we have drawn freely on both Marxist and non-Marxist literature. However, wherever a particular feature has a special significance in Marxist analyses we summarise and assess the relevant Marxist arguments. The coverage of Marxist analyses in this chapter is patchy; we shall have more to say about them later in chapters 3 and 4, especially in the latter. The discussion of this chapter is kaleidoscopic in nature; in order to emphasise this what we have done is to divide the chapter into sub-sections, each dealing with a particular aspect.

## International Competition in Agriculture

The emergence of an international market in agricultural commodities and its effects furnished the background against which the agrarian question was raised and discussed in the SPD. Not only was the protection of domestic agriculture a major political issue in the 1890s but also it was capitalised on by the conservative political parties and other organisations. In 1892 the notorious Bund der Landwirte (Farmers' League), about which we shall have quite a lot to say later, was founded; the Bund campaigned vociferously for protection from cheap agricultural imports and indeed did achieve notable successes. The campaign of the Bund, however, went well beyond the demand for tariffs and thus higher prices for agricultural commodities. Soon after its formation it managed to carve out a place for itself as the representative of not only big farmers, who dominated its leadership, but also of peasants and small farmers.[1] The Bund and its political allies, the conservative political parties, were not the only political force in the countryside. The Catholic Zentrum (the Centre Party) had an important following in South and West Germany, in fact the areas of small farms and the middle peasantry.[2] The general point is that when the SPD came to discuss the agrarian question the countryside was already dominated politically either by the conservative parties or by the Zentrum; and the issue of tariffs and protection from cheap agricultural imports furnished one of the grounds for the emergence of an anti-socialist alliance between these parties.[3]

It was not just Germany but also other countries of Western Europe – France, Britain and Denmark – which felt the impact of international competition and had to accommodate themselves to the extensive market in agricultural commodities which had developed in the last quarter of the nineteenth century. In fact the impact was sufficiently widespread and strong to be generally referred to in the literature as the crisis of European agriculture. The creation of the international market itself was a result of not one but a number of different factors, some of which were interrelated.

First among these was the extension of the area under cultivation in the US, Russia, Eastern Europe and India. The largest expansion took place in the US where the end of the Civil War and the passing of the Homestead Act (which granted allotments of free land to settlers) led to a massive increase of the cultivated area, and to a lesser degree a similar expansion took place in Russia in the 1860s.[4] Given the immense size of both countries and the fact that virgin lands were far away from the centres of consumption in North-Western and Central Europe, the expansion was contingent on the development of transport, both internal (the railway network) and international (mainly shipping).[5]

In general terms what the extension in the transport network and the related decrease in the cost of transportation did was to increase the area on which a centre of consumption could draw. There was indeed international trade in agricultural commodities before the spread of the railways and the introduction of steam ships; but in the first half of the nineteenth century Britain was the only major European country which regularly depended on imported grain. And even in the case of Britain the initial dependence on imported grain was minor compared to what became the rule later in the last quarter of the century. The point in fact is that a heavy dependence on imported grain was just not feasible, for neither the existing transport facilities nor the surplus of grain left for sale would have permitted it.[6]

Besides the factors on the supply side – the development of the transport network and the increase in cultivated area – there were also important factors on the demand side which led to the extension of the international market. With a few notable exceptions all European countries followed the same pattern: either full or near self-sufficiency in food coupled in some cases with exportable surplus to start with, then agricultural production not keeping pace with the increase in domestic demand connected with increase in population and incomes, and finally dependence on imported agricultural commodities. The pattern when specified in fine detail has not been identical and obviously has not coincided in time in different countries. France has been one notable exception among European countries because, except for a brief period in the last quarter of the nineteenth century, she has been self-sufficient in the main items of food. Apart from France, however, Britain, Germany, Denmark and later Russia, Romania and Hungary have all followed the pattern in its general outline. And today we see the repetition of the same pattern in the Third World; there are a large number of Third World countries which were once net-exporters but are now net-importers of grain.

The point, however, is not to enunciate a historical law but to indicate that the extension of the international market in agricultural commodities was as much due to changes in the consuming countries as it was due to the developments in the countries with large tracts of uncultivated land. For most countries of North-Western and Southern Europe dependence on imported grain became a necessity in the last quarter of the nineteenth century. So far as Germany was concerned within a decade (1865–75) it turned from a grain exporting to a grain importing country. In fact earlier on in the 1850s Germany (or rather Prussia) was a major exporter of grain and Danzig prices then set the European standard.[7] But by the 1890s, when the SPD came around to discussing the agrarian question, the import of grains had already become an established feature and there was no question then of regaining self-sufficiency. This was taken for granted even by the parties and organisations which demanded protection from the import of foreign grains, since they never demanded an outright ban on imports but just an increase in the price of imported agricultural products.

The immediate reason for the transformation of Germany from a grain exporting to a grain importing country in the 1860s and the 1870s was that domestic production did not keep pace with the increase in demand. But one cannot take the transformation to imply that German agriculture was stagnant in the second half of the nineteenth century. The phenomenon of domestic production of agricultural goods not keeping pace with their demand in the economy was, as indicated earlier, fairly general; as a result it cannot be simply attributed to the peculiar organisational features of German agriculture (like the dominance of Junker estates in the production of grain). German agriculture was heterogeneous elsewhere in Europe; and though it was not as efficient as, for example, Danish agriculture, it did pioneer some of the important innovations of the last century like the use of artificial instead of natural fertilisers. By the turn of the century Germany had developed an elaborate system of education in agronomy.[8] Not only was there a steady increase in productivity but also a slight initial increase in cultivated area. These were, however, not sufficient to satisfy the increase in demand. Apart from the increase in population a change in taste also contributed to the dependence on imported grain. For example, rye was a staple grain in Germany and remained so, but over time the consumption of wheat increased resulting in higher imports since Germany did not produce much wheat.[9]

The factors mentioned thus far merely indicate how and why an extensive international market in agricultural commodities came to develop. The main factor leading to what has been generally termed the 'crisis of the European agriculture' was the decrease in the price of grains which accompanied the extension of the market. From the mid 1870s onwards prices of grains – those of barley, oats, rye and wheat – fell more or less steadily till 1896;

and it was only in 1912 that they surpassed their level of 1870. The time profile of prices during this period conformed to what is termed a Kondratiev cycle.[10] Moreover, the decline in prices was not restricted to the countries like Britain which had free trade in grain, but it also took place in countries like Germany which, from the 1880s onwards, started imposing tariffs on imported grain.

Yet a decline in price by itself does not constitute a crisis; so what exactly did the crisis consist of? The literature unfortunately is not very clear on this. The crisis of European agriculture could be taken to mean the effects of either an absolute or a relative decline in agricultural incomes.

But the decrease in prices by itself was not sufficient to cause either of the two unless it was coupled with increasing or constant costs, insufficient rise in productivity, rise in industrial wages and the like. To a varying degree these things did happen in European countries. The essential feature of the crisis was not so much an absolute decline in agricultural incomes as a decline relative to incomes in industry and urban areas. When looked at in this way the crisis was peculiar to European countries with developed capitalist industry. Varga (1969, p. 267), the eminent Hungarian Marxist economist, emphasises the local nature of the agricultural crisis and points out that there was no crisis then in the Americas and Australia, the regions exporting agricultural commodities. What the agricultural crisis in Europe did was to further widen the economic gap which already existed between the countryside and the cities. The crisis, one may note, was as much due to industrial development as to international competition in agricultural commodities. And it is the increase in economic disparities between industry and agriculture which is essential to understanding the effects which the decrease in agricultural prices had in different countries, effects like emigration from the countryside and so on.[11]

The decrease in prices did not affect all sections in the countryside in the same way, for the incidence of international competition and thus its effects were not evenly distributed over different commodities. Competition was, as Kautsky points out in *Die Agrarfrage* (ch. 10, sec. c), much more severe in grain than in meat, vegetables and dairy products. In fact dairy producers in the cases where they used cereals as animal feed gained from the international competition, because that meant a decrease in the cost of feeding animals. The uneven incidence of international competition had a special regional significance for Germany since most of her grain came from the estates to the east of the Elbe. The eminent German agronomist, von der Goltz, pointed out it was the estate owners rather than the small and medium farmers of South and West Germany who felt the main blast of competition.[12] For the latter did not have that much grain to sell. It was because of this, and the fact that conservative parties in Germany were anchored to the economic and political position of the estate owners or Junkers, that the demand for tariffs on imported agricultural goods came to be predominantly associated with political conservatism, an association which was not always the case in Germany.

Further, the effects of the emergence of the international market and resulting competition were different in different European countries. On the one hand, agriculture in Britain and Denmark rearranged itself around the international market, though not in the same way. On the other hand, Germany and France tried to insulate their agriculture from international competition by levying tariffs on imports. The reasons for these differences in response have to be looked for in the differences in the structure of agriculture as well as political forces in these countries.

In both Germany and France the end of self-sufficiency and the downward slide of prices along the Kondratiev cycle coincided; as a result agriculture in both these countries was exposed to stiff international competition right from the beginning of the period of dependence on imports. But Britain, as indicated earlier, was dependent on imports well before the rapid decline in prices. Further, British agriculture was already adjusted to the lack of protection from cheap imports from 1846, when the last of the corn laws was repealed.[13]

Denmark was unique among European countries in that just when the international market in agricultural commodities was developing it pioneered new organisations, such as producer and marketing cooperatives, and new techniques of production, such as the mechanical butter separator, which helped to guarantee a uniform standard. These organisational and technical innovations helped Danish farmers to take advantage of the change in the structure of world agriculture because of the colonisation of virgin lands and the decrease in grain prices.[14]

Both in Britain and Denmark the composition of production changed from cereals towards dairy and meat production under the pressure of competition in the grain market. This to a limited extent also happened in Germany. But the change in Britain was, unlike in Denmark, coupled with the dereliction of much of the farm land and a massive contraction in the size of agriculture both in terms of area cultivated and the number of men employed. In Denmark the change resulted in a very prosperous agriculture which was both highly specialised and export oriented. Though both Denmark and Britain retained free trade in grain the reasons for it were different in the two countries. British agriculture suffered from the effects of international competition but after the repeal of the corn laws agricultural interests were not powerful enough to secure tariff protection for themselves. Although agricultural interests were powerful in Denmark, protection was not economically relevant there. Danish farmers who specialised in dairy products and meat for exports, which most of them did after 1875, in fact benefited from the decline in grain prices rather than suffered from it. Thus unlike in other European countries there was no crisis in Danish agriculture.[15]

However, before we get on to the discussion of the political forces which secured the imposition of tariffs in Germany in 1880 it is as well to consider the significance of international competition from the point of view of capitalist development.

One of the recurrent themes in the Marxist literature of the 1880s and the 1890s is that the days of small and middle peasantry in Europe are numbered. It is, for instance, there in Engels' *Peasant Question in France and Germany* (cited in the previous chapter). Wilhelm Liebknecht, a prominent leader of the SPD, in a speech to the Brussels congress of the Socialist International (1891) prophesied that American corn would ruin the small farmers of Germany and thus drive them to the ranks of the proletariat. It was in American competition that he saw the best possible guarantee for the triumph of socialism.[16] The belief in the imminent disappearance of the peasantry was not so much a deduction from observed events as an extrapolation from the way in which competition had already brought about the ruin of small producers in industry.

In a number of Marxist writings market competition is automatically assumed to be a struggle between capitalist and pre- or semi-capitalist organisations of production whereby the former eliminates the latter. In a number of cases that is indeed the case. In the case of industrial goods it could with justification be argued that competition at a certain stage was really competition between large scale capitalist industry and small scale handicraft industry and what it did was to eliminate the latter from the main branches of production. But strictly speaking the same cannot be said of competition in the international market for agricultural goods in the last quarter of the nineteenth century. Engels' prediction of the rapid disappearance of the small and middle peasantry did not materialise, and this was recognised by Marxists. In his *Die Agrarfrage* Kautsky concludes that there is no discernible tendency for small farms and thus peasantry to disappear (ch. 7, sec. a).[17]

But it is not so much the fact of non-realisation of prediction, as the inappropriateness of the classification of international competition in agricultural commodities of the last quarter of the nineteenth century in terms of struggle between capitalist and pre-capitalist modes of production which is essential. The competition which European agriculture faced came as much from the semi-feudal and semi-capitalist estates of Russia and the countries of Eastern Europe, like Romania, as indeed it did from the efficient family farms of the US. Kautsky in *Die Agrarfrage* does recognise the mixed origins of the international competition when he divides the exporters of agricultural commodities into newly colonised countries – the US and Australia – and countries characterised by oriental despotism – Russia (ch. 10, sec c). According to Kautsky, the competitiveness of the former derived from the natural fertility of newly colonised land as well as the absence of feudal traces. In contrast the competitiveness of the latter rests on the peasants' low level of living and their urgent need for cash to pay taxes and rent and thus their willingness to accept whatever prices the market would offer.

Kautsky's argument is of particular interest because it implies that competitiveness need not rest on technical efficiency and that less efficient semi-capitalist farms, in terms of capitalist accounting,[18] may well out-compete more efficient capitalist farms. Further, one may note that the argument *mutatis mutandis* can be applied to an economy where capitalist farms coexist with peasant farms. This is in fact what Kautsky says when he claims that small peasant farms survive not because they are efficient but because peasants consume too little and work too long. We shall return to this point in chapter 4 when discussing the theoretical writings on the agrarian question.

In all, the implication of these arguments is that the international competition did not have unambiguous consequences for the development of capitalist agriculture. Kautsky did not take the position advanced by Engels but he did, nevertheless, assign a specific outcome to the international competition: it would lead to the development of capitalist agriculture in less developed countries and it would ultimately end in the general crisis of capitalism (pp. 247–8). The second does not rest on any argument but is a reiteration of the belief that capitalism will end one day as a result of its internal contradictions. So far as the first is concerned it rests on an assumption that market relationships are necessarily corrosive of pre-capitalist relations of production, an assumption which cannot be accepted as generally valid. Apart from that Kautsky neglects the effects of the international competition on agriculture in developed capitalist countries. One may note that it was in Britain – the country with no peasantry and a country with developed capitalist farming – that the largest contraction in cultivated area as a result of the international competition occurred. Moreover, in Germany the main incidence of competition was not so much on the peasant farms as on the large capitalist farms.

The capacity of peasants to survive competition, both internal and external, was a subject of dispute in the SPD – a subject to which we shall return in later chapters. But at the present stage the point which needs making is that although the international competition was severe and had far reaching consequences for European agriculture, and although it established a new international division of labour in agriculture, it was not a 'process of natural selection' whereby more efficient capitalist farms replaced less efficient peasant farms. If the peasantry declined in numbers, which it did in a number of European countries, it had more to do with the availability of employment in the urban areas and resulting migration from the countryside than international competition as such. With this we turn to one of the main outcomes of the international competition in Germany: the imposition of import tariffs.

## Tariffs

In the last quarter of the nineteenth century a 'protectionist wave' swept the capitalist world. All the major capitalist countries, with the exception of Britain, erected tariff walls to shield their own native producers of agricultural and industrial commodities. The switch towards greater protection was not due only to the development of an international market in agricultural commodities. It was as much due to the development of capitalist industry in countries like the US, Russia and Italy – countries which were previously agricultural or only semi-industrial – and the emergence of international competition in manufactures which that implied.

Germany imposed tariffs on industrial and agricultural goods in 1879 and that was just the beginning of a series of protectionist policies lasting till the First World War. But tariff protection was not a new phenomenon in Wilhelmine Germany, for the very constitution of Germany as a unified country out of a large number of German speaking states was based on a customs union. Nevertheless, for almost twenty years before the introduction of tariffs Germany or the constituent states of the Zollverein (customs union) maintained low tariffs on imported goods. It is interesting to note that this was also the period when Germany was transformed into a major industrial country in competition with Britain in a number of areas of industrial production. Therefore, contrary to what is normally believed, the major part of the initial spurt of capitalist development in Germany took place under liberal rather than protectionist policies. The protectionist ideas of List had lost whatever political force they had had by the 1860s.[19]

The introduction of the 1879 tariffs had both economic and political significance. Economic, because agriculture for the first time became the subject of tariff protection. Earlier on in the 1860s there was a low tariff on agricultural imports but the question of protecting domestic agriculture just did not arise; for Germany, as pointed out earlier, was then an exporting rather than an importing country and the cheap American and Russian grain had yet to flood the market. In fact till 1875 grain prices were lower in Germany than in England.[20] Therefore, so far as tariff policies were concerned, the tariff bill of 1879 constituted a break because before then, especially during the protectionist phase in the 1840s and the 1850s, it was the protection of industry rather than of agriculture which was the main aim of such policies.

Besides their economic significance the tariffs imposed in 1879 were of crucial political importance. The passing of the tariff bill was contingent on the emergence of a conservative (representing the Junkers) and right wing liberal alliance in the Reichstag, an alliance which displaced the political liberals and free traders who had till then dominated parliamentary politics. The tariff bill, it will be remembered, was preceded a year earlier by the bill which banned the Social Democratic organisations; and the two bills, despite the absence of any obvious connections between them, were politically linked. In fact, the Anti-Socialist Law cemented the alliance which eventually supported the tariff bill.

However, the tariff bill was in addition supported by the Centre Party – a party which occupied a nodal position in the Reich. Apart from the SPD the party was the only one which had a mass base, especially in South and West Germany, the areas where small and middle peasants dominated the rural landscape. Though the party was not an agrarian party it did command widespread support in the countryside and though there was no peasant party in Germany the Centre Party, of all the other parties, could be said to be a representative of the middle and small peasants. The party did not support the Anti-Socialist bill when it was first presented, but it did so eventually; and its support for the tariff bill was the beginning of the right–centre alliance which dominated parliamentary politics in Wilhelmine Germany and which underlay the later tariff policies.[21]

But in the political arena it was not just political parties which fought out the battles for and against tariff protection; in addition to them, organisations representing specific economic groups like industrialists and farmers were also among the major participants. In fact a special feature of politics in the Reich was the growth of such organisations parallel to political parties. They did not contest elections but, none the less, had a formative influence on parliamentary politics and government policies. Apart from the Bund der Landwirte (Farmers League) most of these organisations were founded in the 1870s. The foundation of the Reich in 1871 opened up a field of political representation in which all kinds of organisations proliferated. Both the Central Association of German Industrialists and the Association of Tax and Economic Reformers (in fact a conservative association strongly biased in favour of the estate owners) were founded in 1876. There were others besides these two, for example, the Association of Steel and Iron Industrialists. Among them the Central Association was politically the most influential; but it was not what is usually termed an 'economic pressure group', an organisation set up just to influence the programme and behaviour of existing political parties.[22] On the contrary in the 1890s and later it functioned very much as an autonomous political organisation which played a central part in the change of governments and had a direct say in the drafting of the 1902 tariff legislation (named after Chancellor von Bülow).[23]

The formulation of tariff policies apart, the existence of such non-electoral yet political organisations raises a more general issue. Usually the determining political role which such organisations play is taken as a sign of the frailty of parliamentary democracy and their existence is accounted for in terms of the non-democratic forces at work in society. That is justified, but the essential point is that the field of political representation in parliamentary democracies is not restricted to electoral organisations; usually electoral representation is just one form of political representation which coexists with the other forms, e.g., the representation of a specific category of economic agents by the kind of organisation we have just been discussing. Moreover, these organisations were not part of the pre-democratic inheritance of Germany, but instead they arose and prospered with the development of parliamentary democracy in Germany. Paradoxical though it may seem, electoral and parliamentary politics in the Reich itself created a place for non-electoral and non-parliamentary organisation, like the Central Association representing the industrialists and the Bund representing the farmers. Parliamentary democracy in the Reich was indeed feeble in that the Reichstag had limited budgetary powers and it was the Kaiser who appointed the Chancellor — that was just a part of the reason why non-parliamentary 'economic interest groups' could play such an important part in the change of Chancellors and legislative process.

The tariff bill of 1879 granted protection to both industry and agriculture; both these sectors of production were, as they always are, highly differentiated and heterogeneous and the incidence of tariff protection was unevenly spread over different branches of production. In agriculture the main items subject to duty were grain and meat, while among industrial goods it was mostly iron and steel goods, on the one hand, and textiles on the other which attracted tariffs.[24] Gerschenkron in his seminal *Bread and Democracy in Germany* has argued that the list of goods chosen for protection represented an alliance of rye and iron, but this characterisation is only partially correct. In agriculture the East Elbian grain producers were the main beneficiaries of the tariffs for they produced most of the grain and it was in grain that international competition was at its most severe. Though small and middle peasants did benefit from the duty on meat they either did not gain much from the duty on grain or in some cases they even lost by it. That benefits from grain duty were very unevenly distributed was widely recognised and not just by agronomists. For instance Chancellor Höhenlohe stated in 1895 that holdings under 12 hectares (i.e. 87 per cent of holdings according to the 1895 agricultural census) had no corn to sell, and in a large number of cases they were even net buyers of corn.[25] The uneven distribution of tariff protection remained true not only for the 1879 bill but also for successive tariff revisions in the 1880s and 1890s.

In 1885 and 1887 the tariff rates were revised upwards; the upward revision did not affect the duty on industrial goods but only those on agricultural goods, especially grain. What the two revisions did was to turn an initially moderate degree of protection into a high one. The characteristic feature of the tariff rates of the 1880s was that they were fixed unilaterally. In the 1880s a number of European countries led by France concluded bilateral trade treaties with each other; but Germany kept out of such agreements and conducted its trade on the basis of 'most favoured nation status' – granting a country as favourable terms as granted to any other country in return for the same treatment.[26]

German industrial exports grew steadily throughout the 1880s, and by the end of the decade it was clear that Germany had to conclude bilateral treaties with its main trade partners in order to ensure that its industrial exports did not come up against the high tariff walls which European countries were erecting. Thus the 1890s was the era of bilateral treaties and it was in relation to these treaties that the economic interests of agriculture and industry – or more accurately, particular sections of these two branches of production – diverged. Furthermore, it was the conclusion of some of the bilateral treaties which furnished the ground for the establishment of the Bund in 1892, which started its eventful and demagogic career by whipping up support against the treaties which had yet to be ratified.

The bilateral treaties – termed Caprivi treaties – had to be biased in favour of industrial exports and take the form of a decrease in tariff on agricultural imports. For they were nothing more than an exchange of concessions between Germany and her trading partners; and the nature of the exchange was determined by Germany's pattern of trade. The countries with which such an exchange took place were either industrial (like Switzerland or Belgium) or predominantly agricultural (like Austro-Hungary, Italy, Romania and Russia).

Now it is clear from the list that the exchange of concession in most cases had to take the form of Germany lowering the tariff on its agricultural imports in return for other countries lowering their tariff on German industrial exports. Further, it was grain – in particular rye and wheat – rather than meat and dairy products which accounted for the bulk of agricultural imports and also it was grain which enjoyed heavy protection in the 1880s. On the export side it was iron and steel, chemicals and machinery which were most important. Given this composition of imports and exports, the exchange of concessions had to take the form of a reduction in duty on imported grain in return for other countries reducing their tariffs on the products of heavy and chemicals industries.

Therefore what the exchange of tariff concessions did was to drive a wedge between the economic interests of export industries and agriculture. Moreover, the implication was that the drive for industrial exports, which was necessary for the continued growth of industry, was not consistent with the desire to reduce the dependence on imported grain which the proponents of the 'agrarian state' wanted. It was this inconsistency which underlay the controversy which broke out in the 1890s as to whether Germany should be predominantly an industrial or an agricultural state. Besides, the process of exchange of concessions also makes it clear that the demand for free trade on the part of export oriented industries was no less parochial than the demand for tariffs on agricultural imports.

To start with the political support for the Caprivi treaties was overwhelming. In fact the first series of treaties with Belgium, Austro-Hungary, Switzerland and Italy were passed by the Reichstag with huge majorities. This was partly due to the fact that none of these countries were major exporters of grain to Germany.[27] The spectacular electoral victory of the Social Democrats who were hostile to tariffs further strengthened the free trading position. However, the second set of treaties with the major exporters of grain to Germany – Romania and Russia – came under increased opposition, but they too were ultimately passed.

It was soon after the first set of treaties and a sudden dive in grain prices that the Bund der Landwirte, which we referred to earlier, was founded in 1892. The Bund was not a political party (in the sense that it did not contest elections) but in its activities it was overtly political. For instance in the Reichstag elections of 1893 (soon after its foundation) the Bund took an active part – it campaigned for and against candidates depending on their attitude to the protection of agriculture. The Bund was not aligned to any particular political party, it could rather be termed a political holding company. Like an industrial holding company it cast its net wide and tried to spread its influence across party lines and it eventually succeeded. In its political outlook the Bund was unmistakably reactionary and it did not restrict its campaign to the questions of agriculture; it conducted a virulent campaign against the SPD on general political grounds as well as on the party's opposition to tariff protection. In fact the foundation and the growth of the Bund coincided in time with the SPD's attempt to win the countryside; it was in 1893 that the Social Democratic agitation on land had reached its peak and it was in the election of that year the SPD had hoped to capture a large slice of the rural vote.[28] However, we leave this aside for the next chapter.

Though the conservative politicians played a central part in its foundation and its functioning the Bund was not organised like the conservative. parties. Unlike them the Bund was a mass organisation committed to as wide a membership as possible; in fact within a year of its foundation it had managed to recruit 200,000 members. That the Bund was dominated by the Junkers is indeed true, but to treat simply as an organisation of Junkers would be to miss the essential point: it was both a conservative and a populist organisation and it is this combination which made it a novelty in Wilhelmine Germany. The Bund's organisations

## SOME ASPECTS OF GERMAN AGRICULTURE

and activities were not restricted to the east of the Elbe (the region of Junker estates) but were spread over the whole of Germany. Even early on in its existence the Bund conducted campaigns in peasant-dominated Bavaria, and it was these campaigns which caused a large number of the Reichstag members of the firmly non-Junker Centre Party to vote against the trade treaties with Romania and Russia. As a result of the Bund's propaganda campaigns by the end of the 1890s the situation had become such that the members of the Reichstag from rural constituencies had to support tariff protection for agriculture so as not be outflanked by the Bund.[29]

Most, though not all, of the Bund's propaganda relating to agrarian matters concerned the price and import of grain; so a high point in its activities was the presentation of the Kanitz motion. In 1894 an East Elbian landowner, Kanitz, proposed setting up a state monopoly which would import grain and sell it at prescribed prices – i.e. the average of prices ruling between 1850 and 1880. The proposal, though repeatedly presented in the Reichstag, was never accepted. The essence of the proposal was to guarantee a high price for grain regardless of those ruling in the world market; the period by reference to which the prescribed price was to be calculated was deliberately chosen to guarantee a price well above the ruling prices. For as pointed out earlier the price of grain had only started falling in 1875 and it fell more or less steadily till 1896. In its effects and implication the Kanitz proposal bore a striking resemblance to the Common Agricultural Policy (CAP) of the European Common Market; for the main object of the CAP is to maintain agricultural prices at a preset level with a view to benefit the producer rather than consumers of agricultural commodities.[30]

It has been pointed out by a number of authors that the tariff duty on grain far from benefiting the small and middle peasant actually harmed them – this was widely recognised in the 1890s not only by politicians like Höhenlohe (quoted above) and Caprivi but also by peasant organisations like the Bavarian Peasant League.[31] And it was partly out of the recognition of this fact that the Centre Party was solidly opposed to the Kanitz proposal. If that was the case then one may ask why peasant organisations supported the protection of agriculture which favoured grain producers, and why peasants joined the Bund's crusade in favour of protection which was also directed in favour of grain producers. Gerschenkron argues that the peasants' support for the Bund and tariff protection was based more on their irrational notions about agriculture and their ignorance than on their economic interest[32] – an argument very similar to that of Max Weber. Weber treated the history of tariff protection from 1879 onwards as the history of two opposing tendencies in German society, one feudal and the other bourgeois. And tariffs on agricultural imports for him did not just signify a policy which favoured the Junkers but also what he termed feudalisation – cultural and political domination by the Junkers. This view of tariffs was coupled with the argument that German agriculture consisted of two distinct halves and thus there was no such thing as the common interest of agriculture. The implication was that the Junkers had foisted their own particular economic interests on to the rural population as a whole through their cultural and political domination.[33]

Weber is perfectly correct when he points out that German agriculture was not homogeneous and the economic interests of peasants (themselves a very heterogeneous group) do not coincide with those of the Junkers. But that does not imply that either free trade or low tariffs were in their economic interest. What the peasants' economic interests called for was a tariff policy which protected, in addition to grain, commodities like meat, dairy products, fruits and vegetables. In short, commodities which were more important to peasants than to big farmers; and moreover a policy which set the tariff rates on these commodities high enough to offset the effects of a duty on grain on their cost of production. It is not that the commodities which figured high in peasants' marketable surplus were not protected; on the contrary they were, but it was only after 1902 that the rates on these commodities were set high enough to offset the effect of the grain duty on their costs of production.

As for the imposition of tariffs signifying feudalisation, the duty on imported grains did benefit the Junkers and the imposition of tariffs in 1879, as indicated earlier, did presuppose a change in political alliance. But the essential point about the tariff policies in Wilhelmine Germany was that they emerged out of the confluence of diverse economic interests, disparate and at times contradictory political forces, and distinct and often unrelated factors. For instance the reform of the finances of the Reich and the nature of Germany's trade relation with other countries played as important a part in the formulation of tariff policies as a number of other factors relating to Junkerdom. Further, as pointed out above, the demand for free trade on the part of export industries in the 1890s was as much based on parochial economic interests as the Junker's demand for protection; the general point being that there was no straightforward correspondence between protection and political reaction, on the one hand, and free trade or low tariffs and political progressiveness on the other.

However, the question still remains, how did the Bund manage to become a representative of agriculture as a whole given the diversity in the countryside? Though the economic interests of the small and the middle peasants were not the same as those of the large farmers to the east of the Elbe, they were never counterposed to each other in the economic and political divisions which accompanied the formulation of successive tariff policies. The division was more between the economic interests of exporting industry and those of agricultural producers producing for the domestic market, or between rural producers and urban consumers of agricultural commodities, than between different sections in agriculture. Further, the peasantry itself was not a homogeneous economic group but was differentiated both by size of the holding and region; in addition and more importantly, the peasantry, unlike the Junkers, did not constitute a distinct political force. There were political parties in Germany which could be identified with the Junkers, such as the Conservative Party, but there was no such party so far as peasants were concerned. The Centre Party, though it had a base among the peasants of South and West Germany, as indicated earlier, was not a peasant party; rather it was a political party based on the regional differences which were overlaid with the religious differences. Therefore the conclusion in general terms is that the political divisions in Wilhelmine Germany did not differentiate between the peasants and the Junkers. Economic and political divisions, the essential point is, are constituted in different planes and prima facie there is no reason why the two should correspond. So the answer to the question posed here is that the emergence of the Bund and its success as the representative of agriculture as a whole was due to the fact that the peasantry was not an autonomous political force, and that the difference between the economic interests of the peasantry and the Junkers was overshadowed by other divisions which were politically more pertinent.

We have so far avoided the discussion of the Social Democratic attitude to protection, in particular to agricultural protection. This can now be considered briefly.

The SPD's *Landagitation*, which we shall discuss in detail in the next chapter, ran more or less concurrently with discussion and political activity around the Caprivi treaties, together with the foundation of the Bund and its campaign in favour of protection. The SPD, however, did not have any specific policy towards the protection of agriculture taken on its own. Its attitude to tariff policies derived from a general hostility to any kind of tariff protection either of agriculture or of industry. It, for instance, supported the Caprivi treaties on the ground that they implied a decrease in tariffs and thus a reduction in the cost of living. The party's commitment to free trade remained unquestioned throughout most of the 1890s – a period when most of the political parties were divided internally on the issue of protection. And it was only at the 1898 Congress in Stuttgart that there was a full scale discussion and a questioning of the party's attitude towards tariff policies; but that did not lead to any change in the established policy. The party's hostility to tariff protection provided the Bund with a convenient target. In fact by the end of the 1890s, when most of the political parties had succumbed to the protectionist crusade, the Bund's propaganda was that the main enemies of agriculture then were no longer traditional free traders (presumably because so few of them were left by then) but the Social Democrats.[34]

On the doctrinal plane the SPD's attitude could be regarded as a repetition of the support Marx had given to free trade in 1848.[35] Marx's support for free trade was not unqualified; but on balance he came out in favour of free trade on the grounds that it would lead to a further development and a geographical extension of capitalism by eliminating archaic methods of production and organisation. However, it is not the effects of free trade on capitalist development as such but their political implications – increase in the size of the working class and extension in the domain of antagonism between capital and labour – which led Marx to support free trade. But later in the 1880s Engels in his introduction to the speech qualified Marx's position that free trade is necessarily progressive; the introduction, though meant

SOME ASPECTS OF GERMAN AGRICULTURE    39

for the American audience, was republished in *Die Neue Zeit*. Engels' basic argument, which had a greater relevance to the tariff controversies in the Caprivi era, was that the dispute between free trade and protection was essentially one between different sections of the ruling classes; and as such it was not directly relevant to socialists. The implication, nevertheless, was not that socialists should remain indifferent to trade policies, a position which the SPD adopted earlier on in the 1870s; on the contrary the implication was that they should take sides, but on the basis of its effects on things like the rate of accumulation, the cost of living of workers and the level of employment. What Engels did was to put free trade on a par with protection and thus treat the choice between them as an object of economic calculation.

It was Kautsky who *ex post facto* at the Stuttgart Congress of 1898 provided a theoretical justification for the SPD's commitment to free trade. The justification was negative in that it was based more on the pernicious effects of tariff protection than on the positive features of free trade; in fact, there was no reference to the progressive political character of free trade. The general argument against tariff protection was nothing more than a variation on the argument which List had used in the 1840s to justify the protection of German industry; that is, German industry had passed the age of infancy and thus it did not need protection for its continued growth. In addition the argument was that tariff protection for already mature German industry would do less for its development than for strengthening the price cartels which had already established themselves in different branches of German industry.[36] Besides this the Social Democrats were opposed to tariffs on the grounds that the revenue from them was used for the army and the navy. From the point of view of the finances of the Reich the reimposition of tariffs in 1879 had been a great success: for by the 1890s they (mostly duties on imported grain) contributed about a half of the revenue of the Reich – hence the link between tariffs and militarism. The SPD's opposition to protection may have been unpopular in large sections of the countryside but it did bring the party more votes in urban areas. In 1903 the Social Democrats campaigned against the von Bülow tariff rates – the replacement for the rates set under the Caprivi treaties and invariably higher than them – and succeeded in enlarging their share of the vote.[37]

By 1897 the price of grain and other agricultural commodities had started rising but that did not dampen the protectionist propaganda of the Bund. And, as indicated just now, the replacement of the Caprivi treaties by von Bülow treaties led to an increase in tariff duties both in agricultural and industrial commodities. However, in the late 1890s the propaganda of the Bund was not restricted to the decline of prices, it also included the shortage of labour arising out of the migration of rural inhabitants from the countryside to the cities.

What was in all the effect of tariff protection on German agriculture? Tariff protection did initially lead to a slight increase in cultivated area but it did not lead to self-sufficiency.[38] Without tariff protection agriculture would have been smaller both in terms of the area cultivated and of the number of men employed. Further, what the structure of protection did was to bias the composition of production in favour of grains, in particular rye which was cultivated on East Elbian estates, and away from products like meat and dairy products. Tariffs, in general, did not increase the cost of living; because agricultural prices in Germany fell despite them. The essential point is that tariff protection could at best only insulate German agriculture partially, because, as we shall see in the section on emigration from the countryside, it was not only international competition but also the development of German industry which induced changes in German agriculture.

**The Prussian Road**

At this stage it is instructive to change tack and turn to the emancipation of serfs in Prussia in the first quarter of the nineteenth century, which, though far from contemporaneous with the events with which we are concerned, is, none the less, of interest for a variety of reasons. The emancipation as it happened in Prussia and the ensuing development of capitalist agriculture has acquired the status of a paradigm in Marxist analyses of agrarian relations. Lenin, for example, in his *Development of Capitalism in Russia* arranged his discussion of the development of capitalist agriculture around the distinction between the American and the Prussian path. The distinguishing feature of the latter, according to Lenin, is the internal transmutation of the landlord economy into a capitalist economy. In other accounts the Prussian emancipation has been counterposed, as the model of liberation from above, to the emancipation of peasants which took place in the wake of the French Revolution, in turn regarded as the model of emancipation from below.[39]

Besides its paradigmatic value, the emancipation of serfs in Prussia is of interest to the structure of agriculture three-quarters of a century later, for it exercised a determinant influence on the distribution of land into units of production then. In fact the existence of large Junker estates and the relative absence of a peasantry in Prussia at the end of the nineteenth century was directly linked with the way in which serfs were liberated at the beginning of the century. In broad outlines the distribution of land determined at that time tenaciously outlived the events of intervening years. In addition it was not only the institutions and relationships which the emancipation changed but also those which it managed to evade – the hold of landlords on the local government in rural areas – which make it relevant.

What did the Prussian reforms, whose accomplishments and failures have acquired such significance for historians – Meinecke[40] for instance – actually consist of? So far as land and rural inhabitants were concerned the reform consisted of the series of laws and edicts passed in the first quarter of the nineteenth century after the defeat of the Prussian army at the hands of Napoleon in 1807. These laws concerned both the status of men as citizens and as economic agents and the division of land between the peasants and the landlords. The first of these edicts, named after Stein and issued in 1807, made the serfs who were tethered to the land and to their lords into free men by fiat. However, it was the law passed in 1816 and named after Hardenberg which laid down the rules for the partition of land between landlords and their dependent subjects, and thus created a new form of property to replace feudal property.

But the emancipation of the serfs and the definition of property rights were not the sole concern of the reforms; these were also associated with the reform of the fiscal system, the army, the educational system and the administrative apparatuses of the state. In some cases the military defeat by itself necessitated a change; for instance the heavy indemnity which Prussia had to pay to France forced her to change her tax system.[41] The reforms of the army (attributed to Scharnhorst) and the educational system (attributed to Humboldt) like the agrarian reform also became paradigms; they created a model bourgeois army and educational system. The essential feature of Scharnhorst's reform was to create a national army based on universal conscription and an army which established its own hierarchy rather than duplicating the existing hierarchy of feudal ranks. Similarly Humboldt's reforms set out to build a unified educational system which encompassed all, rather than just one, categories of citizens.[42] When the agrarian reforms are looked at in relation to all other reforms with which they were coupled, it becomes clear that the change in the feudal relations of production was neither an exclusive nor, more importantly, a determinant locus of change. The reforms could be regarded, as indeed they are by some, as window dressing on the part of the ruling class of a feudal state after its ignominious defeat;[43] but the problem with this view is that it is Junker centred, i.e., it takes their economic and political position as the measure of all change. True, that reforms far from diminishing the economic power of the Junkers actually increased it; and not only that, they also left the control of the local government and the administration of justice in the rural areas in the hands of estate owners. But it is equally true that the reforms changed the organisation of the army and the educational system in ways which did not favour the Junkers, and which consequently make it difficult to classify them as window dressing on the part of the ruling class.

However, to return to the reforms which concerned the serfs and property in land: the serfs who were made into free men by the reforms were tethered to their lords through a variety of obligations, economic, judicial and personal; and their patrimony did not just consist of things but also obligation and servile duties. Depending on their status and capacity, they had to render services to the lord of the domain by hand (*Handdienst*), by the use of their plough oxen (*Spanndienst*) and by having their wives and children work in the lord's household (*Gesindedienst*). This last form of service survived till the end of the nineteenth century; it was common then for an agricultural labourer's wife and children to perform various unpaid services in the employers' household.[44] And the form in which a serf rendered services to the landlord acquired a great importance during the reforms for they determined whether or not the serf was entitled to property in land.

Prior to the reform there was no well defined and exclusive

ownership of land; instead the property in land was characterised simply by use-rights in land. Furthermore, these rights were quite diverse and cannot be reduced to a single form. Some serfs were like freeholders in that they (either *Erbpächter* or *Erbsinsleute*) had an unrestricted and inheritable right of use of land; while others (*Zeitpächter*) for instance had only a non-inheritable right of usage. In addition the right of usage was not necessarily exclusive.[45] The commons (*Gemeinheiten*) for example, were open to use by a wide variety of rural inhabitants, though not to everyone. *Mutatis mutandis* this was also true for arable land in that persons other than the cultivator also had the right of use of the stubble. Apart from these there was an important difference between the right of usage and the kind of ownership with which we are familiar, namely, not even the unrestricted and inheritable rights of usage were transferable by sale.[46]

The absence of fixed proprietary exclusiveness characteristic of the conception of ownership in Roman Law, and the medley of rights of usage – some overlapping and some mutually exclusive – were complementary to the web of servile obligations to which the serfs were subject. In fact pre-reform property in land was not defined just by the right of usage which a serf had, in a general sense the relation between the man and the land, but in addition by the duties he performed for the landlord and the relations between men. Pre-reform property relations were thus an assemblage of intertwined relationships between men and things, on the one hand, and relations between men, on the other. The dissolution of this form of property therefore involved not only a delineation of an exclusive and alienable ownership in land but also the separation of the two forms of relationship – a separation which is characteristic of the bourgeois conception of property and which has not always existed. Just as duties and obligations together with the right of usage defined the property in land so far as serfs were concerned, the claims which estate owners had on the serfs and land in their domain (*Rittergut*) defined the nature of property in land which they had.

Now given that the servile duties which the rural inhabitants performed were complementary to the right of usufruct it became clear that the emancipation of serfs was not just a humanitarian measure but, what is more important, a necessary component of the emergence of a new form of property in land.

The serfs did not get their freedom as a gift; they had instead to obtain it through a *quid pro quo* transaction. In return for the commutation of services the serfs had to pay monetary compensation – partly as lump sum and partly in the form of a perpetual land tax – as well as ceding either a part or the whole of land which they possessed. Serfs who had heritable usage of land and who owned draught animals and thus rendered service by ploughing the fields of the estate owners (*Spanndienst*) got full possession of the two-thirds of their land by ceding a third to the landlord. As for the others (those with non-inheritable rights and without draught animals), they were first considered entitled to a part of the land which they possessed, while later amendments deprived them of whatever meagre claim of ownership they had. The process of exchange between serfs and estate owners, officially termed regulation, was not accomplished immediately; there were still peasants in 1850 who were waiting for their status to be regulated. Those who were not entitled to land further suffered because the law (*Bauernschutz*) which protected their right of usufruct was no longer enforced after 1816; as a result a large number of them were evicted from their lands – a process termed 'putting down of peasants' (*Bauernlegen*).[47]

The reforms freed a large number of serfs, not only of their obligations and their servile status but also of their land; and it increased both the money capital and the land in possession of the Junkers. In cases where the reforms favoured serfs it was only the *Spannfähig* – those who owned oxen and thus were relatively well off – who benefited. It is often said that the Prussian reformers had an opportunity of creating a large and independent peasantry which they missed by biasing the exchange in favour of the Junkers; and that the creation of a large peasantry would have avoided the problems which arose later due to the grossly unequal distribution of land. That may be so but the point is that the creation of a self-subsistent and economically independent peasantry, and the retentions of the Junker estates, were not mutually consistent. This was not simply because a larger share of land settled on by the peasantry would have meant a smaller share for the Junkers' estates. The Junkers needed a regular supply of labour to work on their farms if they were to survive economically; in the pre-reform period this was guaranteed by the services which the serfs had to perform either by their hands or with the help of their beasts. In the post-reform period, on the other hand, it was the peasants who did not qualify for property in land and thus were evicted from their land who formed the reservoir of labour for the Junkers. The creation of a large and self-subsistent peasantry would have undermined the foundations of the Junker economy by depriving it of a readily available and cheap supply of labour.[48] It is then not just in the first quarter of the nineteenth century but later on too that the ready availability of labour remained crucial to the survival and prosperity of the Junker estates; in fact one of the biggest problems which the Junkers faced in the 1890s was the shortage of labour in the countryside.

In conclusion what one can say is that the reform had a dual character and it is this duality which makes it relevant to the conditions which prevailed in the rural Prussia of the last quarter of the nineteenth century. The reform obviously extended even further the large share of land which the Junkers already possessed; and it thus created a situation whereby a relatively small number of estates accounted for most of the arable land. In addition to that the reform kept most of the rural population dependent on the same class to which they were enserfed before the reform. As a result for most of the rural inhabitants the emancipation from serfdom did not immediately signify any great change in their social and economic conditions. The freedom which the reform bestowed on the serfs acquired an economic significance only later when ex-serfs started putting their freedom to use by migrating in large numbers from the countryside. The large scale migration, either to the US or to the cities in rural Prussia to the east of the Elbe, did not start until as late as the 1860s. The implication in general terms is that neither the dispossession of a large number of serfs, nor the granting of freedom to serfs to migrate or to sell their labour power, by themselves revolutionised the conditions in the East Elbian countryside; they only started to have effects later when the German cities, as a result of capitalist development, and the open spaces in the US, started to suck labour from the countryside. But for those who remained in the countryside the conditions of employment, as we shall point out later, retained in some ways a striking resemblance to serfdom.

The method employed by the Prussian reform is also of general relevance. We pointed out earlier that the serfs were not granted but had to purchase their freedom and, in the few cases where they qualified for it, the ownership of the land which they already possessed and cultivated. The reform, in other words, took the form of a commercial contract between the estate owner (*Rittergutsbesitzer*) and the serfs. But as contracts go it was a strange one: it involved transactions in things which contracts in bourgeois societies presuppose, namely, the freedom of the parties to the contract and the exclusive ownership of things. That is what made it an imaginary and fictitious contract despite the semblance which it had of being a *quid pro quo* and thus a fair exchange. Thus it had a specific function, namely, to give recognition to the economic privileges which the estate owners had under the *ancien regime* by giving them a different form.

In fact the abolition of servile obligations and status by setting up a mythical contract was not peculiar to Prussia. Initially during the French Revolution in 1789 the edicts distinguished between 'personal' and 'real' obligations; the former, which included *corvées, mainmorte*, gestures and practices affirming the superior status of the *seigneur*, were regarded as violent impositions and were therefore abolished without any compensation. The latter, which included taxes and rent paid to feudal lords, were regarded as having been established through a contract between feudal lords and servile peasants and thus liable to abolition only by a *quid pro quo* payment. In fact the existence of the contract was taken for granted unless proved to the contrary; and in essence that contract was no different from the contract which the Prussian serfs supposedly entered into when they surrendered their freedom to the feudal lords and agreed to serve them in a variety of ways, a contract which they had to undo by entering into yet another contract after the Prussian reforms. In both cases the requirement that the obligations be redeemed rested on the reference to a mythical contract. In the end the French peasants did not have to redeem even their 'real' obligations; after peasant uprisings they were simply abolished by decree in 1792.[49]

References to such mythical contracts however are not restricted to the agrarian reforms of the eighteenth and nineteenth centuries. All land reforms, where rights of use and restricted possessions are converted into an exclusive and alienable property and where a compensation is paid, implicitly refer to some such mythical contract. In fact this is implied by the very principle of a *quid pro quo* compensation in that situation. Such contracts, though mythical, none the less perform a very specific and well defined function, namely, they determine the distribution of the new form of property in the image of the distribution of the old form of property and thus maintain a continuity between the different regimes of property.

In all, what did the Prussian road consist of? The Prussian reforms created capitalist property in land but under terms favourable to the Junkers and to a lesser degree to the well off peasants, the *Spannfähig*, who qualified for the ownership of land. The reforms and the later events left some of the feudal privileges (like the hunting monopoly and the hold of the Junkers on the rural local government) untouched. The Junker domination of the *Gutsbezirke*, the units of rural local government, though formally abolished in the early 1890s, actually survived well into the twentieth century; and the Junkers retained judicial power over their labourers till the 1870s when the patrimonial courts were abolished. The political power of the Junkers at the national level indeed rested on the institutionalised power which they had in rural areas. Further, though the reforms abolished servile obligations the rural labourers remained in a state of abject dependence on the estate owners who employed them; even at the turn of the century their wives and children were forced by the established custom to perform unpaid work in the estate owner's house (*Gesindedienst*).[50] Capitalist agriculture did indeed develop in the Prussian countryside and unlike English landlords the Junkers themselves became capitalist farmers. In contrast to England where capitalist farming developed on the basis of lessee cultivation, the leasing of land was not common in Prussia; the Junkers were resident rather than absentee landlords. However, capitalist agriculture in Prussia or rather Prussia to the east of the Elbe remained marked by feudal privileges and practices.[51]

Yet one has to take care not to treat the Junkers as the embodiment of feudalism. Initially the Junkers were obviously economic agents defined by feudal relations of production, but these relations did change and so did the nature of the category 'Junkers'. When the SPD came to discuss the agrarian question in the 1890s the Junkers were not feudal lords but capitalist farmers. But when Max Weber talked of the feudalisation of Germany in the last quarter of the nineteenth century he equated feudalism with the Junkers and often feudalisation, for him, meant nothing more than a policy which favoured agriculture.[52]

A related problem arises when the Prussian reform is treated as the paradigm of the 'feudal' path to capitalism – or as Marx termed it 'the path of compromise' – and then counterposed to the reform brought about by the French Revolution, in turn treated as the paradigm of the revolutionary or the bourgeois path to capitalism. Such a juxtaposition carries with it the assumption that reforms which favour the feudal lords follow the former road while those which favour the peasants the latter path – the assumption is clearly there in Soboul, for instance. But this assumption, which most Marxists would regard as uncontroversial, does in turn seem to rest on a contention which is not so uncontroversial. That is, just as feudal lords embody feudal relations of production so peasants embody bourgeois relations of production, if not in fact at least in *potentia*.

The contention is open to the obvious objection that the peasants who were involved in the reforms were as much the creatures of feudal relations as the feudal lords themselves. The *Zeitpächter* or the *Spannfähig*, for instance, were as much products of feudal relations as the Junkers; and of course the same holds for the French *seigneurs*, the *laboureurs* or the *manouvriers*. In addition the argument is that it was not just the feudal lords whose interests were served by feudal relations. Apart from rent and feudal exactions which benefited the feudal lords, institutions like the commons, or laws like the *Bauernschutz* (the Prussian law which protected peasants from eviction) were also the constituent parts of the feudal relations. The abolition of the commons or the right to stubble which took place not only in Germany but also in France and elsewhere, hurt the poor peasants more than anybody else in the countryside. For they owned little land and were thus dependent on those rights for the grazing of their cattle. The general point is that there is no reason to assume that peasants are opposed to feudal relations *in toto* and that the line of division between feudal and bourgeois relations runs along the line which separates changes which favour the feudal lords from those which favour the peasantry.

That the peasantry itself can be enveloped in feudal relations and institutions is clearly recognised by some Marxists, especially by Kautsky and Lenin. The interesting point about Lenin is that unlike Marx he counterposes the Prussian road not to the French road but to the American road. The peculiarity of the American case, and what distinguishes it from the French case, is the complete absence of rural differentiation connected with feudal relations and institutions.

But once it is accepted that feudal relations should not be identified with the feudal lords the exact status of the two roads becomes unclear. That the reform brought about by the French Revolution was different from the Prussian reform does not leave any room for dispute, but the characteristics of the two roads are not well defined. Is the revolutionary road to capitalism shorter than the feudal road? Not necessarily, for the reforms which favour the peasantry are not always conducive to the development of capitalist agriculture. Here it is instructive to compare Prussia with France. The development of capitalist agriculture in Prussia was not any slower than in France; in fact, in a number of areas, e.g. education in agronomy, the use of artificial fertilisers etc, France lagged behind Germany in the latter half of the nineteenth century. Further the parcellisation of land in the French countryside, which was in part determined by the way in which the French peasants were liberated by the revolution, though it helped to keep a larger percentage of the population on the land than elsewhere in North-Western Europe was, none the less, a barrier to the development of capitalist agriculture.[53]

There are two points which need to be made by way of drawing together this discussion. First, the line of division between the revolutionary path and the path of compromise does not necessarily run parallel to the line separating the changes which favour the development of capitalist agriculture from the ones which do not. And, second, there is no reason to presume that changes which favour landlords necessarily perpetuate feudal relations and institutions, albeit in a different form.

In this context it is interesting to look at the role which agronomy played in the Prussian reform. Albrecht Thaer, the father of agronomy in Germany, played a central part in drafting the Prussian reform laws, in particular the law which divided up the commons into private plots (*Gemeinheitsteilung*) introduced in 1821. He opposed the protection of peasants from eviction and the maintenance of the commons on the grounds that they hindered the development of rational agriculture. The aim of agriculture, for Thaer, was not just production but, as he put it, 'to make profit or money by the production and sometimes by the processing of vegetable and animal substances'. In fact what Thaer called for was the development of commercial agriculture, and the realisation of the aim which he set for agriculture presupposed exclusive proprietary rights in land and that the owner of the land was able to change its use and the organisation of production according to the requirements of profit. It was because of these that he opposed *Bauernschutz* and the commons. In fact Thaer was the only agronomist to have opposed the commons; agronomists of the new school in pre-revolutionary France denounced them as 'vestiges of ancient barbarism'. Though the laws which Thaer helped draft favoured the Junkers, he was an apologist neither of the Junkers nor of feudal agriculture. Quite the opposite; his *The Principles of Rational Agriculture* published between 1809 and 1812 was no less than a compendium of how to bring about technical and organisational changes in feudal agriculture.[54] And the ideas of Thaer were not universally accepted; in fact, they were opposed by romantics and reactionaries like Adam Müller who very much wanted to retain the 'personal relationship in agriculture'.

It is this which led Simon (*The Failure of the Prussian Reform Movement*) to remark that while liberals and reformists tended to favour landlords (especially the commercial farmers among them) romantics and reactionaries were the most staunch supporters of the laws and regulations which protected the economic positions of the peasantry. In fact, the connection between Thaer and the Prussian reform was not accidental. For everywhere in Europe it was the break up of feudal agriculture which opened up the space for agronomy – a discourse which, like medicine, straddled a number of disciplines such as biology, physiology and chemistry as well as organisational and commercial questions. And throughout it was the agronomists who were the most trenchant critics of feudal agriculture.

At the end of this discussion it is necessary to add a qualification and make a general remark. Though we have talked of the Junkers, the serfs and the peasants none of these denote homogeneous categories. We have already indicated that there were important differences among the serfs and what the reformers did was to use some of the existing differences to create new differences like the self subsistent peasantry, on the one hand, and dependent peasants without land on the other. Similarly, the Junkers were themselves differentiated and they were divided in their attitude to the reform laws.[55] Further, there was an important difference between revolutionary France and reformist Prussia. The opposition in France was between the *seigneurs* and the peasants while that was not so in Prussia. The principal opposition there was between a section of the Junkers who were allied with reformist administrators like Stein, Hardenberg, Scharnhorst, Thaer, Humboldt etc, on the one hand, and the romantics and reactionary Junkers on the other. The point is that the lines of divisions in Prussia were just not the same as those in France and that is why the French Revolution cannot be simply counterposed to the Prussian reforms.

**Rural Labourers and the Flight from the Land**

The downward slide of cereal prices which had started in the mid 1870s finally came to a halt in the mid 1890s; in fact cereal prices started to rise in 1897 and continued to do so more or less till the First World War. But the Bund, as before, kept up its campaign for higher tariffs. The emphasis of its propaganda, however, shifted from protection against foreign competition to the shortage of labour in the countryside (*Leutenot*) arising out of the migration of rural inhabitants towards the cities.[56] Count von Kanitz, the mover of the notorious motion to nationalise the grain trade, attacked the industrialists for robbing the land of its rightful cultivators. 'Every adult labourer', he said, 'represents a considerable capital which we have laid out, [sic] yet when the people are grown up they offer their labour to the industry, which thus reaps where it has not sown.'[57]

The flight from the land, *Landflucht* as it was called, was not a new phenomenon in Germany; there had been a massive migration of rural population since the 1860s, first to the US and then principally to the German cities. Nor was the flight from the land a peculiarly German phenomenon; it was, as indeed it is now, a natural correlate of the development of capitalism. English farmers and agricultural labourers, for instance, deserted the countryside in large numbers in the last quarter of the nineteenth century when English agriculture started to contract under the pressure of international competition.

Yet there was something specific about rural – urban migration in the Germany of the 1890s. The migration was then seen as a product of the economic and social conditions of rural labourers. The emphasis, in other words, was not so much on the pull of the cities but rather on the push of the rural areas. A large number of studies, ranging from Weber's survey of the conditions of rural labourers to *Verein für Sozialpolitik*'s analysis of the causes of emigration from rural areas, catalogued the oppressive conditions of employment and the poverty of the labourers in the Junker estates of East Elbia. The studies singled out these factors, rather than the better conditions which awaited rural emigrants in the cities, as the main cause of flight from the land.[58]

Flight from the land in the 1880s and the 1890s had a specific pattern of its own; unlike previous migration most of it was from the districts where Junker estates dominated the landscape. The emigrants from the rural areas then, as Weber emphasised, were not for the most part peasants but rural labourers. It is these two features of the pattern of the flight from the land – its origin in East Elbia and the fact that it consisted of rural labourers rather than independent peasants – which gave it a wider significance. Just as in the case of international competition in agricultural commodities, the effects of emigration were not evenly spread over the whole of agriculture or over different regions. Their incidence was concentrated on the Junker estates.[59] The issue of rural migration, like the issue of protection from foreign agricultural imports, thus became linked with estate agriculture, and the study of the causes of emigration in turn became a study of the anachronistic conditions which prevailed in the Junker estates.

Kautsky interpreted the significance of the pattern of rural emigration in terms of its implication for the extension of capitalist agriculture and the survival of peasant agriculture. According to Kautsky, it imposed a constraint on the expansion of capitalist agriculture, while it had little or no effect on peasant agriculture. For peasant farms, especially small and medium ones, Kautsky argued, often had a surplus of labour and thus did not suffer from a shortage of hands. They suffered rather from a shortage of land.[60] One may as well note the paradoxical feature which Kautsky by implication attributed to rural emigration: though it fuelled the development of capitalist industry it also stifled the growth of capitalist agriculture.

What gave the flight from the land an additional significance was the fact that it was coupled with the immigration of Polish labourers in those provinces of Prussia which German labourers were fleeing, the very provinces which already had a substantial Polish population and which successive German governments wanted to Germanise. Weber,[61] fervent nationalist as he was, termed this exchange of Polish for German population as a process of 'denationalisation'. Emigration from the rural areas in the 1860s till the 1880s did not have racial associations, because it did not create any vacuum to be filled by the influx of foreign labourers.

The destination of rural emigrants started to change in the 1880s. Earlier on it was emigration overseas, especially to the US, which accounted for a large part of rural emigration. However, by the start of the 1890s German emigration to the US had started to taper off, and by the end of the 1890s the whole of overseas emigration had decreased to a fraction of its former level. For instance overseas emigration declined from 120,000 in 1891 to a mere 24,000 in 1899. Likewise the origin of rural emigrants underwent a change in time. To start with, the emigrants of the 1840s till the 1860s came from South-West Germany, an area characterised by fragmentary land holdings. But from the 1870s onwards the rural emigrants predominantly came from rural provinces of Prussia in the east, the region of large estates.[62]

The decrease in the rate of overseas emigration in the 1890s did not mean a decline in the number of rural labourers leaving the countryside, but simply that they were going to German cities rather than overseas. During the period 1885–1900 German industry, which was already fairly developed in the 1870s, grew more or less steadily. At the time of the Caprivi treaties in the early 1890s Germany was already a major exporter of manufactured goods, and by the late 1890s Germany had overtaken Britain in steel production, the production of heavy machinery and electrical goods.[63] In the 1890s the export of goods had grown as though to replace the export of men. In fact the needs of industry had grown to the extent that it led to the influx of foreign labourers, especially Polish; around the turn of the century there were substantial pockets of foreign labourers in the steel and coal industries. So in general terms it was the rapid expansion of German industry which became in the 1890s the principal force attracting rural labourers. Hence the hostility of the agrarians to the continuing development of German industry and the debate which counterposed the interests of industry to those of agriculture, or rather to those of estate agriculture.[64]

Thus the estate agriculture of East Elbia at the end of the nineteenth century came under pressure from two different sources – the international grain market and the domestic labour market, in particular the urban labour market catering for the needs of the industry. The pressure on Junker agriculture to change therefore came more from events outside agriculture in German cities than from internal competition within German agriculture. It is for this reason that the problems of agriculture were discussed in the 1890s in relation to either tariffs or the migration of labour to the cities. This cannot be too heavily emphasised, since it means that it is not at all legitimate to talk of autonomous dynamics of capitalism in German agriculture. This indeed is one of the main themes of Kautsky's *Die Agrarfrage*, in which he argues that impetus for change in agriculture does not come from inside but from outside, from industry and urban areas. However, we leave this aside for discussion in chapter 4.

We shall turn now to the two questions: who were the emigrating rural labourers and what were their conditions of employment like?

The rural labourers did not form a homogeneous group. Some were landless while some others, as Kautsky points out, were themselves small peasants who sold their surplus labour to the estate owners or even to other peasants. Their tenures of employment were also varied; some of them were seasonal while some others were regularly employed.[65] And besides these there were important regional differences in the laws and customs which underlay the employer and employee relationships in rural areas; these varied from one constituent state of the Reich to another.

In the rural districts of Prussia the *Instleute* were the mainstay of the regular labour force in the rural areas. These labourers were hired by the year and they were paid partly in money and partly in kind (*Naturalien*) and at times they also got a strip of land to cultivate for their own consumption. Further, the *Instleute* were often housed by the estate owners, and whether or not they were had an important bearing on their relationship with their employers. In fact some of them were by prevailing standards in the countryside fairly prosperous and in some cases they themselves employed labourers. Basically they furnished regular field labour and in addition their wives and children performed various kinds of work on the estate.[66]

It was not just the *Instleute* but also their families which were employed. The relationship between them and the estate owners was anchored in the *Gesindeordnung*, introduced in 1810 so that the landlords could retain the use of the labour of their ex-serfs (families included) in forms not much different from those which prevailed before the emancipation. The essential point, however, was that the *Gesindeordnung* put the rural labourers on a par with the domestic servants; in fact the law applied to everyone who was housed by the employer. To be treated as a *Gesinde* (house servant) in particular meant that the labourers' wives and children were required to perform various unpaid services in the employer's house or estate. And, moreover, that they could not form an association, a trade union for instance, to further their economic demands. In addition to the obligations imposed on them by the *Gesindeordnung* labourers as well as peasants in rural Prussia were required to perform what was termed 'the hand and span' service in connection with the execution of rural works.[67]

The *Gesindeordnung* was, however, not peculiar to Prussia; similar laws existed in other states of Germany. Both Saxony and Bavaria had their own variants of the law; in fact, the Bavarian *Gesindeordnung* was even more restrictive and onerous than the Prussian one. What a *Gesindeordnung* implies, and that is what makes it of general interest, is a distinction between a 'personal' and a commercial relationship of employment. The house servant embodies the former and to be treated as one is to be denied rights like the right of association which are taken as correlates of the latter relationship. The treatment of an employee as house servant was not peculiar to Germany; the systematic distinction between servant–master and employer–employee relationship was only introduced in Britain, for instance, in 1871.[68]

For Weber the economy of Junker estates was characterised by patriarchial relationships and, for him, the *Instmann* was the embodiment of that relationship. In the 1890s, however, it was the *Instleute* who were migrating in large number to cities and that for Weber was ominous for Junker estates. For according to him just as the migration of labour destroyed the Roman Latifundia so the migration of the *Instleute* would destroy the Junker estate. However, the emigration of the *Instleute* did not lead to the destruction of the Junker estates; they were replaced by seasonal labourers, mostly of Polish origin.

In fact, to a degree the Junkers benefited from the substitution of seasonal for regular labour. Poles and the labourers of other

Slav nationalities were only employed for part of the year – they normally came in spring and left in autumn. Further, coming from countries poorer than Germany they were willing to work for lower wages. These labourers were housed in barracks on the large estates and they were ruthlessly exploited and did not enjoy any legal protection from the employers. The substitution of seasonal for regular labour fitted in with the change in the composition of output of large estates in favour of field crops like sugar beet; for such crops required seasonal rather than regular labour. However, seasonal labourers were not a perfect substitute for regular labourers; certain tasks (looking after the animals) and certain products (meat and dairy products) required regular rather than seasonal labour. In a more general context the emigration of regular labourers and their replacement by seasonal labourers did not improve working conditions in the countryside; on balance if anything they made them worse. For the seasonal labourers had even fewer rights and even less legal protection than the *Instleute* whom they replaced.

The answer to the question 'what made the German labourers leave the countryside?' may seem obvious now – their economic and social conditions. These were obviously crucial, but it needs emphasising that there would have been migration even in the absence of the oppressive conditions of living and employment in the countryside.[69] For there would still have been an economic gap between the city and the countryside. Though the difference between urban and rural incomes was a major determinant of migration, its influence on different sections of the rural population was not the same. For, as Weber emphasised, the emigrants for the most part were not independent peasants or the poorest sections of the countryside but rather the relatively well off *Instleute*. But it was the latter who bore the brunt of the oppressive *Gesindeordnung*.

Apart from that it needs pointing out that there is an important difference between the respective positions of peasants (those who own the land they cultivate) and agricultural labourers, which on its own would tend to make the migration of the latter quantitatively more important than that of the former. That is, agricultural labourers have to migrate as families while peasants can migrate individually leaving certain members of the family behind to tend the family land. Thus *ceteris paribus* emigration from those districts where agricultural labourers predominate will be higher than from those where land-owning peasants dominate. Weber found this to be the case but he chose to explain it all in terms of psychological dispositions.[70]

One needs to be explicit here and emphasise that it was not just the oppressive conditions of living and employment in rural areas taken in isolation but rather the glaring difference between such conditions in rural and in urban areas which was in fact the main cause of emigration from the countryside. In matters of industrial and social legislation Germany was as advanced as any other country in Europe. In fact the social legislation of the 1880s introduced during the phase of what was termed 'State Socialism' became a model of social legislation in other capitalist countries. But the important point is that very few of the industrial and social laws applied to the countryside. For instance, unlike industrial establishments agricultural estates were not subject to any public inspection; insurance against accidents and sickness did not apply to agricultural labourers and so on. Moreover, as pointed out earlier, agricultural labourers did not have the right of association. In the Germany of the 1890s agriculture and industry, as it were, constituted two distinct social and economic estates, each with it own laws and its own conditions.[71]

This glaring discrepancy not only had implication for the migration of labour but also for political organisation. We pointed out in the previous chapter that the SPD just after its legislation was an almost exclusively urban party and in fact remained predominantly so even after its agitation on the land (discussed in the next chapter). But that was not just because the SPD had privileged industrial labourers in its programmes. It also had to do with the fact that the kind of organisations and groupings – like factory based organisations, social groups and neighbourhood committees – from which the party drew its support were absent in rural areas. And there were formidable obstacles to the setting up of such organisations.

For a start the rural inhabitant did not have the right of association. Besides this the rural population was spatially dispersed; moreover, rural labourers, the section of the rural population which the SPD had singled out to appeal to, were politically as well as economically dependent on estate owners. If the rural labourer was an *Instmann* then he lived on the estate and even if he did not he came under the jurisdiction of the *Gutsbezirk*, the unit of local government in rural Prussia which the Junkers dominated. The conditions in other parts of Germany were different but that difference does not affect the general argument that the urban bias of the SPD was not just grounded in doctrine but more importantly in the rural–urban divide which characterised Germany at that time.

The emigration of rural labourers posed a special problem for the SPD since it resulted in a decrease of the very section of the population which the party had singled out as its potential supporters.[72] Not only was the problem that the regular labourers were not firmly tethered to the countryside, but also that the seasonal labourers who replaced them could not be won over easily. For most of the seasonal labourers were Polish and not German, and they were in Germany for only a part of the year. Of all the political parties the SPD was the only one which campaigned for better conditions and legal protection for foreign labourers working in Germany; but the party did not succeed in acquiring a stronghold amongst them.[73] One most important consequence of the massive emigration out of the countryside was that it undermined the continuity of political work on the land; for often it was the politically conscious who chose to flee the oppressive conditions on the land. A large number of rural workers who migrated to towns did eventually support the SPD but that support was often not translated in the number of seats which the party had in the *Reichstag*, for the electoral boundaries were drawn on the basis of 1867 and 1871 censuses and were not revised with the changes in the distribution of population from rural to urban areas. The result was that the two parties with large rural support, the Centre Party and the Conservative Party, had a much larger share of parliamentary seats than their share of the total vote. It was these two parties that were indirectly the main beneficiaries of rural–urban migration from the 1890s onwards. For despite the decline in their electoral support they managed to retain their parliamentary strength.[74]

## Rural Indebtedness

The indebtedness of the farmers was yet another component of the Bund's propaganda about the plight of German agriculture. Over time rural indebtedness, both in absolute terms and in terms of the ratio of debt to the value of land, steadily increased.

Though it was taken as such by agrarians, the increasing debt was not by itself either a sign or a cause of crisis. For arguably the increase in indebtedness was just a consequence of the extension of monetary and credit relations to agriculture, or more specifically of the fact that an increasing numbers of buyers were resorting to mortgage credit.[75] Most of the rural indebtedness was in the form of mortgage credit; so its increase was connected with the increase in the value of land mortgaged rather than with an increase in investment on land.

Kautsky (*Die Agrarfrage*, ch. 5, sec. c) took the increase in mortgage credit to imply that the ownership of land was progressively passing into the hands of mortgage banks. This, for him, had a double significance. On the one hand, it meant the separation of the ownership of land from its management – a feature which he regarded as an essential condition for the nationalisation of land. In interpreting the significance of mortgage credit in this manner Kautsky was putting the German land tenure system, characterised by the absence of the leasing of land, on a par with the English system, in which leasing was common. On the other hand, the increase in the area of mortgaged land, Kautsky thought, would make it easy to nationalise land. For that would only entail the nationalisation of a handful of mortgage banks rather than a large number of farmers. We leave these arguments at this point and come back to them in chapter four.

An important feature of rural indebtedness was that it was not evenly spread over different types of farms and thus over different regions. Though indebtedness was not restricted to farms of a particular size, *pro rata* or in terms of the gearing ratio (debt to the value of land) indebtedness increased with the size of the farm and it was, therefore, higher in the rural provinces of Prussia than in other parts of the country. Thus indebtedness was more of a problem for the large holdings of the Junkers than for other farmers.[76]

A large debt obviously meant a large debt service cost, but also a large fixed cost which did not vary with the variations in the revenue. This was crucial because it made estate farmers especially susceptible to fluctuations in income. A large gearing ratio, in addition, implied that the economic interests of large estate owners essentially lay in a continuous increase in land prices. An interesting feature was that land prices were tied to tariff protection; estate owners, in a number of cases, used increases in tariffs as an occasion to sell their estates. This was what happened after the passing of the Bülow tariffs in 1904 which increased tariffs on agricultural imports. Further, not only tariffs but also the policies of the settlement commission (*Ansiedlungsgesellschaft*), a public body which bought lands offered for sale with a view to keeping them in German hands, kept the price of land high in the eastern provinces of Prussia.

If the Junkers faced a crisis due to indebtedness it was on account of revenue, because of a decline in grain prices, not keeping pace with the increase in mortgage payments, because of speculation and the resulting increase in the price of land. It was this mixture of rising land prices and decreasing grain prices which led to a sudden jump in the number of foreclosures in the mid 1880s. Some Social Democrats (Parvus,[77] for instance) saw indebtedness rather than international competition in the grain market as the main cause of the crisis of estate agriculture. But the two were not mutually exclusive. The point is that the Junkers were particularly vulnerable to any decrease in grain prices because of their high indebtedness. The Bund constantly demanded relief from the burden of indebtedness and to that effect suggested the nationalisation of mortgage debts, a demand which orthodox Social Democrats like Kautsky opposed.[78]

**Differentiation in the Countryside**

German agriculture, as elsewhere in Europe, was highly differentiated, constituted as it was of farms ranging from tiny vegetable and fruit patches to large estates which were among the largest in Europe. Yet differentiation in the German countryside had its own specific features. The contrast in the size of the farms, especially in the east, was greater and more striking than elsewhere in Europe. Further, the differences had a strong regional character.

When describing the differences in the countryside one is interested in characteristics such as the amount of labour employed, the source of labour (family or the labour market), the composition of output, the extent of dependence on the market and whether or not agriculture is the principal or just a subsidiary or yet another activity. However, information on these is often not directly available; instead what is usually available is the distribution of farms into groups divided according to their area. One reason is obviously that while property in land in most countries occupies a privileged status and is thus registered and documented, the same is not true for property in agricultural implements, livestock and other things which as well as land have an important bearing on the characteristics of the farm. Thus the discussions about the differences among the units of production in agriculture assume the form of a hermeneutic: the land at the disposal of the farm in addition to the importance which it has in its own right becomes an index of other characteristics. This indirectly is one of the reasons why the controversy as to whether or not large farms are more efficient than small farms never seems to stop or be resolved – we shall have something to say about this controversy later in chapter four.

There were three agricultural censuses during the period when the agrarian question was discussed in Germany: those in 1882, 1895 and 1907.[79] Kautsky discussed the first two in his book. The data in these censuses were organised according to the area of the farm divided into the following 6 categories:

1) farms up to .5 hectare
2) from .5 ha to 2 ha
3) from 2 ha to 5 ha
4) from 5 ha to 20 ha
5) from 20 ha to 100 ha
6) over 100 ha

These categories, however, can be collapsed into three categories which are perhaps closer to the kinds of differences in which Marxists have been interested. The first two taken together for the most part contain dwarf holdings or fragmentary farms – we shall come to the economic significance of such holdings shortly. The middle two categories taken together constitute the most heterogeneous category in that they contain both small and fairly sizeable peasant farms as well as commercial farms specialising in particular commodities. The last two, as the first two, are fairly unambiguous in that they represent large farms.

Let us look at the picture indicated by the contents of three censuses. For instance for the distribution of the total number of farms and the total cultivated into farms of different sizes according to the 1882 Census, see Table 2.1.

TABLE 2.1 Analysis of 1882 Farm Census data

| Category | Number of farms as percentage of the total | Combined area as percentage of the total |
|---|---|---|
| Above 20 ha | 5.8 | 55.5 |
| From 20 to 2 ha | 36.2 | 38.8 |
| Up to 2 ha | 58 | 5.7 |

The general picture is one of extreme inequality. Of the 5 million enterprises covered in the census a clear majority of them were tiny; in fact so tiny that something like 3 million of them constituted only 5.7 per cent of the total cultivated area. The large farms, on the other hand, were on average so large that only about 180,000 (a very small proportion of the total) of them spanned over a half of the total area. In fact, the two distributions, as can be seen from the table, are mirror images of each other – both of them are heavily tilted towards one of the extremes.

Assuming that self-subsistent and independent peasantry (in the sense of having enough land to sustain the household) falls in the middle two categories, it is clear that there was a substantial peasantry in Germany; but it was, as we shall see later, very unevenly distributed over the regions. Despite this the single most striking feature of the distribution is still the coexistence of large numbers of fragmentary holdings with a small number of farms occupying most of the land, a feature to which Kautsky pays a more or less exclusive attention in his analysis.

How did the two distributions change over the 25 years covered by the three censuses? Exact figures apart, the notable feature of the three censuses taken together was that there was little change. Kautsky notes this in *Die Agrarfrage* (ch. 2, sec. b) and argues that it does not imply the absence of change, instead that changes concern what different types of farms sell in the market and the kind of economic activities which they carry out, and thus are not registered as changes in the size distribution of farms. The figures for changes in the distributions can be seen in Table 2.2.

SOME ASPECTS OF GERMAN AGRICULTURE 63

TABLE 2.2 Changes in the size distribution of farms 1882–1907

| Category | Change in the percentage of the total number (1882–1907) | Change in the percentage of the total area (1882–1907) |
|---|---|---|
| Above 20 ha | −0.8 | −4. |
| From 2 to 20 ha | −0.1 | +4.1 |
| Up to 2 ha | +0.9 | −0.3 |

What Table 2.2 gives is the bird's eye view of the change, which though not the same as the detailed picture is not far removed from it. We have left out the 1895 Census but doing that does not under-represent the change. For the changes between the first two censuses are generally in the same direction as those between the last two. The same is also true for the components of each of the three categories.

Over the quarter of a century covered by the three censuses, the number of farms increased by around half a million (approximately by 9 per cent) and, as one can infer from Table 2.2, most of this increase was in the category of dwarf holdings (up to 2 ha). That increase in the total number by itself would have meant a decrease in the average size of the farm on the grounds that the same amount of land was divided among a larger number of farms. There was, however, a slight increase in the total cultivated area between 1882 and 1895; but then there was, more or less, an equal decrease during the period between the last two censuses (1895–1907).

One would normally attribute this increase in the number of farms to the parcellisation of a given area of land which accompanies a growth of rural population. But the point is that over this period the total of the population dependent on agriculture decreased.[80] The two facts taken together may seem paradoxical; but the number of farms is not directly linked to the size of population dependent on agriculture. To establish a link between the latter and the former one has to take into account the status of farms which are being counted. For the present purposes that status is specified by two features: the nature of land tenure and the purpose of cultivation.

So far as the farms in the category 'up to 2 ha' – the category where most of the increase took place – were concerned, they were either owner-occupied or occupied by agricultural labourers who received a strip of land as part of their wages. Moreover, given that the average size of the farm in this category was around ½ ha the aim of cultivation was to satisfy the needs of the household, rather than to produce for the market. Farms up to 2 ha, then, were generally extensions of small peasant households; the implication is that the increase in the number of farms was linked to the proliferation of autonomous households.

When explaining what might have led to this proliferation one needs to take into account a not so obvious point that the factors which affect the size of the rural population do not all have the same effect on the number of autonomous households. A natural increase in population coupled with the division of land on inheritance will lead to a corresponding increase in the number of autonomous households and thus the farms linked to those households. But emigration from the countryside often does not lead to a decrease in the number of households and thus the number of farms. For emigrants are often single individuals rather than whole families, who reduce the size rather than the numbers of the households.[81] What this asymmetry of effects means is that a natural increase in rural population, even when coupled with a more than offsetting emigration from rural areas, can be sufficient to lead to a parcellisation of land and thus an increase in the number of farms. This asymmetry of effects is further reinforced by a feature peculiar to agriculture to which Kautsky draws attention: while there is no physical restriction on the division of land, the consolidation of several farms into one is subject to such a restriction. The reason is that the latter usually makes economic sense if the farms in question are contiguous to each other.[82]

These factors can only account for the increase in the number of owner-occupied rather than all the farms in the category 'up to 2 ha'. In addition the increase must have been due to an increase in the number of labourers who were given a patch of land by their employers. Not all agricultural labourers were, however, given land; and those who were not, as Kautsky points out, had very little personal freedom. They could not marry and set up a household. The massive flight from land, especially by those who fell into this category, may have led employers to grant land to landless labourers and thereby increase the number of labour-occupied farms. We leave aside the significance of the increase in the number of farms in the lowest category for discussion later in this chapter and turn now to changes in other categories.

Over the period 1882–1905 there was an increase in numbers in the category '2 to 20 ha' and a decrease in the highest category 'above 20 ha'. One would expect farms in these two categories, unlike those in the lowest category, not to be labour-occupied. Further, given the relative absence of leasing in Wilhelmine Germany one would expect them to be mostly "owner-occupied". What the predominance of owner-occupation suggests is tnat the sub-division of land on inheritance must have been the main factor responsible for changes in these categories. Although at first sight it may seem paradoxical it can account for both the increase and the decrease in the numbers.

The point is that the sub-division of farms on inheritance not only affects the numbers in the category in which they happen to be to start with, but also the numbers in the categories of smaller farms below them. For the sub-division may reduce the size of a farm to the point where it filters down to the category below. Each category may thus gain farms from the categories above and likewise lose some to the categories below. The actual change in each category will then depend on the balance of losses and gains as well as the increase due to the sub-divisions which keep the farms in the same category. The balance can be either positive or negative except at either end of the range because the lowest category (up to 2 ha) cannot lose and the highest category (farms above 20 ha) cannot gain from the other categories. What this means is that as a result of sub-division of inheritance the numbers in the highest category can decrease while those in the lowest category can only increase. As for the numbers in the middle categories they can either decrease or increase, depending on the balance.

Details aside, an interesting general implication of the argument is that a natural increase in population coupled with the sub-division of land will by themselves change the size distribution of land and bias it more and more towards smaller farms. If we accept Kautsky's point about the difficulty in consolidating small farms then it becomes clear that partible private property in land is itself a mechanism for the perpetuation and even proliferation of small peasantry.

However, in Wilhelmine Germany not all landed property was divided up on inheritance, especially so the large estates of East Elbia.[83] A high proportion of the estates were subject to *Fideikomiss*, the restriction being that their historical boundaries had to be preserved. According to Kautsky, something like a half of the Prussian estates were entailed, and not only that but the proportion of entailed estates increased in the last quarter of the nineteenth century. The aim of the institution obviously was to pre-empt any attempt on the part of the future generations to divide up the estate. None the less, the *Fideikomiss* could not stop the number of large estates from decreasing. But the decline would have been even greater without the institution of the *Fideikomiss*, especially in view of the indebtedness of large estates and the forced sales to which this led in some cases. Though there was a peasant counterpart of the *Fideikomiss* in the form of the *Anerbenrecht*, by and large entailing was restricted to the higher end of the scale; and its net result, apart from other things, was to maintain the unequal distribution of land.

Before moving on to discuss the regional differences in German agriculture, one may note the changes in the distribution of the total area amongst farms of different size in Table 2.2. Those changes, though still small, are greater than the changes in the distribution of the total number. In addition, the two sets of changes are not in the same direction. For instance, it can be seen that the share of the lowest category in the total area decreased, despite the fact of both an absolute and a relative increase in the number of farms in that category. In part the converse is true for the middle category. Kautsky explains both these by the merger of small with larger farms of the middle category. In addition to that one can also account for the increase in the share of medium sized farms in the total area by the process of filtering: one would expect the farms which filter down from the highest to the middle category to be larger in size than those which filter out of it to the lowest category.

How were the different types of farms geographically distributed? With a few notable exceptions farms above 100 ha were confined to the provinces to the east of the Elbe, the only major exception being the Duchy of Anhalt in Middle Germany. With slight amendments the same was true even lower down the scale in farms from 20 to 100 ha. By and large in South and West Germany farms did not exceed 20 ha, and for the most part they were considerably smaller than that. So in general terms North and East Germany was the land of large estates while South and West Germany was the land of small farms.[84] But this was only one aspect of geographical distribution and the one which is commonly known. There were others which were equally interesting.

In nearly all the East Elbian provinces the landscape was either dominated by estates larger than 100 ha or fragmentary holdings less than 2 ha. The self-sufficient peasantry was a rarity in these provinces. Farms of less than 2 ha were not peasant but what both Lenin and Kautsky termed the proletarian farms. Families attached to these farms, as Kautsky emphasised in *Die Agrarfrage* (ch. 8), did not subsist just by cultivating the fragment of land which they possessed but by selling their labour to the large estates under whose shadows they existed. In a large number of cases these small farms were created by estate owners themselves when they gave their labourers the use of a strip of land. What this meant is that estates and dwarf holdings did not compete with each other in the market for agricultural commodities, but stood in a complementary relation to each other: the latter supplied labour to the former.

Fragmentary or dwarf holdings, unlike large and middle farms, were not local to any particular region. With a few exceptions they were densely spread over the whole countryside. But since in the case of these holdings cultivation was a household activity, the range of other activities carried out by the households stationed on such holdings crucially depended on whether they were in industrial or in agricultural regions. If they were in the latter they functioned as the reservoir of the agricultural labour force. On the other hand, fragmentary holdings in the industrial regions, especially those in the vicinity of cities, were more diverse in character; for they had a much greater range of activities open to them. Another interesting feature of Germany was that the provinces in which large farms dominated had either very little or no industry. The line of division between the industrial and agricultural regions coincided fairly closely with the line separating the regions of large estate from those of medium and small farms. Details aside, it is true to say that the river Elbe was not only a geographical landmark but also a structural divide in German agriculture.[85]

The discussion so far, but for a few tangential arguments, has been exclusively concerned with the size of the farms. So we turn now to the question of association between the size of the farm and its other economic and social characteristics. The essential point is that in the case of arable land the distinction between large and small farms is in actual fact a distinction between a wage labour and a family labour farm. Roscher (apart from other things an agronomist) focuses on this point when he defines a large farm not in terms of its size but in terms of the fact that it employs wage labour.[86] In a similar vein the Erfurt programme and Engels (*The Peasant Question* . . .) define a small farm as one which is large enough to sustain the family in question. This definition of small farm obviously excludes fragmentary holdings, since they are not large enough to sustain the family on their own. According to the censuses of 1895 and 1907 only about a tenth of the household holdings up to 2 ha were completely dependent on the cultivation of land, the rest participated in other activities for their sustenance.

Suggestive though these definitions are, the main problem with them is that they do not lead to an unambiguous correspondence between the area of the farm and classifications 'large' and 'small'. To take the definition of a large farm first: the employment of wage labour not only depends on the area of the farm but also on a number of other factors like the level of mechanisation, the composition of the output and the size of the family. For instance, a vineyard of 2 ha may heavily depend on regular wage labour while a grain farm of over 10 ha may do without it and just need seasonal labour.[87] As for the notions of family labour or a farm large enough to sustain the family, the main problem is that the family is, as Chayanov repeatedly emphasised, a highly variable entity.[88] Not only is the size of the family defined in terms of kinship boundaries variable, but also the size of the family labour available to work on the family labour farm may have no pre-given relation to the former. For when the labour market is well developed and there are ample opportunities for migration to cities the size of the family labour force may well vary without any variation in the size of the family as a kinship unit.

The point of these qualifications, however, is not that the area of the farm is of no use whatsoever; rather that its significance is highly context-specific. The 1907 Census contained a fairly detailed sample survey of the sources of labour used on farms of different sizes. What turns out to be the case is that farms of all sizes, even those smaller than 2 ha, employed wage labour of some kind. This, by the way, is very much in line with the sample surveys of agriculture in other countries; in India for instance. The general feature seems to be that, unlike in industry, in agriculture there is no firm dividing line between enterprises which employ wage labour and those which confine themselves to the family labour. The results of the sample survey can best be described by Table 2.3.

TABLE 2.3 Survey of employed labour

| | |
|---|---|
| 1. Farms above 100 ha | Negligible amount of family labour and nearly all wage labour |
| 2. Farms from 20 to 100 ha | Predominantly wage labour |
| 3. Farms from 10 to 20 ha | The balance distinctly in favour of family labour |
| 4. Farms from 2 to 10 ha | A very small amount of wage labour |
| 5. Farms up to 2 ha | Nearly all family labour |

One can draw a number of straightforward conclusions from this table. The firms in the first two categories were capitalist farms, in which family labour confined itself to the supervision of wage labour. Referring back to the first two tables we can say that capitalist farms spanned just over a half of the total cultivated area. Category 3 is of special importance, for it came nearest to being independent and self-subsistent peasantry. The farms in these categories on average accounted for 7 per cent of the total farms and 17 per cent of the total cultivated area. Category 4 may be said to have consisted of small peasants, those who, except in particular cases like wine producers, were quite poor and had to depend on either the sale of labour or other activities to supplement their income.

Lenin, in fact, wrote an article on the 1907 Census and commented in detail on the findings of the sample survey.[89] It was, however, Category 5 which he singled out for special comment. The central finding of the survey, for him, was that of 3,378,509 farms contained in that category only 14 per cent of them were economically independent and the rest regularly depended on the sale of their labour. Holdings in this category were on average $\frac{1}{2}$ ha in size and a substantial proportion of them were occupied by the agricultural labourers who received the use of a patch of land in lieu of wages. Thus Lenin's main argument was that 'farms less than 2 ha' do not so much represent farms as proletarian households that possess a parcel of land.

This argument, which was the same as advanced by Kautsky in *Die Agrarfrage*, was in fact highly original and departed from the traditional Marxist characterisation of what constitutes a wage labourer. We shall assess this argument in chapter 4. However, it is important here to note the general implication of it: that capitalism can develop in agriculture without any necessary increase in the number of landless labourers, and accompanied by the continued survival or even multiplication of small holdings. Thus according to Lenin's criterion for identifying agricultural proletariat the increase in the number of the holdings up to 2 ha in the 25 years between 1882 and 1907 was not an increase in the number of peasants, as revisionists like David and Bernstein (of whom we shall have more to say in chapters three and four) argued, but an increase in the size of the agricultural proletariat.

It is at this stage best to draw the two strands of the discussion together by way of a conclusion. Though the change in the distribution of the total number of farms and the total area into farms of different sizes was relatively minor, there was, nevertheless, an important change in German agriculture. Capitalist development of agriculture did not take the form of an extension in the area occupied by large capitalist farms; instead it took the form of an increase in the intensity of cultivation and thus a lowering of the threshold where wage labour started to become important.[90] Though there was no survey of the sources of labour in the censuses of 1882 and 1895, the extent of the dependence of wage labour in the category 'farms from 10 to 20 ha' was higher than generally expected. In addition to an increase in the intensity of cultivation there was also a significant change in the composition of output. East Elbian estates, as Kautsky points out, branched out from cultivation to the processing of agricultural produce, brewing and the refining of sugar.[91] We leave the discussion of capitalist development in German agriculture at this, and come back to it later in chapter four.

Now after this long discussion of various aspects of German agriculture one may want to raise the question: what briefly were the main features of German agriculture and the economy pertinent to the agrarian question?

To start with there was the fact of international competition and the emergence of an extensive market in agricultural commodities in the last quarter of the nineteenth century. But it was not so much this in isolation as the German response to it in the form of successive tariff policies, and the way in which such policies served as the point of encounter between economics and politics, which was of central importance. Essentially, tariff policies not only had economic effects but they also furnished the ground for the emergence of alliances between political parties, the Anti-Socialist alliance of 1878–9, for instance, and political organisations representing various economic interest groups, Bund der Landwirte, for example.

However, it needs emphasising that it was not just important to the international market in agricultural commodities but also to the changes within the German economy itself. The agrarian question was raised at a time when the structure of the economy was rapidly shifting in favour of industry. Paradoxically then agriculture assumed political importance precisely at a time when its importance in the national economy was steadily declining – a fact which Kautsky singled out for a special emphasis in *Die Agrarfrage*. The growth of German industry led to a steady increase in urban incomes as well as in the volume of employment. It offered the rural inhabitants an opportunity of walking more or less straight into a job.

One of the essential features of the German economy then was the urban–rural gap, not only an economic but also a political and social gap. It leads to a massive flight from the land; what gives it an additional importance is the fact that the SPD was, as Kautsky candidly pointed out, a predominantly urban and industrial party.

Finally there was the fact of the regional diversity of Germany. While North and East Germany was dominated by large estates, agriculture of South and West Germany was composed mainly of small and medium size peasant farms. The economic divisions characteristic of a factory could be easily applied to the former but not to the latter.

# 3 *Landagitation*

Just twelve days after the expiry of the Anti-Socialist Law in October 1890 the SPD held its congress in Halle.[1] The rapidity with which the party managed to do this points to the fact that it not only survived the period of banishment but actually managed to thrive during it. Party literature was distributed widely during the period of illegality, especially in the late 1880s; and though the party itself did not contest elections during that period, known Social Democrats did. They used election campaigns as occasions for spreading general Social Democratic propaganda. From the Reichstag elections of 1884 onwards the share of votes cast for Social Democratic candidates steadily increased. In fact it was the spectacular increase in the share of votes cast for them in the elections of February 1890 which forced the government to let the Anti-Socialist Law lapse. As compared to the 1887 elections the number and the share of votes cast for Social Democratic candidates in 1890 almost doubled. With a fifth of votes cast for it the SPD became the largest parliamentary party, though not in terms of its share of seats in the Reichstag.[2]

The congress in Halle was thus not a congress of a party trying to pick up the pieces after a long exile but of a mass electoral party. The three main issues which concerned the party then were: the formulation of a new programme to replace the Gotha programme, how to devise a party organisation suited to legal existence and finally the formulation of future tactics and strategy.[3] We pointed out in chapter 1 that the party had already decided in 1887 to replace the Lassallean Gotha programme with a Marxist programme. That was, however, what the party did at the Erfurt congress, a year after the Halle congress – hence the name the Erfurt programme. Devising a new party organisation was an urgent issue, because the efficient and comprehensive organisation which the party had built up during the period of illegality could not be carried over to the period of legality. For the laws which governed the formation and functioning of organisations – political or otherwise – were, like so many other laws in Imperial Germany, not federal but state laws and each state had its own brand of such laws. The accession to legal existence had its costs too: the party could no longer circumvent laws as it had done during the past but had to start obeying them. The party organisation, though of great interest, is not relevant here so we leave that aside.[4]

What is, however, of interest here is the regional diversity of Germany in the 1890s. That diversity did not just consist in the differences in the structure of agriculture, to which we referred in the previous chapter, but also variations on the political and legal plane. Imperial Germany had a system of universal suffrage but only for the Reichstag; the system of elections to state assemblies (Diets) varied from state to state. In Prussia (by far the largest state), for instance, elections to the Prussian Diet were through the notorious 'three class system', a system of open rather than secret ballot and not based on the principle of 'one man one vote' but instead on 'each man according to his taxes'. For under the system the electorate was divided into three sections, each accounting for a third of the total income tax collected, and each with equal voting power. Though Bernstein suggested as early as 1893 that the SPD contest the Prussian Diet election, the party did not do so till the late 1890s and it was only in 1908 that the Diet had its first Social Democratic members. Other states had systems of universal suffrage, but Saxony too adopted the Prussian system as soon as Social Democrats started doing well in state elections.[5] The system of election to the State Diets would not be of crucial importance but for the fact that laws concerning associations, maintenance of public order and the *Gesindeordnung* (discussed earlier) were made and administered by state rather than federal agencies.

The point is that the SPD's spectacular success in the Reichstag elections had a very limited significance, for political power was not concentrated but, on the contrary, dispersed in institutions and apparatuses based on very different rules and regulations. The domain of competence of the Reichstag was very limited indeed and the regional diversity of Germany was a necessary correlate of the particular form of dispersion of political power which characterised the country. The dilemma which confronted the party throughout the pre-First World War period was that it was an outstandingly successful mass political party in a country which was far from democratic and in a country in which parliamentary elections had a very cramped place. It is this dilemma rather than the deviations from Marxism which give the revisionism and reformism which broke out in the SPD of the 1890s their significance.[6]

The other two tasks which faced the party, namely, the drawing up of a Marxist programme and the formulation of future tactics and strategy, were interrelated. However, as we shall point out later the relationship between the Erfurt programme and the party's policies was not necessarily a paradigmatic relationship between 'theory' and 'practice'. It was in Halle that the party leadership launched the slogan of 'branching out on the land'. But what was the status of the '*Landagitation*' on which the party was about to embark and where did it fit in the party's strategy and tactics?

*Landagitation* was not merely a response to events in the countryside. As is clear from the last chapter German agriculture was undergoing a rapid change and indeed felt the impact of what was happening in the countrysides beyond and in the cities within the German boundaries at the time of the launching of *Landagitation*. But neither was the international competition in grain and in other agricultural commodities, nor for that matter the flight from the land in response to the oppressive conditions in the countryside, the principal reason for launching *Landagitation*. In fact at that time rural areas in Germany were still politically underdeveloped and this remained the case even later when agrarian issues became prominent and when the Bund had gathered enough support to become a major political force. The plight and oppression of rural labourers acquired prominence not as a result of any political ferment in the countryside but as a result of the movement of population out of the countryside and consequent attempts to locate the causes of that movement. In this respect Wilhelmine Germany was different from the Russia of the turn of the century when Russian Marxists were discussing the agrarian question, or from the China of the late 1920s when Mao Tse-Tung went out to investigate the peasant movement in Hunan. Indeed Wilhelmine Germany was also different from the as yet non-unified Germany of 1848 when peasants in several regions rose against the servile obligations to which they were still subject and the financial liabilities which they had acquired in return for their freedom.[7] This was crucial, for the countryside by itself did not offer issues which *Landagitation* could take up and thus one of the main problems for the SPD was how to gain a toe-hold in rural areas.

Instead the SPD's interest in the rural areas was electoral. Of the fifth of the total votes cast for Social Democratic candidates in the 1890 election very few came from rural constituencies; and of the ones which did most were from the small towns placed among rural constituencies. The German countryside at the beginning of the 1890s had just over a third of the total population,[8] being at that time in electoral terms an exclusive domain of either the Conservative or the Centre Party or to a lesser extent of the National Liberal Party. In addition to that the electoral importance of the rural constituencies in the 1890s and even later up till the Weimar Republic far exceeded their weight in population. For the electoral boundaries in the North and the East were drawn by reference to the 1867 census and by reference to the 1871 census in the South. The tenacious refusal to alter the electoral boundaries in response to the massive movement of the population out of the rural areas obviously meant that the share of the parliamentary seats of the three parties with support in rural constituencies was much greater than their share of the total votes. A glaring example of the discrepancy is given by the voting figures in 1890: the SPD with 20 per cent of the total votes had only 9 per cent of the parliamentary seats while the Conservative Party, which was anchored in the rural districts of East Elbia with only 12.5 per cent of the votes, had a bit more than 19 per cent of the parliamentary seats. This is not an isolated instance that such a discrepancy remained true not only for the Conservative Party but also, in fact more so, for the Centre Party.[9]

The rural constituencies were therefore of particular value to the SPD for a variety of reasons. First, they were an as yet untapped reservoir of potential supporters and voters. And second the capture of rural constituencies was seen as part of the strategy to take on the bourgeois parties in their own hinterland. Bebel in his speech from the platform talked of breaking the hold of the Centre party on the rural areas of South and West Germany – an aim which was, as we shall see later, never realised.

The attraction of rural areas to the SPD in terms of electoral calculations is obvious: votes from the countryside given the bias in the electoral system would have yielded a more than proportional return in the form of parliamentary seats. But in addition the rural areas offered a special challenge to the SPD. For the amassing of votes in the urban areas, especially those with a Protestant majority, had not been a major problem. Thus Bebel boasted 'Wherever a factory chimney rises, there you will see socialists being made'.[10] But that Social Democratic propaganda was wasted on peasants was commonplace then and indeed later. Schaeffle (a prominent critic of Marx) predicted that Social Democracy would, as he put it, 'dash itself in pieces against the anti-collectivist skulls of the peasants and against peasants' sons in military uniform'.[11] This kind of sentiment was not restricted to the critics of Marxism and Social Democracy; Vollmar (a leading reformist in the ranks of the SPD) in the Frankfurt congress of 1894 argued that the peasantry would never accept Social Democratic or collectivist ideas, and that it was Social Democracy that would have to reconcile itself to the peasants' ideas.[12] In fact after a few years of *Landagitation* the whole of the party came around to recognising that Social Democratic propaganda was not easily digestible by the rural inhabitants. However, we leave this aside for later discussion. Further, the connection between the peasantry and the army was widely recognised. Engels in a letter to Liebknecht wrote that to win the land labourers would be at the same time to win the ace regiments of the Prussian army; and thus it would be, as Engels saw it, a sure guarantee against the physical repression of the SPD.[13]

Not only was the 'branching out onto the land' regarded as necessary and urgent but also eminently possible within a very short period of time. Engels in the same letter to Liebknecht talked of winning the land labourers within three years, and this optimism was not restricted to Engels, far away as he was from the battlefield.[14] *Landagitation* was not so much thought of as a 'long march' as a short campaign which would yield victories quickly. Indeed this optimism was not restricted to *Landagitation*, the leaders of the party talked of ultimate victory as if it was just on the horizon. This is crucial, for it is in striking contrast to what came to be generally accepted from the mid 1890s onwards; it was the realisation that final victory was elusive and that there was still a long and uncertain road ahead which furnished the background for the emergence of reformism and revisionism within the party.

Given that *Landagitation* was not a response to particular

events in the rural areas but was instead a central component of the SPD's strategy for political power, a series of questions are raised. What was the general political strategy of the SPD? What place did the elections occupy in that strategy? What was the connection between the party's electoral strategy of which *Landagitation* was an essential component and the Marxist Erfurt programme?

Contesting elections at various levels remained the centrepiece of SPD strategy and non-parliamentary activities of the party were more of a complement than a substitute for them. But the leaders of the party were not, to use the term Lenin used for some Russian Marxists, 'parliamentary cretins'. On the contrary they were very much aware of the restricted role which elected bodies played in the German political life; indeed there was a full scale discussion of the limitations of the Reichstag and state Diets and the restricted significance of electoral victories both in the Halle and the Erfurt congresses. There were sections in the party, especially '*die Jungen*' (the youth) from Berlin and Magdeberg, who were resolutely opposed to what they saw as the growing parliamentarisation of the party after the lifting of the Anti-Socialist Law.[15] But, as emphasised in the first chapter, the non-parliamentary path to socialism did not exist. The threat of the Government using force hung over the heads of the Social Democrats. In fact throughout the 1890s and later in the period up to the First World War Social Democrats and party organisations were constantly harassed in the form of imprisonment, arbitrary rulings and whimsical interpretations of laws.[16] Not only was the threat of violence ever present but also it was clear to the SPD that it could not wrest political power by force. A striking instance of the restricted room for manoeuvre which the SPD had is provided by the Erfurt programme itself. Republican and anti-monarchist as the party was, it could not formally demand a republic for the fear of committing *lèse majesté* and thus risking another ban.[17]

If the non-parliamentary path did not exist, the parliamentary path or rather paths, for there was not one but many, were not well charted. The strategy of the final take-over of power was vague, in fact it was less strategy than wishful thinking. The party leaders saw parliamentary elections not so much as a way of moulding and influencing government policies, but more as a means of disseminating social democratic ideas and policies demonstrating the extent of pupular support for them and *ipso facto* hostility towards the existing political and economic order. For example Liebknecht in his reply to the 'youth' who were critical of the parliamentarisation of the party in the Erfurt congress said that 'I am – in fact all of us are – of the opinion that the centre of gravity of our party is not in but outside the Reichstag, and that our activity in the Reichstag, until the time we acquire a decisive influence there, should be principally concerned with propaganda'.[18]

The acquisition of political power was conceived in terms of a show of force – not physical force but the force conferred by mass support. Just after the Halle congress Bebel outlined the strategy in the Reichstag to acquire such an overwhelming majority in favour of Social Democracy that no force would be able to stop it from assuming political power. The link between the amassing of an overwhelming majority and accession to political power was not made clear; indeed it could not be made clear, as Bebel pointed out in his very widely read *Socialism and Women*.[19] The same argument was repeated by Kautsky in his commentary on the Erfurt programme (reprinted in English as *The Class Struggle*) when he argued that depending on circumstances socialist revolution could take diverse forms, including a peaceful and non-violent form. In addition he argued that

> Neither is it necessary that the social revolution be decided at one blow; such probably was never the case. Revolutions prepare themselves by years or decades of economic and political struggle; they are accomplished by constant ups and downs sustained by the conflicting classes and parties; not infrequently they are interrupted by long periods of reaction. (*The Class Struggle*, p. 91)

It is a commonplace, especially among more recent German writers on German Social Democracy such as Mathias, Lehmann and Steinberg, that the Marxism of Kautsky and indeed that of the whole of German Social Democracy was heavily adulterated with evolutionism and thus for them socialist revolution was more of a 'natural event' – something whose timing could be calculated and thus predicted – than a 'social event' which did not lend itself to calculation and prediction. Leaving aside the problematic nature of the distinction between natural and social events, this characterisation is not accurate. The question 'what form would the assumption of power take?' was never properly answered, it kept on cropping up throughout the period up to the First World War. Though various answers were given to the question, not only in the Erfurt congress but also much later in the Jena and Mannheim congresses in 1905 and 1906 when the use of a general strike as a political weapon was discussed, they always retained a tentative character. And it is for this reason that Kautsky decided to write *Der Weg zur Macht* (*The Road to Power*) in 1909.[20] Contrary to what is suggested by some German writers on the SPD, the party leaders did not regard the capture of political power as a subject of calculation and they either avoided answering the question of the capture of power or gave, for the most part, nothing more than a general answer. In fact, Engels in his comments on the Erfurt programme tried to pose the awkward question 'what form would the capture of power take?' and thus implicitly criticised the leaders of the party for neglecting the question. It was in these comments that Engels specified the winning over of small peasantry and rural workers and the neutralisation of the army as the two necessary requirements for the victory of socialism in Germany.

Furthermore, contrary to what is normally believed now as a result of the critique of the Second International by Korsch, Lukacs and Luxemburg, neither Kautsky nor other leaders or theorists of the party were mechanistic or economistic in the sense that they assumed that economic changes and events *by themselves* would bring about a socialist revolution. Not only did the Erfurt programme affirm that the struggle for socialism is of necessity a political struggle but also the very organisation of the party and the way in which it functioned emphasised the primacy of political activity. True, the political activities which the party carried on, for example education and propaganda, may not be exactly termed revolutionary political activities by the left critics of the Second International; but those activities were political, none the less. A satisfactory treatment of the Second International is yet to be written; for the ones which exist, especially those written by Marxists, are too much conditioned by the splits which the First World War and the Russian Revolution precipitated.

However, like other Marxists, Kautsky, the Erfurt programme and other theorists and leaders of the party, including Rosa

Luxemburg and Bernstein, were economistic in the sense that they assumed that it was economic changes taking place under capitalism itself which would provide the preconditions for transition to socialism. But this assumption was not peculiar to the Second International; it is to be found in Lenin, for instance. We cannot go into a detailed discussion of this here so we turn back to our original concern, namely the tactics and the strategy of the SPD in Wilhelmine Germany. Though, as argued above, the relation between the amassing of support (especially electoral support) and accession to political power was left vague, the former was assumed to be tethered to the economic tendencies within capitalism.

It is here that the Erfurt programme becomes directly relevant.[21] The programme consisted of three parts: the preamble, the general political and social demands and, thirdly, specific demands concerning the conditions of work and the terms of the labour contract between employers and the wage labourers. The preamble itself consisted of a series of thematic statements and a list of the tendencies of capitalism. The tendencies which the preamble listed and which have since then become famous and regarded as an integral part of Marxism were:

1) the dispossession of labourers from the means of production,
2) the displacement of small by large enterprises,
3) the disappearance of the middle strata and the polarisation of population into wage earners, on the one side, and capitalists on the other,
4) increasing misery and uncertainty on the part of the population and, finally,
5) the intensification of class struggles.

The assumption was that these tendencies were inscribed in the very structure of capitalism and were obviously related; for the first three are simply different facets of the same phenomenon. Small enterprises were defined in the programme as those in which labourers themselves owned the means of production while large enterprises were those which employed wage labour. So the displacement of small by large enterprises is in effect an institutional counterpart of the dispossession of labourers from the means of production. As for the progressive disappearance of the middle strata this was implicit in the first two, for the middle strata were normally assumed to consist of the self-employed. The last two tendencies are in turn related since increasing misery and uncertainty could be regarded either as a cause or a correlate of sharpening class struggle. Thus schematically speaking the programme postulated two main tendencies: the polarisation of society into a handful of capitalists on the one side, and the appearance of a large number of individuals who had nothing to sell but their labour power on the other and, in addition, the deepening of economic crises and the sharpening of class struggles.

The tendencies listed in the preamble could be traced back to Marx's *Capital* but their status by virtue of the fact that they appear in a political programme is different. For the preamble was not a piece of economic analysis and thus not subject to any criteria for the validation of such analyses. Further, the tendencies by appearing in the preamble acquired a political significance which they did not have in *Capital*, at least not in a direct sense. That is, they pointed to the fact that transition to socialism is not only necessary but also feasible. Necessary, because the only lasting solution to the crises of capitalism is the collective ownership of the means of production. Feasible, because capitalism through its functioning enlarges the size of the working class which is revolutionary *in potentia*, if not in fact. The political significance associated with the tendencies is crucial for it implies that to question the tendencies is to question either the necessity or the feasibility of transition to socialism. This is the reason why Marxists, at least those who want to defend orthodoxy, have always been sensitive to the questioning of the validity of the tendencies, no matter how ill-founded or shaky they may be.

An instance of this is provided by Bernstein's *Evolutionary Socialism*. The policy recommendations of the book apart, a large part of it questions whether or not the tendencies listed in the Erfurt programme are being realised. Much of what Bernstein says apropos the tendencies (the middle strata do not show a tendency to disappear, in certain branches of production small enterprises are standing up to large enterprises, the distribution of income and wealth is becoming less rather than more unequal, economic crises are losing their earlier severity) though not necessarily correct or false is, when such points are taken individually, relatively innocuous. Yet Bernstein's book provoked a strong reaction in the form of a series of articles by Kautsky in *Die Neue Zeit* and a pamphlet by Rosa Luxemburg – *Reform or Revolution*. But neither the strength nor the nature of the response can be understood without reference to the political themes associated with the tendencies. In fact both Kautsky and Luxemburg were less concerned with the specific questioning of the tendencies by Bernstein than with its general political implication that, after all, transition to socialism may not be either feasible or necessary. Indeed Bernstein set out to question the tendencies precisely because the Erfurt programme has conferred on them a general political significance.

The growth of support for the SPD was linked within the party to the realisation of tendencies; in fact the propaganda and educational work of the party was centred on expositions of the tendencies of capitalism. In rural areas, for instance, the party's agitational work consisted of telling peasants that their days were numbered and that there was no hope for their survival in the face of competition. The assumption in the early 1890s was that the tendencies were going to unfold themselves at a rapid pace and thus, as Bebel predicted, the party would soon be able to amass enough support to overwhelm all opposition to it. The assumption was not unwarranted because within the three years from 1887 to 1890 the party had almost doubled both the share and the number of votes cast for it in the Reichstag elections. But the SPD never did manage to acquire overwhelming support; its share of the total votes in the Reichstag elections of 1912 (the highest it got in the pre-First World War period) was just above a third at 35 per cent. By the late 1890s it was clear that capitalism was not behaving as had been expected, and it was this relisation which furnished the background to Bernstein's questioning of orthodoxy. But the belief in the rapid realisation of the tendencies did have important effects on the party, especially in relation to the question of compromise and the way in which the policy of the party was assessed and discussed internally.

A striking feature of the SPD in the 1890s was its unwillingness to enter into any kind of deal or compromise with other parties, to undertake actions which could be construed as supporting either the Imperial or the state governments, or to make formal concessions. The debates around whether or not to participate in the elections to the Prussian Landtag or whether or not to vote for state budgets provide telling examples. Given the three class system of elections, the SPD on its own could not hope to get much more than a third of the total votes in most of the constituencies. For the supporters of the SPD were by and large confined to the third class – the class containing the majority of the population who by virtue of their poverty and low income accounted for a third of the taxes collected and thus only for a third of the total votes. It was clear that Social Democratic candidates could only get elected to the Prussian Landtag by entering into alliance with other parties, especially National Liberals and the Centre Party in certain areas. Bernstein suggested such an alliance in an article in *Die Neue Zeit* in 1893 and Bernstein's suggestion was discussed in the Cologne congress of the same year but it got no support on the grounds that it would mean entering into a compromise with bourgeois parties. But eventually the party came around to accepting the necessity of contesting the Prussian Landtag elections and thus of entering into an electoral deal with other parties. The change, however, was not easily accepted. The principle of participating in the election was accepted in the Hamburg congress of 1897, but electoral alliances with other parties were not sanctioned in principle till three years later in the Mainz congress of 1900.[22]

The debates concerning whether or not Social Democratic members of the state assemblies should vote for state budgets followed a similar pattern. The SPD faction in the Reichstag never voted for the Imperial budget on the grounds that most of the Imperial expenditure went to finance the military. However, the Social Democratic faction in the Bavarian Landtag voted for the state budget as early as 1894 on the grounds that state expenditure did not go to finance the military but instead social welfare and education, expenditures to which the SPD was not opposed in principle. But the Frankfurt Congress of 1894 laid down the general principle of opposing both the Imperial and state budgets. The controversy around voting for or against budgets erupted once again in 1901 when the SPD members of the Landtag of the Grand Duchy of Baden voted for the state budget and Rosa Luxemburg denounced them for deserting fundamental socialist principle. The party, however, did not side with Rosa Luxemburg and passed a resolution in the Lübeck congress of 1901 allowing the SPD members of various Landtagen a choice of voting for or against state budgets.[23]

In relation to both the issues, i.e, entering into an electoral alliance with the bourgeois parties and support for state budgets, it was the Social Democrats from South Germany, especially those from Bavaria, who broke ranks and acted in defiance of the principles laid down at national party congresses. In fact they were organised into separate parties. In addition to the SPD there were Social Democratic parties of Bavaria, of Württemberg, of the Grand Duchy of Baden and of Alsace-Lorraine. The Bavarian Social Democratic Party was led by Vollmar who questioned both the policies and the programme of the SPD right from the beginning of the period of legality.[24] It was not only in relation to the two issues mentioned here that the Bavarian party acted independently but also in relation to *Landagitation*. The party adopted an agrarian programme of its own (about which we shall have something to say later) which contrary to the prevalent view in the SPD was very sympathetic to the peasantry.

The unwillingness of the party to enter into any kind of alliance with other parties in the 1890s and its intransigence obviously rested on the belief that the unfolding tendencies of capitalism, in conjunction with educational and propaganda work, would over time swell the ranks of party supporters and therefore put the party in a position where it would be able to exercise power and influence on its own. However, this belief started to be questioned from the mid 1890s onwards, first in relation to the postmortem of *Landagitation* and then in relation to other issues, like participation in state elections and support for particular legislative measures etc. By the turn of the century many of the cardinal principles of the party had buckled under the pressure of political expediency.

Before we turn to *Landagitation* proper it is necessary to dispose of two questions and draw the threads of the argument together. The two questions are as follows: what was the relation of the Erfurt programme to agriculture and the rural areas and, second, what were the specific demands of the programme and what was their relation to the preamble?

The tendencies listed in the Erfurt programme, in particular those concerning the dispossession of producers from the means of production, the displacement of small by large enterprises and the disappearance of the middle strata, were of direct relevance to agriculture and rural areas. When the Erfurt programme was drafted and discussed Germany was already among the few major industrial countries, and the small enterprises which existed in

Germany were for the most part in agriculture. The large scale industry by then had established its pre-eminence in most branches of industrial production, especially in heavy manufacturing and mining. So far as industry was concerned it was assumed – not just by Marxists but also by the critics of Marx like Sombart – that some if not all of the tendencies had already worked themselves out. In fact it was changes in agriculture which were regarded as the source of verification of the tendencies. It was Sombart who claimed that changes in agriculture would falsify the Marxist contention that the tendencies were universally valid, a claim which was repeated by the revisionist critics of the party's attitude towards the peasantry, e.g. David. In fact, part I of Kautsky's *Die Agrarfrage*, as he himself makes clear, was a riposte to this claim. It was for this reason that changes in agriculture acquired a wider significance and a large part of the debate around the agrarian question consisted of technical issues, like whether or not large farms were more efficient than small farms and whether or not the census data on the size distribution of farms showed that the peasantry was disappearing. We shall discuss these issues in the next chapter when we come to the theoretical debates on the agrarian question. But the main point is that the discussion of agriculture and the peasantry had a dual facet to it: it was, on the one hand, concerned with the extension of the political work of the party in the countryside and on the other hand, as a result of the special significance which agriculture had *vis à vis* the preamble of the Erfurt programme, it became a discussion of the strategy of the party and of the programme itself.

As for the specific demands in the programme, they were few and divided into two parts.[25] The first consisted of general political and social demands which encompassed all citizens – demands like universal suffrage in all elections, the removal of all restrictions on the right of association, the provision of universal education and medical care etc. The second consisted of demands formulated with a view to what was termed *Arbeiterschutz* (protecting workers). It included demands for an eight hour working day and prohibition of the employment of children, demands relating in general terms to the sale of labour power and the conditions of work in productive establishments. Of these demands only one directly set out to protect the interests of rural inhabitants, the demand for the abolition of the

*Gesindeordnungen* and their replacement by a single set of labour laws applying to both industry and agriculture. However, protection was extended to rural inhabitants, to use a distinction which was commonly employed in the SPD, only in their capacity as sellers of labour and not as peasants or owners of land no matter how small a piece of land they owned. In response to the criticism of the party's attitude towards the peasantry the Frankfurt party congress of 1894 appointed an agrarian commission which was delegated to suggest additions to the list of specific demands. The commission, as we shall see later, did suggest demands like the easing of the burden of mortgage credit for inclusion in the programme; but a year later the Breslau congress rejected every one of the commission's suggestions. Thus as before the party decided not to give recognition to the economic interests of rural inhabitants *qua* owners of land.

What was the relation between the Erfurt programme and the policies and the tactics of the party? The policies and the tactics of the party were not completely mapped out by the programme; only at specific points did the two overlap. Implicit in some of the recent analyses, especially those from Germany, is the argument that the teleological conception of history outlined in the preamble of the Erfurt programme and the writings of Kautsky predisposed the party towards revisionism and reformism well before Bernstein set out to question the party's programme and policies.[26] It is true that revisionism – in the sense of questioning the validity of the tendencies attributed to capitalism – and reformism – in the sense of recommending alliance with other political parties and accepting some of the government policies as reasonable rather than opposing all of them – were present in the party well before Bernstein's questioning. But by itself that had nothing to do with a teleological conception of history. It is as much present in 'revolutionary' Rosa Luxemburg's *Reform or Revolution* as it is in Kautsky's writings; the teleological conception of history is not an exclusive trade mark of either revolutionaries or reformists or revisionists. Bernstein, in *Evolutionary Socialism*, set out to question the path of the development of capitalism sketched by Marx and Marxists only to replace it by yet another teleology.

It is not that the Erfurt programme and the conception of the development of capitalism embodied in the programme and shared by the party leaders in the 1890s had no effect on the policies and the political disposition of the party. It did, but only on specific issues; and the two issues on which it had a discernible effect were, first, compromise and coalition with other political parties and, second, the recognition of the economic interests of the 'middle strata', especially the peasantry, and the extension of support for them. The two were related in the sense that the latter would have been pointless without the former. The party now and then did enter into an informal or implicit alliance with other parties on specific issues, but the belief in the iron and blind laws of capitalism themselves eventually providing the conditions for transitions to socialism made it impossible to have any systematic and comprehensive discussion of compromise with other political parties and organisations. It is an open question as to what German Social Democracy would have achieved had it entered into an alliance with other parties but the disposition against making no concessions at a formal level put an end to whatever possibility there was of continuing *Landagitation*. With this comment we now move on to the form and the trajectory of *Landagitation*.

The call of the party leaders to branch out on the land in the Halle congress was enthusiastically taken up by party members throughout the country. In fact systematic *Landagitation* began in the winter of 1890–91 soon after the Halle congress. The immediate response of provincial party branches and the constituent parties in South and South-West Germany was to appoint committees to plan and suggest ways of agitation on land. For instance, just a few months after the Halle congress the Württemberg Social Democratic party – as pointed out earlier Württemberg like Bavaria, Baden, and Alsace-Lorraine had its own Social Democratic party – in its own party congress appointed what was termed a *Landorganisation*.[27]

The form of *Landagitation* was in most respects predetermined before it even started. Concentrated as the support for the party was for the most part in large cities and to a minor degree in small towns, *Landagitation* had to take the form of urban party members, in particular industrial labourers, going out to the countryside. As we pointed out earlier, very few of the votes cast for the party in 1890 came from rural areas and those which did in fact came from small towns. The banning of the party, though it did not succeed in stopping its growth, did nevertheless manage to confine Social Democratic organisations and thus support to urban industrial centres. Emigration drained the countryside of whatever occasional Social Democratic support it may have had. The countryside was thus an alien land for the party members.

Not only did the party not have rural bases from which it could branch out, it approached the countryside for electoral and other reasons not directly connected with events there. So the two problems which the party faced in the countryside were: whom to approach and on what basis? The solution to the first problem was straightforward in the areas where the rural population was clearly divided between landowners and agricultural labourers, as indeed was the case in the rural districts to the east of the Elbe. But not so in South and South-West Germany, for in those areas it was the peasantry which dominated the landscape. The peasantry, as pointed out earlier in the discussion of the structure of German agriculture, was (and indeed always is) a heterogeneous category; it ranged from the owners of fragmentary holdings who treated cultivation as a secondary activity to those who were quite well off and depended on regular wage labour for a substantial proportion of labour used on their land. Differentiated though the peasantry was the lines of divisions which traversed it either did not coincide with the ones which Social Democrats used or did not have immediate political relevance and thus did not provide an anchor for *Landagitation*.

Take for instance the division between wage labourers and capitalists or their employers, for not all employers were capitalists. This division so far as large scale industry was concerned yielded a clear cut and economically significant distinction, provided capitalists were assumed to include not only the owners of capital but also managers, supervisors and the like (as Marxists normally do). Workers, in that context, were set apart from capitalists by the way in which their wages were determined, the places which the tasks they performed occupied in the hierarchical order which underlay the division of labour, and the level of their incomes. Indeed similar factors separate present day industrial workers from their capitalists. In addition what is crucial is that those factors were in a large number of cases politically pertinent, in that they furnished the grounds for political mobilisation and organisation.

But the same was not true in the rural areas of Germany where wage labour was intertwined with family labour, as was the case in South and West Germany. We have already pointed out that all categories of peasants depended on wage labour, but obviously not to the same degree. So far as the small peasantry was concerned the peasant was often no better off than the labourer he employed. And as Kautsky and Max Weber pointed out small peasants were often worse off than agricultural labourers employed by big farmers. The point in general terms is that though the tactics of protecting the immediate economic interests of workers (tactics enshrined in the specific demands put forward in part II of the Erfurt programme) could, as they did, serve as the basis of *Landagitation*, in the regions of large estates they were often irrelevant and, in the regions where small and middle peasantry dominated, often counterproductive. The party did not have anything to offer by way of putting forward specific demands to protect their economic interests to the peasantry as owners of land. The Bavarian and South German Social Democrats did want to rectify that; we shall have something to say about that later.

Not only did the party have nothing to offer to the peasantry: the specific demands it put forward in the economic interests of workers (which naturally encompassed agricultural labourers) like the eight hour working day, regular holidays and even the demand for the abolition of the *Gesindeordnungen* went against the economic interests of peasants. The status of these demands *vis à vis* small and middle peasant employers was different from that *vis à vis* large farmers, estate owners and large industrial employers. Small and middle peasants often worked the same number of hours and under the same conditions as their employees. If agricultural labourers worked longer than an eight hour day and did not have regular holidays and days of rest so did their employers, if they happened to be small and middle peasants. Kautsky in his *Die Agrarfrage* singled out the fact that small peasants worked immensely long hours for special emphasis; but he set his face against making any concessions to the peasantry.[28] The argument is therefore that the distinction between employers and employees in small farms did not have the same significance as it had elsewhere and the party, in singling out agricultural labourers for economic protection, was in fact discriminating against small and middle peasants. True, the same demands also implied a bias against large industrialists, estate owners and large peasants and farmers. But there was a crucial difference: these categories of economic agents were not regarded as potential supporters or allies of Social Democracy, while small and middle peasants were. And furthermore, it is questionable whether it was, given the intertwining of family and wage labour, possible to appeal to and organise agricultural labourers in opposition to and in separation from their employers when the latter happened to be small and middle peasants.

There is a wider problem at issue here and it is as well to bring it out briefly. In an economy where conditions of work and the nature of employment differ, any general demand concerning the conditions of work and the terms of employment will run into the inevitable problem of not being appropriate in certain conditions. Exactly the same problem as outlined here also arises in relation to small scale industries and small scale establishments in distributive trades. But one may also take into account that the recognition of differences and the adjustment of demands accordingly does not make the political task any easier. For tailoring the demands concerning the conditions of work and the terms of employment to the place of employment gives rise to the criticism that such a practice condones poverty and squalor in small scale establishments. What needs recognising here is that there is a problem which does not lend itself to a straightforward solution.

To revert to our original two questions concerning the target of *Landagitation* and what was to be the basis of appeal to the rural inhabitants regarded as potential supporters of Social Democracy. To the east of the Elbe *Landagitation* was directed towards agricultural labourers and elsewhere it was, despite the problems which we just outlined, oriented towards both agricultural labourers and small and middle peasants. In addition the *Landagitation* at least initially was based more on general political propaganda than on specific economic demands. In addition to the two problems indicated in the form of the two questions *Landagitation* came up against a determined opposition by the parties which dominated the countryside, administrative and repressive state apparatuses, and the church and the clergy. The countryside was not a *tabula rasa*, and *Landagitation* was like a war as characterised by von Clausewitz, i.e., movement in a resistant medium.

The propaganda activity which formed the main component of *Landagitation* took the form of urban workers going to the countryside and spreading Social Democratic ideas and its programme by word of mouth or by distributing written material. These propaganda visits for obvious reasons had to take place on Sundays and were for purely physical reasons restricted to the countryside in the vicinity of towns where the SPD already had a base of supporters. Often what was termed the 'red cavalry' on foot and on bicycles followed the advance detachment dispatched by train.

The Sunday agitators did not meet just indifference but active hostility in villages. They had great difficulty in procuring meeting rooms for landlords and were under constant threat of withdrawal of licence if they let their rooms to Social Democrats, so they had to hold their meetings in the open air. Not only that, Sunday agitators were harrassed, often beaten up or had dogs set on them. For instance, in response to the party's call for a meeting fifteen kilometres from Bielefeld on a piece of land owned by a Social Democratic worker in a village, Pastor Iskraut organised a counter demonstration and occupied the piece of land with the help of his supporters, and some fanatic peasants beat up those who had come to attend the meeting including women and children.[29] A delegate from Mönchen-Gladbach in the Cologne congress of 1893 recounted that during the election campaign a few months earlier they were greeted outside villages, as he put it, by both the terrestrial (the police) and celestial (priests) army who set their dogs on them.[30] Another common tactic employed by rural authorities was to use laws, both current and old laws which had long fallen into disuse, against Social Democratic agitators. In Prussia the formation of local organisation was banned under the Law of association, open air meetings were banned as a threat to public order and landlords who, despite warnings from the authorities, let their rooms to Social Democrats found themselves prosecuted for some infraction of the laws. The Prussian police often used the Press Law of 1851 to arrest those distributing material in public places without prior permission. And a resort to time consuming house-to-house distribution was met with the laws regulating activities on the Sabbath.[31]

*Landagitation* in the form of general political propaganda continued for almost three years after the Halle congress. But very soon it was realised that the countryside did not lend itself to be conquered so easily and that initial calculations regarding the time it would take to gather sizeable support in rural areas had been far too optimistic. In the Berlin congress of 1892 there were complaints about the shortage of appropriate material for distribution in the countryside and the general lack of coordination of agitation on the land. However, *Landagitation* only came in for a comprehensive critique a year later in the Cologne congress of 1893, a number of events setting the stage for it.

The beginning of 1893 saw the formation of the Bund der Landwirte and the rise of agrarian demagogy centred around the demand for tariff protection. Later in the summer of the same year there were elections to the Reichstag, the first the SPD had fought as a legal organisation since the 1870s. Given that the interest in the countryside was electoral the elections became a test of the success of *Landagitation*. In addition the election campaign coincided with the onset of an exceptional drought which struck all categories of cultivators.

The SPD increased its share of the total votes over that obtained in the 1890 election, although the increase was minor (from 20 to 23 per cent) relative to the spectacular increase it had experienced earlier (from 10 per cent in 1887 to 20 per cent in 1890). The small size of the gain was in fact a great disappointment, for while Engels in a letter to Kautsky had talked in terms of two and a quarter or two and a half million votes (i.e. between 30 and 33 per cent of the total), in the event the party fell well short of the 2 million mark.

Disappointment was not only that a negligible proportion of the small increase originated in the rural constituencies but also that general result of the election did not provide any cause for joy to the party either. For side by side with the SPD the Conservatives, the *Zentrum* and the Anti-Semites had also increased their share of the votes. The first two, as we pointed out earlier, hegemonised the rural areas. What the election made clear was that the two and a half years of *Landagitation*, contrary to the hopes placed on it, did not even loosen the grip of these two parties on the countryside.[32]

It was against this background that the Cologne congress in the autumn of 1893 was held. Apart from the disappointment over the election result, the question which dominated the congress was how should the party conduct *Landagitation*? The printed material provided for agitation came in for trenchant criticism on the grounds that it was dominated by general political and theoretical issues like the tendencies of capitalism, the law of value etc., issues which were either of little or no interest to the rural population. The key issue was, however, not the technical and organisational failings but the chances of success of *Landagitation*, which on principle did not offer anything to the peasantry by way of special demands on their behalf. Bebel speaking for the leadership of the party reaffirmed the position of the party towards the peasantry, according to which it had nothing to offer to the peasantry except the prediction that sooner or later it will go under. However, Bebel in a letter to Engels, who was expecting to hear of a spectacular victory, acknowledged the difficulty of conducting agitation among peasants by merely outlining to them their bleak and hopeless future. 'I heard farmhands saying: you have made clear to us bluntly that you are not able to help us, but we do not want to go under, and that is why we vote for the Anti-Semites. The Antis promise to help us.' Bebel also candidly pointed out in the same letter that the cold logic of Social Democratic predictions about the future of the middle strata (*Mittelständen*) stirs no response among that 'narrow minded class of men'.[33]

But nothing specific was decided at the Cologne congress except to hold a full scale discussion on the *Landagitation* and the agrarian question in the next year's congress (held in Frankfurt). None the less, it had become clear at the congress that the main question which faced the party was: what specific concession was it willing to make to the peasantry? Though the central party organisation was committed to a neutral stance towards the peasantry, as outlined in the Erfurt programme and pronouncements of party leaders like Bebel and Kautsky, the Southern German Social Democrats were not. And since it was Vollmar, the leader of Bavarian Social Democracy, who led the attack against the party's stance towards the peasantry at the Frankfurt congress it is interesting to consider the experience of *Landagitation* in Bavaria briefly.

Unlike in Prussia it was not just the rank and file but also the local party leaders who participated in *Landagitation* in Bavaria and elsewhere in South and West Germany. Vollmar had openly come out in favour of compromise with the governments (both local and Imperial) and other parties and in favour of what he termed 'practical politics' as early as 1891 – well before revisionism and reformism had become widespread in the party. Obviously, with an eye to the fact that Catholicism was firmly established in the Bavarian population (77 per cent of which was then rural) Vollmar tried in vain to tone down the commitment to secularisation of public life which was incorporated in the Erfurt programme.[34]

The Bavarian Social Democratic Party in its Regensburg congress of 1892 had adopted a programme of its own which in a number of fundamental respects departed from the Erfurt programme.[35] And it was on the basis of this programme that the party fought the 1893 election to the Bavarian Landtag. Unlike the national party the Bavarian party put the peasantry and the workers at par with each other and declared itself to be the party of all labouring people rather than just the proletariat. And instead of adopting a neutral stand towards the peasantry the Bavarian Social Democrats pledged themselves to struggle for the amelioration of the economic conditions of the peasantry.

The Bavarian Social Democrats justified their *Bauernfängerei* (peasantism) on a number of different grounds. First, peasant property was argued to be different from capitalist property in that it did not rest on the exploitation of labour – not a novel argument since it would have been accepted by orthodox party theoreticians like Kautsky. Second, peasants, in general, were no better off than workers; in fact, they shared the same conditions of life, poverty and uncertainty about future prospects. Once again this argument was not a hallmark of reformism; for in *Die Agrarfrage* Kautsky argued that small peasants were in fact worse off than agricultural labourers. Third, to the question 'what interest does Social Democracy have in helping the peasantry to survive?' the answer was: the destruction of the peasantry would merely swell the reserve army of the unemployed and thus put downward pressure on wages and, in addition, that Social Democracy could never hope to gain political power without the support of the peasantry. The point is that these arguments were not very different from those put forward by the orthodox theorists. There was, however, one orthodox argument which was missing: that the days of the peasantry were numbered and that no power could stop them from disappearing. But the point still remains that the *Bauernfängerei* was not anchored to arguments radically different from those put forward by orthodox Marxists.

As for the specific demands to ameliorate the economic conditions of the peasantry, they were drawn up on the basis of the following requirements. First, demands should not be prejudicial to the interests of agricultural labourers. Second, they should not be contrary to the economic interests of the population as a whole. As a result of this, the Bavarian Social Democrats firmly came down against tariffs on agricultural imports. And, finally, the demands should not move against the tide of economic evolution and thus prejudice the transition from private to social property. As far as Kautsky was concerned the last requirement ruled any support for the peasantry as property owners; for he assumed that transition to socialist organisation of production would take place on the basis of large scale production and not on the basis of small scale peasant production. This in fact was the assumption which underlay Kautsky's writings on the agrarian question. In contrast revisionists and reformists maintained that peasants were not only holding their own against large capitalist farms but also that peasant property was consistent with a transition to socialism. The specific demands which the Bavarian Social Democrats put forward were: 1) nationalisation of mortgages, 2) state monopoly of agricultural credit, 3) reduction of the rate of interest on mortgages, 4) state provision of agricultural insurance and 5) the maintenance and protection of communal property and communal rights. The first four demands are self-explanatory; the significance of the fifth lies in the fact that both communal property and communal rights were of particular importance to small peasants.

The Bavarian Social Democrats fought both the elections to the Reichstag and the Bavarian Landtag in 1893 on the basis of a programme and a campaign, in which Vollmar played a prominent part, biased in favour of the peasantry. In the Landtag elections the Social Democrats gained five seats and thus entered the Bavarian Landtag for the first time.[36] In addition, in one particular constituency in the Reichstag election in which Vollmar had himself campaigned, the votes cast for the SPD almost doubled from 9.6 per cent in 1890 to 18.9 per cent. Elsewhere too the SPD registered gains but its share of the total votes still remained derisory. Overall, the Bavarian *Landagitation* left the towering dominance of the *Zentrum* over the countryside untouched. Nevertheless, Bavarian Social Democrats had gathered enough support to demonstrate to the rest of the party that a policy favouring the peasantry could bear results.

The agrarian question and *Landagitation* was the main item on the agenda of the Frankfurt congress of 1894;[37] the main attack on the party's policy towards the peasantry and the form which *Landagitation* had taken thus far came from Vollmar and

Schönlank, a representative from Thuringia. Detailed criticisms of *Landagitation* aside, the main line of attack was that the SPD could not hope to win the rural population, of whom a sizeable portion were peasants of some kind, by merely outlining the trajectory of development of capitalism and pointing to a socialist future. Vollmar declared that the peasantry could only be won over on the basis of demands which were of immediate relevance to them. There was more than just pragmatism and the dislike of theoretical speculations concerning transition to socialism at stake in Vollmar and Schönlank's attack. The attack was directed at the fundamentals of the SPD strategy and it was two pronged. First, what was implicitly questioned was the assumption that Social Democrats could gather enough mass support for socialism to, as Bebel had earlier put it, overwhelm all the opponents of Social Democracy. When Schönlank argued that 'the medicine of socialism has to be administered to peasants in homeopathic doses, otherwise it will kill them', he was in effect questioning the possibility of gathering a sizeable support for socialism in rural areas. The argument in fact was more general, because, *mutatis mutandis*, it could be extended to the urban petit-bourgeoisie, which was exactly what Bernstein did later. Complementary to this fundamental questioning was the positive recommendation that the practical work of the party should be geared more towards immediate demands and issues affecting different sections of population and less towards the distant issue of transition to socialism. The implication was that the party should adopt a heterogeneous and diverse strategy in its practical work instead of the strategy which the party had followed till then. That strategy was the one implicit in the Erfurt programme and it consisted in restricting the activities of the party to those issues which bore a discernible relation to the struggle for socialism.

Despite the strong reaction which Vollmar and Schönlank's attacks provoked, the congress accepted its implications for the party programme and the stance towards the peasantry in the form of a resolution. The main components of the resolution which was adopted by a huge majority were: first, the recognition of the need for immediate reforms to alleviate the current distress of the peasantry and agricultural labourers and thus the necessity of a special agrarian programme consisting of specific demands to be added to part II of the Erfurt programme. Second, the recognition that the protection of the peasant should cover him not only as citizen but also as cultivator and owner of land. And, finally, the appointment of an agrarian commission to draw up specific proposals for discussion and adoption at the next congress (held at Breslau in 1895).

The resolution was a victory – though short lived – for Vollmar and the reformists. The agrarian commission consisted of fifteen members and was divided into three sections each consisting of five members. The division followed the regional differences in the structure of agriculture. One section was assigned the region to the east of the Elbe, the land of large agricultural estates coexisting with small parcels of land belonging to agricultural labourers; the other, central Germany (Saxony, Thuringia, Oldenburg, Brunswick, Westphalia and Hanover), a region characterised by middle and large peasant farms; and the third section was assigned South Germany, the land of small peasant farms. Each section drew up a specific programme and a report which later formed an ingredient of a general report and programme produced by the commission as a whole. The agrarian commission not only included Vollmar and Schönlank but also the two main political leaders of the party, Bebel and Liebknecht. But it did not include Kautsky; it was he who launched the main and eventually successful offensive against the very project of a special agrarian programme.

The commission published its report and the list of specific demands to be incorporated in the Erfurt programme in June 1895 (four months before the Breslau congress). Many of the demands had already figured in the agrarian programme of Bavarian Social Democracy and the most important and contentious of the demands in their general outline were as follows:

1) The conservation and an increase in the public property in land (state property, communal property etc), in particular forests and water.
2) Handing over the state lands (which occupied a substantial area) to agricultural cooperatives or to small peasants for cultivation.
3) The state provision of credit.
4) The nationalisation of mortgage banks and mortgage debt and a reduction in mortgage rate of interest.
5) The state provision of insurance against various risks.

6) The maintenance and extension in the communal rights of pasture, collection of forest wood.³⁸

The two essential features of these demands are, first, extension of the economic role of the state and, second, strengthening of communal rights and property (including cooperatives). Though the peasantry was, for the most part, not specifically mentioned in the demands, the distribution of benefits implied by the demands were heavily biased in favour of the peasantry. For instance the strengthening of communal rights was meant to be of special benefit to small peasants because their economic survival crucially depended on such rights.

The whole project of a special agrarian programme to protect the peasantry and the specific recommendations of the commission came under attack well before the Breslau congress in the autumn of 1895. Very soon after the Frankfurt congress Engels' article *The Peasant Question in France and Germany* was published in *Die Neue Zeit*. Though the article was a critique of the Nantes programme of, as Engels put it, 'the French Socialist of the Marxian trend'; it was meant for the consumption of German Social Democrats. What it set out to do was to lay the ghost of peasantism (*Bauernfängerei*) which had raised its ugly head at the Frankfurt congress. Engels put his magisterial authority behind the neutral stance which the SPD had taken before it decided to appoint the agrarian commission. To the question 'What, then, is our attitude towards the small peasantry?', Engels frankly replied 'Neither now nor at any time in the future can we promise the small holding peasants to preserve their individual property and individual enterprise against the overwhelming power of capitalist production.' And Engels was perfectly prepared to accept the consequences of this neutral stance. Referring to big and middle peasants, Engels said 'If these peasants want to be guaranteed the continued existence of their enterprises we are in no position whatever to assure them of that. They must then take their place among the Anti-Semites, peasant leaguers [the reference is to the Bund der Landwirte] and similar parties who derive pleasure from promising everything and keeping nothing.'³⁹

It was Kautsky who launched a point by point attack in the form of a series of articles in *Die Neue Zeit*⁴⁰ on the proposals of the agrarian commission after their publication. The attack was directed at the two essential features of the proposal mentioned above, extension in the power of the state and the strengthening of communal rights and property. Kautsky opposed the former on the basis of what has since then become the classic Marxist conception of the state: that it is the instrument for perpetuating the political dominance of the ruling classes (which for Kautsky included both the capitalists and the Junkers). The argument was that any increase in the power of the state necessarily implied an increase in the power of the ruling classes. The argument did, for Kautsky, allow for certain exceptions; but only in cases where the extension could only be to the interest of the working class. The examples of the exceptional cases were: the demands for the regulation of the conditions of work and the terms of employment and restrictions on the employment of children and the like. All these demands were already incorporated in the Erfurt programme. And, obviously, the nationalisation of mortgage companies and the state provision of agricultural credit did not fall into the category of justifiable extensions of the power of the state.

Kautsky was opposed to the demand for preservation of communal rights and property on the grounds that they helped prolong an outmoded and inefficient organisation of production. In fact, Kautsky's argument against communal rights and property was exactly the same as the one which agronomists like Thär used against such institutions. This is important; the classic Marxist position that large scale farming is efficient while small scale is anachronistic and inefficient – a position iterated in *Capital*, in the writings of Engels, Kautsky and Lenin – is a position grounded in agronomy. For Kautsky, not only was peasant production inefficient but also there was no justification for a socialist party helping it to survive.

Kautsky could see no justification for a special agrarian programme and he rightly pointed out that the proposals of the commission undermined the foundation of the Erfurt programme and the terms on which the party had conducted its work and gathered support among the population. Kautsky is often accused of being doctrinaire and theoretically inflexible; that may have been so, but he was right that the commission's recommendations amounted to a fundamental departure from the policy of the party. And Kautsky was not the only one who held this opinion.

Kautsky's critique and Engels' magisterial intervention had

already shifted the balance against the proposals of the agrarian commission. The opponents of the proposals at the Breslau congress of 1895 merely reiterated the positions which Kautsky had already put forward in his article. In fact the commission did not so much present and explain the rationale behind the proposals as defend them against Kautsky's specific critiques. To the critique that an extension in the power of the state implies an increase in the domination of the ruling class, Bebel and Liebknecht replied that the state is not a homogeneous entity and thus an increase in state intervention (not just in the domains which Kautsky had specified) should not be rejected prima facie. This type of argument has become the natural complement of the kind of argument advanced by Kautsky. And to the point that communal property and communal rights under capitalism merely help perpetuate an anachronistic organisation of production, the reply was that communal property instituted under capitalism, contrary to what Kautsky had assumed, could form the basis for the development of socialist property and, in addition, such a form of property helped convince individualistic peasants of the benefits of collective organisation of production.

Despite all the defence put up by Bebel and Liebknecht congress overwhelmingly rejected the commission's proposal. However, the congress did pass a proposal recognising that 'agriculture has its peculiar laws, differing from those of industry, which must be studied and considered if Social Democracy is to develop an extended operation in rural districts'. The Breslau congress put an end to *Landagitation* and deflected efforts to the theoretical plane. In fact theoretical writings on the agrarian question flourished after the congress as the pages of *Die Neue Zeit* amply demonstrate, and it was then that Kautsky started working on *Die Agrarfrage*, his *magnum opus* which appeared four years later.[41]

The end of the *Landagitation* did not mean an end of the SPD's political work in the countryside; that continued, but only as a part of general activity to increase the support for the party. And support for the SPD did increase in rural areas over time especially to the east of the Elbe. For instance, in the 1898 election the party displaced the National Liberal to become the third largest party in the countryside and in the election after that in 1903 it replaced the Conservatives as the second largest party in the countryside.[42] But the SPD did not manage to dislodge the

Centre Party from its commanding position in the rural areas of Catholic Germany. However, one should not wholly, or even predominantly, attribute the lack of success in the rural areas where the peasantry dominated the landscape (also the areas of support for the *Zentrum*) to the inability of the party to adopt a pro-peasant programme. It is questionable whether the mere adoption of a pro-peasant programme would have been sufficient to tilt the balance in favour of the SPD. This doubt rests on two specific factors. First, the Bavarian and other Southern German Social Democratic parties were fairly autonomous of the central party organisation and they were perfectly capable of following a pro-peasant programme and strategy and indeed did so. The Bavarian party reaffirmed its pro-peasant programme in 1896, a year after the Breslau congress. Second, the SPD not only had difficulty in gathering the support of Catholic peasants but also, which is important, of Catholic industrial labourers. It was as late as the 1912 election that the SPD managed to displace the Centre Party as the largest party among the industrial labourers of the Catholic Ruhr valley and Westphalia.[43]

The rejection of the agrarian commission had a more general significance and that was what made the Breslau congress an important landmark.

*Landagitation*, as pointed out in the beginning of this chapter, was the central component of the SPD's strategy to capture political power and its end thus meant an admission that the strategy outlined at Halle and at Erfurt was based on a gross miscalculation. The party rejected the reformism and revisionism implicit in the agrarian commission's proposals in the name of orthodoxy; but the failure of *Landagitation* had already undermined the strategy implicit in the orthodox stance. The Breslau congress did not put an end to reformism and revisionism; all that happened after Breslau was that they made their appearance in relation to other issues – issues like whether or not to vote for state budgets, whether or not to contest Prussian elections, whether or not to support the subsidy to shipbuilding etc. We leave the political field at this juncture and turn to the theoretical writings on the agrarian question.

# 4 Theoretical Writings on the Agrarian Question

At the Breslau congress the SPD, as it were, exchanged agitation on the land for theoretical work. Theoretical writings on the agrarian question flourished after the congress and they covered a wide range of issues; the tendencies of development in agriculture, the effect of foreign competition on domestic agriculture, and differences between industry and agriculture. But of these it was around the last issue that the controversy between the 'revisionists' and the 'orthodox' – though not very precise and revealing terms but nevertheless useful as short hand – was indirectly centred. Technical though the issue of 'whether or not large farms are more efficient than small farms' was, it acquired a political significance because of the association that it had to questions like 'is the peasantry disappearing fast enough to make a pro-peasant posture redundant?' We shall have a great deal to say about this issue in this chapter.

Besides a large number of articles in Social Democratic periodicals like *Die Neue Zeit* and *Sozialistische Monatsheft*, the theoretical work on the agrarian question resulted in two massive tomes: Kautsky's *Die Agrarfrage* and David's *Sozialismus und Landwirtschaft*. The former is deservedly recognised as a Marxist classic; the latter, which is a revisionist riposte to Kautsky's orthodox analysis is, however, not so well known. *Die Agrarfrage* appeared in 1899 (4 years after the Breslau congress) and more or less at the same time as the other Marxist classic, Lenin's *Development of Capitalism in Russia*. The Social Democratic literature is so large that it is impossible for us to survey it all in this one chapter. As a result we have decided to settle for a detailed discussion of Kautsky's book; for the reason that it is not available in English and, more important, that it is comprehensive enough to include in it nearly all the issues raised in the theoretical writings. An additional excuse for being selective is that we shall be publishing a selection of articles on the agrarian question as a companion to this volume.

It is clear from our earlier discussion that Kautsky's book is a product of a specific political conjuncture. Yet the manner in which the book is written and the way in which it has been assessed by Marxists and non-Marxists alike has tended to obscure the link which the book undoubtedly has to contemporary political events and other writings on the question. Though the book appeared after a heated controversy around the agrarian programme and various issues related to agriculture Kautsky left out any mention of his Social Democratic opponents. The preface and part II of the book, which is devoted to agrarian programmes, do refer to the Breslau congress but only in passing. It is not that the book just happened to appear amidst political and theoretical controversy relating to the agrarian question; its arguments, what is included in it and the distribution of emphases cannot be understood except in relation to the controversy. One could characterise *Die Agrarfrage* as a polemical book written in a non-polemical style.

It was the non-polemical presentation of the book which seriously influenced its assessments, especially the later ones. *Die Agrarfrage* was hailed as volume IV of *Capital*, a praise which detached the book from its conditions of production and placed it on a pedestal. The praise, however, though *appellation controlée*, was not exclusive to this book: it was also applied to Hilferding's *Das Finanzkapital*. It is, moreover, not just adulatory; it carries within it a particular, and one may add questionable, conception of the relation between *Capital* and later Marxist classics. We shall get around to explaining why in the concluding chapter to this book. Now to turn to the book itself.

Kautsky distinguishes between two forms of discourses on agriculture: the analysis of specific situations and of tendencies.[1] For him it is the former which is essential for formulating agrarian programmes and political strategies. In contrast the analysis of tendencies is wider in scope: it is not restricted to any particular national economy. Though he does not conceive of it in this way the distinction between the two forms of discourses amounts to one between intranational and international analyses. The task of a theorist, according to Kautsky, is to look for general tendencies of social evolution – which are supposedly the same in all capitalist countries. Hence the reason for equating the analysis of tendencies with international analysis. But, Kautsky goes on to argue, though the tendencies of evolution in all capitalist countries (in particular those in agriculture) are the same everywhere, the form in which they are realised may well vary from one country to another. So far as agriculture is concerned the explanations for variations in the form of realisation of tendencies have to be looked for in factors such as differences in geographical location, climatic factors, historical conditions and the balance of political forces between different classes.

To Kautsky the distinction is relevant because he sees *Die Agrarfrage* primarily as a theoretical book – it is subtitled *A Review of Tendencies of Modern Agriculture*. Part II of the book, however, is directly concerned with the question of formulating a Social Democratic agrarian programme. Though the book is interspersed with the analyses of particular facets of German agriculture, yet there is relatively little of that given the conditions in which the book was written. Just in this respect the contrast between *Die Agrarfrage* and Lenin's *Development of Capitalism in Russia* could not be greater. For the latter is more or less exclusively concerned with Russian agriculture and industry; in terms of Kautsky's distinction Lenin's is an analysis of a specific situation rather than of tendencies.

There is nothing novel about the methodological distinction which Kautsky makes; it is similar to the ones between empirical and abstract and between particular and general. It is, therefore, not the distinction itself but the way in which it operates in the book which is of interest. Kautsky uses the distinction to mark out the boundaries of the book; but it is, in fact, more than just an abridged description of the table of contents of the book. *Die Agrarfrage* itself contains the analyses of specific situations in Germany as well as in other capitalist countries like France, Britain and the US. Given the distinction, the question is what is the relationship between such analyses – schematic and selective though they are – and the analysis of tendencies, which is supposedly the main object of the book? The point is that the distinction has implications for the relationship between the various components of the book itself and it is that which makes the distinction relevant for us.

The tendencies of evolution which Kautsky discusses in the book have a mixed ancestry, most of them are taken as givens while a few are derived from the analyses of the book. The empirical analyses of the book and the tendencies are not connected by a process of induction; in particular the former are not used to validate or invalidate the latter. This may seem to imply that empirical analyses of the book are pointless; but they are not. For Kautsky they have a double significance: first, they indicate the form in which tendencies are realised and, second, they furnish the explanations of why tendencies of evolution are not realised in particular situations. The second of these, one may note, only makes sense when tendencies are not regarded as empirical generalisations. Since most of the tendencies which Kautsky discusses are taken by him as givens, the question for him is not so much 'what are the tendencies of evolution in agriculture?' but rather 'how do particular factors at work in capitalist economies hinder the realisation of tendencies?' The discussion of the supposed tendency of large farms to replace small farms provides a particularly apt example of this. Kautsky is not interested in the question of whether or not one could speak of such a tendency – a question which was central to his revisionist critics like David and Bernstein – but instead in identifying the factors which stop large farms (shown to be more efficient) replacing less efficient small farms.

Before we discuss the effects which this procedure has, it is worth noting that Kautsky adopts exactly the same procedure that Marx does when discussing the tendency of the rate of profit to fall in volume III of *Capital*. For what Marx does is first to derive the tendency by reference to technical changes which involve the substitution of machines for labour, and then discuss other factors like the cheapening of raw material prices and increase in the rate of exploitation of labourers which might stop the rate of profit from falling. This procedure gives rise to the riposte that if the supposed tendency is always coupled with the factors which counteract it, then there is no more reason to term it the tendency for the rate of profit to fall than the tendency for the rate of profit to rise, or even to remain constant. However, within the terms of *Capital* such a change of the name of the tendency is not possible because Marx's procedure rests on a hierarchy of determinations. The factors which make the rate of profit fall are regarded in *Capital* as more fundamental than those which might keep it constant or raise it. Such a hierarchy of determinations is also implicit in Kautsky's procedure and it is that which makes his distinction between the two types of discourses significant.

Implicit in Kautsky's distinction is the conception of national economies, or rather agriculture in different countries, as vehicles for the realisation of tendencies which are not tethered to any particular capitalist economy. Thus for Kautsky the significance of the features which give agriculture in a particular economy its specific character solely consists in what they imply about the realisation, or the nonrealisation, of the tendencies in question. As a result of this Kautsky completely neglects those features which are not related to the tendencies he outlines. For instance he more or less completely neglects the middle peasantry and regional differences which, as we saw earlier, characterised German agriculture for the reason that they are not pertinent to the tendencies, such as the proletarianisation of the peasantry, in which he is interested. In effect, the tendencies of social evolution discussed in *Die Agrarfrage* act there as a filter: they determine the content and the orientation of what Kautsky terms the analysis of specific situations. A related consequence of the distinction adopted by Kautsky is to limit the degree to which the analysis can differentiate between the agriculture of different capitalist countries. For if the specificity of agriculture in a particular capitalist country consists in its having factors which help or hinder the realisation of tendencies which are supposedly valid for all capitalist countries, then the implication is that differences between the agricultural sector of different capitalist countries amount to them being at the different stages of realisation of the tendencies.

Given what it is meant to be, *Die Agrarfrage* is organised around a number of tendencies. We pointed out in the previous chapter that the preamble of the Erfurt programme was a catalogue of the tendencies of the development of capitalism, some of which, like the proletarianisation of independent producers and the replacement of small scale by large scale production, are carried over in the book. However, unlike in the Erfurt programme there is no presumption in the book that the tendencies are necessarily realised. In fact one of the main conclusions of *Die Agrarfrage* is that the path of evolution sketched in the Erfurt programme is not completely valid for agriculture. In general terms just this much was already acknowledged at the Breslau congress in 1895, when it was affirmed that agriculture has its own laws of development different from those of industry. In some respects *Die Agrarfrage* can be regarded as an attempt to elaborate and to back up this claim.

But had the book confined itself to doing just that it would not have provoked the controversy which it did. For both the 'revisionists' and the bourgeois critics of Marxism argued, as one would expect, that the Marxist laws of development at least do not apply to agriculture. Kautsky in addition to that went on to claim (by implication) that the fact of the peculiarity of agriculture does not undermine the political calculations implicit in the Erfurt programme: it was economic changes themselves which would generate preconditions for transition to socialism. It was this claim which made the book orthodox and controversial and it rested on two types of arguments. First, the validity of political calculations does not depend on each sector of the economy following the path of development sketched in the Erfurt programme. Further, Kautsky argued, the path of development taken by agriculture is of limited significance in the overall context. For not only is industry the leading sector of the economy, its relative importance would continue increasing over time. The implication then is, as Kautsky outlined in the conclusion to the theoretical section of the book, that the fact that agriculture does not generate preconditions for transition to socialism is not of great political significance. For Kautsky it is industry and urban areas which are the sites of major political and economic changes and it is from there that changes in agriculture initially originate.[2] But soon after the publication of *Die Agrarfrage* Bernstein in his famous *Evolutionary Socialism* set out to challenge even the assumption that at least changes in industry and in urban areas are generating preconditions for transition to socialism.

Apart from this the second strand of argument in Kautsky is that the path of development of agriculture does not diverge from that taken by industry as much as it seems or has been claimed to do. Though unlike in the latter, there is a discernible tendency in the former for large scale to replace small scale production, there is, nonetheless, in agriculture as in industry a steady extension of capitalist production, proletarianisation and even an increasing concentration of property in means of production (land). These processes, runs the underlying theme of Kautsky's argument, take a form different in agriculture from that in industry. The extension of capitalist production in agriculture, for example, does not take the form of an extension in the area occupied by large capitalist farms – as *mutatis mutandis* it does in industry – but rather a proliferation in the range of activities carried out by large farms. Referring to East Elbian estates Kautsky points out that a large number of them have branched out in manufacturing activities like the distillation of alcohol and sugar refining. He terms this process 'industrialisation of agriculture' and regards it as one of the most important components of *Die Agrarfrage*.[3]

Similarly the process of proletarianisation takes a specific form in agriculture. Unlike in industry it does not necessarily take the form of the dispossession of labourers from means of production; Marx, however, tended to regard the two processes as identical. For Kautsky as well as for Lenin, the proletarianisation of the peasantry usually takes the form of peasant households not possessing enough land to sustain themselves and thus being forced to sell their labour. One may note that unlike in Marx the unit of analysis is not the individual but the household. For Kautsky as for Lenin a proletarianised peasant household is characterised by the following two features: it sells labour rather than commodities and hence the cultivation of land is just a household activity.[4] The novelty of this conception lies in its implications. The first is that proletarianisation is not necessarily coupled with the disappearance of the units of production organised along non-capitalist lines – peasant farms, that is.

In addition the implication is that the relation between capitalist and peasant farms is not so much one of competition as of complementarity. For given Kautsky's conception of small peasants as proletariat *sui generis*, he assumed that the latter sells labour to the former rather than that both types of farms are selling identical or similar agricultural commodities and thus competing against each other. The nature of the relationship is of great significance because it implies the absence of the mechanism – market competition – by which, as Marx assumed, capitalist organisations destroy pre-capitalist organisations of production. Thus, in effect, what Lenin and Kautsky end up doing is separating the process of proletarianisation from the process of destruction of pre-capitalist organisations and their replacement by capitalist organisations of production. This separation constituted an important departure from what Marxist analysis – in the form in which it was embodied in the Erfurt programme – had till then taken for granted: that the two processes are tethered to each other. This departure raises the question 'what is the mechanism, if any, by which pre-capitalist organisations of production are destroyed in agriculture?'; but neither Lenin nor Kautsky answered it.

Not only does the process of proletarianisation as conceived by Lenin and Kautsky leave open the possibility of a peaceful coexistence of capitalist with peasant farms, but also the 'peasant proletariat' which it creates is not on a par with the industrial proletariat. For both Marx and Marxists have linked transition to socialism with the proletariat on the grounds that the latter – devoid of means of production as it is meant to be – has no interest in the private ownership of means of production. But this argument is only relevant to the industrial proletariat and not to the 'peasant proletariat' who strictly speaking cannot be said to be uninterested in the private ownership of land. Kautsky recognises this in *Die Agrarfrage* when he points to the two different personae of the small peasantry: sellers of labour and owners of land.[5] Now the end result of the argument is that though one can speak of the process of proletarianisation – or, what amounts to the same thing, an increase in the extent of participation in the labour market – taking place in agriculture, one cannot equate with it the effects (either economic or political) which Marx and Marxists have traditionally associated with the process of proletarianisation.

As for the concentration of property in land, this too, according to Kautsky, happens despite the fact that there is no tendency for large farms to replace small farms. Kautsky's demonstration of this relies on the distinction between the concentration of titles (either juridical or effective) to landed property and concentration in the sense of an increase in the proportion of total land area occupied by large farms; and it concerns the former rather than the latter. The argument, schematically speaking, is that with the extension of mortgage credit and increase in the frequency of the sale and purchase of land the proportion of mortgaged land in the total has steadily increased which, as we pointed out in chapter two, did happen in Germany.[6] This, for Kautsky, amounts to a concentration of titles to landed property on the grounds that most of mortgage credit is advanced by a handful of banks (as indeed was the case in Germany) and therefore it is they rather than cultivators who are the real owners of the land. As in the previous case here too Kautsky separates the two processes – of concentration of ownership in the means of production and of increase in the size of units of production – which were till then assumed to be inextricably mixed together in industry; and as before, in the process of separation he ends up changing the significance of the process in question. The concentration of property in land, so Kautsky thought, would make the task of nationalising land, an essential component of any socialist transformation of agriculture, easier because that would require the nationalisation of only a handful of mortgage banks.[7] But such a concentration, it is essential to note, does not produce large capitalist farms which can be more or less immediately converted into socialist farms, assumed by Kautsky and other orthodox Marxists like Lenin to be by definition large. The concentration of landed property thus leaves open the problem of consolidating small farms into large socially owned farms and therefore it does not create all the conditions for transition to socialist units of production. But this changes the significance which concentration had for Marx and Marxists: it by itself creates one of the economic conditions for transition to socialism.

Now what should one make of Kautsky's argument that the tendencies of social evolution are for the most part the same in agriculture as they are in industry, though their forms of realisation are different in the two sectors? One could regard the argument and the analyses on which it rests as a desperate attempt to immunise the analyses which underlie the Erfurt programme, of which Kautsky was a main architect, from criticisms by revisionists. There is an element of that in Kautsky's analyses but it would be wrong to dismiss his analyses on that ground. The analyses, of which we have given a sketch here, are in parts highly original and, more important, they are valuable regardless of their relation to the Erfurt programme. Further, we have seen that the similarity which Kautsky seeks to establish between the tendencies of evolution in agriculture and in industry is more formal than real (identity in terms of effects). Kautsky's analysis of the proletarianisation of the peasantry, for instance, remains valuable regardless of its relation to the tendencies mentioned in the Erfurt programme, and whatever similarity it has to the process of proletarianisation as conceptualised in the Erfurt programme is, as we just said, more formal than real. Nevertheless, Kautsky's attempt to establish a homology between the tendencies of evolution in agriculture and in industry and thus sustain the arguments of the Erfurt programme does have effects on his analysis: in particular what it does is to put emphasis on formal similarities and either underplay or even neglect the differences between the two sectors.

The controversy between the 'orthodox' and the 'revisionists' both before and after the publication of *Die Agrarfrage* was, however, centred around one issue: the relative technical efficiency of large and small farms. This seemingly technical concern was endowed with a wider economic and political significance because large and small, as we shall see, were assumed (usually implicitly) to be associated with other characteristics like the form of organisation of production. So what is of interest here is not so much the correlation between size and technical efficiency but the wide range of issues which were raised in the context of the comparison between large and small farms.

The important feature of Kautsky's analysis is not the argument that there is no discernible tendency for large farms to replace small farms but the fact that he separates the question of survival of different types of organisation of production from their relative efficiency. Till Kautsky's book it was normally taken for granted that it was the less efficient forms of organisations of production which disappear leaving the more efficient forms of organisation to survive and flourish,[8] as though economic mechanisms and forces sifted out more efficient forms of organisations of production for propagation. What is at issue here is the notion of 'natural selection' as applied to economic and social changes. Such a notion, as has been pointed out by a number of authors, has never been very precise and that is true for Marxist as well as non-Marxist uses of the notion.[9] But what is of interest to us is just the presumption that there is a relationship between survival and relative efficiency and the significance which it managed to acquire, rather than the exact mechanism by which economic forces select out the types of organisations of production for survival.

Kautsky as well as other orthodox Marxists always remained committed to the position that large farms (synonymous with capitalist farms) are more efficient than small farms, in turn regarded as a synonym for peasant farms. That the latter survive, Kautsky explained by separating the question of survival from that of technical efficiency, because of factors specific to agriculture: the finiteness of land, the lack of a complete separation between the household and the farm and the practice of granting the use of a strip of land in lieu of money wages. The revisionist position, in contrast, was that peasant farms are more efficient than large farms; it was the tenacious survival of peasant farms which, for them, provided the evidence in support of this claim. The revisionist argument, one may note, kept technical efficiency tethered to survival. The dispute between the 'orthodox' and the 'revisionists' about the relative efficiency of large and small farms, heated and labyrinthine as it was, raised two types of questions. First, which of the two sides is correct? Second, how did a technical question come to occupy the central position in what was essentially a political argument?

There is, strictly speaking, no single answer to the question of whether or not large farms are more efficient than small farms. For the size of the farm is just one of the features which affects its efficiency, which itself can be defined in a number of distinct ways; the question, therefore, is loose enough to accommodate a wide variety of answers. Yet both parties gave a precise answer to the question; but they did so by making assumptions which concerned not the size but other features of farming. We shall have something to say about the assumptions which Kautsky makes later. It is, however, the second rather than the first question which is more important here. What made technical efficiency a political issue was the assumption, which both the 'orthodox' and the 'revisionists' shared, that it was only the more efficient organisations of production which could form the basis for the development of socialist organisations of production. In turn its implication was that a Social Democratic agrarian programme should not favour the continued survival of inefficient organisations of production (small or peasant farms, according to Kautsky) on the ground that they are obstacles to the development of a socialist agriculture. Thus the dispute about the relative efficiency of large and small farms was, in effect, a continuation of the earlier dispute centred around the Agrarian Commission report in 1895: how far should Social Democracy go supporting the economic interests of the peasantry?

The revisionist position, which found its most comprehensive expression in David's writings, was that large scale production though efficient in industry was not so in agriculture.[10] Given the peculiarities of agriculture like the dispersion of production over a large area and discontinuities in the production cycle due to climatic changes, David argued that it was small scale owner-cultivation rather than large scale capitalist cultivation which had the edge in terms of efficiency. The revisionists not only argued for a programme which favoured the peasantry but also their position had definite implications for the organisation of future socialist economy. Unlike the orthodox who stood for the social ownership of means of production in all economic spheres, industry as well as agriculture and commerce, the revisionists questioned the necessity of socialising the whole economy and took the view that the private ownership of means of production when coupled with self-employment, as in peasant or artisan production, was perfectly consistent with socialism.

Though concerned with the question 'whether or not peasant production is consistent with socialism' the contestants, especially the orthodox, avoided the issue which became important later in the Soviet Union and elsewhere: how to transform an agriculture dominated by the peasantry into socialist agriculture? This would have been a non-problem for the revisionists but not so for the orthodox. In assessing the orthodox arguments one needs to take into account the two facts: the tenacious survival of peasant production in the face of all kinds of changes and, second, all the cases of socialist transformation of agriculture that we know of have taken place, not on the basis of large scale capitalist farms, but of medium or small scale peasant farms. The point then is that even if one can manage to establish the technical superiority of large scale farms that has little relevance to the problem of the construction of a socialist agriculture.

Before we go on to describe the specific arguments of *Die Agrarfrage* it is as well to list the tendencies and themes around which the book was organised.

1) There is no pronounced tendency for the size distribution of farms to change over time.[11]
2) Efficient though large farms are there is no tendency for them to replace the small farms.[12]
3) The motive forces which transform agriculture do not originate in agriculture but in industry. It was industry which destroyed rural industry and it was political ferment in urban areas which led to the destruction of feudalism.[13]
4) Agriculture by itself does not produce conditions for transition to socialism; such conditions, however do exist, in industry and in urban areas.[14]

5) Changes in agriculture there certainly are, but they concern what farms of different sizes produce, sell, the magnitude of indebtedness and migration from the countryside rather than the size distribution of farms.[15]
6) The peasantry will be ultimately destroyed by the combination of internal (increase in the size of the peasant household) and external (competition from capitalist farms and from overseas and the availability of employment in industry and in urban areas) factors.[16]

The starting point of Kautsky's analysis is not capitalist agriculture, with whose tendencies of evolution he is principally concerned, but the self-sufficient peasantry and feudal agriculture, grouped under a wider category termed natural economy. That discussion is centred around a very specific notion of self-sufficiency, which not only Kautsky but also other Marxists like Rosa Luxemburg and Lenin, have used as the central feature of pre-capitalist economies (usually termed natural economies by early Marxists). A unit of production is regarded as self-sufficient when it itself produces what it consumes, a notion which though self-evident is not as neutral as it might seem. This innocuous notion of self-sufficiency, however, acquires a special significance when particular effects are attributed to it. Self-sufficiency, according to Kautsky as well as other Marxists, confers 'immortality' on units of production and social organisations; for, the argument is, in that case they themselves reproduce the conditions of production, barring natural calamities and disasters.[17]

It needs no argument to see that 'natural economy' is too slender a notion to support any comprehensive analysis of pre-capitalist economies. The essential point is that the notion of self-sufficiency makes no reference to the forms of property and contours of units of production. A self-sufficient unit of production could refer to any of the following: a slash and burn tribal organisation, a unit of cultivation based on communal property, a peasant farm based on family labour and private property in land or a farm cultivated by share-croppers or serfs. Yet Marxists have widely used the notion when comparing pre-capitalist economies with a capitalist economy, as Kautsky does in *Die Agrarfrage*, or analysing the effect of the relationship between the two types of economies, as Rosa Luxemburg does in *The Accumulation of Capital* (ch. 27).

What the notion of natural economy does is to put pre-capitalist economies in a particular relation to capitalist economies and thus chart a path of transformation of the former into the latter. What needs noticing is that a natural economy is the one in which markets for goods and, naturally, also for labour are absent – precisely the features which by their presence characterise a capitalist economy. Market relationships, for Kautsky and other Marxists, not only spin a web of personal interrelationships but also corrode pre-capitalist relationships and organisations and lead to their replacement by capitalist relations and organisations. In all, what the notion of natural economy does is to put market relationships at the centre of the analysis, and thus make the history of the transformation of pre-capitalist into capitalist economy a history of the extension of market relationships. This is what Kautsky does in a sketchy fashion and others such as Rosa Luxemburg have done in a greater detail. Pre-capitalist economies may be devoid of market relationships in specific cases but they are a great deal else besides. Further, market relationships are not as corrosive of pre-capitalist relationships as they are automatically assumed to be when the latter are gathered together under the banner of natural economy. In fact some pre-capitalist economies can easily accommodate market relationships without undergoing any major change. Marxist historians, like Kula in his study of Polish feudalism, point out, though not without an element of surprise, that the development of grain markets rather than weakening the feudal relations strengthened them.[18] The element of surprise, however, has its origin in the assumption that market relations are by themselves corrosive of feudal relations.

Kautsky's discussion of feudalism[19] is piecemeal and is striking by virtue of the fact that it does not mention the social relations of feudalism like the form of payment of rent and the legal and economic relations which tether the peasants of a feudal society to their lords. In fact Kautsky's discussion of feudalism and of self-sufficient peasantry is less an analysis of specific types of non-capitalist economies than a device to bring particular features of capitalism into relief. For instance, Kautsky argues that feudalism, like other modes of production, only has the ability to sustain no more than a certain size of population, and once that limit is reached feudalism gives way to another mode of production (capitalism) which can carry on with the task of sustaining the population too big for feudalism; thus he points not so much to the cause of transition from feudalism to capitalism as indicates by analogy that there is a limit to technical developments under capitalism which, when reached, will lead to transition to socialism (ch. 3). The argument itself is a variant of Marx's statement and is based on a dialectic of the economic and the demographic which in its general structure is the same as that in the Malthusian argument.

Kautsky's discussion of feudal agriculture and self-sufficient peasantry leads on to a description of what Kautsky terms modern agriculture. And like the earlier discussions this too displays some peculiar features. It is, for instance, centred around a diverse assortment of phenomena like meat production, crop rotation, the use of machinery and fertilisers, bio-chemical processing of agricultural produce and agronomy. Now and then there are interesting observations on particular issues: for example he points out that in comparison to the fallow system crop rotation enlarges the cultivable area as well as the choice of crops available to cultivators, thus enabling them to tailor their cropping pattern to the pattern of market demand.[20] But the striking feature of the discussion is its neglect of organisational features like the systems of land tenure, and whatever reference there is to such features is in the context of a contrast between the significance attached to the area of the unit of production under feudalism and capitalism respectively.

Under feudalism, Kautsky points out, the methods of cultivation used on estates are no different from those on small peasant farms. For the former are cultivated by the very peasants who cultivate the latter and with the help of the same tools that they employ on their own farms. But in contrast, he goes on to argue that the methods used on large capitalist farms and on small peasant farms are often not the same. The former, for example, may be more mechanised and better informed about agronomy than the latter. The implication of the argument, it is this which makes it interesting, is that controversy concerning the relative technical efficiency of large and small farms is only relevant in the context of capitalism, and that it is the implanting of capitalism in agriculture which creates the contrast between the farms of different sizes.[21]

Yet the size of farms is not the only organisational feature of agriculture; it is not even the most important in all cases. The incidence of capitalist relations and new agricultural technology does not, one needs to emphasise, just depend on the size of the farm. The implanting of capitalism in agriculture may create differences between the farms of different sizes but the point is it also drives a wedge between farms situated in different regions and between farms with different cropping and ownership patterns. The size of the farm is just one out of a number of distinct axes along which the differentiation of agriculture under capitalism takes place. Kautsky accuses bourgeois writers on agriculture of overemphasising the size at the cost of other features of farming; in fact Kautsky's own analysis is open to exactly the same criticism.[22] This overemphasis mars a fair proportion of his analysis and devalues his arguments, many of which are potentially very valuable and interesting. A particularly striking example of this is provided by his comparison of large and small farms to which he devotes one full chapter.

The main point is, however, that neither in the chapter 'Modern Agriculture' nor in the one which follows it, 'Capitalism in Modern Agriculture', does one, except for tangential remarks, get an adequate analysis of the organisational features of modern agriculture. The latter chapter is for the most part no more than a reformulation of the concepts of *Capital* like value, surplus value and tendencies like the falling rate of profit. Out of this reformulation the only bit specifically related to agriculture is that which concerns rent (both absolute and differential) and the price of land. Following Marx, Kautsky argues that differential rent arises from the fact that under capitalism identical commodities sell at the same prices regardless of differences (like those in the fertility and the location of soil) in the condition under which they are produced. Absolute rent, in contrast, arises out of the private ownership of land, a feature which for Kautsky as well as for Marx is not an essential component of capitalism. Thus the former is capitalist and the latter 'non-capitalist'; and it is the nature of the latter which, as we pointed out earlier in chapter one, for Marx provides the rationale for the nationalisation of land under capitalism.

Homologous to the two types of rents there are, for Kautsky as for Marx, two types of personages in capitalist agriculture: the landlord and the capitalist farmer. Though the two can be represented by one and the same person, as in the case of owner-cultivation, the tendency in capitalist agriculture is, according to Kautsky, for the two to be distinct. Thus Kautsky like Marx takes lessee-cultivation to be the paradigm of capitalist agriculture. It has been pointed out already, and is recognised by Kautsky himself, that the leasing of land (unlike in England) was not common in Germany. But Kautsky takes the view that this does not affect the realisation of the tendency but just the form in which it is realised. This type of argument is, as we have seen, quite common in Kautsky; and it is that as land changes hands more and more of it is mortgaged and mortgage payment takes on the same character as rent. The essential point of the argument is that the mortgage bank stands in the same relation to the 'owner-cultivator' as does the landlord to the lessee-cultivator. In Germany, Kautsky claims, mortgage banks are the real owners of agricultural land.[23] This is, however, not quite true, as we shall see.

This argument, to which we have referred in several places, like a number of Kautsky's other arguments is ingenious; and it extends the domain of validity of Marx's claim that capitalism separates the owner from the cultivator of the land beyond the English case on which it seems to be exclusively based. But as in the case of a number of arguments we have cited earlier, the proletarianisation of the peasantry and the concentration of the ownership of means of production, the homology which Kautsky establishes between the English and the German case is more formal than real.

From the point of view of the financial burden it imposes on the cultivator mortgage payment may indeed be identical to rent. But this is not sufficient to establish a complete identity between the two; there still remain a number of crucial differences between the leasing and the purchase of land on mortgage. To start with the ownership of land by a mortgage bank by its very nature is transitory: it passes to the cultivator after a certain number of years. Kautsky's claim that the proportion of mortgaged land will keep on rising depends on the unspoken and not so innocuous assumption that the area of the newly mortgaged land exceeds that of the mortgaged land about to pass into the hands of the cultivator. Further, the respective positions of the two types of cultivators are not the same. For instance, a rise in the price of land because of the correlated increase in rent is to the disadvantage of the lessee; but not so for the cultivators already in possession of mortgaged land. For mortgage payments depend not on the current price of land but on the price at the date of its purchase as well as on the rate of interest. The latter, like the owners of land, in fact, gain from a rise in the price. Apart from these differences one needs also to note that, for Marx as for Kautsky, the whole pertinence of the fact that the owner of land is not the same as its cultivator consists in the presumption that it furnishes the social basis for the nationalisation of land. Referring back to the discussion of the nationalisation of land in the first chapter, here one simply needs to note that one cannot see why the possessors of mortgaged land, like the lessees, would be in favour of the nationalisation of land – a measure which, notwithstanding Kautsky's assumption, cannot be carried out by just nationalising mortgage banks.

However, we leave Kautsky's discussion of the capitalist character of modern farming at this and move on to his comparison of large and small farms, to which we have made frequent references.[24] Here we shall restrict ourselves to those specific features of the argument which have not been mentioned earlier.

Kautsky does not just assume but in fact demonstrates the superiority of large over small farms. The demonstration relies on a number of distinct types of arguments. First, there are the arguments which rely on the indivisibility of agricultural machines and buildings beyond a certain degree. The superiority of large farms lies in the more intensive use of machines and building that they make. Second, the larger the size the greater the possibility of specialisation of labour, a classical explanation of the beneficent effect of large scale production. Then, finally, there are the arguments which ground the superiority of large farms in the fact that they find it easier to obtain credit and a better price for their produce.

In his arguments Kautsky does not use any particular type of farm, in terms of its organisation, location and cropping pattern, as the point of reference; they, in fact, are presented as if they are universally valid. But they are not, as even a cursory testing of them would show. To take the last set of arguments first: that large farms have an advantage both in the credit and the commodities markets may be true in a large number of situations; yet, the point is, that has nothing to do with the size as such but with the way in which credit network and marketing are organised. For instance the cooperative provision of marketing and credit services can neutralise the disadvantage from which small farmers suffer. In fact just at the time when Kautsky was writing, Denmark had already developed a highly efficient and market oriented small scale agriculture with the help of the cooperative marketing and processing of produce.[25] As for the second type of argument, it is true that large farms have a greater possibility of employing trained personnel and thus using more scientific techniques of cultivation than small farms. But the actual importance of this advantage crucially depends on institutional factors like the scale and the coverage of agricultural extension services. In the case where the rural population is educated and agricultural extension services comprehensive, small farms may have exactly the same access to new techniques as large farms. The point in general terms is that what seems to favour large farms turns out in a number of cases to depend on something other than the size.

As for the first set of arguments, it is true that buildings and machines do not vary continuously with the size and to that extent they may be more intensively used on large than small farms. But the actual incidence of the economies of scale will crucially depend on the extent to which machines are used and their technical characteristics; and these in turn will depend on the cropping pattern. It is, for instance, well known that grain production lends itself to mechanisation more easily than dairy production, horticulture or market gardening. The incidence of the economies of scale is, it is necessary to note, not only uneven but it also influences the respective cropping patterns of large and small farms: it often turns out that large farms are biased in favour of crops which lend themselves to mechanisation while small farms are in favour of labour intensive and high value crops. Two implications follow from this, both of them damaging to Kautsky's argument. First, the size required for the efficient utilisation of the means of production varies greatly from one crop to another; a point which Kautsky himself recognises when he says that while a vineyard of only 3 ha is considered big a 100 ha grain farm only counts as medium sized. Second, the dependence of cropping pattern on the size and the uneven incidence of the economies of scale over different crops implies that the relative efficiency of large and small farms may depend on the criterion by which it is measured. It is, for instance, known that small farms often come out more efficient than large farms if the measure of efficiency is the value of output per hectare and *vice versa* when the measure happens to be the output per man.[26]

Now it is clear that large and small are vague categories, though not meaningless. The farms which Kautsky compares under the headings of large and small are, one must be reminded, not just different in size but also different in organisation. Small and big are meant to be peasant and capitalist farms respectively. The comparison is further complicated by the fact that peasant and capitalist are as elastic as categories as are large and small. Though Kautsky does not define it explicitly, a peasant farm presumably refers to a family labour farm and a capitalist farm to one worked by wage labour. The mode in which farm labour is procured, though of central importance, does not exhaust all the characteristics relevant to a comparison between peasant and capitalist agriculture. A peasant farm, one may note, can be anything from a highly market-oriented farm abreast with the latest technology to a primitive farm turned over to the satisfaction of household needs. Similarly, a capitalist farm can be anything from a highly mechanised and modern farm to a semi-feudal estate like the Junker estates of East Elbia. What the heterogeneity of the two categories means then is that the result of comparison between the efficiency of peasant and capitalist farms will crucially depend on the examples used as the standard of reference.

It is, however, not entirely clear what the referent of Kautsky's discussion is. The comparison itself, though interspersed with examples, is presented as if it does not depend for its validity on any specific type of farm; but, as is clear from our discussion here, that is definitely not so. However, Kautsky's insistence, mollified to some degree later,[27] that large farms are more efficient than small farms and the latter cannot overcome their disadvantages even by forming cooperatives raises for him the question: how do small farms manage to survive?

Small farms, the argument is, manage to survive through very hard work and meagre consumption. Small peasants, the argument continues, are often worse off than agricultural wage labourers. The implication of the argument is that the support for the continued survival of the peasantry unwittingly becomes a support for the perpetuation of onerous work and poverty in the countryside, an implication which is clearly directed against the revisionist supporters of the peasantry. These arguments are not specific to Kautsky; they are supported by observation culled from a wide variety of sources.[28] That small peasants live in conditions of abject poverty seems to be as valid as any general statement about a heterogeneous category could be. But the point is that it does not depend for its validity on the claim that large farms are more efficient than small farms.

Kautsky's aim, however, is not just to draw attention to the poverty of peasants but to establish a causal connection between that poverty and the size of the farm. That small peasants survive does not, for Kautsky, mean that they are efficient in some technical sense but that they are wretched. It is possible to establish this connection, though not with the same degree of certitude and definiteness as in Kautsky, without having to subscribe to an all-embracing technical superiority of large over small farms. The argument is that the standard of living of a peasant household obviously depends on what it manages to produce for sale or for its consumption, which in turn depends on the area of the family farm, besides other factors like the methods of farming and the size of the family labour force. Stated in this loose form the statement is incontrovertible; for to deny it would imply that land as a factor of production is irrelevant to agriculture. One may, however, note that for the purpose of this statement it is not just the area of the peasant farm but that relative to the size of the peasant family, the land to labour ratio, which counts. But usually the area and the ratio seem to keep generally in step with each other.

But Kautsky was not concerned simply with making non-controversial statements; he wanted to demolish the case for structuring agriculture around small peasant farms, a case argued by David as well as by leading bourgeois agronomists like Sering. In terms of Kautsky's arguments, the 'peasantists' utopia' would end up perpetuating abysmally low levels of consumption and overwork not only by adults but also by children. Notwithstanding the lacunae in his arguments, Kautsky has a point which is best brought out by the following variation on his argument.

Poverty and drudgery are relative concepts; the bench-mark used for assessing their extent thus ought to and normally does depend on the structure of the economy. In an economy where industry has firmly implanted itself and the majority of population lives in urban areas, as indeed was the case in the Germany of the 1890s, the bench-mark arguably ought to be incomes and work practices in urban areas. This is, in fact, the bench-mark which has been commonly used in such economies, in other capitalist countries as well as the Germany of the 1890s. For the migration from the countryside to the cities is a universal feature of capitalist development and it is the rural–urban economic gap which is one of main determinants of that migration. Now the essential point is that small or medium peasant farming *qua* paradigm of agricultural organisation has to be assessed in terms of its ability to generate income and patterns of work comparable to those in urban areas. What one can argue, especially given the fact of a continual increase in income and reduction in the hours of work in urban areas, is that the ability of an agriculture centred around small and medium sized peasant farms to do so is extremely limited.

Such an agriculture, one can further say, may not only perpetuate but in fact widen the economic gap between rural and urban areas over time. In relation to the Germany of the 1890s one may recall that over a half of total farms were no more than 2 hectares in size (see chapter two), a size on average too small to generate incomes anywhere near urban incomes in an advanced industrial country. The recent experience of Western European countries shows that small and even medium sized peasant farms tend to become poverty traps;[29] and attempts to bridge the rural–urban economic gap have eventually to take the form of replacing such farms with more mechanised, larger and sparsely manned farms. This argument can alternatively be put in terms of the efficiency comparison between large and small farms: what the growth of incomes and change in work pattern in urban areas does is to shift the emphasis in agriculture towards output per man (a criterion directly related to personal incomes and which *ceteris paribus* favours larger farms), and away from output per unit of land (a criterion which tend to favour small farms because of their labour intensity).

What, however, needs questioning is the assumption that there is an ideal type of agricultural organisation independently of the structure of the economy, an assumption which underlies Kautsky's arguments in favour of large farms as well as revisionists' arguments in favour of peasant farming. We leave the discussion of large and small farms, to which we have devoted more than proportionate space, at that and move on to what follows it in *Die Agrarfrage*.

The descriptions of the poverty and drudgery of small peasant households by itself only partially explains how they tenaciously manage to survive in the face of capitalist development. For one could point out that the same is true for handicraft and small scale manufacturing and yet they do not seem to display the same resilience as peasant agriculture. One of the main arguments of *Die Agrarfrage* is that the survival and even the proliferation of small peasant farms has much to do with the peculiar characteristics of agriculture as a branch of production, an argument which is intermittently elaborated in the three chapters following the one which compares large with small farms.

Besides its heavy dependence on climatic and other natural factors, the peculiarities of agriculture have much to do with the special feature of land as a factor of production. It is the fact that land as a factor of production is location specific, as well as the oft repeated truism that the area of cultivated land in already inhabited countries cannot be increased significantly, which in different guises play a central role in a variety of Kautsky's arguments.[30] The latter in conjunction with the fact of the private ownership of land is what, for Marx, is responsible for absolute rent. What we shall do now is to describe briefly Kautsky's arguments by arranging them around these two facts.

That the quantity of land cannot be increased gives the holder of land a power to exclude the non-holders from engaging in agriculture, a power which possessors of those means of production whose quantity can be increased (in particular industrial means of production) do not have. What this means is that peasant farms by occupying a substantial portion of available land set a limit to the extension of capitalist agriculture. Here a contrast with artisan production would best bring out the point at issue.

The means of production in possession of artisans do not set any barrier to the development of large scale capitalist industry; for in principle the quantity of such means of production can always be increased. In fact one can go even further and argue that it is in most cases irrelevant for the development of capitalist industry because machines and tools used by capitalist industry are often just not the same as those used by artisans. The argument then is that capitalist manufacturing can set itself up and develop independently of pre- or semi-capitalist artisan manufacture. Correlatively there is no necessity for the capitalist development of manufacture to take the form of the internal transformation of artisan into capitalist manufacture. Often the only point of contact between capitalist and artisan industry is the market for finished goods, a contact which in a large number of cases proves fatal for the latter.[31] In this connection it is interesting to note that Marx when analysing the rise of capitalist industry leaves out the existing structure of handicraft and artisan production and concentrates on the following two: the existence of the labour market and the concentration of money capital in a few hands.

But the case of agriculture is very different. Both capitalist and pre-capitalist agriculture, for a start, are centred around the same factor of production: land. Given this and the non-extendability of land, the development of capitalist agriculture can only take two forms: either the internal transformation of pre-capitalist into capitalist farms or pre-capitalist farms ceding the land in their possession to capitalist agriculture. The details of the actual process of its development aside, the essential point is that capitalist agriculture cannot develop independently of the existing pre-capitalist agriculture. It was this dependence which Lenin (in the Preface to *The Development of Capitalism in Russia*) recognised more clearly than Kautsky.

Now to return to the survival of small peasantry. In the case of small peasant farms their internal transformation into capitalist farms is, for the most part, ruled out because the area at their disposal is, generally speaking, too small to support a capitalist enterprise where labour as well as other means of production are imputed costs.[32] Such a transformation is not only possible but does take place in the case of medium or large peasant farms and landed estates. In addition peasant farms do not easily lend themselves to annihilation by external factors. Peasant farms by the mere fact of their existence limit the expansion of capitalist farming and thus competition from that source. Finally, peasant farming unlike, for example, artisan production has a great capacity to adapt itself to market forces.

It is here that another dimension of agriculture as a branch of production becomes relevant. Land is the site of a wide variety of productive activity; as a result agriculture is never as specialised as branches of manufacturing. Apart from that, important as food is among the items of personal consumption, especially so when its level is low, agriculture can be turned over to the satisfaction of the needs of the household in a way which branches of industry cannot be. Cultivation can become, as indeed it does according to Kautsky, part of the chores of a peasant household; but, for instance, artisan production cannot be because the article it produces may at best account for a very small proportion of household consumption. In all, a secret of the survival of peasant farms is the malleability that it has as a result of the multifarious nature of agricultural activity itself.

Survival, however, does not mean the absence of change; it simply refers to the fact of the continued existence of small farms. This brings us to another theme in Kautsky's argument: the change as a result of the development of capitalism takes the form less of a redistribution of land than of change in the composition of what farms of different sizes respectively produce and sell, as well as relations between them. Small farms, Kautsky's argument is, sell labour rather than commodities; and they are thus complementary to large farms which buy labour.[33] This constitutes, for Kautsky, the process of proletarianisation of the peasantry, a process which we discussed earlier and which is premised on the parcellisation of land arising out of an increase in the population dependent on land. Large farms, on the other hand, branch out into ancillary activities like the brewing of alcohol and the refining of sugar, a process Kautsky termed the industrialisation of agriculture.[34]

There are a few more features which can be discussed in relation to the two properties of agricultural land which we have singled out: non-extendability and immovability. Of such features the three which occupy an important place in *Die Agrarfrage* are: systems of land inheritance, parcellisation of land, and obstacles in the way of shifting the size distribution of farms in favour of large farms. All of these in fact dovetail into the ones we have already discussed.

The systems of inheritance which establish a connection between the past and present distribution of land occupy a central place in agriculture. But it is not clear exactly why. For one may retort that this is exactly what such systems do in the case of those means of production whose quantity can be increased or, more specifically, industrial means of production. Implicit in Kautsky's analysis of the systems of inheritance is the argument that they automatically assume a special importance in agriculture because of the relatively limited degree of freedom that there is for changing the distribution of agricultural land. The distribution of reproducible means of production can, one may note, change simply as a result of the way in which additions to the inherited stock are distributed. But obviously that cannot be so in the case of land since there is no addition to the inherited stock. In the case of land that the essential point is that all changes in its distribution have to take the form of a redistribution in the inherited stock – a restriction which by itself assigns central importance to the way in which inherited stock is distributed and hence to the systems of inheritance. In addition to all this, it is relevant to take into account that the formation of joint stock companies in industry and commerce has more or less completely eliminated the influence of inheritance on the structure of companies, something which has not happened on a significant scale in agriculture.

A recurring theme in Kautsky as well as in Marx is that private property in land perpetuates irrationalities in the distribution of land – both in the way it is distributed among farms and among individuals. Inheritance, which is the ghost of private property, is essential to this process. What the inheritance of land does, according to Kautsky, is to select individuals for the possession of land not on the basis of their suitability to agriculture but on the basis of the accident of their birth.[35] The main target in this argument is not so much small and medium farms as large landed estates which, in the Germany of the 1890s, though they were relatively few in numbers occupied most of the land area. Inheritance, moreover, may influence the distribution of land among farms in a direction which takes it further away from the one required by rational agriculture.

To see how this might happen we need to divide the systems of inheritance into the ones which keep the land intact and those that divide up the land among heirs.

The system of entail, which usually affects only the farms at the top end of the scale, came in two different versions in Germany: *Fideikomiss* (the aristocratic version applying to the East Elbian estates) and the peasant version *Anerbenrecht*.[36] It was, however, the former which was more important and what it did, in general terms, was to slow down the division of estates which would have happened naturally as a result of the increase in population and the frequency of bankruptcy. This in itself for Kautsky, given his arguments about the technical superiority of large farms, should have constituted a step towards the development of rational agriculture. But he, and indeed others like Max Weber,[37] regarded *Fideikomiss* as anachronistic because it perpetuated the estates built around feudal traditions and which in a number of cases were too large to be managed as one single unit.

The systems of inheritance which divide up the land, in contrast to entail, affect the whole spectrum of the size distribution and in the main what they do is to shift the size distribution towards the lower end. As explained earlier in chapter 2, in the case where rural population is growing this type of system of inheritance builds in the size distribution a tendency towards an increase in the share of small farms in the total. This in terms of Kautsky's analysis has two effects: a progressive proletarianisation of the peasantry and, second, the proliferation of farms beyond the level needed to sustain a rational cultivation of land. In all a combination of the two systems would freeze the top end of the distribution and lengthen the tail at the expense of medium sized farms.

The other feature of land is its immovability which, in Kautsky's view, makes it difficult to create a large farm out of a number of small ones. For that is only possible when the small farms in question are contiguous to each other. Thus by implication Kautsky points to an asymmetry: given private property in land, the parcellisation of land is much easier than its centralisation.[38]

This more or less finishes the coverage of notable specific arguments in part I of *Die Agrarfrage*, the theoretical section of the book.[39] It is as well to raise here the general questions which Kautsky tries to answer by way of conclusion to that section of the book: what form would the development of capitalist agriculture take, what will eventually happen to the peasantry and, finally, what actual form would the development of socialist agriculture take?

What Kautsky terms 'latifundia' play an important part in his answers to these questions.[40] Latifundia in Kautsky's sense are not a feudal relic but a modern development; an industrial and agricultural conglomerate. These, according to Kautsky, started to develop in the last quarter of the nineteenth century in the form of large estate owners acquiring more farms, usually not in order to enlarge the area of the parent farm, and undertaking manufacturing activities like brewing and sugar refining. This was a process to which we referred earlier and which Kautsky termed the industrialisation of agriculture. Thus a latifundium was not an integrated unit of production but instead, like a modern corporation, a unit of management and ownership composed of a number of units of production. The reasons for which Kautsky attaches what seems an inordinate importance to such organisations are: first, by bringing a number of farms (covering a fairly large area) under one management they facilitate a rapid diffusion of rational methods of cultivation and lead to mechanisation and the employment of specialised labour, in short the effects associated with the economies of scale; second, they bring about an integration of agriculture and industry.

What the modern latifundia do, according to Kautsky, is to spread the benefits of large scale farming in a situation where private property in land makes it difficult to combine together a number of small farms into a large one, and it leads to a situation where the boundaries of farms are determined by the exigencies of cultivation rather than just by the facts of ownership. For Kautsky the modern latifundia are not only agents of the development of capitalist agriculture but also the foundation of future socialist agriculture. Though he does not spell it out explicitly, Kautsky does conceive of future socialist agriculture as consisting of one giant latifundium enveloping the whole of agriculture and enveloping a wide variety of industrial activities.

The peasantry, according to Kautsky's prognosis, will dissolve itself. Incapable of matching the levels of income offered by industry and modern agriculture as peasant agriculture is, it will shrink as a result of the desertion of the peasants themselves. The essential point is that Kautsky regards peasant agriculture as an obstacle to development of both capitalist and socialist agriculture. Peasant agriculture does not, according to Kautsky, play a positive part in the evolution of socialist agriculture. A socialist government, as conceived by Kautsky, will not expropriate the peasantry but wait for it to dissolve itself voluntarily. It is this view of the peasantry and peasant agriculture which is a central component of Kautsky's discussion of agrarian programmes to which we now turn briefly.

That discussion starts with a sceptic note by asking the question: does Social Democracy need an agrarian programme?[41] It will be recalled that four years earlier in 1895 (at the time of the Breslau congress) Kautsky had argued against having a special agrarian programme. In fact part II of *Die Agrarfrage* is centred around the question of whether there is a need of revising the position taken at the Breslau congress? In general the answer, for Kautsky, is no.

The essential consideration for Kautsky is the point of

incidence of a proposed Social Democratic agrarian programme. If by agrarian programme one means a programme principally catering for the interests of the peasantry then, in terms of Kautsky's arguments, that cannot be a Social Democratic agrarian programme. For, the argument runs, there is no more reason for Social Democracy to support peasantry than any other propertied section of the population – small entrepreneurs and shopkeepers.

An agrarian programme is, however, acceptable to Social Democracy if its point of incidence is the agricultural proletariat. But here on the basis of the previous discussion one would point out that in terms of Kautsky's own arguments peasantry and agricultural proletariat are not mutually exclusive. Kautsky does take the overlap between the two categories into account, and distinguishes between peasants as proprietors and as labourers and argues that a Social Democratic programme would only cater for peasants in their latter capacity.

The demands which in Kautsky's view Social Democracy could legitimately make fall into three categories; first, demands concerning the terms and conditions of employment and living of agricultural labourers; second, demands for abolishing the remaining feudal institutions and privileges; and finally, demands for the democratisation of political institutions and the extension of personal rights to the whole population. There is, however, a notable absence from the list of demands supposedly in line with the principles of Social Democracy: the nationalisation of land.[42]

We pointed out in chapter 1 that land nationalisation, according to Marx, was not only feasible but in fact necessary for the development of capitalist agriculture. Kautsky opposes land nationalisation on the grounds that such a measure rather than weakening the position of the Junkers, who in his view already dominated the state apparatuses, would strengthen it. For similar reasons Kautsky is also opposed to the demand for the nationalisation of mortgages with a view to decreasing the burden of mortgage payments, a demand put forward by the Bund but also by some Social Democrats. In general terms Kautsky is opposed to any extension in the domain of intervention of the state except in those areas where it could only work to the advantage of the working class or would be in the interest of the population as a whole, such as the regulation of the conditions of work and the nationalisation of forests and water.

In all, except on particular issues, Kautsky wanted Social Democracy to maintain a neutral but not an indifferent stance towards agriculture. Social Democracy, in his view, ought to be interested in the tendencies of the development of capitalist agriculture but it should not influence the course of that development. He wanted the SPD to be candid and recognise that in essence it was an urban and a proletarian party.[43]

At the end of this long description of the arguments of *Die Agrarfrage* one may want to raise general questions such as what is one to make of the book? what precisely is its significance? is it anything more than a product of specific political and economic conjuncture which has no value other than as an archive? All these questions ultimately come around to the question of the mode of utilisation or reading of the book. Since there is no one correct mode of utilisation of the book we can do no more than to list the two which are pertinent to our purposes.

One can indeed read the book as an archive. The aim in that case is to place the book in the context of the conditions of its writings and to construct around it the network of political events, political programmes and theoretical writings of which it is a part. This is one of the things that we have done in these four chapters.

But that is by no means the only use one can make of the book and other writings on the agrarian question. One can read the book as an assemblage of arguments, concepts and other discursive entities which may lend themselves to use in relation to contemporary concerns like the development of capitalist agriculture in the Third World countries of today. We have a few suggestions to make to guide the use of the book as a box of tools.

One should not, for a start, take the claim of the book (made in its subtitle) that it is the analysis of the tendencies of modern agriculture, at its face value. The essential point is that *Die Agrarfrage* is not a coherent and unified analysis of such tendencies. Tendencies of evolution indeed play an important part in structuring the book; but they are more often than not used as clamps to hold disparate things together, to force them into shape and to filter out the features not directly relevant to political programmes. They, with the exception of a few, are not the end-products of the analysis of the book. What one must then do is to devalue the claim that such and such tendencies are realised, albeit in a distinctive form, in agriculture. The value of such claims is more political than analytical.

Once the straitjacket of tendencies is removed, one can use the wealth of analysis and insights that there is in the book in different forms. One of the aims behind going through the specific arguments of the book as we have done in this chapter is to indicate the value of particular analyses taken on their own.

In addition we suggest that one should not take *Die Agrarfrage's* claim to be a Marxist classic to mean that it is an elaboration of what is already there, at least in *statu nascendi*, in Marx's *Capital* and other writings of Marx and of Engels. One might say that we have gone out of our way to emphasise the differences between Kautsky's, Marx's and Engels' analyses. The aim, however, is not to single out Kautsky as an errant Marxist (a charge which is too easy now to level against him, given his denunciation by Lenin as reformist and revisionist) but to point to the differentiated nature of Marxism itself, even of its most orthodox variety. It is in these differences, we may suggest, fearful of attracting the wrath of the guardians of the faith, that the potential of the further development of Marxism lies.

# 5 Social Democracy and the Agrarian Question

The agrarian question has a paradoxical feature: agriculture and rural populations came to be noticed and to constitute a decisive political force precisely at a time when their weight in the economy was steadily decreasing. This feature characterised not only the German economy but also other European economies such as those of Belgium, France and Italy. But the agrarian question was not just a response to economic conditions and events; these indeed did play a crucial part but they cannot account for the manner in which the agrarian question was raised.

What we have argued is that in Western Europe the agrarian question was intimately connected with the rise of parliamentary democracy. It is necessary to note that questions concerning the countryside as an arena of political struggles and the economic state of agriculture, the ensemble of questions which together form what we have termed in this book 'the agrarian question', were posed to political parties rather than to anybody who happened to be interested in the countryside and agriculture. Broadly speaking in Western Europe in general and in Wilhelmine Germany in particular the agrarian question was conditioned by two sets of factors: first, the emergence of an extensive market in agricultural commodities and the resultant international competition and, second, the birth of parliamentary democracy and the related formation of new political forces (in the form of political parties and mass political organisations anchored in parliamentary politics). Both these factors, one may note, originated outside rather than inside the countryside.

Though we have discussed it in relation to a Marxist party, the agrarian question was not addressed exclusively to Marxists and Marxist political parties. So far as Marxism was concerned rural areas did have peculiar features which singled them out, features connected with the fact that non-capitalist relations in one form or another tenaciously survived in the countryside. Though these features presented other Marxist parties as well as the SPD with special problems it was not these which conferred upon rural areas the political importance acquired at the turn of this century. The factors responsible for the emergence affected non-Marxist parties and organisations too, albeit in a different way.

The countryside was an unknown territory to the SPD; but not because agriculture with its embellishments of non-capitalist relations did not fit into the Marxist theoretical schema. The difficulties which the party faced had their origin in non-doctrinal factors. They were not due to the fact that the party could not find a place for the peasantry and small scale agriculture in its political programme, as indeed it did not when it rejected the Agrarian Commission Report at the Breslau congress in 1895; the SPD would have found it difficult to gain a toe-hold in the countryside with any kind of programme. German Social Democracy was in fact founded on a specific range of organisations, party branches, social and cultural associations and trade unions. Not only did such organisations not exist in the countryside, but they were difficult to establish there because of the way in which agricultural production was organised and because of the political control exercised by the sections of population hostile to the SPD. Therefore, the fact that the Erfurt programme mentioned only agricultural labourers and not other sections of the rural population in its economic demands, was not the main barrier to Social Democracy's winning all over the countryside.

Here a number of points are pertinent. The debate whether or not to append a special agrarian programme to the Erfurt programme, one may recall, took place not before the start of *Landagitation* but after it had failed in its aims. Thus the course of *Landagitation* was not affected by doctrinal disputes before and after the Breslau congress. Moreover, the fact that the party came to reject the pro-peasant stance at the Breslau congress did not imply that the whole party organisation accepted the official position. Southern German Social Democrats for legal reasons were organised into separate parties; and these were fairly autonomous in their functioning and their choice of the terms on which they conducted their political propaganda. We pointed out that the Bavarian Social Democrats had adopted a pro-peasantist programme in their congress in 1892 and conducted their political work in the countryside on the basis of that programme. But the important point is that Southern German Social Democrats were no more successful in amassing support in the countryside than were their comrades elsewhere.

This proposition must be qualified, for while *Landagitation* was a failure, the electoral support for the SPD steadily increased over time; in 1903 the party displaced the Conservative Party as the second largest party in the countryside. But the point which needs to be made is that the relative lack of support for Social Democracy in the countryside cannot be explained in terms of the party not having a programme sympathetic to the peasantry. Indeed programmes do have an importance of their own but in the case of Wilhelmine Germany they do not seem to have been decisive in the failure to achieve the ambitious targets which the SPD had set for itself at the beginning of the 1890s. In assessing the effectiveness of the party's political work in the countryside one has to keep in view the following two general facts. First, the party had overestimated the speed with which it could gather support not only in rural but also in urban areas. Second, some of the barriers which the party encountered in rural areas were not confined to it alone. For instance, the party found it relatively difficult to win over the Catholic population of South and West Germany, among urban workers as well as rural inhabitants.

That it is difficult to establish political organisations in the countryside is a commonplace. In the *Eighteenth Brumaire of Louis Napoleon* Marx compared peasants to a sack of potatoes, a collection of disparate things which just happens to be assembled together. But the difficulties which the SPD faced in the countryside were of a different order altogether. It was not that the rural population of Wilhelmine Germany was unorganised and disparate. On the contrary they were subject to a wide variety of organisations and control, more so than their urban counterparts. Further, the foundation and the spectacular growth of Bund der Landwirte as a mass organisation points to the existence of possibilities for the establishment of political organisations in the countryside. The difficulties which the SPD faced concerned the obstacles which existed in the way of the establishment of Social Democratic organisation rather than organisations as such.

The establishment and the growth of the Bund may be taken as a pointer to the space which the SPD could have occupied had it followed a policy sympathetic to agriculture and rural population. But the point is that the space which the Bund occupied could never have been occupied by the SPD. For there was an essential asymmetry between the position of the SPD and the position of non-Social Democratic organisations, especially that of the Bund. They could thrive in the countryside on the basis of existing institutions and relations, an opportunity which was not open to the SPD. A Social Democratic organisation had to furnish its own foundation and develop by circumventing the existing socio-political framework. The argument, in general terms, is that a Social Democratic organisation could not compete with non-Social Democratic organisations simply by offering a more appealing political programme.

Moreover, it was not just that a Social Democratic organisation could not flourish in the countryside but also that the very nature of Social Democracy put constraints on the type of rural Social Democratic organisation which could be established. For the Bund was a self-proclaimed parochial organisation of agrarian interests; it made no claim to represent any other economic interest. In contrast the SPD was a nation-wide organisation committed to representing not one but a number of different sections of German society. This together with the fact that it was an urban and industrial workers' party in its orientation precluded the establishment of a Social Democratic organisation which could compete with the Bund as the purveyor of a programme favourable to agriculture. One should emphasise that this was not a corollary of the indifferent position which the party came to adopt towards the peasantry and small scale agriculture. Even with a revisionist agrarian programme, as for instance that suggested by the Agrarian Commission, the party would have found it impossible to be a match for the Bund. Thus the belief that the German Social Democrats could have cut the ground from underneath the Bund had they been less doctrinaire and more in tune with reality – a belief which is implicit in both Mitrany's *Marx Against the Peasants* and Gerschenkron's *Bread and Democracy in Germany* – rests on a gross over-estimation of the power of political programmes and the neglect of the constraints implicit in the very structure of German Social Democracy.

In effect what we have done in this book in general terms is to devalue the importance of theoretical stances and political programmes. It is not that we consider them irrelevant but rather that they are of a specific significance and that the work and the functioning of a party or an organisation is not completely hegemonised by them. If this is accepted then the implication is that the attitude and the political stance of Marxist political organisations towards agriculture and the peasantry cannot be explained just in terms of doctrine and deviations from it.

Backed by the writings of Engels and Kautsky one can speak of an orthodox position towards the peasantry, but that did not remain unchanged over time. Both Engels and Kautsky argued for a neutral stance towards the peasantry and small scale agriculture but further east in Russia, unlike in Germany and Western Europe, it was not just the revisionists but also the orthodox who talked in terms of aiding the peasantry. There the orthodox position was to aid the peasantry in its struggle against the feudal lords and the remnants of feudalism. And since then this position has remained a more or less standard Marxist position towards the peasantry. It is true that the Marxist orthodoxy has always been hostile to the idolisation of the peasantry but that stance, it is important to note, is consistent with a wide variety of positions towards agriculture and the peasantry. It is also true that Marxist orthodoxy has never accepted that a peasant organisation of production can be an integral component of a socialist agriculture, but that refusal too is consistent with a wide variety of policies towards agriculture. The assessment of Marxist policies towards the peasantry and agriculture is too much dominated by the Russian experience; but it needs noting that the transition from peasant to socialist agriculture has taken not one but a large number of different paths, from that of forced collectivisation to the reliance on peasant initiative to form cooperatives and communes.

The conditions which different Marxist parties have encountered have been very different. The first Marxist parties were all urban and industrial parties in the sense that they were anchored in cities and among industrial workers. Their interest in agriculture took the form of branching out from the cities to the land, a fact which is not only true for the Western European but also for the Russian Social Democratic parties. But this line of progression changed later on. In some Asian countries the sequence was reversed: in China and in Vietnam the Marxist parties instead of branching out from the cities to the land first consolidated themselves in the countryside and from there went on to engulf the cities. The position of the rural areas in those Asian countries was very different from that of rural areas in Europe.

In Western Europe the rural areas were an inhospitable territory for the growth of Marxist parties and it was the cities which provided the conditions for their establishment and development. It was exactly the reverse in the case of China and Vietnam. The general political environment in the two cases was completely different. In European countries one is for the most part concerned with parliamentary democracy; in the case of China and Vietnam, with civil war and colonial and semi-colonial rule. The main point behind alluding to the experience of Asian countries is to question the all-too-common assumption that Marxism and Marxist organisation are congenitally hostile to the peasantry and always an alien force in the countryside.

Now finally to turn to the tendencies of development in agriculture: it is true that economic tendencies in agriculture were different from those in industry – a fact which was not only acknowledged by the critics of Marx but also, as we pointed out, by his supporters. But what is not clear is the exact pertinence of this difference. It is true that the growth of industry was coupled with the emergence of features which furnished a fertile ground for the rise of Social Democratic organisations in Europe. But a lot of such features had more to do with the rise of parliamentary democracy than with the development of industry as such. Apart from that, as is clear from our discussion, the difficulties which the SPD faced in establishing itself in the countryside had no direct connection with economic conditions there; they had more to do with the social and political order in the countryside. Here one may note that the SPD had as much difficulty in establishing itself in the regions of large estates as in those of small and medium sized farms.

There was a lively theoretical debate on issues relating to agriculture within the SPD. But these debates had a specific significance of their own and little direct relevance to the problems of rural areas. These debates did concern what may seem contemporary issues, like whether or not large farms are more efficient than small farms and whether or not the latter were being displaced by the former. But these debates, as we pointed out, had more to do with the question of whether or not peasant agriculture and the private ownership of means of production was consistent with socialism – an issue far removed from current problems of agriculture – than with the actual developments in agriculture.

# Notes to Part 1

## 1 The Agrarian Question

1. Engels, *The Peasant Question in France and Germany*, in Marx and Engels *Selected Works*, (1970), vol. III, p. 457.
2. Clapham (1968), pp. 159 and 209; von Waltershausen (1920), p. 460.
3. For an account of the vicissitudes of the First International see Marx, letter to Bolte, in Marx and Engels *Selected Works* (1970), vol. II; de Laveleye (1884), ch. 9.
4. Hunt (1964), ch. 1; Russell (1896), Lectures V and VI; Nettl (1965); Michels (1962).
5. The two constituent factions of the party were: (1) the Allgemeiner Deutscher Arbeiterverein, founded by Lassalle in 1863, and (2) the Sozialdemokratische Arbeiterpartei, founded at Eisenach in 1869 – hence the name 'Eisenachers'. For a short history of the party, see Russell (1896).
6. Engels, Foreword to the *Critique of the Gotha Programme*, in Marx and Engels (1970), vol. III.
7. Engels, letter to Bebel, ibid.
8. In fact the SPD had been banned in Prussia since 1876. See Lidtke (1966), p. 53.
9. Dawson (1881), ch. 14.
10. For a short account of the debate within the party see ibid., pp. 260–2. The role and significance of parliamentary activity remained a subject of discussion during the period of illegality as well as after that period. For an account of the discussion during the 1880s see Lidtke (1966), ch. 5. For the later period during the 1890s see Milhaud (1903), pt. V.
11. von Vollmar (1977), pt. III.
12. Lehmann (1970), pp. 9–11.
13. Lidtke (1966), p. 279.
14. For an assessment of Lassalle see Bernstein (1893), ch. 10.
15. Lidtke (1966), pp. 45–6.
16. For an account of Schulze–Delitsch movement and its relation to the socialist movement see Dawson (1881), pp. 135–44.
17. For a non-Marxist but still a socialist discussion of cooperatives see Oppenheimer (1896). For a Marxist assessment of cooperatives see Kautsky (1899), pt. I, ch. 6, sec. c, as well as Vandervelde (1913).
18. For a detailed discussion see Lidtke, ch. 6.
19. de Laveleye (1884), ch. 9 and Cole (1954), ch. 6.
20. For an assessment of the Marxist analysis of classes see Cutler et al. (1977).
21. Marx, *The Nationalisation of Land*, in Marx and Engels (1970), vol. II.

22. Marx invokes the authority of agronomists when discussing the barrier which private property imposes on the rational cultivation of land. See *Capital* (1966), vol. III, p. 167.
23. This view in fact pervades the whole discussion of rent in vol. III of *Capital*.
24. For instance see *Capital*, vol. III, p. 618.
25. Gratton (1971), ch. 1.
26. Kautsky (1899), pt. II, ch. 1, sec. d.

## 2 Some Aspects of German Agriculture

1. Kitchen (1978), ch. 9, p. 211.
2. The epithet Catholic should not be taken literally; the Centre Party was not a confessional party. In fact as it became important politically in the 1890s it loosened its ties with the church. Furthermore, it had Protestant support in some areas of South-West Germany. For a brief characterisation of the Centre Party see Blackbourn (1976), esp. sec. 1.
3. Ibid.
4. Johnson and Kroos (1956), ch. 11; Kautsky (1899), ch. 10, section a to d.
5. Kautsky (1899). For a general survey of the development of the railways and shipping see Ashworth (1975), ch. 2, sec. IV.
6. A. G. R. Porter wrote as late as 1851, 'An inconsiderable state . . . may exist under circumstances which oblige it to be habitually dependent on the soil of other countries for the food of its inhabitants; but this can never be the case with numerous people.' A statement cited in Clapham (1968), p. 209, and it was backed by an elaborate calculation showing why a habitual dependence on the part of Britain was not feasible.
7. Clapham (1968), pp. 210–11.
8. Clapham (1968), pp. 47–52 and 214–21; Kitchen (1978), pp. 203–6. The quantitative estimates of the increase in efficiency are given in Dillwitz (1973).
9. Dawson (1914) emphasises this point which is overlooked by other authors.
10. Lewis (1978) traces the Kondratiev price swing, pp. 24–8. The price series up to 1890 are given in Buchenburger (1893), vol. 2. For the later period see Ashley (1920), pp. 64, 68 and 85.
11. This particular feature is singled out for special emphasis by Lewis (1978). A similar argument is also implicit in Kautsky's *Die Agrarfrage* (part 1, ch. 11) when he emphasises that industry is a leading and agriculture a lagging sector of the economy.
12. von der Goltz demonstrated in *Geschichte der Landwirtschaft* that the depreciated price level primarily affected the crops produced by the East Elbian estates and that the farmers of Bavaria and Schleswig-Holstein where pig and cattle breeding was common did not experience a crisis at all. Walter in *Schriftens des Vereins für Sozialpolitik* further showed that only 15.5 per cent of Bavarian farmers' income in fact came from grains. These demonstrations are cited in Barkin (1970), p. 193.
13. Chambers and Mingay (1966), pp. 157–61.
14. Westergaard (1922), pp. 66–9.
15. For a general account of developments in Danish agriculture see Wester-

gaard (1922), pp. 66–80. For an unorthodox interpretation of the changes in English agriculture see Fletcher (1965).
16. Cited in Kitchen (1978), p. 206.
17. Varga (1969), pp. 261–74 for an assessment of the Marxist analyses of the agrarian crisis of the last quarter of the nineteenth century and its comparison with the agrarian crisis of the 1920s.
18. Kautsky (1899), ch. 6, sec. b. Paradoxically this is the same point which Chayanov makes in his famous *The Theory of Peasant Economy* (1966).
19. Ashley (1920); Dietzel (1903); Kindleberger (1951).
20. Buchenburger (1896), vol. II, p. 557.
21. This point is emphasised by both Blackbourn (1976) and Rosenberg (1943).
22. Kitchen (1978), pp. 135–49.
23. Dietzel (1903), p. 375.
24. Ashley (1920), p. 62.
25. Dawson (1904), p. 76.
26. Dietzel (1903).
27. Dawson (1904), ch. 7.
28. Bürger (1911), esp pp. 138–48; Barkin (1970), pp. 61–2; Kitchen (1978), pp. 210–11.
29. Pühle (1975).
30. On the Kanitz motion see Barkin (1970), pp. 89–94.
31. Farr (1978).
32. Gerschenkron (1966), pp. 73–6.
33. For an account of Weber's position see Mommsen (1959), pp. 105–7; Barkin (1970), p. 197.
34. Bürger (1911), pp. 138–48.
35. Marx (1975) *Speech on Free Trade, Collected Works* 6 and Engels (1969) 'Zolltariff und Freihandel', Marx Engels *Werke*, Band 21.
36. For an account of the discussions at the Stuttgart Congress see Milhaud (1903), pt. v, sec. 2, ch. 3, sec. 2.
37. On the Social Democratic victory see Barkin (1970), p. 247.
38. Dillwitz (1973).
39. Soboul (1976), Introduction.
40. Meinecke (1948). For Meinecke the key to German history was the inability of the country to abandon the *Obrigkeitstaat* (authoritarian state) for a *Gemeinschaft* (commonwealth state) and the Prussian reforms were, for him, an apt instance of this inability.
41. Prussia after its defeat had to pay France 120 million francs in indemnity, a sum which was too high for the Prussian Government to raise by means of the existing taxes. An important feature of the reform was the overhaul of the tax system which was first proposed in 1812. See, for instance, Koselleck (1967), p. 167.
42. A short account of the reforms is to be found in Koch (1978), ch. 8.
43. Anderson (1974), for instance, says that 'Yet it was a traditional ancien regime which attended the Congress of Vienna (1815), in company with its neighbours Austria and Russia', p. 272.
44. For a brief account of the differences among serfs and the services which they performed see Clapham (1969), p. 37.
45. See, for instance, Simon (1971), p. 91.

46. In law there was no free trade in land before the edict of 1807, though there were covert sales and purchases of land before then. See Simon (1971), p. 25.
47. A detailed discussion of the reform laws is to be found in Simon (1971), ch. 6. Also see Clapham (1969), ch. 2.
48. Oppenheimer (1896).
49. A brief account of the reforms brought about by the French Revolution is to be found in Duby (1976) ed., vol. III, ch. *'La Revolution et l'Empire'*.
50. See, for instance, Rosenberg (1966), p. 219 as well as Dawson (1914), p. 31.
51. The fact that the Junkers were resident rather than absentee landlords was of great significance to Max Weber. He explained the differences between Eastern Germany and South-Western Germany in terms of the fact that landownership was resident in the former and absentee in the latter. See Weber (1967).
52. Mommsen (1959), ch. 5.
53. For a synoptic view of French agriculture see Bloch (1966), ch. 7.
54. An account of Thaer's ideas is to be found in Frauendorfer (1963), pp. 206–75.
55. Simon (1971), ch. 2.
56. Dietzel (1903).
57. Cited in Dawson (1914), p. 287.
58. The study in question was by von Philippovich (1892).
59. Between 1890 and 1895 populations in all Prussian provinces with the exception of the three industrial provinces (Berlin, Westphalia and Rhineland) decreased. The rural provinces of Prussia were the ones which constituted the land of large estates. The statistics of the change in population are to be found in Barkin (1970), p. 198. Not only that, even where migration was from rural provinces of Prussia the outflow from the districts where large estates dominated was heavier than from the ones where peasants were more important. This was what Weber found from his empirical enquiries on the conditions of rural labourers in Prussia; a brief account of his findings is to be found in his *Antrittsrede* (1958).
60. Kautsky (1899), pt I, ch. 7, sec. f and ch. 9, sec. e.
61. Weber (1958).
62. Walker (1964), passim.
63. See, for instance, Barkin (1970), ch. 3.
64. Barkin (1970), passim.
65. Dawson (1914), ch. 14.
66. Weber (1979); Dawson (1914), pp. 280–3.
67. Dawson (1914). Stadthagen (1900) gives a list of the laws to which agricultural labourers were subject.
68. For a general discussion of the contract of employment see Wedderburn (1971), ch. 2.
69. Weber (1958), pp. 2–25.
70. Ibid.
71. The list of laws and social provisions which applied to industrial but not to agricultural labourers is to be found in Dawson (1914), p. 283.
72. Saul (1975), p. 171.
73. Dawson (1914), ch. 14.

74. Russell (1896) gives an instance of the over-representation of rural areas, Lecture vi, sec. 1.
75. For a brief account of the growing indebtedness see Dawson (1914), pp. 245–6 as well as Kautsky (1899), pp. 85–91.
76. A detailed description of the extent of indebtedness in different areas is to be found in Buchenburger (1893), pp. 29–39.
77. Parvus (1896), esp. pp. 818–27.
78. Kautsky (1899), pt ii, ch. 1, sec. d.
79. A comprehensive summary of these censuses is to be found in Dillwitz (1973).
80. Kautsky (1899), pp. 217–18.
81. As pointed out by Kautsky the structure of the labour force in rural areas was not the same as that in urban areas. The proportion of 15–40 age group was much higher in the latter than in the former, which in part must have been due to the migration of single individuals rather than whole families. For statistics see Kautsky (1899), p. 219.
82. Pt. i, ch. 7, sec. c.
83. Kautsky (1899), ch. 9, sec. c.
84. Dillwitz (1973).
85. Ibid.
86. Augé-Laribé (1912), ch. 3.
87. Ibid.
88. Chayanov (1966).
89. Lenin (1963), *Collected Works*, vol. 16, pp. 427–46.
90. Max Sering, a conservative agronomist in his critique of Kautsky's *Die Agrarfrage*, singles out the increase in the intensity of cultivation for special emphasis, and uses the point to explain why the trend is towards a greater efficiency of peasant farms. Sering (1899).
91. Kautsky (1899), pt. i, ch. 10, sec. e.

## 3 Landagitation

1. Russell (1896), p. 116.
2. Lehmann (1970), p. 279.
3. Russell (1896), p. 116.
4. Russell (1896), Lecture v; Milhaud (1903), pt. iii.
5. Schorske (1955), ch. 2, sec. 5; Milhaud (1903), pt. v, ch. 2, sec. 3. On the power of the states see Craig (1978), ch. 2.
6. Dawson (1914), ch. 21.
7. Hamerow (1958), ch. 9.
8. von Waltershausen (1920), p. 426.
9. Lehmann (1970), p. 16.
10. Cited by the famous Belgian socialist Vandervelde, in Ensor (1910), p. 219.
11. Cited in Lehmann (1970), p. 17.
12. Milhaud (1903), pp. 308–9.
13. Cited in Lehmann (1970), p. 17. Also see Marx and Engels *Selected Works* (1970), vol 3, pp. 475–6.
14. Cited in Lehmann (1970), pp. 17 and 58.

15. Milhaud (1903), pt. v, ch. 1, 2; Steinberg (1976), p. 65.
16. Russell (1896), Lecture v; Milhaud (1903), pt. IV, ch. 1, 2.
17. Marx and Engels *Selected Works* (1970), vol. III, p. 435.
18. Cited in Milhaud (1903), p. 188.
19. Milhaud (1903), pt. v, chs. 1 and 2.
20. Schorske (1955), pp. 42–53 and 111–15.
21. Reprinted in Russell (1896), pp. 137–41.
22. Milhaud (1903), pt. v, ch. 2, secs II to IV.
23. Ibid.
24. Milhaud (1903), pt. III.
25. Kautsky (1895), esp. p. 560 for comments on the relation between the proximate and the ultimate demands.
26. Steinberg (1976); Gustafsson (1972); Matthias (1957).
27. Lehmann (1970), pp. 19–20.
28. Kautsky (1899), pt. I, ch. 6 sec. b.
29. Lehmann (1970), p. 29.
30. Milhaud (1903), p. 80.
31. Saul (1975).
32. Lehmann (1970), p. 58.
33. Lehmann (1970), p. 61.
34. Lehmann (1970), pp. 67–73.
35. Milhaud (1903), pp. 302–8.
36. Lehmann (1970), p. 36.
37. Milhaud (1903), pt. v, sec. II, ch. 4; Russell (1896), Lecture VI, sec. II.
38. Milhaud (1903).
39. Marx and Engels *Selected Works* (1970), vol III, p. 473.
40. Kautsky (1895).
41. Milhaud (1903).
42. Saul (1975), p. 176.
43. Droz (1974), ch. 1.

## 4 Theoretical Writings on the Agrarian Question

1. Kautsky (1900), Preface to the French edition of *Die Agrarfrage*.
2. Kautsky (1900), pt. I, ch. 11.
3. Kautsky (1900), Preface to the French edition, as well as pp. 359 and 459 on modern latifundia, which Kautsky regarded as the model of capitalist enterprise in agriculture.
4. Kautsky (1899), pt. I, ch. 8.
5. Kautsky (1899), pt. II, ch. 1, sec. b.
6. Kautsky (1899), pt. I, ch. 5, sec. c.
7. Kautsky (1899), pt. I, ch. 4, sec. b. Mortgage credit, according to Kautsky, creates one of the essential conditions for the formation of socialist agriculture; see, p. 298.
8. Kautsky (1899), p. 163.
9. Winter (1964).
10. David (1895).
11. Kautsky (1899), pt. I, ch. 7, sec. a, and also p. 298.

# NOTES

12. Kautsky (1899).
13. Kautsky (1899), pt. I, ch. 11, sec. a.
14. Kautsky (1899), pt. I, ch. 11, sec. b.
15. Kautsky (1899).
16. Ibid.
17. Kautsky (1899), pt I, ch. 2.
18. Kula (1976).
19. Kautsky (1899), pt. I, ch. 3.
20. Kautsky (1899), pt. I, ch. 4.
21. Kautsky (1899), pt. I, ch. 6, sec. a.
22. Kautsky (1899), pt. I, ch. 11, sec. a.
23. Kautsky (1899), pt. I, ch. 5, sec. c.
24. Kautsky (1899), pt. I, ch. 6.
25. Westergaard (1922), pp. 66–80 and Kautsky (1899), pt. I, ch. 6, sec. c. Kautsky, however, does acknowledge the advantages of cooperatives, and he does agree that in principle they are capable of overcoming the disadvantages of small size. But he argues that it does not happen in practice; for usually it is medium and large farmers who derive benefit from cooperatives.
26. See, for instance, Sen (1975), Appendix C.
27. Kautsky (1899), pt. I, ch. 7, Sec. d.
28. Kautsky (1899), pt. I, ch. 6, sec. b.
29. See, for instance, Franklin (1971).
30. Kautsky (1899), pt. I, ch. 7, sec. c.
31. Kautsky (1899), pt. I, ch. 7, secs b and c.
32. Sen (1975), appendix C and Kautsky (1899), pt. I, ch. 8, sec. a.
33. Kautsky (1899), pt. I, ch. 8, sec. a. For a classification of small enterprises see pp. 299–300.
34. Kautsky (1899), pt. I, ch. 10, sec. c.
35. Kautsky (1899), pt. I, ch. 9, sec. c and also ch. 11, sec. a.
36. Kautsky (1899), pt. I, ch. 9, sec. c.
37. Mommsen (1959), ch. 5.
38. Kautsky (1899), pt. I, ch. 11.
39. Ibid.
40. Kautsky (1899), pt. I, ch. 7, sec. c and also ch. 11, sec. b.
41. Kautsky (1899), pt. II, ch. 1.
42. The list of demands is to be found in Kautsky (1899), pt. II, ch. 1, sec. h. On the nationalisation of land see pt. II, ch. 1, sec. d.
43. Kautsky (1899), p. 349.

# Bibliography to Part 1

Anderson, P., *Lineages of the Absolutist State* (London: NLB, 1974).
——, *Considerations on Western Marxism* (London: NLB, 1976).
Ashley, P., *Modern Tariff History: Germany, United States and France* (London: Murray, 1920).
Ashworth, W., *A Short History of the International Economy Since 1850* (London: Longman, 1975).
Augé-Laribe, M., *L'évolution de la France agricole* (Paris: Armand Colin, 1912).
Banaji, J., 'Summary of Selected Parts of Kautsky's *The Agrarian Question*', *Economy and Society*, v (1976) 2–49.
Barkin, K. D., *The Controversy over German Industrialisation 1890–1902* (Chicago: Chicago University Press, 1970).
Bernstein, E., *Ferdinand Lassalle as a Social Reformer* (London: Swan and Sonnenschein, 1893).
——, *Evolutionary Socialism* (London: Library of Socialism, 1909).
Blackbourn, D. G., 'Class and Politics in Wilhelmine Germany: The Centre Party and the Social Democrats in Württemberg', *Central European History*, vol. IX (1976) pp. 220–49.
Bloch, M., *French Rural History* (London: Routledge and Kegan Paul, 1966).
Buchenburger, A., *Agrarwesen und Agrarpolitik*, 2 vols (Leipzig, 1893).
Bürger, C., *Die Agrardemagogie in Deutschland* (Berlin, 1911).
Chambers, J. D. and Mingay, G. E., *The Agricultural Revolution 1750–1880* (London: Batsford, 1966).
Chayanov, A. V., *The Theory of Peasant Economy* (Homewood, Ill.: R. D. Irwin, 1966).
Clapham, J. H., *Economic Development of France and Germany 1815–1914* (London: Cambridge University Press, 1969).
Cole, G. D. H., *Socialist Thought – Marxism and Anarchism 1850–1890* (London: Macmillan, 1954).
Craig, G. A., *Germany 1866–1945* (London: Oxford University Press, 1978).
Cutler, A., Hindess, B., Hirst, P. Q. and Hussain, A., *Marx's 'Capital' and Capitalism Today Vol. I* (London: Routledge and Kegan Paul, 1977).
David, E., 'Ökonomische Verschiedenheiten zwischen Landwirtschaft und Industrie', *Neue Zeit*, Jg. 13 Band 2 (1895) pp. 448–54.
——, *Sozialismus und Landwirtschaft* (Berlin: Verlag der Sozialistischen Monatshefte, 1903).
Dawson, W. H., *German Socialism and Ferdinand Lassalle* (London: Swan Sonnenschein, 1881).
——, *Protection in Germany* (London: King and Son, 1904).
——, *The Evolution of Modern Germany* (London: T. Fisher Unwin, 1914).

Dietzel, H., 'The German Tariff Controversy', *Quarterly Journal of Economics* vol. XIX (1903) pp. 365–416.
Dillwitz, S., 'Die Struktur der Bauernschaft von 1871 bis 1914', *Jahrbuch für Geschichte*, Band 9 (1973) pp. 47–127.
Droz, J. (ed.), *Histoire générale du socialisme*, vol. II (Paris: P.U.F., 1974).
Duby, G. (ed.), *Histoire de la France rurale*, 4 vols (Paris: Editions du Seuil, 1976).
Engels, F., 'Zolltariff und Freihandel', in Marx–Engels *Werke* Band 21 (1969) pp. 360–75.
Farr, I., 'Populism in the Countryside: 'The Peasant Leagues in Bavaria on the 1890's' in R. J. Evans (ed.) *Society and Politics in Wilhelmine Germany* (London: Croom Helm, 1978) pp. 136–59.
Fletcher, T. W., 'The Great Depression of English Agriculture', *Economic History Review*, second series vol. 18 (1965) pp. 562–75.
Franklin, S. H., *Rural Societies* (London: Macmillan, 1971).
von Frauendorfer, S., *Ideengeschichte der Agrarwirtschaft und agrarpolitik in deutschen Sprachgebiet*, vol. 1 (Munich: DLV Verlaggesellschaft, 1963).
Gerschenkron, A., *Bread and Democracy in Germany*, 2nd. ed. (New York: Howard Fertig, 1966).
Gratton, P., *Les luttes de classes dans les campagnes* (Paris: Editions Anthropos, 1971).
Gustafsson, B., *Marxismus und Revisionismus* (Frankfurt: Europäische Verlagsanstalt, 1972).
Hamerow, S., *Restoration, Revolution, Reaction: Economics and Politics in Germany, 1815–1871* (Princeton: Princeton University Press, 1958).
——, *The Social Foundations of German Unification* (Princeton: Princeton University Press, 1969).
Hunt, R. N., *German Social Democracy, 1918–1933* (New Haven: Yale University Press, 1964).
Johnson, E. A. J. and Kroos, H. E., *The Origins and Development of the American Economy* (New Jersey: Prentice Hall, 1956).
Kautsky, K., 'Unser neuestes Program', *Neue Zeit* Jg. 13 Band 2 (1895) pp. 557–65, 586–94, 610–24.
——, *Die Agrarfrage* (Stuttgart: Dietz, 1899) French ed. (1900) reprinted Maspero, Paris, 1970.
——, *Der Weg zur Macht* (Frankfurt: Europäische Verlagsanstalt, 1972).
Kindleberger, C. P., 'Group Behaviour and International Trade', *Journal of Political Economy*, vol. LIX (1951) pp. 30–46.
Kitchen, M., *The Political Economy of Germany 1815–1914* (London: Croom Helm, 1978).
Koch, H. W., *A History of Prussia* (London: Longman, 1978).
Koselleck, R., *Preußen zwischen Reform und Revolution* (Stuttgart: Ernst Klett Verlag, 1967).
Kula, W., *An Economic Theory of the Feudal System* (London: NLB, 1976).
de Laveleye, E., *Socialism of Today* (London: Field and Tuer, 1884).
Lehmann, H. G., *Die Agrarfrage in der Theorie und Praxis der deutschen und internationalen Sozialdemokratie* (Tübingen: J. C. B. Mohr, 1970).

Lenin, V. I., *Collected Works*, 45 vols (Moscow, 1960–71).
Lewis, W. A., *Growth and Fluctuation* (London: George Allen and Unwin, 1978).
Lidtke, V. L., *The Outlawed Party. Social Democracy in Germany, 1878–1890* (Princeton: Princeton University Press, 1966).
Luxemburg, R., *The Accumulation of Capital* (London: Routledge and Kegan Paul, 1963).
——, *Reform or Revolution* (New York, 1970).
Marx, K., *Capital*, 3 vols (Moscow: Progress Publishers, 1966).
Marx and Engels *Selected Works*, 3 vols (Moscow: Progress Publishers, 1970).
——, *Collected Works* (Moscow: Progress Publishers, 1975)
Matthias, E., 'Kautsky und der Kautskyanismus', *Marxismusstudien*, vol. 2 (1957) pp. 165–97.
Meinecke, F., 'The Year 1848 in German History: Reflections on a Centenary', *Review of Politics*, vol. x (1948) pp. 475–92.
Michels, R., *Political Parties* (New York: Free Press, 1962).
Milhaud, E., *La democratie socialiste allemande* (Paris: Alcan, 1903).
Mitrany, D., *Marx against the Peasant* (London: Weidenfeld and Nicolson, 1951).
Mommsen, W. J., *Max Weber und die deutsche Politik 1890–1920* (Tübingen: J. C. B. Mohr, 1959).
Nettl, J. P., 'The German Social-Democratic Party 1890–1914 as a Political Model', *Past and Present*, no. 30 (1965) pp. 65–95.
Oppenheimer, F., *Die Siedlungsgenossenschaft* (Leipzig: Duncker und Humblot, 1896).
Parvus 'Der Weltmarkt und die Agrarkrisis', *Neue Zeit*, Jg 14, Band 1 (1896) pp. 197–202 *passim*.
von Philippovich, E., *Auswanderung und Auswanderungspolitik in Deutschland*, Schriften des Vereins für Sozialpolitik, Band 52 (Leipzig: Duncker und Humblot, 1892).
Pühle, H. J., *Agrarische Interessenpolitik und preussischer Konservatismus im Wilhelminischen Reich 1893–1911*, 2nd ed. (Bonn-Bad Godesberg: Verlag Neue Gesellschaft, 1975).
Rosenberg, H., 'Political and Social Consequences of the Great Depression of 1873–1896 in Central Europe', *Economic History Review*, vol. xxvii (1943) pp. 58–73.
——, *Bureaucracy, Aristocracy and Autocracy* (Boston: Beacon Press, 1966).
Russell, B., *German Social Democracy* (London: George Allen and Unwin, 1896).
Saul, K., 'Der Kampf um das Landproletariat', *Archiv für Sozialgeschichte*, Band 15 (1975) pp. 163–208.
Schorske, C. E., *German Social Democracy, 1905–1917* (Cambridge Mass.: Harvard University Press, 1955).
Sen, A., *Employment, Technology and Development* (London: Oxford University Press, 1975).
Sering, M., 'Die Agrarfrage und der Sozialismus', *Jahrbuch für Gesetzbung, Verwaltung und Volkswirtschaft*, Jg. 23 (1899) pp. 1493–1556.
Simon, W. H., *The Failure of the Prussian Reform* (New York: Howard Fertig, 1971).

Soboul, A., *Problèmes paysans de la révolution 1789–1849* (Paris: Maspero, 1976).

Stadthagen, A., 'Ausnahmerechte gegen die ländlichen Arbeiter in Deutschland', *Neue Zeit*, Jg. 18 Band 1 (1900) pp. 388–98.

Steinberg, H., *Sozialismus und deutsche Sozialdemokratie* (Berlin: Dietz, 1976).

Stolper, G., *The German Economy 1870 to the Present* (London: Weidenfeld and Nicolson, 1967).

Vandervelde, E., 'Socialism and Capitalistic Transformation of Agriculture', in R. Ensor (ed.), *Modern Socialism* (London: Harper and Brothers, 1910) pp. 198–219.

——, *Le coopération neutre et la coopération socialiste* (Paris: Alcan, 1913).

Varga, E., *Beiträge zur Agrarfrage* (Hamburg: Verlag Carl Hoym, 1924).

——, *Krise der Kapitalistischen Weltwirtschaft* (Frankfurt: Europäische Verlagsanstalt, 1966).

von Vollmar, G., *Reden und Schriften zur Reformpolitik* (Berlin: Dietz, 1977).

Walker, M., *Germany and the Emigration* (Cambridge Mass.: Harvard University Press, 1964).

von Waltershausen, S., *Deutsche Wirtschaftsgeschichte 1815–1914* (Jena: Verlag von Fischer, 1920).

Weber, M., *Gesammelte politische Schriften* (Tübingen: J. C. B. Mohr, 1958).

——, 'National Character and the Junkers', in H. Gerth and C. W. Mills (eds) *From Max Weber* (London: Routledge and Kegan Paul, 1967) pp. 386–96.

——, 'Developmental Tendencies in the Situation of East Elbian Rural Labourers', *Economy and Society*, vol. VIII (1979) pp. 172–205.

Wedderburn, K. W., *The Worker and the Law* (Harmondsworth: Penguin Books, 1971).

Westergaard, H., *Economic Development in Denmark* (London: Oxford University Press, 1922).

Winter, S. G., 'Economic "Natural Selection" and the Theory of the Firm', *Yale Economic Essays* (1964) pp. 225–72.

# Part 2
# Russian Marxism and the Peasantry 1861–1930

# Introduction

Part 2 shifts the discussion from late nineteenth-century Germany to Russia between 1890 and 1930. Whereas German Social Democracy has become associated with the economism and reformism of the Second International, Russian Social Democracy found its realisation in the Revolution of 1917 and came to represent revolutionary socialism. It has been argued in Part 1 that this schema opposing the revolutionary practice of the Russian party to the reformist practice of the German party is largely a construct of a history which ignores the political and economic conditions within which the respective organisations worked. In particular, arguments have been advanced which demonstrate the fallacy of treating the theoretical work of German socialists as the elaboration of a 'Classical Marxism' laid down in the writings of Marx and Engels.

In turning now to Russian Social Democracy these arguments will be repeated and extended. Following principles laid down already, emphasis will be placed on the ensemble of political, economic and social conditions which determine the nature of the problems confronting Social Democracy. It is usual in the treatment of Russian Marxism to associate its development with the political history of one man – Lenin. The history of Russian Marxism to 1917 is too often constructed around Lenin and the party he is supposed to have created, the statements of Lenin being treated as though they are an invariant and adequate representation of Bolshevism. Such accounts in effect canonise the writing of Lenin and the analyses that he made of Russian conditions, alternative accounts then necessarily assuming the status ascribed them by Lenin.[1] The problem with such writing is that the teleological narrative that it sets to work elevates the line followed by the victors of October 1917 into a Marxist orthodoxy against which all dissenters are registered as non-Marxist deviants.

In particular, Lenin's analysis of the development of Russian capitalism, constructed as it is as an alternative to Narodnik accounts, is treated as the realisation of a Marxist orthodoxy established prior to and independently of Lenin's work. For example, it has been suggested that the *Development of Capitalism in Russia* is simply an application of the principles of *Capital* to the Russian social formation.[2] As we shall see, this overlooks the radical differences between the work of Marx and of Lenin, but more significantly it consigns dissenters from Lenin's analysis to the camp of 'non-Marxists'. One of the main arguments that will be developed in chapters 7 and 8 of Part 2 is, however, that Lenin's political adversaries had as much right to the label 'Marxist' as he; and that furthermore, in doctrinal terms, Lenin's work is often far less orthodox than that of his opponents. Russian Marxism of the late nineteenth and early twentieth centuries will be shown to be characterised by a state of *competition* between different political tendencies, all of which invoke the names of Marx and Engels in seeking to establish their credentials. Since in many cases this was far from the mere adoption of convenient slogans, it would be wrong to impose order on this situation by either simply using the opinions of Lenin, or some other device, to establish 'true' from 'false' Marxism. What has to be stressed is that 'Marxism' cannot be treated as a coherent body of doctrine from which deviations can be clearly identified.

Of course one of the ways that this problem could be solved is by reference to the writings of Marx and Engels themselves, a resort to a supposedly unsullied source whose heritage has been, paradoxically, one of disagreement and division. If we turn to their writings on Russia, however, we find that from the late 1870s Marx and Engels did follow a more or less consistent line – of general support for the Narodniks, and for revolutionary terrorism especially. The reason for this was that Marx in particular believed that the Russian working class would not form an appreciable political force in the foreseeable future, and that in the meantime the only viable course of radical politics was one of terrorist action against the Tsarist autocracy. As will be shown in chapter 6, this judgment was seriously flawed, and Social Democracy developed in Russia out of a rejection of the advice proffered by Marx and Engels.

Just as the political writings of Marx and Engels do not form a coherent theoretical totality on which their heirs could draw, so

Marx's analysis of capitalist development in agriculture provided no firm basis for the elaboration of a 'Marxist analysis' of Russian conditions. Those socialists who sought in the later nineteenth century to use Marx's work as a guide for their work in the countryside had necessarily to build on fragments, and this process naturally bred divergences and disagreements. The body of work so produced cannot be evaluated by reference to an original source in Marxism, whether it be in *Capital* vol. III or the *Eighteenth Brumaire*. Neither is it justifiable to suppress this heterogeneity by the imposition of a teleological historical proof which elevates the work of Lenin as the embodiment of revolutionary rationality. If Lenin's work is to be properly evaluated, it is necessary to be able to judge competing work independently of Lenin's criticisms of it, for these naturally reconstruct the object of criticism.[3]

The strategy adopted in the following chapters is to pose the 'agrarian question' for Russian Social Democracy as a series of issues constituted under quite distinct conditions. At the theoretical level this involves the agrarian analyses of Lenin; at the political level it concerns the calculations involved in the formulation and revision of an agrarian policy for Russian Social Democracy; and as a problem of economic policy, it concerns the operation of state administrations in a variety of conditions, partly not under their control, and partly created by the administrative apparatuses themselves. The 'agrarian question' is not therefore synonymous with 'the peasantry' as a pre-given and identifiable population whose existence suffices to give rise to political and economic controversy. The 'agrarian question' rather simply indicates a series of persistent, but diverse, problems posed on a number of levels to Russian Social Democracy first as an embryo political organisation, then as an arena of theoretical debate, and finally as the custodians of state power.

# 6 Russian Agriculture 1860–1900: Some Effects of the Emancipation Settlement

In the later nineteenth century, agriculture was the primary occupation of nearly two-thirds of the Russian population, and even in 1913 this sector contributed 45 per cent of the National Income. Pre-revolutionary Russia was dominated by a backward peasantry which farmed the land in almost medieval fashion, and which was considered by many contemporary socialists as the bulwark of Russian autocracy and a barrier to political change. It would be wrong however to treat this section of the population as either a unitary mass, or as a rural, traditional sector which shackled the possibilities of political and economic development. As the Bolsheviks were to establish, any revolutionary change which did not take into account the aspirations of sections of the peasantry would be doomed to failure, and we shall later show how this position distinguished Bolsheviks from Mensheviks after the split in Russian Social Democracy.

In this chapter we are concerned primarily with certain aspects of Russian agricultural development, but it must not be assumed that to talk of 'agriculture' is equivalent to a discussion of the Russian peasantry – setting in motion a series of oppositions like agriculture/industry, peasant/worker, rural/urban. All too often these axes are either explicitly or implicitly treated as specifications of the problems of economic development, the 'peasant question' being one of how quickly a rural, agricultural peasantry can be transformed into an urbanised, industrial working class which will provide the labour force for a continuous process of economic growth. In pre-war Russia, economic development took the form not of an increasing *separation* of activity along these lines, but rather of their *integration*. The reasons for this can principally be found in the 'backward' character of the late nineteenth century Russian economy, but whereas Gerschenkron has argued that this 'backwardness' was an asset for the industrialisers, it can perhaps be suggested that the problems that beset the Russian economy resulted in the adoption of solutions that themselves perpetuated unevenness and obstacles to development.[1]

A prime example of this can be found in the relation of industrial and agricultural enterprise. It is well-established of course that these often either shared a work-force through the year, or existed in a complementary relation; peasants without enough land flowing to industrial employment, and workers laid off simply drifting back to the land. What has not been given so much attention is that well into the twentieth century major sections of industry were located in rural areas. In 1902 for instance more than half of Russia's industrial plant, and 58 per cent of its labour force, was located outside towns and cities. This was not simply an indication of the predominance of small industry in rural areas: it was most pronounced in the case of establishments employing more than 1000 workers. 90 per cent of the labour-force employed in mining and metallurgy, and 66 per cent of that employed in manufacturing, was located in rural areas. Of all the main industries, only paper-making and printing had more than 40 per cent of its labour-force in urban areas.[2]

The engagement of peasants in small-scale handicraft and other handworking occupations was emphasised by Lenin as we shall see, and such involvement of peasant producers in non-agricultural activities (usually part-time or during the winter months) is a common feature of predominantly rural economies. The model of capitalist industrial development supplied by England however indicates that with industrial advance, industrial enterprises are either centralised in already established urban areas, or what are initially rural locations rapidly become urbanised. In the urban setting, individual enterprises contribute to a web of relations which promote specialisation and competition generating the increasing differentiation of town and country, drawing a national population away from the land and into the towns.

In Russia on the other hand almost the reverse was the case: new industries were often established in rural locations because they could there draw on a skilled labour-force (from handworking industries), the land was cheaper, and less formality was required in seeking legal clearances. Some businesses of course developed either out of domestic concerns, or large serf-based factories but in all of these cases, the scale of operations was not, as in Germany or the United States, an indication of industrial advance, but rather of the backwardness of Russian conditions. In late nineteenth century Russia, *integration* rather than *specialisation* characterised the expansion of businesses, the weakness of the commercial and communications infrastructure forcing concerns into the backward and forward integration of their operations, and their concentration often in giant factories.[3]

The constant involvement of the rural population in industrial employment demonstrates the fallacy of equating the 'peasantry' with 'agriculturalists' in general. However, in Russia the land did play a crucial role in the structure of the economy by virtue of the manner in which a majority of the population was, through bonds with private landlords and village communities, tied to specifiable plots of land.[4] The Emancipation legislation of the early 1860s altered this connection, and set in train a number of processes which on the one hand strengthened the shackles of household and community on the working population, and on the other undermined them. As we shall see later, the measures that were introduced were far more than an 'agrarian reform', but the apparent decisiveness of the legislative amendments to rural relations enabled later writers to treat '1861' as the point of collision between feudal and capitalist systems, without requiring a more sophisticated treatment of the process of disintegration and reorganisation of the rural economy that can in fact be traced back to the later eighteenth century.[5]

The timing of the Emancipation legislation was largely dictated by the developing crisis in the Russian economy which was brutally highlighted by the defeat of the Russian Army in the Crimean War. The social and political system which was often described as the most reactionary in Europe showed itself incapable of effectively confronting the modern armies opposing it; further, the antiquated army based on levied peasants serving twenty-five years could not be adequately supplied or reinforced through the almost non-existent transport system. The reforms which followed this should not however be conceived as the means for dismantling the old feudal order and laying the foundation for a new capitalist one. The Russian social order had existed with political, social and economic crises for decades, and the economic measures taken in the early 1860s were dictated more by political considerations than economic problems. Struve for example in his study of the Russian feudal economy argued that far from the internal development of serfdom producing its own collapse as a system of production, it in fact reached a peak of production in the 1850s.[6] Despite what in retrospect appeared appallingly wasteful uses of labour, the advantages at an economic level of introducing wage labour were quite dubious, since as far as the lords were concerned their estates, producing 90 per cent of commercial grain in the early nineteenth century,[7] harvested and distributed this product with free labour. As Lyaschenko points out, the effects of this can be traced in the instabilities of the grain prices in time and space; the lords, not 'knowing' their production costs, were prepared to make all sorts of reductions in price to exchange their 'free' product for cash. The fluctuations in price that are taken as the sign of an agricultural crisis represent on the contrary the typical form assumed by commercial relations in a predominantly feudal economy, where the formation of prices is subject to a number of factors such as regional isolation and absence of market institutions. These and other conditions combine to ensure a diversity of local prices whose fluctuations can be quite fortuitous, and in no way reflect general economic conditions.[8] The economic reforms of the early 1860s were not aimed primarily at the creation of a specific type of economy, but must instead be understood as an attempt to stabilise a political order characterised by aristocratic debt and peasant unrest. The measures which were introduced had no uniform impact, the regional divergencies in the development of commercial and feudal relations dictating the form the local settlement would take.

Towards the end of the eighteenth century, and partly consequent on certain reforms which made gentry engagement in agricultural production possible, two broad regions emerged in European Russia: a North-Central primarily non-agricultural sector, and a Central-Southern 'black-earth' agricultural sector which with the improvement of communications was able to transfer grain to the north and then abroad.[9] Landlords exploited the serf labour under their control either in the form of dues or money payment (*obrok*), or in the form of forced labour or corvée (*barshchina*). The latter predominated in the black-earth region, where it was the labour of the serf which, while it was free of cost to the landlord, was of value in working his land. In areas of poorer soil the serfs tended to render dues in money or in kind, although figures indicate that twice as many private serfs were engaged in corvée as rendered dues.

It would be wrong however to treat the pre-Emancipation peasantry as if characterised by the private ownership of serfs, for a substantial section of the rural population consisted of state serfs, whose conditions were distinct from those just mentioned, and who were dealt with under separate legislation of 1863. The origin of these serfs who had no master but the state has been outlined by Crisp,[10] and she emphasises that while in some ways their relation to the state was similar to that of the private serf to his master, the impersonal nature that this assumed rendered it in many ways a formality. Thus land was possessed in a similar manner, but state serfs tended to treat their land as their own, selling it and bequeathing it to members of their family. The fact that laws were repeatedly promulgated forbidding this only underlined the prevalence of the practice.[11] Unlike the private serfs, the state serfs were defined in the Code of Laws of 1832 as 'free rural dwellers', possessing legal and political rights, able to buy land and change their place of residence. Measures were adopted in 1843 to promote the emigration and resettlement of state peasants under conditions which removed liability even for military service and taxation.[12] The engagement of the serf population in commercial transactions on their own account was not however limited to state serfs; by the mid-nineteenth century some private serfs had begun to engage in trade, and established the rights to sue in a court of law on their own account. While some even purchased land, this was done in the name of their owners, and much of the conflict that arose out of the Emancipation settlement can be traced to debt-ridden landlords reneging on the unenforceable ownership of land by private serfs and simply appropriating serf land as their own property.

The rise of indebtedness among landowners in the nineteenth century led not to a collapse of feudal relations, but to their intensification. Despite the adoption of such measures the overall level of debt steadily increased, the average debt on a mortgaged serf being 69 roubles in 1856, while the total number of serfs mortgaged rose to 7.1 million (66 per cent of the total) by 1859.[13]

The loans that were raised in this fashion from state credit agencies were used mainly for daily expenditure, gradually increasing the proportion of estate income that was devoted to the maintenance of the aristocracy's daily life at the expense of the estate economy. From the 1840s proposals for the abolition of serfdom were made to the government which in the terms of settlement involved means of liquidating this debt, the provision of the peasants with land being conceived primarily as a way of providing the landlords with capital.

The Statute of Emancipation promulgated on 19 February 1861 concerning the 22 million private serfs (53 per cent of the serfs in Greater Russia) was in effect aimed at this twin resolution of the political problem. The compromise that was established was however so unclear, and was to be worked out in such diverse situations, that the Statute itself was in places contradictory and opaque. Delayed in its communication to the public until the Lenten season, when the peasantry were thought to be less prone to drink and violence, it was read out from the pulpit by the local priest; usually barely more literate than his congregation, and like them believing that the land belonged to them of right, he therefore was liable to read into the Statute such a sentiment. Those who argued that such provisions were not contained in the decrees often then claimed that the real provisions were yet to come, or that the local officials were falsifying the Tsar's will. The subsequent passive rebellions and riots occupied large forces of troops in the three months following its reading, although by June the activities of peace mediators began to show in the decline of disturbances reported.[14]

Under the terms of the Emancipation, the serf was required to accept an allotment of land for the time being, and pay for it. The state undertook to advance to the landlords the major portion of the price of the allotment, and the former serfs were committed to repay directly to the state the major part of the assessed price (in the form of redemption payments), while a proportion was paid to the former owner.[15] The peasants therefore received land, and the landlords money – but the peasants were forced to pay for what they customarily regarded as theirs, while the manner in which allotments were established and assessments made introduced further antagonisms into an already unequal situation. Land was not assigned to individuals, but to households which were members of a commune, which was jointly responsible for the redemption payments and taxation. These 'traditional institutions' of Russian peasant life were reinforced under the terms of the Settlement so that the state could secure the payment of dues owed to it. Unfortunately however, the legislation misconstrued the nature of the commune as a collective agency, and by its operation created entirely artificial 'communes'.

It was only in the early eighteenth century that the commune assumed a central role in rural life, when it was made responsible for the rendering of taxes and military service. This was one aspect of the legislation introduced at this time which established a serf economy at a time when in Western Europe its last vestiges were disappearing. As we shall see in the following chapter, the commune was conceived by radicals in the later nineteenth century as the epitome of a primitive communism that could under certain conditions form the basis for a direct transition to a communist society. The self-governing aspects of the commune that were held to be a portent of the future were however in many instances of dubious merit, for investigations carried out during the 1830s indicated that many of the village assemblies met outside public houses, votes being bought with drinks and the wealthier peasants putting up pliable poorer candidates for the official positions.[16] Moreover, the communal productive functions of the *mir* were limited to the regular re-allotment of strips of land – work was not performed in common outside the household, nor were implements shared. This last aspect was to be of crucial importance in the alleged 'revival' of the commune during 1917.

Prior to the Emancipation then, the village community had constituted the collective agency for the division of ploughland, pasture and woods; in some cases households belonging to one commune also had rights in another through the division of its holdings of ploughland and pasture, and such cases serve to illustrate that communes were not simply geographical entities (congruent with a village or group of villages), but were rather collective agencies constituted through rights in land. While this meant that some households were members of more than one commune, any problems arising could be dealt with by various adjustments. The terms of the Emancipation settlement however treated communes as if they were simply geographical entities, making no provision for multiple membership on the part of households. It further introduced an artificial unity in the cases of serfs settled on the lands of a large landholder – for the convenience of the owner, these were placed in single communes, often disrupting the actual relations that had prevailed before the Settlement. Additional subsidiary arrangements further complicated these already diverse dispositions, which were then all called by the same name, *selskoe obshchestvo*, given a separate parliament of householders, and left to regulate the political and economic affairs arising from the Emancipation. As Robinson emphasises, the Statutes of 1861 did not clearly recognise or name the land-commune and assembly as such, extending this later to the State peasants in exactly the same fashion. The Emancipation settlement then created a formal and an informal distribution of property relations which of themselves could be potentially divisive of the emancipated serfs. A distinction which it did preserve however was between repartitional communes and those with hereditary household tenure.

Allotments were assigned to households on the basis of the number of 'revision souls' to be found in each commune for the census year 1858, and norms of land area were fixed according to local conditions. In particular, the landlords were given the right to make 'cut-offs' where the old allotments exceeded the local norm established, and demand a reallocation of holdings where there was an intermixture of lord's and peasant land. The peasant household then in general found itself either with too little land for subsistence (in the good agricultural regions) or with land above what was wanted but which had to be accepted and paid for. In other words, in areas of good agricultural land the landlords ensured that the settlement terms provided them with available wage labour for their own land, and in the regions of poor soil the landlords could divest themselves of waste land in return for inflated prices supported by the Government. In this way the peasants in the black-soil region were deprived of 25 per cent of the land that they had previously farmed, and in many cases were still burdened under the terms of the reform with obligations of labour or money payment.

While by European standards the overall average size of peasant holdings was quite large, the methods of cultivation employed were such as to reduce the yields of the various products in the different parts of Russia. In most areas three-field strip farming predominated, with the repartitional communes reallocating the strips periodically among the households. Such a system of repartition leads to the repeated scattering of any one household's holdings, and even where hereditary tenure was the rule, the dispersion of the strips concerned was maintained by the commune, all the household heads being required to assent for a consolidation to be effective. The scattered nature of the land farmed by any one household obviously introduced problems in cultivating it, imposing limitations on the disposable time and means of production that could be deployed. In many cases the commune determined the cycle of crops, and the subordination of the household to this institution strictly limited the farming initiatives that it could take. On the other hand, the conditions of the Emancipation settlement, in which insufficient land or inflated redemption dues confronted the peasant household, made it imperative that measures be taken to improve the returns from the productive activity of the household. In some areas the restrictions of poor agricultural land turned the household increasingly to domestic handicraft production, while in others, given the limitations on the productivity of communal land often stripped of its water-courses or forest, households increasingly turned to renting the land needed. In 1883 a Peasants' Land Bank was founded with the object of providing credit facilities for the purchase of land, although the credit made available to the peasantry in this way never matched that supplied to the nobility.

The economic forces imposed by the terms of the Emancipation forced peasant agricultural production increasingly to the marketing of crops which would realise some return in cash, and the rise in grain prices in the early 1880s stimulated this movement. However, as has been outlined earlier, the prices of grains, particularly wheat, began at this time to be increasingly determined by the conditions of a world market dominated by the development of the American West. On the other hand manufactured goods bought with any cash left over from taxes and dues and subsistence were priced according to protectionist government policies, denying the agricultural producers the inverse advantages of falling grain prices with the extension to a world market. By the mid-1890s rye and oat prices were half what they had been in 1880, while the population in the countryside had grown by half since 1867.

The deteriorating situation of the peasant population during this period can be gauged partly by the rising price of land, as competition for badly needed extra land intensified and drove the prices up, and from the fall in number of households with only one or two horses. During the decade of the 1890s, figures indicate that the number of three-horse households fell by 35 per cent, while the number with none at all in European Russia rose by 22 per cent. While key statistics therefore indicate a steady deterioration in the conditions of the Russian peasantry towards the end of the nineteenth century, it would be a mistake to conceive this as a universal phenomenon for the rural population as a whole. While the responsibility for the collection of dues and taxes fell on the commune as a collective entity and thus tended to homogenise the emerging differences between member-households, the growth of relations of land renting and wage labour took place not only between emancipated serfs and landlords engaged in commercial farming, but also increasingly among the peasant population itself. To read therefore the increasing arrears of redemption payments (which by 1896-1900 rose to 119 per cent of the annual assessment, despite a series of reductions and deferments) as an index of rural destitution in general would be to ignore the actual diversity of conditions that this trend concealed.

Both Robinson and Gerschenkron have suggested that, given the instruments available to the state to enforce payment of dues, the actual increase in the level of arrears recorded during the 1890s can only be interpreted as an index of the inability, rather than refusal, of the peasant to pay. Combined with other indicators, such figures are used to suggest the presence of a developing economic crisis in the peasant economy associated with a steady worsening in the material conditions of the peasantry in general. At the same time that arrears were steadily mounting, however, the revenue from indirect taxation was also rising, and the centrality of items like kerosene, matches and candles as producers of tax revenue indicates that rural consumption of these items was rising to some degree, independently of the increase in rural population. One writer has suggested that this trend points to a general improvement in the conditions of the peasantry over this period, although this appears to be based on a failure to properly take account of the far higher *per capita* urban consumption of these products.[17] On the other hand, the rapid growth of the domestic market for cotton goods in the 1890s does indicate that significant sections of the population were supplied with the means to make such purchases.

To pose the relative poverty or affluence of the rural population as a whole in this fashion does however obscure the prevailing social and economic relations which define the nature of 'poverty' or 'affluence'. It can be argued that the use of statistics on the possession of horses by household as indices of rural poverty as above obscures such relations. Far from indicating a general crisis of the peasant economy, they can be interpreted as indices of the shift of sections of the peasantry from reliance on subsistence agriculture as a primary occupation to handicrafts, local industry, agricultural wage labour or even renting. A survey commissioned by Witte in the later 1890s showed for example that large numbers of households consumed all their harvested grain and obtained the cash that they required from handicraft production. In this way households switched their cash production out of an increasingly internationalised grain market into the fabrication of furniture, toys and musical instruments where even on an international market they could compete effectively with factory production. In addition to this, it was possible under the prevailing laws governing the movement and employment of household members to hire out labour from the household for agricultural or industrial purposes and treat the wages arising from this as a component of household income.

Indices of rural poverty therefore can be argued to be related not to the actual welfare of the population concerned, but are rather suggestive of divisions within this rural population and alterations in productive activity. While on the one hand a household might have divested itself of its draught animals and thus appear to be driven into destitution, on the other hand the engagement of its members in manufacturing or agricultural wage labour might very well result in a marked improvement in the material conditions of a household. Significant sections of the rural population then could be argued not to have been in the later 1890s confronted with the problems of rural poverty, but instead with the different problems of wage labour and petty commodity production.

The increase in the size of the population in the later nineteenth century has already been noted. It was indeed considerable: the population of European Russia grew by 15 per cent between 1858 and 1867, and by 48.5 per cent 1858–97. In the rural areas it has been argued that this resulted from the calculation on the part of households that the more members they had, the greater the entitlement of land at redistributions. On the other hand, the rise in population itself inhibited redistributions of communal land since those with land were reluctant to part with any of it. The sheer overpopulation of certain parts of Russia was however recognised as a critical problem, and Maslov in his *Agrarian Question in Russia* identified it as the most important factor in Russian rural conditions.[18] Sections of the peasantry sought to ameliorate their difficulties by renting parcels of land in addition to their Emancipation allotments, and it was later observed that this led to a feature of the Russian economy whereby the larger the plot of land was, the less likely it was to be rented.[19]

Shortage of agricultural land for the peasant population was also recognised as a problem by the Government, who developed specific policies aimed at the settlement of a surplus population in the Far East, Siberia and Asiatic Russia. By 1894 between 8 and 9 million peasants had been resettled beyond the Urals, representing a movement over which the Government never had total control. A significant proportion of emigrants in any one year during the later nineteenth century were always irregulars, that is, settlers who had not gone through the proper procedures before departing from their original place of residence. It proved impossible for these peasants to be returned to their starting points, and so they became in effect second-class regular emigrants who did not necessarily benefit from the inducements provided by the Government administration. In May 1905 the Resettlement Administration, which had up until then been a section of the Ministry of Interior, passed into the Ministry of Agriculture, which was at the same time re-named Chief Administration of Land Settlement and Agriculture. The policy of migration thus became linked institutionally with the agrarian reforms which were to be introduced a few months later, presenting a double approach to the problems of Russian agriculture.[20] By this time, the process of Siberian resettlement had been speeded up by the opening of the Siberian Railroad, and the railways in general had seriously affected the process of internal migration and colonisation, opening up remote areas and reducing overland journeys from a matter of months to one of days.

Crisp goes so far as to suggest that if one critical feature of the later nineteenth century economy is to be isolated, then the prime place usually accorded the Emancipation settlement should instead be given to the building of the railways.[21] The existence of a rail transportation network certainly transformed the Russian economy, where roads were poor, rivers shallow, and the distances from inland areas to coastal waters immense. In the later eighteenth century the chief grain supplying areas were the less rich soils in the vicinity of centres of consumption; the produce of the better soil in the central region was generally not marketed because of transport difficulties.[22] The opening up, and partial creation, of the Central Agricultural Region by the railways made possible the sale of crops which had hitherto either been abandoned or had rotted: grain output rose by 70 per cent in the period 1860-80, and exports increased by a factor of 3.3.

The uneven development of the railway network naturally affected the manner in which new markets for grain were created, and the relationship between producing and consuming regions thereby constituted. The immediate effect of railways was, however, to raise the price of agricultural produce for the producer on the spot, benefiting agriculture in their vicinity. But in reducing the cost of transport over long distances, the cost of hauling produce to the railway line became comparatively more significant in the costs of the producer. In this way the railways came to have a decisive impact on the distribution of farming systems throughout Russia.[23]

By the end of the century in England virtually the only modern and competitive sector in agriculture that had survived the effects of international competition was the liquid milk trade, reliant on the railways to deliver fresh milk to urban areas.[24] In a similar fashion in Russia major consuming centres drew on dairies up to 320 km away, but which were disposed in a narrow strip of land no more than 30 km wide. Beyond this dairy farmers were forced to produce butter, but this in turn required greater financial outlay and modifications to farm organisation. Potatoes, as a bulky product, only travelled any distance if they were produced close to a railway line, although in this case there were possibilities of converting such produce on the spot into starch or spirit.

The situation for grains was no different, and the development of Russia's exports in the latter part of the century was based heavily around the sale of rye, wheat and barley. One Populist theoretician, Nicolai-on (Danielson, the translator of *Capital* and correspondent of Marx), identified the construction of railways and the creation of credit as the two main instruments by which the Tsarist government sought to transform the 'communal' peasant economy by capitalist means. In an article first published in 1880, he describes the process by which rail transport and credit contrive to strip the peasantry of their grain and ship it abroad to pay for the alien development of a capitalist enclave by the state. Nicolai-on identifies the establishment of major credit institutions in Russia with the period in which railway construction gets under way, and suggests that the principal traffic carried by the new railways is either workers engaged in search of agricultural work, or grain. In 1869 grain accounted for 33.4 per cent of railway freight; in 1876, 42 per cent.[25] Month by month he pieces together the cycle of activity in the economy by an investigation of the flow of traffic on the railway, both passenger and freight, concluding that railway traffic is conditional on agricultural production.[26] A study of the movements of money between merchants and banks further shows that credit operations are determined largely by agricultural produce and its movement. Nicolai-on argued that unlike in the West, where the railways were developed as a means for the marketing of factory goods, in Russia they functioned primarily to channel grain into foreign markets. Capitalist development, which for Nicolai-on in Russia meant industrial development, was held to be parasitic upon, and external to, the Russian communal economy, and was a creature fostered by the policy of the state.

As we have seen, the problem with this position is that it ignored the fact that many of the 'traditional' elements of Russian communal life were just as much creations of state policy as the 'modern' ones. While Nicolai-on was right to emphasise the impact of railways on the structure of the Russian economy, the manner in which he conceived this economy had important political consequences for the kind of socialist perspectives that it engendered, as we shall see in the following chapter. During the 1890s a debate developed between Social Democrats and Populist theoreticians over the fate of Russian capitalism, a debate which drew on the conditions outlined above as evidence in favour of diverse analyses of the future of the Russian economy and of Russian socialism. More than this: they both drew on the writings of Marx and Engels for theoretical guidance, attempting to combine the insights of their masters with the problems of Russian economic development, adapting in their own way the analysis that Marx had made of English capitalism to the possibility of the development of a Russian capitalism. Having briefly outlined some of the features of the economy which was the subject of controversy, we can now turn to a more direct consideration of the politics of Russian Marxism, and the nature of the agrarian question that it confronted.

# 7 Russian Marxism and the Agrarian Question

Herzen, perhaps the founding 'Russian Populist', was criticised by Marx in *Capital* for having discovered the commune not in the Russian countryside, but in a book written by a German, August von Haxthausen's *Studies on the Interior of Russia*, published in Germany between 1847 and 1852. Haxthausen had been invited to study Russian peasant conditions by the Tsar, and his account of his investigations identified the source of social cohesion in Russia as the peasant commune, with its hierarchical, patriarchal organisation. In earlier reports that he had made to the Prussian throne in his status of adviser on agrarian relations Haxthausen had identified the slavic farming communities (*Gemeinden*) of Pomerania as a stabilising factor during the upheavals of the early years of the century, providing a traditional social order into which individuals could be integrated without posing the threat of revolutionary disorder.[1] The vision of the relation of traditional peasant organisation to general social stability clearly appealed to the Russian autocracy when it was translated into Russian conditions. But it also appealed to radicals like Herzen who saw instead the possibility of a specifically Russian national solution to the problems of democracy and change. It was therefore rather unfair of Marx to mock Herzen in the way that he did, since it is clear that what Haxthausen 'discovered' in Russia was merely that for which he had sought in vain in Prussia.

Chernyshevsky, representing a newer form of Russian populist thought than that associated with Herzen, later criticised the inherent conservatism of Haxthausen's work; but when liberal economists suggested that the commune was not a natural creation of Russian history but rather was founded legislatively by the state, he strongly denied this and supported the notion of the commune as a fundamental and natural Russian social institution, whose existence made possible the development of society in a manner distinct from that characteristic of Western Europe.[2] To this end Hegelian dialectics were summoned in support of a view of the commune, not just as a last vestige of an anachronistic social order, but rather as the inevitable end of social development. Analogies from zoology, geology and philology were deployed to demonstrate that 'in its form, the highest stage is similar to the initial stage'.[3] Carefully chosen instances of technological development were then used to suggest that the commune was the ideal form for its introduction and development, any failure in contemporary practice being explained by the existence of peasant poverty. In this way Russia would show the West the way to further social development, avoiding the short-lived European concentration on railroads and industrialisation.

The development of Russian socialist thought at this time around the idea of the commune as the kernel of a future Russian socialist order was reinforced by the development within the First International of demands aimed at the introduction of communal property in land.[4] Most significant perhaps was the *Manifesto to Rural Workers* written by J. P. Becker and published by the Propaganda Committee of the International Workers' Association in Geneva in 1869 and 1870, which saw the salvation of small proprietors, self-employed cultivators and wage-labourers alike in the reclamation of their common rights in the land and the establishment of communal enterprises. In effect, the immediate recommendations that Becker made (small proprietors to pool land and implements, landless to be made members of the cooperative with the same rights, indemnities for capital input of original proprietors)[5] were aimed at establishing in Western Europe the kinds of institutions that existed in Russia, albeit in a socialist environment. The Russian populists in many ways saw themselves in advance of European socialists by the fact of their homeland possessing the germs of such a future society already, necessitating only the overthrow of the Tsarist autocracy for the foundations of this society to be laid. As they became acquainted with Marx's work this position was further developed, by treating *Capital* as an effective analysis of what could be avoided in Russia – the ramifications of capitalist development.

This sentiment was shared by the Russian censor, who first of all permitted imports, and then publication of *Capital* in Russian, principally on the grounds that its analysis did not apply to

Russia.[6] It was also shared by Marx, who, in a letter to the editor of the populist journal *Notes on the Fatherland* drafted in 1877,[7] in which he criticised the manner in which a recent defence of his work had been conducted by Mikhailovsky, stated unambiguously his opinion that if the course set in 1861 were followed, then Russia would lose the greatest chance ever available of avoiding the 'fatal vicissitudes' of the capitalist system.[8] As we will see below, this line, though qualified, was one adhered to by Marx and then Engels until the 1890s, allied to a Blanquist approach to the Russian state.[9]

Mikhailovsky, Danielson and Vorontsov, the three leading Populist theoreticians of the Russian economy, all acknowledged their debt to Marx's analysis of capitalism, although they differed in the conclusions that they drew in the Russian context. The first took Marx's analysis of the division of labour and interpreted its progress in capitalist society as destructive of human relations, the progress of society being therefore counterposed to the progress of individuals which Mikhailovsky saw as the essence of human progress. This was allied to a conception of 'social welfare', so that while he did not oppose the development of factories, banks, railways and so on in principle, he only conceived them as progressive if they improved the welfare of the people.[10] In this case 'the people' was predominantly the Russian peasantry, which was identified in such analyses with the future of the Russian nation as a whole.

The other two writers were perhaps more conventional economists, basing their arguments on forms of social and economic development rather than a theory of humanity, and differing on the question of the measures appropriate to the reform of the economy. In the previous chapter Nicolai-on (or Danielson) has already been introduced as providing a novel analysis of the place of railways in Russia's economic development. He had in fact formulated this account after Marx had requested some information from him on Russian banking, and he corresponded steadily with first Marx and then Engels after the former's death.

A major feature of Nicolai-on's treatment of Russian economic relations was the counterposition of capitalist production to 'people's production', in which the development of capitalism was parasitic on goods produced by 'the people' and also resulted in their direct impoverishment in terms of their consumption of grain.[11] Capitalist production in Russia was for Nicolai-on characterised as the turning of people's products into commodities within the process of circulation in the capitalist sector. 'People's production' was not and could not be for him capitalistic or commodity based. But this was not simply an expression of an economic romanticism, conceiving a rural, agricultural peasantry as engaged in natural processes alien to the artificial productions of capitalism. 'Capitalist agriculture' was for Nicolai-on a reality – but in England and Europe, not in Russia.[12] The distinguishing feature of Russian conditions was that the people still possessed the land, and could always concentrate on expanding the product of the land if industrial employment slumped.

Associated with other studies that he undertook, Nicolai-on concluded that capitalism was in Russia the creation of a state apparatus, and not an indigenous form, the manner in which capitalist development was being promoted threatening to destroy the old economic system without providing any reliable alternative social foundation. Capitalism and its allied technology would in this way destroy the very domestic markets that it needed for its own growth.[13] If Russia was to avoid such a fate then agriculture and industry must be merged in the hands of the immediate producers on the basis of large-scale production. The establishment of a planned, socialist system would enable agriculture and industry to develop together without the crises and breakdowns inherent in capitalist development. The political condition for such a perspective was the destruction of the Tsarist autocracy.

Much of the foundation of Nicolai-on's arguments came from Vorontsov's *Fates of Capitalism in Russia* which was published in 1882, although here the analysis of the problems besetting the Russian economy was linked to demands such as the transfer of gentry lands to the peasantry, the reduction of levels of taxation, and the making available of cheap credit. Vorontsov, unlike Nicolai-on, addressed such demands for reform directly to the state, attempting to alter the established policy of forcing the peasantry to pay for a process of industrialisation that was contrary to their interests. As far as agricultural production went, the existence of capitalist forms was restricted to cases where large-scale farms employed dispossessed labour. Cultivation by small proprietors not separated from their means of production were thus non-capitalist by definition, even if such small enterprises were dependent on capitalist markets for the sale of their produce and the continuation of production. In many ways of course this line of argument is faithful to the arguments advanced by Marx concerning the process of primitive capitalist accumulation, in which the dispossession of direct producers is treated as central to the process of formation of capitalist relations. Following such indications, Vorontsov could counterpose the peasant commune to capitalist development, and further suggest that the existence of the commune with its land and implements represented an 'advantage of backwardness' in which the technical benefits of the West could be directly incorporated into the communal relations of the East, charting a specific and non-capitalist path of development for Russia.[14]

In a review of the Russian edition of Nicolai-on's *Russian Economy after the Peasant Emancipation* (1893), Struve succinctly summarised its argument as centring on the proposition that capitalism was impoverishing Russia, instead of contributing to the rapid growth of national income as in Western Europe. He argued that the principal error of both Vorontsov and Nicolai-on was to equate capitalism in general with *industrial* development, and then describe the decline of the peasantry as the outcome of inappropriate (capitalist) forces.[15] Signs of collapse in the peasant economy (such as the renting of land, failure to repartition, migrant wage-labour, shortage of land) could be read by Populist economists as the result of forcing the agricultural sector to pay for a state-supported process of industrialisation that was itself parasitic on the viability of the agricultural sector. It is clear that these writers did not develop such arguments from a romanticist conception of the peasantry; they did however suggest that rural conditions showed the possibility of a non-capitalist path of development. Furthermore, these ideas were firmly based on Marx's analysis of capitalist economy that was to be found in *Capital* Vol. I.

As Struve emphasised, the maintenance of this position required that peasant communes were treated as though they were immune to capitalist relations, and came into contact with them only through the depredations of industrial production. But the fact that this was an unreal assumption had been graphically demonstrated in Russia by the well-known attempts of the nobleman Engelhardt who had established model communes on his estate during the 1870s and 1880s. Despite all efforts at self-reliance, these communes continually found a need to resort to the employment of hired labour to fulfil their tasks, and in addition to this the democratic organisation of successive communes collapsed as individuals rose to domination over the rest. The wages received by local peasants employed on these model communes were used by them to rent more land and increase their production of cash crops. Engelhardt eventually despaired of these attempts to influence the course of the Russian economy by the power of individual example, concluding that every peasant was at heart a *kulak*.[16]

It must be stressed at this point that the analysis of the Russian economy just outlined was one which drew heavily on Marx's work, and which construed itself as the introduction of Marx's analysis of capitalist forms to Russian conditions. This was a view that was not only prevalent among certain sections of the Russian intelligentsia, but was one that was to a great extent shared by Marx himself. If an official imprimatur suffices for the identification of theoretical filiation, then it is this Populist version of the development of the Russian economy, and the place within this process of the commune and the peasantry, that must be recognised as the genuine Marxist article. But of course the provenance of discursive forms can neither be established by reference to letters of recommendation, nor by the beliefs of the authors of nineteenth-century texts on the Russian economy.

The support that Marx gave to the Populist conception of the future possibilities of Russian socialism was to a large extent based on his tendency to view occasional crises as terminal, a kind of political Micawberism. Thus for example the internal conflicts engendered by the Russo–Turkish war were conceived as bringing Russia to the edge of revolution; writing to Sorge in 1877 Marx stated that 'all sections of Russian society are in complete disintegration economically, morally and intellectually. This time the revolution will begin in the East, hitherto the unbroken bulwark and reserve army of counter-revolution'.[17]

While distancing himself from some of the analyses of Russian capitalism proposed by the Populists, he shared their view that the commune could, if not first destroyed by external forces, become the basis of a regeneration of Russia along socialist lines. The Political conditions for this eventuality were two-fold: the destruction of the Tsarist autocracy, and a supporting proletarian revolution in the West. The first principle led him to support terrorist attacks on the autocracy, sharing the Populist conception that with the removal of the leading elements of the autocracy the political order that sustained it would crumble.

The most extensive argument that Marx presented along these lines is to be found in the drafts of the letter that he sent in reply to Vera Zasulich's request for his opinion on the place of the village communes in the future development of Russia. Emphasising the probability of a course of political and economic development in Russia which was distinct from that being followed in W. Europe, he based this judgement principally on an analysis of communal property forms, from which he concluded:

> In fact from the purely economic point of view Russia can only find a way out of the cul-de-sac in which she finds herself through the development of the village communes; it would be vain to seek a way out through English relations of tenure, since this is contradicted by all the agricultural conditions of the country.[18]

In the following year, 1882, Marx and Engels wrote a short preface to the second Russian edition of the *Communist Manifesto* in which this line of thought was made more public, emphasising the political necessity of simultaneous revolutionary outbreaks in East and West for the commune to form the basis on which a communist society could begin to develop.[19] Marx, and then Engels after the former's death in 1883, continued to conceive of the decisive problem in Russia as the removal of the autocracy, long after Plekhanov and others (as will be seen) had decided that revolutionary terrorism was obsolete, and that for any change in Russia a workers' movement had to be created. Indeed, Engels expressed his adherence to the 'activism' of such politics in 1885 in a letter to Zasulich (now an associate of Plekhanov in the Emancipation of Labour Group) when he stated his belief that Russia was nearing its '1789', and that the balance could easily be tipped by a small group of activists:

> ... if ever Blanquism – the fantasy of overturning an entire society through the action of a small conspiracy – had a certain justification for its existence, that is certainly in St. Petersburg.[20]

While such activists might be entirely misguided, their action would alone suffice to set in motion a reaction throughout the whole of Russian society that would liberate it from the chains which held it in check, and allow it to follow its own (non-capitalist) path to socialism and communism. In arguing this line, Engels implicitly denigrated the activities of the Emancipation of Labour Group, whose existence had been earlier deprecated by Marx as marginal to Russian circumstances, exiled as they were in Geneva.

While Engels later confided in correspondence to Danielson that he considered the commune to be on the wane[21] it is perhaps interesting to consider the position he had advanced in an earlier series of articles published in *Der Volkstaat* in April 1875. These were written as a response to Tkachev's accusation, in his *Open Letter to Friedrich Engels*, that Engels was ignorant of Russian conditions, and that if he were better informed he would know that a social revolution was more likely and simpler in Russia than in the West. The reason for this, suggested Tkachev, was that while there was no urban proletariat, there was no bourgeoisie either, so that the workers only had to struggle against political power, and not the power of capital. The Russian state furthermore was a monolith without any economic roots, lacking the organised social interests that could protect it when threatened.

These articles by Engels were later published as the pamphlet *Social Relations in Russia*, and in them Engels poured scorn on the primitive analysis of capital and the state that Tkachev put forward. He did this by showing first that there existed in Russia diverse groups whose interests were defended by the state, and that the idealistic picture painted by Tkachev of the *artel* (industrial collective) and commune overlooked the emergence of exploitative relations within them. Considering the results of the 1861 settlement, he stated that:

> there is no country like Russia where, at the very onset of bourgeois society, the parasitic forms of capitalism are so developed, its webs entwining the whole country and population.[22]

Having shown that the *artel* is often either a temporary commercial expedient, or subordinate to moneylenders and merchants, Engels goes on to argue that the commune is no unique

Russian institution, but rather a primitive survival of previous Indo-Germanic communal forms. The separation of the communes one from another was in addition the sign of their incorporation into a form of oriental despotism, Tsarist autocracy. As Engels pointed out, most communes were simply communally redivided but farmed individually, and that the future development of Russia would see their rapid demise.[23]

This scathing attack on romanticist conceptions of primitive communism depended on the viability of treating relations of exploitation as undifferentiated and unambiguous *signs of capitalism*, and as we shall see this was replicated in certain arguments in the 1890s. In an 'Afterword' to a second edition of the pamphlet published in 1894, Engels recapitulated Marx's various statements on the commune while emphasising that nowhere had agrarian communism produced anything except its own collapse. The 'revolutionary optimism' that he had shared with Marx in the early 1880s had, he argued, been predicated on the imminent possibility of a revolutionary outbreak in Russia, and that if a revolution was to occur in Russia in the 1890s, it would be easier because a section of the population had absorbed the intellectual conclusions of capitalist development, not because of the survival of a primitive communist form.[24]

Engels' position on Russian conditions during the 1870s was therefore distinct from that adopted by Marx around 1879, and the assumption of a similar line by Engels at this time involved him in an alteration of his previous assessment as embodied in *Social Relations in Russia*. We shall see below that in fact the development of a Russian Marxism drew primarily on the authority of this earlier work of Engels, and not on the authority of Marx's words themselves. But this 'Russian Marxism' is not something that can be deduced from the writings of Marx and Engels on Russia, and the previous discussion has shown that if the words of Marx are held to be constitutive of Marxist orthodoxy, then the orthodox Marxists of the 1890s turn out to be the Populists, rather than the Social Democrats. But Russian Marxism is something more than the espousal of a particular social and economic analysis and the use of certain terminology: it involves a commitment to forms of organisation and agitation that characterise Russian Social Democracy. Insofar as a genealogy of Russian Marxism can be identified, it is one whose source is not the writings of Marx but rather the work of

Plekhanov and the group of emigrés that formed around him in the 1880s. The establishment of a Marxist orthodoxy by this group was not licensed by reference to the kinds of statements from Marx and Engels that we have just outlined; it rather consisted in the creative reformulation of certain of Marx's political and economic analyses in a fashion that was tacitly rejected by Engels until shortly before his death.

Plekhanov, who was to become the 'Founding Father of Russian Marxism' and then later a 'Menshevik revisionist' became first involved politically with the Land and Liberty movement in 1876, but by 1879 he had detached himself from this organisation on the grounds of his opposition to terrorism as a political tactic. He then became for a short while a leading member of the Black Repartition movement; following its suppression by the police he moved to Geneva in January 1880, to become one of the leaders of the Russian emigration. He had at this time begun to study Russian conditions, increasingly moving from Populism and a faith in the Russian peasantry with his reading of Flerovsky and Orlov[25] in particular. In 1881 he became convinced that the prospects of political change in Russia were limited to the development of a bourgeois–constitutional monarchy, associated with the development of capitalist relations in agriculture and industry. Further, the failure of terrorist politics in this year – the assassination of the Tsar, far from leading to the collapse of Tsarist autocracy, actually resulted in the consolidation of the political order – marked for Plekhanov the death-throes of an obsolete form of revolutionary politics. If the revolution was to be made in Russia, Plekhanov concluded, it would be necessary to construct a new basis for political work, both practically and in theory. In September 1883 the Emancipation of Labour Group was formed with the intention of laying the foundations of a new revolutionary politics.[26]

This necessarily involved a rejection of the positions held at this time by Marx and Engels on Russia, and Plekhanov turned instead to Marx's analysis of Germany in 1848 (dealing as it did with a semi-feudal, agrarian state in which constitutional democracy appeared the most advanced form that was likely to be established), and Engels' *Social Relations in Russia*. Using the *Communist Manifesto*'s outline of revolutionary politics based on the possibilities in W. Europe in the late 1840s, Plekhanov elaborated Engels' analysis of capitalist development and political change for the Russia of the 1880s. As has been noted above, *Social Relations in Russia* placed relatively little emphasis on the possibilities of an agrarian communism forming the basis of revolutionary change in Russia, and further stressed the importance of the existence of a bourgeois class for the development of a revolutionary struggle.[27] Marx and Engels in their earlier work had advocated an alliance between the proletariat and the progressive bourgeoisie against the feudal order, an alliance in which the proletariat would first compel their allies to participate in the making of a bourgeois revolution before in turn seizing power themselves on this basis.[28] This conception was taken over by Plekhanov, and the future of revolutionary politics in Russia was thereby shifted from the shoulders of the peasantry *qua* 'people' to those of the emergent working class, in alliance with liberals and bourgeois radicals.

The first complete formulation of this position can be found in Plekhanov's article *Socialism and the Political Struggle*, written in 1883 as a critique of *Narodnaya Volya*, and as the assertion of the necessity for a new departure in Russian revolutionary politics. Having outlined Marx's and Engels' conceptions of politics and the economy, Plekhanov concluded by stressing the fact that constitutional democracy, not socialist revolution, was what figured on the political agenda, and that in order to achieve this the task of Russian revolutionaries was to build a workers' party. This did not however involve a rejection of the peasantry as a political force, but rather concerned an assessment of the likelihood of the rural population taking a political initiative compared with the possibilities presented by industrial workers:

> Let us make a reservation to avoid misunderstandings. We do not hold the view, which as we have seen was ascribed to Marx's school rather than it existed in reality, and which alleges that the socialist movement cannot obtain support from our peasantry until the latter has been turned into a landless proletarian and the village community has disintegrated under the influence of capitalism. We think that on the whole the Russian peasantry would show great sympathy for any measure aiming at the so-called 'nationalisation of the land'. Given the possibility of any at all free agitation among the peasants [i.e. under a constitution], they would also sympathise with

the socialists, who naturally would not be slow in introducing into their programme the demand for a measure of that kind. But we do not exaggerate the strength of our socialists or ignore the obstacles, the opposition which they will inevitably encounter from that quarter in their work. For that reason, and *for that reason only*, we think that for the beginning they should concentrate their main attention on the industrial centres.[29]

One of the most important features of this passage is that it clearly rejects the idea that dispossession of the peasantry is a necessary condition for the involvement of sections of a peasant population in a socialist movement; and in so doing, argues that such a conception of proletarianisation is not a Marxist dogma. As we shall see below, Lenin took over and elaborated this conception, although this has been obscured by the later assumption among Marxist writers that it was necessarily revisionist to suggest that dispossession was not a necessary condition of capitalist development.

However, while Plekhanov rejects the apparently 'orthodox' Marxist doctrine according to which the dispossession and consequent proletarianisation of the peasantry is a condition for their engagement in a revolutionary alliance with an urban proletariat, there is a persistence in his account of a unitary, undifferentiated conception of the category 'peasantry' *qua* object of political calculation. Thus for example Plekhanov considers the appeal of demands for land nationalisation to the peasantry in general, rather than to sections of rural small producers identified by political and economic analysis. The alliance of the 'peasantry' and the 'workers' compounds this lack of differentiation, treating the peasantry as a mass perhaps not far removed from the Narodnik idea of the peasantry as 'the people'; in addition, the nature of the demands adopted by such a political alliance are conceived in terms of the urban workers including items of interest to the peasantry in a programme that they have already established.

While such criticisms can be made of these early formulations of a Social Democratic agrarian policy, it would be wrong to conceive that these statements were primarily theoretical in nature and therefore subject only to theoretical evaluation. Plekhanov's proposition that an urban working class should be the only force capable of assuming the political initiative in a country where such a class was barely in evidence involved a radical break with established Russian radical thought. Further, the persistence of a unitary category of 'the peasantry' within these formulations did not in fact seriously affect the political perspective that was developed; all it amounted to was a rejection, for the time being, of a central role for the peasantry in party work. What concerns us here is the manner in which this analysis of the peasantry was developed by Plekhanov, and how it could lead him to such a radical revision of the traditional Populist conceptions of the tasks confronting Russian revolutionaries.

*Socialism and the Political Struggle* did not contain any detailed comments on the nature of the Russian economy and its development; these are to be found in *Our Differences*, a defence of *Socialism and the Political Struggle* and the Emancipation of Labour Group against criticisms raised in the journal *Vestnik Narodnoi Voli*. Published in 1885, the introduction of this piece immediately confronts the question of the inevitability of capitalist development in Russia, and reviews the arguments of Chernyshevsky, Bakunin and Tkachev on the possibilities contained in the Russian rural commune. Plekhanov argues that the Emancipation had ended any possibility there might have been for the kind of transition envisaged by Chernyshevsky, while the romanticist notions of 'peasant communism' adhered to by Bakunin and Tkachev removed the necessity for their considering the actual developments taking place in the 'communal economy'.[30]

There then follows a lengthy exposition of the form of capitalist development that Russia was undergoing, beginning with a rejection of the Populist arguments concerning the insufficiency of domestic markets for the effective functioning of a capitalist economy. Plekhanov does this by arguing that in France, Germany and America markets were *created* for the goods produced by their new industries, principally through the implementation of restrictive trade policies on the part of the state concerned. Such an argument also counts against the proposition, outlined above, that capitalist development in Russia was simply a creation of the Tsarist state which had no real basis in the Russian economy, emphasising the role of state intervention in monarchies (Colbert's France) and democratic republics (post-bellum America) alike.

Writers such as Vorontsov had also suggested that the Russian working class, on which Plekhanov placed so much emphasis, scarcely existed. Plekhanov immediately points out that the figures produced by Vorontsov and others relate only to workers employed in established factories, ignoring completely the non-factory industrial workers in the various handicraft industries. A number of such industries are then cited, such as weaving and spinning, which while being handicraft based are in fact run on capitalist lines. This enables Plekhanov to suggest that competition between certain types of handicraft industrial enterprises and factory enterprises is not between independent producers on the one hand and capitalists on the other, but between big and small capitals.[31] The employment of hired labour in domestic enterprises leads to an increasing involvement of rural producers in industrial production, in some cases placing agricultural labour in second place with respect to overall household income. While the Narodniks blame the dereliction of some areas of land on 'poor agricultural conditions', Plekhanov argues that the more certain returns from capitalist industrial production, either as entrepreneur in the case of the rich peasant, or as labourer in the case of the small, encourages the development of trades such as shoemaking and cotton fabrication:

> The decline of agriculture and the disintegration of the old 'foundations' of the peasant *mir* are the inevitable consequence of the development of handicraft production, under the *actual* conditions, of course, not under the *possible* conditions with which our Manilovs console themselves and which will be a reality we know not when.[32]

Capitalist commodity production, then, is proceeding apace in Russian town and country, according to Plekhanov, undermining the 'natural economy' of the Russian commune. The development of a money economy associated with this assists in the destruction of communal land tenure, the village community being unable to adapt effectively to new conditions.[33] There follows a general discussion of the decline of village organisation, concluding with a consideration of the decay of redistribution of the communal lands and its relation to the development of inequalities, and particularly the emergence of *de facto* individual rights in land. The trend in the Russian rural economy is towards the establishment of capitalist relations, affecting large as well as small farms. Attempts to check this development by the abolition of large scale agriculture would have no permanent effect on this tendency, since the production of grain as a commodity by small producers subjects them equally to the 'implacable laws of commodity production'.[34] These laws will in due course necessarily give birth to the capitalist entrepreneur and the rural wage-worker. Small versus large farms does not indicate independent producers versus capitalists: it is rather a question of the big versus the small bourgeoisie. In conclusion, Plekhanov poses a rhetorical question:

> If, after all we have said, we ask ourselves once more: Will Russia go through the school of capitalism? We shall answer without any hesitation: why should she not finish the school she has *already begun*?[35]

The subordination of the peasantry to the industrial proletariat in the future work of revolutionary organisation in Russia is not therefore based in Plekhanov's analysis on an opposition of a traditional peasantry to a progressive emergent urban proletariat. On the contrary, it is argued that the 'natural economy' of the peasantry is being rapidly eroded, and that a process of change is under way in the countryside that will eventuate in the establishment of capitalist relations as the dominant relations of production and distribution. This is shown both in the prevalence of domestic handicraft industry as a means for the support of increasing numbers of peasant households, and in the decay of communal forms of land tenure. What Plekhanov maintains, however, is that this process of capitalist transition is incomplete in contemporary Russia, and that furthermore the forms of organisation that it gives rise to militate against small peasants and rural workers becoming an effective political force. The task of building Social Democracy in Russia therefore necessarily falls to the industrial proletariat, or more precisely, it is the task of the Social Democrats to constitute the working class as a political force.[36] It is true that in different drafts of a programme for Russian Social Democracy (discussed in the following chapter) Plekhanov increasingly inclined to a view of the peasantry as a bulwark of absolutism, until he took the position in *The Duty of Socialists in the Famine* (1892) that the bourgeoisie and the proletariat were the sole revolutionary forces, describing the 'muzhik' as the basis for thousands of years of Eastern despotism.[37]

To a certain extent however such a development is a result of a purely political evaluation of a kind that is absent from *Our Differences*, which while consisting of a relatively general description of the Russian economy undifferentiated by region or sector, does seek to establish in a systematic fashion certain economic forces at work. Drawing heavily on the analyses of Vorontsov and other Populist writers, Plekhanov re-organises the evidence that they introduce into an alternative image of Russian capitalist development, one which relies heavily for its outlines on Engels' *Social Relations in Russia*. The anti-Populist analysis that results from this in turn provided the foundation for Lenin's own investigations of the tendencies governing the Russian economy, and while his writing clearly goes far beyond that of Plekhanov, it is important to note that texts such as the *Development of Capitalism in Russia* belong to an established political and theoretical tradition, developing the work already produced within it rather than founding an alternative.[38]

The point of departure for Lenin's early work on the Russian economy is the necessity of providing a clear refutation of Narodnik theories of economic development, which by the 1890s were associated with the work of Vorontsov and Danielson, as well as being promoted by the journal *Russkoye Bogatstvo*. During this decade the denial of the possibility of capitalist development in Russia, and more significantly perhaps the central role ascribed to peasant institutions in the regeneration of Russian society, became increasingly debatable even for many Narodniks. Argument gravitated therefore away from these traditional concerns toward the proposition that capitalism must necessarily choke in Russia for want of a home market, a proposition that became the major target of criticism both from Social Democrats and from Legal Marxists. As will be shown, the contention that Russian capitalism would fail to find a home market rests on a conception of a unitary body of consumers ('the people') too poor to purchase the goods produced by capitalist enterprises, and thus in itself denies the possibility of differentiation and the existence of antagonistic classes within this unity. The question of the 'home market', or in more abstract terms, 'the market question', therefore, is simultaneously the peasant question, even though the polemics that it gave rise to apparently concerned only factors such as distribution, crises and realisation. Lenin's *Development of Capitalism in Russia* can appear to be divided between abstract investigations of the Russian home market, and statistical accounts of peasant production and commodity exchange; but if it is recognised that the stake in the debate on the home market is the fate of the Russian peasantry, it becomes easier to comprehend the sometimes arcane structure of this work.

While the Narodnik 'defence' of the peasantry shifted therefore in the 1890s to questions of capitalist realisation, rather than maintaining this defence more directly, there was in the closing years of the century a revival among students of conceptions of the importance of the peasantry for revolutionary change that in many ways recapitulated basic theses of Populist thought.[39] This eventuated in 1902 with the formation of the Socialist Revolutionary Party, a party which identified itself with the peasantry and which was seen by many as 'neo-Narodnik'.[40] It is sometimes suggested that Lenin's polemics on agrarian issues were projected against adversaries of his own construction, that the 'Narodism' he savaged had perhaps disappeared almost twenty years earlier. While certain Narodniks availed themselves of this argument[41] it would be wrong to interpret changes of position or partial retreats as constituting a dissolution of a Populist trend, since these shifts were in fact the preliminaries to the establishment in the early 1900s of a party which itself was to claim Marxism as a heritage.

Between 1893 and 1900 Lenin worked on a number of studies which fall broadly into two groups: detailed evaluations of recently published material on Russian economic development, and criticisms of the theory and politics of Narodism. These two strands come together in the *Development of Capitalism in Russia* (henceforth DCR) which in a sense constitutes a summary of the agrarian writings of the previous years; but it is worth briefly considering these earlier pieces before moving on to DCR.

The first item in the *Collected Works* is in fact a review essay written in 1893 on Postnikov's *Peasant Farming in South Russia*, entitled by Lenin 'New Economic Developments in Peasant Life'. The concern of the essay is to evaluate the material furnished by Postnikov on the emergence of economic differences among the peasantry and to establish the form in which relations obtain between these different groups. The work of Postnikov is seen by

Lenin as an advance on earlier summaries of Zemstvo statistics in that a false aggregation of different regions and conditions is avoided, and that furthermore sustained criticism is made of the conception of the village community as a homogeneous entity. Postnikov argues that villages are increasingly differentiated by household, and that an assessment of the peasantry must begin from the proposition that village communities are characterised by a division into distinct economic groups.

Lenin's essay takes up this point and investigates the manner in which these real divisions can best be articulated from the available statistics. Several indices are considered: stock and implements held by a household, the allotment of arable land per household, the area of land under crops, and so on. The last is held to be the most crucial index of the economic status of the household, since the amount of allotment land is only a function of the number of males in the household.[42] From an examination of such indices, Postnikov forms the opinion that there is a tendency to the formation of large farms, and that these larger units will in time displace smaller ones. Lenin considers this a premature assessment:

> ... to prove the inevitability of small farms being ousted by large ones, it is not enough to demonstrate the greater advantage of the latter (the lower price of the product); the predominance of money (more precisely, commodity) economy over natural economy must also be established; under natural economy, when the product is consumed by the producer himself and is not sent to market, the cheap product does not encounter the more costly product on the market, and is therefore unable to oust it.[43]

We saw in the previous chapters that this question of the viability of small as opposed to large farms was as often as not considered primarily from the standpoint of agronomy, that is from regard to the technical characteristics of different scales of enterprise. Lenin on the other hand argues here that such an approach is inappropriate, since while it might be shown that the large farm enjoys technical and organisational advantages not available to the small farm, it is only via capitalist competition that the confrontation between such units takes place. Variations in regional conditions, and differing arrangements for the production of income for the enterprise, can both easily nullify what appear to be overwhelming advantages enjoyed by the large farm, and as is stressed here, it has also to be considered whether the agricultural products of the smaller farms are in fact deployed as revenue producers.

The question of the tendency of capitalist development to result in the annihilation of small by large scale enterprise, which as we have seen, occupied a specific place in the agrarian debates of German Social Democracy, is not considered an important issue by Lenin. Instead, he regarded the structure of activities of the peasant household as of prime importance, deriving from this the means for the evaluation of the extent of differentiation among the peasantry. The relative size of farms, and the bearing on this of arguments drawn from agronomy, is thereby subordinated to a consideration of the factors that contribute to, or inhibit, the differentiation of peasant households, such as which lease land, which have access to credit, which hire out or employ wage-labour, which have inadequate draught animals, and so on. Postnikov divided peasant households into three groups according to the freedom of the household head to conduct farming with respect to the number of draught animals owned:

1. Households owning full team, with two adults and a part-time worker in the household;
2. Households 'yoking' with one another for field work;
3. Households with no animals, or only one, which hire animals from others – or alternatively let their land for a part of the harvest and have no cultivated land of their own.[44]

Lenin considered however that Postnikov did not fully draw the conclusions that followed from this:

> Postnikov did not raise this question of the character of the economy of the bottom group of peasants, and did not elucidate the relation of outside employments to the peasant's own farming – and this is a big defect in his work. As a result, he does not adequately explain the, at first glance, strange fact that although the peasants of the bottom group have too little land of their own, they abandon it, lease it; as a result, the important fact, that the means of production (ie. land and implements) possessed by the bottom group of peasants are

qualitatively far below the average, is not linked up with the general character of their farming. Since the average quantity of means of production, as we have seen, is only just enough to satisfy the essential needs of the family, it necessarily and inevitably follows from this fact – the fact of the poor peasants being deprived of their fair share – that they must seek means of production belonging to others to which to apply their labour, ie. they must sell themselves.[45]

The emergence of wage-labour is therefore derived by Lenin from a series of other relations in the rural economy, and is not treated as a mere sign of capitalist relations. For Lenin, the existence of wage-labour in the economy of rural Russia is indicative of a process of differentiation, but a process which does not depend for its rate of development on *dispossession* of the peasants. To be a wage-labourer seeking industrial or agricultural employment does not mean that one has no land, rather that the household from which such a worker comes either cannot support its members on the land available, or does not possess the means needed to farm the allotment effectively. What is taking place in the Russian countryside according to Lenin is not the differentiation of *individuals*, but rather the differentiation of *households*. The main problem under conditions where the basic rural unit is not the person as economic and political agent, but the household, is not the growth of a *landless* proletariat, but the formation of *households with insufficient land*. The significance of this distinction for political and economic calculation is great, since it assumes a greater degree of rural heterogeneity than the classification according to possession of land *tout court*. As will be shown in the following chapter, assessment of the draft agrarian policies of Social Democracy requires a recognition of the importance of the progress of differentiation in the countryside for the calculation of class forces. This does not involve simply identifying the existence of a rural proletariat which is assumed to possess similar class interests with an urban proletariat, but rather assessing the conditions that had themselves engendered the process of differentiation.

As can be seen from Lenin's later 'Handicraft Census of 1894–95 in Perm Gubernia and General Problems of "Handicraft Industry"' (1897) the economy was regarded as an object of study that went beyond the requirements of refuting Narodnik publicists. Here Lenin is concerned with the involvement of rural households in capitalist manufacturing, discussing the relation between wage labour and family labour, the relation of income from handicraft activities to that from agricultural activities, and the organisation of industries which relied on domestic detail work. He concludes that this form of industry 'already implies the deep-going rule of capitalism, being the direct predecessor of its last and highest form – large-scale machine industry'.[46] While the writing of Plekhanov outlined earlier consisted of a set of conclusions concerning the capitalist nature of the Russian economy, Lenin engaged in a more thorough examination of the forces at work within this economy for the purpose of calculating likely paths of development. This is most clearly apparent in DCR, but it is worth noting that from the first Lenin concerned himself with research into the minutiae of economic statistics.

He did at the same time of course engage more directly in polemics with Narodnik ideas, producing a series of papers – 'On the So-Called Market Question' (1893), 'What the "Friends of the People" are and how they Fight the Social-Democrats' (1894), 'The Economic Content of Narodism and the Criticism of it in Mr. Struve's Book' (1894), 'A Characterisation of Economic Romanticism' (1897) and 'The Heritage We Renounce' (1897). In these writings Narodnik conceptions of Russian economic development are consistently attacked; in particular the argument that was put forward according to which sustained capitalist development was not possible in Russia since the products of industry would rapidly exhaust the markets available and find no alternatives, is repeatedly refuted. Lenin for instance demonstrates that 'capitalism', for the Narodniks, is an affair of big factories, contrasting with a 'people's production' characterised by small scale and the possession by the producers of the means of production.[47] This small-scale and impoverished peasant industry is nevertheless capitalism, argues Lenin, and the same goes for agricultural production which the Narodniks persist in treating as if it were impervious to capitalist relations.

By equating capitalism with modern industry, and counterposing to it an impoverished domestic consumer market, the Narodniks are enabled to suggest that capitalist development in Russia is faced with a problem of realisation. As Plekhanov had earlier argued, this neglects the manner in which state policy had contributed to the formation of markets for developed western

European capitalist economies, but Lenin generally chooses to rebut the 'so-called market question' by deploying theoretical arguments based on the reproduction schemata of *Capital* Vol. II; or, as in the case of 'A Characterisation of Economic Romanticism', through a critique of the theories of Smith and Sismondi. Such an approach tends to conceal the fact that a condition of existence of the problem itself was a conception of the peasantry as a unitary 'people' separated from and hostile to the development of capitalist relations. As Lenin pointed out, this conception ignored the extent of the engagement of peasant households in capitalist industry through handicraft manufacture, let alone the sale of agricultural commodities to 'industrial consumers'. To equate 'consumption' with personal goods also ignored the production by industry of its own means of production.

Narodnik theory, conceded Lenin, had at one time had a progressive role, in posing the problem of the direction of capitalist development in Russia. The solutions that were proposed to this problem were however quite fallacious, and by the 1890s they were being increasingly led to a 'defence' of the peasant which was reactionary. Their romanticisation of peasant life led for example to a preference for labour services over wage labour, advocating in effect the restoration of feudal relations as a solution to capitalist development.[48] Such arguments revealed a detachment from the nature of the conditions in which 'the people' lived and worked, knowledge of which, argued Lenin, was crucial to the construction of effective Social Democratic politics. The culmination of his work on these problems is to be found in the *Development of Capitalism in Russia*, published in the same year as Kautsky's *Agrarfrage*.

In DCR, detailed arguments based on *zemstvo* statistics come together with the more general polemics against Narodnik theory to produce a definitive rebuttal of those who suggested that capitalism had no real foothold in Russia. As was stated in the 'Preface to the First Edition', 'the author has set himself the aim of examining the question of how a home market is being formed for Russian capitalism',[49] and the work takes the general form of demonstrating how, in all forms of agricultural and industrial production, capitalist relations are increasingly dominant. The existence of these capitalist relations itself provides the markets that the Narodniks deny. The book is divided into eight chapters

RUSSIAN MARXISM AND THE AGRARIAN QUESTION  193

whose titles indicate the structure of the argument:

1. The Theoretical Mistakes of the Narodnik Economists
2. The Differentiation of the Peasantry
3. The Landowners' Transition from Corvée to Capitalist Economy
4. The Growth of Commercial Agriculture
5. The First Stages of Capitalism in Industry
6. Capitalist Manufacture and Capitalist Domestic Industry
7. The Development of Large-Scale Machine Industry
8. The Formation of the Home Market

While we are here concerned principally with the agrarian problem for Russian Social Democracy, this does not mean that this problem is congruent with 'agriculture', nor that the category 'peasantry' is a rural rather than an urban matter. As Lenin makes clear here, the first stages of capitalist developments in industrial production take place mainly in peasant households, and are intricately related to agricultural activities of the household. The formation of manufactories in rural areas is a further development of industrial production, and it is only with the establishment of large-scale machine industry that a specifically urban proletariat emerges. This urban proletariat is however still in many ways peasant-based, partly because of the dominance assigned to the commune in the post-Emancipation settlement and its control over migrating labour. The 'agrarian question' then for Lenin in this context has a dual significance: to what extent are capitalist relations developing in the rural areas?; and how does the consequent relation between agricultural and industrial sectors affect the process of formation of a working-class? It is with the first problem that we will concern ourselves in this chapter, while the second will emerge as of major significance in the next.

In the first chapter Lenin summarises his arguments, outlined in his previous articles, concerning the theoretical errors that lead the Narodniks to argue that a home market is destroyed in the process of capitalist development in Russia, and that in the absence of this home market the alien economic form will wither. A contrast is established immediately between natural economy as a homogeneous economic form, and commodity economy which is conceived as a heterogeneous economic form. The process of movement from one to the other is expressed in the expansion and intensification of a social division of labour which is characteristic of commodity economy. 'Natural economy' is seen as the form of economy advocated by the Narodniks – patriarchal peasant families, village communities and feudal manors in which each economic unit engages in all forms of economic activity. With commodity economy on the other hand the number of separate and interdependent branches of the economy steadily multiplies and 'it is this progressive growth in the social division of labour that is the chief factor in the process of creating a home market for capitalism'.[50] The task for Lenin is thus defined as demonstrating that commodity economy is increasingly established in different branches of economic life, for once established in these branches the development of the division of labour works to conquer these areas for capitalist production and distribution. DCR is therefore neither a comprehensive history of Russian capitalism (of the kind produced by Struve and Tugan Baranovsky) nor an investigation of the structure of Russian capitalism at the end of the nineteenth century. If it were the former, it would be necessary to abandon the Emancipation as point of departure for the 'history' constructed in the text, and if it were the latter it would be necessary to deal with other areas than the purely economic aspects. Lenin states in the 'Preface' that these two limitations are consciously accepted, and it is necessary to heed these to avoid dealing with the book as something over than that which it is.

Having dealt with the Narodnik arguments on realisation and the home market, Lenin proceeds to a consideration of agricultural production, dealing with it in two broad divisions: firstly the peasant economy which is examined in chapter two, and then following this the landlord's economy which is dealt with in chapter three. This distinction was to become politically crucial, for after the 1905 revolution Lenin composed a new Preface for the 1907 edition of the book which specifically identified these two forms of economy as the foundation of alternatives – the revolutionary road and the Junker road – in a transition to capitalism.[51]

Chapter two begins by recapitulating the material drawn from Postnikov which was discussed above, emphasising the importance of differentiation between households within the village community and the increasingly complex relations that this gives rise to. The well-to-do peasants are identified as the major purchasers and hirers of land, turning themselves into small landowners and capitalist farmers at the expense of other members of their communes. The extension of cultivated area by these rich peasants is predicated on the availability of reserves of labour to work it, and accordingly it is possible to locate in the communes poor peasants who have either insufficient land, no stock, or no implements who become wage labourers on the larger farms. Because of the nature of the statistics that Lenin is using, based as they are on varying methods of classification, he is only able to consistently identify the relation of the top to the bottom groups along different dimensions in various regions. The existence of a middle group between the rich and the poor is accordingly a problem, for it can only be consistently identified after the location of the groups on either side of it.

This is an important problem, and was to become a decisive political problem in the 1920s, when a similar difficulty in locating actual representatives of this middle category who were not simply variants of the other two was a major contributing factor in the collapse of NEP agrarian policy. It can be noticed that in working through the statistical examples the middle peasantry is dealt with *last*, since on most indices its statistical existence is predicated on being mid-way between the two other groups which are consequently discursively prior. But in addition to this, the nature of the middle-peasant household is conceived as independent (while fragile), and therefore as a negation of the economic forces that surround it. Consider this summary from the end of the chapter:

> The intermediary link between these post-Reform types of 'peasantry' is the *middle peasantry*. It is characterised by the *least* development of commodity production. The independent agricultural labour of this category of peasant covers his maintenance in perhaps only the best years and under particularly favourable conditions, and that is why his existence is an extremely precarious one. In the majority of cases the middle peasant cannot make ends meet without resorting to loans, to be repaid by labour-service etc., without seeking 'subsidiary' employment on the side, which also consists partly in the sale of labour-power etc. Every crop failure flings masses of the middle peasants into the ranks of the proletariat. In its social relations this groups fluctuates between the top group, towards which it

grativates but which only a small minority of lucky ones succeed in entering, and the bottom group, into which it is pushed by the whole course of social evolution.[52]

The precarious existence of 'independent' farmers in a commodity economy is well-illustrated here, but the future that is assigned to them in capitalist relations is one which contains their inevitable annihilation. Their subordinate discursive existence is reflected in their subordination to the activities of rich peasants except in those years when the crops are good enough to ensure independence for a little longer. But as we have seen in the sections dealing with the arguments in German Social Democracy, conditions can be postulated in which such 'independent farmers' maintain their existence with no immediate prospect of being swallowed up by either of the classes above and below them. For Lenin, the future that he foresees is one which is written into the nature of an agricultural commodity economy, and once this has taken root it will inevitably flourish and realise this basic nature. Capitalist relations are thus ascribed a certain autonomy, for once they appear they proceed almost under their own impulse to dominance of the economy as a whole.

This conception of capitalist development is not a problem when dealing with Narodnik theories, for here all that is required is to show that capitalist relations exist in those very areas considered by the Narodniks to be non-capitalist, and to indicate the likelihood of their further development. If however the issue is the actual configuration of economic forces operating in a specific conjuncture, then this conception of auto-development becomes an obstacle to economic and political calculation. The problem consists in the fact that the period of time within which such forces are realised is in principle incalculable. While the demonstration of the inevitability of the growing dominance of capitalist relations suffices to inflict a theoretical defeat on the Narodniks, serious alterations must be made in the form of analysis if it is to be used as the basis for the formulation of party policy. For a political organisation, the space of time in which various elements in an economy decay and are renewed is at the same time the space of time in which it has to act on these forces. It is therefore necessary to have some means of establishing the opportunities present for organisation and agitation in specific conjunctures. As we have seen in the case of German Social

Democracy, the apparently limitless 'tendencies' of capital that founded its political analysis were closely related to the political problems that it confronted. In the case under consideration here, the 'tendency' for capitalist relations to develop is not grounded in the same way, and consequently requires supplementary conditions if such an analysis is to be of use in the formulation of policy. As will be shown in the following chapter, it was precisely the failure to recognise this problem fully that led to the Social Democrats being overtaken by events in 1905.

The effects of differentiation on the peasantry are demonstrated by Lenin in the second chapter as leading to the formation of two dominant groups, and contrary to the view of the Populists this does not result in the annihilation of a home market, but to the creation of two quite specific ones: among the rural proletariat for articles of consumption, and among the rural bourgeoisie for means of production.[53] The diversity of the activities of both these groups – among the bourgeoisie, for example, engagement in usury and commercial enterprise, among the proletariat special trades – necessarily enlarges the demand for implements, machines and raw materials, while the increasing dependence of all these forms of activity on a money economy in turn implies that personal consumption is also derivative of market relations. Lenin thus utilises his analysis of capitalist differentiation of the peasant economy as a demonstration of the error of Narodnik theory, showing how in the midst of the commune relations of dependence and superordination were being established.

The third chapter is an examination of the landowner's economy, and because of its nature Lenin has to consider the effects of the Emancipation on the agricultural estates. Pre-emancipation conditions are summarised as feudalistic, where the independent farming of the peasant was a condition of the estate economy, the purpose of providing land for such use being to provide the landlord with labour.[54] The predominance of the corvée economy that Lenin outlines is conditional upon the general prevalence of natural economy, in which peasants are provided with land by a lord and tied to it in such a way that the landlord can exercise direct supervision and compulsion in the allocation of work by the peasant. These relations were shattered by the Emancipation, since in the long run the ties of personal dependence were broken, and the provision of land by the landlord in return for labour was also thereby terminated. We say here 'in the long run', for the provisions of the Settlement were such as to legally perpetuate these forms, by granting households use-rights only over allotment land, and not outright title, and various devices were introduced to perpetuate the role of the landlords beyond the term of the transitional arrangements. However as Lenin points out, since the conditions required for capitalist production did not exist and because the corvée system had been undermined rather than destroyed, the form of transition from feudal to capitalist production on the estates was necessarily hesitant and diverse. The failure to provide households in good agricultural regions with sufficient land for their needs (and the removal of pastures and woods from settlement lands) did, as shown earlier, enable the landlord to provide himself with dependent labour.

Two transitional forms are identified by Lenin as most characteristic: the labour service system, and the capitalist system. In the former the landlord's land is cultivated with the implements of the neighbouring peasants, while the forms of payments for this service are varied. The latter system involves hired workers who farm the landlord's land with their own equipment.[55] The capitalist form of landlord farming is judged to dominate in European Russia, while labour service dominates in other parts; the question is then posed, which of these forms is going to eliminate the other? The answer to this is found by Lenin in the usually disregarded distinction between labour service performed by peasants with implements, and that performed by those without. That is, Lenin differentiates between types of agricultural activity and the kind of equipment necessary. In the case of the former, tasks such as ploughing and carting are included, requiring implements and draught animals; while in the case of the latter, the tasks include reaping, threshing and other operations requiring only simple tools. As noted above, the corvée economy is dependent on natural economy for the supply of labour; but without the ties which compel a peasant to work on the lord's land it is necessary to rely on economic need. Those well-to-do peasants who possess implements and draught animals have however no such need, while those who do not possess such means of production do. But this rural proletariat, being no longer so directly bound to the landlord, might prefer to earn wages elsewhere, either in industry or for work on peasant farms.

Lenin deduces that the development of capitalist wage labour undermines the basis of corvée economy, and that therefore landlord's economy is increasingly compelled to assume a capitalist character.[56] This is admitted to be a theoretical deduction made in the absence of adequate statistical evidence, but such evidence as there is can be used to demonstrate the nature of the process, if not its rate of development.

Lenin therefore shows in these two chapters that a dual form of capitalist evolution is under way in Russia: the internal differentiation of the natural economy of the peasantry into capitalists and wage labourers, and the transition of estate farming from a feudal basis to a capitalist one. As we shall see, he came to advocate the political support of the first tendency, which in practice meant advocating that it be furnished with the means for its rapid development. In most cases this was principally land that had been removed by the terms of the Emancipation from the control of the peasantry, or in general the landlords' land itself. The 'revolutionary road' outlined in the 1907 'Preface' saw this transfer of land as the most effective way of smashing the relics of serfdom which the landlords' economy perpetuated, which in turn would lead to an even more rapid development of capitalist differentiation. The alternative to this is the Junker road,[57] in which there is a slow transition to capitalism on the basis of the estates step-by-step breaking the feudal forms which dominate it. In DCR Lenin confines himself to establishing the economic structure of the two forms of capitalist agricultural production and their possible variations, later using these elements in his construction of a Social Democratic agrarian policy which attempted to comprehend the political opportunities of these variations.

The chapter following that on the landlords' economy and its transition summarises the previous discussion into the question: do the changes noted express a growth of capitalism and the home market? This is examined by an investigation of the production of different agricultural goods, noting their requirement for labour and capital, and regional specialisation in grain crops, as well as the demands for the competitive production of vegetables, fruit, flax and dairy goods. It is demonstrated for these and other goods that either their production increasingly assumes the form of commodity production, with an intensive use of hired labour and machinery, or their conditions of circulation as goods are those of commodity relations. In the case of dairying, the care of cattle and the chores of milking were often left to small producers, while the processing of milk into butter and cheese was taken over by local industrial concerns equipped with modern machinery.[58] Flax was likewise left to the peasantry, although the attempt to rent more land furthered differentiation among households, apart from the fact that the product had to be sold as a commodity to manufacturers. It was in grain farming, and certain aspects of stock farming, that technical developments were most available and accordingly these sectors of production became increasingly dominated by capitalist forms of production.

In this chapter therefore, unlike in his previous work, Lenin makes explicit use of agronomy to evaluate the economic possibilities of different agricultural investments, and he is able to show how the course of capitalist development in agriculture proceeds in a different fashion to that in manufacturing. While the latter is characterised by increasing specialisation on one product or part of a product, agriculture does not divide into such distinct branches but merely specialises in one product or another, while adapting other activities to this product, rather than eliminating them. The consequence is that capitalist agriculture is characterised not by the standardisation of industrial products, but by increasing diversity and complexity.[59] This very diversity, among other factors, gives rise to an extensive capitalist market.

Chapters five and six examine the way in which industrial production on a capitalist basis becomes established in peasant handicrafts and transforms the domestic base of such craft production, first into manufacturing, and then into factory production. The development of industry is therefore intricately related to the development of agricultural production, arising in the patriarchal household as a subsidiary occupation to agricultural activities, then in certain trades and areas becoming a major means of subsistence of peasant households, before taking the labour out of the household and into manufactories perhaps owned by rich peasants. This process both independently gives rise to, and draws on, a force of wage labourers who are set to work with machinery (or with hand tools) on detail work that displaces the skills of the artisan production of the household or small workshop. Simple capitalist cooperation is developed in workshops where a number of commodity producers combine under the supervision of merchants or farmers. This in turn grows into capitalist manufacture, and this is in chapter six examined trade by trade.

The purpose of this detailed exposition is to counter the Narodnik view that capitalist production is an artificial element in the Russian economy in contrast to the 'people's production' of the handicraft trades. Extensive forays into material from woodworking, felt, samovar and accordion trades leads to the conclusion that they are characterised in their organisation of production by a division of labour, which in certain cases opens the way for machinery and the elimination of hand production.[60] These enterprises are not 'people's' any more than they are 'artificial': they are developing capitalist enterprises, characterised as such by their internal organisation and by the sale of their products as commodities, and developing indigenously to the Russian economy.

Lenin's outline in this and the following chapter on large-scale machine industry follows closely Marx's account in *Capital* of the development of capitalist industry, but he cannot be accused of having imposed a model of economic development drawn from England and applied without regard to Russian conditions. As noted above, he drew a distinction between the characterisitic form of development of capitalist relations in agriculture and industry, a distinction which rested on the forms of labour available and the characteristics of the enterprise. While David accused Kautsky of conceiving Marx's model of industrial development as a model of capitalist development *tout court* (and in his *Sozialismus und Landwirtschaft* argued this with stupefying laboriousness) the same accusation cannot be levelled at Lenin.[61] The capitalist character of Russian agriculture is derived by Lenin principally from the forms of labour there employed, and the relations into which goods enter on sale by enterprises engaged in cash transactions. The functions of the category 'social division of labour' is used primarily to conceptualise the breakdown of a homogeneous natural economy and express the dispersion of a commodity economy unified by the category 'market'. While 'machinery' plays an important part in the assessment of the level of development of capitalist agriculture, it is not expressive of the extent of capitalist relations, as de Crisenoy suggests.[62]

The final chapter of DCR returns the narrative to the point of departure, the question of the home market and the possibility of its existence with the development of capitalist relations in Russia. The construction of the text as a detailed analysis of capitalist forms permits this resumption of the initial problem to assume a quite different status however. Whereas the initial treatment of the errors of Narodnik theorising on the economy is one which invokes the names of Smith and Marx in a theoretical refutation of underconsumptionist arguments, the final chapter of the book re-establishes this refutation on the basis of the descriptive material that had been presented in the previous chapters. As has been suggested above, this concentration on the home market is simply an expression of the 'agrarian question', for the Russian economy was dominated by rural production and the market for capital and consumer goods is thus located in the countryside. While it should not be thought that the book is directed primarily to the 'peasant question', the actual location of developing industrial and agricultural capitalist relations necessarily focusses primarily on a peasant, rather than a working-class, population.

This structural characteristic does however mean that the text cannot legitimately be appropriated as a model Marxist account of the peasantry and capitalism, for it addresses not the peasantry-in-general, but rather specific problems confronting Russian Social Democracy. Indeed, DCR has remained a work more often gestured towards than investigated by more recent Marxists, its imposing size and complex arrangement perhaps discouraging easy assessment, promoting a general recognition of its existence while at the same time it remains on the shelves unread. The lack of serious assessments of this memorial of late nineteenth century Russian Social Democracy is truly remarkable.

It was stated in passing above that Lenin's text, contrary to casual remarks that it represents an 'application' of the theory of Marx's *Capital* to Russian conditions, is in fact a radically unorthodox work which abandons many of the supposed central ideas of Marxism. Partly of course this idea of the extension of a project embodied in Marx's writings to new areas was encouraged by the stance adopted by Lenin in his arguments with Populist theorists, and also by the manner in which he drew comparisons with Kautsky's *Agrarfrage*. Receiving this book when his own was already in the press, Lenin added a brief précis of it to his "Preface" and stated that he regarded *Agrarfrage* as 'the most noteworthy contribution to recent economic literature' after

*Capital* Vol. III.⁶³ But as we have seen in chapter four Kautsky's book is far from an extension of Marx's economic analysis, and to treat it as such conceals the political and polemical nature of the text. Lenin went on in a review to describe *Die Agrarfrage* as the first systematic Marxist study of capitalism in agriculture.⁶⁴ By associating DCR with Kautsky's text Lenin implied that both were simply applications of Marxist orthodoxy to the economic problems confronting Social Democracy in Germany and Russia.

In both cases this argument has been demonstrated in detail above to be erroneous. If a comparison of the two works is made, major differences can be established very easily. The most obvious is perhaps the way in which Kautsky's book rigorously eschews detailed reference to German economic conditions, while Lenin's is characterised by an overwhelmingly empirical discussion of the impact of capitalist relations on the Russian national economy. The apparent centrality to *Agrarfrage* of questions of the technical efficiency of different types of farming enterprise finds no counterpart in DCR, while Lenin's heavy emphasis on the process of differentiation and proletarianisation is nowhere matched by Kautsky. In fact this concentration by Lenin on the peasantry as composed of increasingly antagonistic households has no direct foundation in *Capital*, although perhaps some authority could be found in Engels' *Social Relations in Russia*. *Capital* Vol. III is often identified as the relevant point of departure for a Marxist analysis of capitalist agricultural relations on account of the space devoted to a theory of capitalist rent, but there is no trace of such work in Lenin's analysis of agricultural capitalism in Russia. Of course there is some treatment of the problem in *Die Agrarfrage*, but as we have shown this is in some ways no more than a ritual gesture towards an orthodoxy that has elsewhere been abandoned.

More important perhaps is the fact that Lenin does not use value categories in his account of the development of capitalist relations in Russia. In recent years the adherence to orthodoxy in Marxist economies has come to be judged very largely on the manner in which questions of the creation and realisation of surplus value, and the mode of its distribution, have been articulated. Critiques of such endeavours are usually met by the guardians of orthodoxy with the accusation of revisionism, or an attempt to demonstrate that such critiques are simply repetitions of the treatment of Marx's theory of value by Böhm-Bawerk and von Bortkiewicz. The orthodoxy that is defended in this way has however no relation to the doctrines espoused by Lenin and Kautsky. In fact Lenin was criticised by a contemporary precisely for his neglect of value analysis in DCR, and in reply Lenin argued that the consideration of Russian capitalism as sectors of productive and unproductive capital, and flows of surplus value, could have no part in the composition of a work of this nature.[65] While Lenin maintained that perhaps such an account could be constructed after a work like DCR had been written, if not before, his failure to develop his analysis of Russian capitalism in this way is itself significant. It can be suggested that the composition of a work like DCR made such an analysis irrelevant, and it is in fact hard to see what purpose it would serve.

In the case of agricultural production the application of value analysis is represented by the introduction of Marx's theory of capitalist rent which modifies certain value categories for the purpose of applying them to capitalist agriculture. Lenin however never deploys such arguments in the studies of Russian economic conditions that he made during the 1890s. When he does employ Marx's theory of rent, it is for a quite different purpose – the establishment and defence of Marxist orthodoxy in theoretical debate. Thus the first detailed exposition of a theory of rent is to be found in Lenin's article 'Capitalism in Agriculture', which is a defence of Kautsky's *Agrarfrage* against criticisms levelled by Bulgakov. These arguments are further elaborated in 'The Agrarian Question and the "Critics of Marx"'.[66] In both these cases, and in later articles, the exposition of a Marxist theory of rent is conceived not as a means of producing specific analysis of capitalist conditions, but rather as a means of establishing a position in debate and demonstrating the theoretical weaknesses of opponents. While the debates that were constructed in this way are of great interest, their indirect relation to problems of the analysis of the Russian economy makes their discussion here only of secondary importance. There are many aspects of Lenin's writings on the agrarian economy that cannot be effectively dealt with in this context, and although there is nowhere an extensive or exhaustive treatment of them it is not the purpose of this book to simply rehearse as a totality Lenin's confrontation with agrarian issues.

This chapter has argued that Russian Marxism, far from being a simple application of Marxist principles to Russian conditions, was a quite specific creation of the revolutionary movement in Russia. As such it cannot be treated as if it has a genealogy originating in the words of Marx, in comparison with which orthodoxy and revisionism can be simply read off as continuation or divergence. The customary reduction of 'Russian Marxism' to the Marxism of Lenin has been shown to obscure the manner in which several of the elements of political and economic analysis in his work are developed out of the work of Plekhanov, who likewise rejected implicitly Marx's pronouncements on the prospects of a revolutionary movement in Russia. Lenin's Marxism was not established as a faithful reproduction of Marx's views on Russia, nor was it an application of Marx's 'model' of capitalist development. Instead, the orthodoxy of Lenin's work is founded in his appreciation of the necessity of constructing in Russia a popular political movement that would successfully challenge Tsarist autocracy. The theoretical studies that he undertook were intricately related to this objective; the development of a popular movement depended on the destruction of Populist theory and the political perspectives that it embodied, such as a defence of landlord economy and a refusal to recognise the progressive aspects of Russian capitalism. The Populists however cannot be regarded as 'anti-Marxist', for even if they had not drawn so heavily on Marx's work, they can be seen in many ways to be more faithful to Marx's actual analysis of Russia than Lenin.

The years of theoretical preparation that Lenin spent during the 1890s in dispute with liberal and Populist economists was conceived not only as time spent on the simple elaboration of a defensible Marxist analysis; it was at the same time a political preparation for the development of a programme for Russian Social Democracy. Basing himself on the analysis of the Russian economy represented by *Development of Capitalism in Russia*, Lenin proceeded to outline the bases of a policy that would enable various classes within this economy to be united around specific struggles. As has already been suggested, the direct use of an analysis that revolved around the refutation of Populist theory involved some problems of calculation that were to become critical during the 1905 Revolution. The discussion now turns to a consideration of the manner in which the agrarian question became in Russia the object of political calculation in the programmes of Social Democracy.

# 8 The Russian Social Democratic Labour Party and the Development of an Agrarian Programme

Strictly speaking, the RSDLP did not have a programme until 1903, the date of its second Congress. The Party however split at this time into two groupings – Bolsheviks and Mensheviks – and as a consequence the political directives embodied in this programme were subjected to divergent interpretation. Furthermore, one of the central issues dividing the two factions came to be precisely the attitude to the peasantry, and thus the agrarian question itself became contested within Russian Social Democracy.

As has been argued above, it would be illegitimate to resolve this divergence by appeal to a higher authority able to legislate on, and identify, doctrinal purity and deviations therefrom. Equally, the use made by subsequent historians of a Bolshevik or Menshevik line (according to political taste) to organise the controversies in the period 1905–8 similarly obscures the political stakes involved and the manner in which specific arguments were constructed. In this chapter it will be argued that the problem of formulating political policy for a Social Democratic movement was one that had necessarily to be solved through a calculation of the possibilities presented by political and economic forces in Russia. Such a calculation could not simply be based on the elaboration of basic doctrines expounded by Marx and Engels, and it will be further suggested that 'Marxism' cannot in this way be treated as if it were a coherent project emanating from the pronouncements of its two major proponents. While the two wings of the RSDLP each claimed a monopoly on Marxist orthodoxy, the status of such claims cannot be resolved by a rationalist appraisal of their theoretical heritage. It must also be recognised that the Socialist Revolutionaries also espoused a form of Marxism, while during the 1905 Revolution a heterogeneous peasant socialist movement emerged which, while not expressing itself on matters of theory, found itself sharing similar policy positions to those of the Russian Marxists.

While it can be suggested that the Social Democrats were at least in agreement over the assumption that the peasantry were not about to disappear, dispute arose over their composition and the status of peasant action in the early stages of revolutionary activity in Russia. While both Mensheviks and Bolsheviks conceived revolutionary action in two broad phases – first the establishment of democratic institutions, and then on this basis the agitation for a socialist revolution – there was a difference over the roles ascribed to the peasantry in each phase. Initially, that is before 1905, the Mensheviks ruled out entirely the peasantry as a progressive political force and regarded them largely as a 'reactionary mass'. The Bolsheviks on the other hand, while conceiving the working class as the major force in revolutionary struggle, argued that such struggle would not succeed unless significant sections of the peasantry were drawn to support the workers through attacks on remnants of feudalism. The importance Lenin ascribed to this last point is indicated by the fact that his formative political years were spent in consideration of the 'peasant question', and a major part of his involvement in the drafting of the RSDLP programme dealt exclusively with the part that sections of the peasantry had to play in the coming revolution.

Lenin's early studies of the Russian economy had produced a detailed analysis of the class structure of the Russian countryside. But as suggested in the previous chapter, the narrative structure within which this economic identification took place inhibited a conversion to a political identification of social classes in specific conjunctures. Just as a Social Democratic agrarian programme could not be read out of an economic analysis of the peasantry (in which it might be thought sufficient for a Marxist to spot the proletariat among the mass of petty proprietors), so also was it impossible to convert DCR into a political manual. Without further investigation of political and social conditions it was not possible to produce a programme that was effective or realisable. The discussion that follows does not pretend to be a complete summary of the issues raised in the period 1884–1907 during debate among Russian Social Democrats of agrarian issues, for the purpose here is not to construct a historical narrative but to emphasise the political problems associated with Russian Social Democracy and the peasantry. It is however to be regretted that the only available published account of the material under consideration below is that supplied in sections of Carr's *History* Vols. 1 and 2.

It must be noted then that in the following pages only a relatively limited number of issues are raised. Prime among them is the nature of the political calculation necessary for the adequate formulation of a Party programme, and the distinction of such calculation from a simple identification of economic classes and forces. Secondly, the confrontation of demands for nationalisation and municipalisation in the period 1905–6 is highlighted as a means of distinguishing Bolshevik from Menshevik policy. The additional variant demand for *division* of land among the peasantry espoused at this time by sections of the Bolsheviks is not discussed, since this does not serve to isolate a factional difference. Finally, it should be noted that only limited use has been made of Lenin's *Agrarian Programme of Social Democracy in the First Russian Revolution 1905–7* which, while being a major (and neglected) text, could not be discussed in detail here without disturbing the limitations that have necessarily to be imposed.

As outlined in the previous chapter, the Emancipation of Labour Group was formed in 1883 with the objective of developing an organised working class movement which would make possible a struggle for the establishment of a constitutional monarchy. The drafting of a programme coincided with the formation of the Group, and the *Programme* published in Geneva succinctly formulated conceptions that were later elaborated in *Socialism and the Political Struggle*. This draft emphasises the complexity of the task facing socialists in a country characterised by the existence of a nascent capitalism and the vestiges of 'obsolescent patriarchal economy', a situation intensified by a consequent underdevelopment of the middle class, making it necessary for the working class to lead the struggle for political reforms. A series of reforms are proposed which are associated with the establishment of a democratic constitution; once achieved, such a constitution will enable a further development of revolutionary organisation and make possible the introduction of a series of economic demands which in general promote capitalist development.

This two-step conception of the coming struggle, the establishment of a democratic political order being the condition for the further development of economic reforms, places distinct social classes in different relations. The first stage consists of a socialist intelligentsia organising advanced sections of workers, and then together with them leading liberal elements in Russia in a struggle for political rights. The second stage introduces the peasantry as a political ally, for as we have seen it is argued that the nature of the peasant economy is such as to militate against its engagement in progressive and sustained struggles under conditions of an absolutist regime. This is stated clearly at the end of the draft programme:

> The Emancipation of Labour group *does not in the least ignore the peasantry, which constitutes an enormous portion of Russia's working population.* But it assumes that the work of the intelligentsia, especially under present-day conditions of political struggle, must be aimed first of all at the most developed part of the population, which consists of the industrial workers. Having secured the powerful support of this section, the socialist intelligentsia will have far greater hope of success in extending their activity to the peasantry as well, especially if they have by that time won freedom of agitation and propaganda.[1]

It is then immediately stated that this position would have to be amended in the event of an independent revolutionary force emerging from among the peasantry, but this reservation is of the nature of a qualification rather than a definite proposal. The immediate political struggle is to be one led by the socialist intelligentsia and the advanced sections of the working class. It is only on the achievement of democratic rights that the economic reforms, at whose head stands a proposal for a 'radical revision of our agrarian relations' (comprising measures aimed at freeing the peasantry from the burdens of the Emancipation), and which also conclude with a demand for state assistance to production associations,[2] can begin to be enacted.

A revised version of the draft was published in Geneva in 1888 under the title *Draft Programme of the Social Democrats*, and while the political and economic demands were virtually identical with those of the earlier version just outlined (the exception being the addition of a demand for universal state education) significant alterations were made in the preamble to the programme. Whereas the previous draft had viewed the peasantry essentially as a neutral force in the fight for democratic reforms, here they are postulated as reactionary and hostile to Social Democracy and its objectives. The post-reform conditions are held to have resulted in both a disintegration of the commune, and the survival of those aspects of it that bind the peasant to the state and enslave him to the rich. This form of attachment to the land blocks the political development of the peasantry and retains their perspective within the bounds of the village world, which is still essentially a patriarchal order. Consequently socialist demands, which would benefit them more directly than most other social groups, find hardly any support among them, and this 'political indifference and intellectual backwardness'[3] becomes defined as the 'main bulwark of absolutism'. So long as the peasantry are defined by liberals as 'the people', then the putting forward of 'popular' demands by the liberal bourgeoisie is confronted with popular indifference. The emergence of an industrial proletariat from the ruins of a village economy on the other hand makes possible the development of progressive agitation:

> Whereas the ideal of the village community member lies in the past, under conditions of patriarchal economy, the political complement of which was tsarist autocracy, the lot of the industrial worker can be improved only thanks to the development of the more modern and free forms of communal life.[4]

No mention is made in this draft of the possibility of an independent revolutionary movement among the peasantry, and further the condition of the allegiance of the peasantry to a revolutionary movement is that the workers adopt demands that are equally favourable to the peasants and the workers. The return of the Social Democrat worker to the village as agitator is the means by which the peasantry will be incorporated into a popular movement, and the working class is described as a force drawing the poor peasantry along in its wake.

This second draft therefore places the entire future of the revolutionary movement squarely on the shoulders of Social

Democratic workers, who are themselves responsible for the development of a peasant movement. This subordination of the peasantry, conceived as the passive recipients of a politics established elsewhere by industrial workers, and consequently as supporters rather than partners in revolutionary action, is one that is often held to characterise Marxism's general approach to the peasantry (cf. Mitrany). The alleged failure of Marxism in this respect is often ascribed to the fact that *Capital* is a work that deals only with industrial capitalism, and that in the absence of further guidance Marxists have since the nineteenth century persisted in transferring a model of class formation and organisation appropriate to the industrial working class unaltered to the peasantry. These arguments have been expounded and criticised in earlier chapters, and it can be seen on reflection here that to regard the position adopted toward the peasantry in the 1888 programme as a result of transferring a general model of capitalist development to the Russian countryside would be quite erroneous. In this second draft the peasantry are 'written off' as a revolutionary force in the coming political struggle because of the character of political and economic forces in Russia, in particular the role of the Tsärist autocracy in perpetuating peasant institutions under the terms of the Emancipation. The subordination of the peasantry, indeed the conception of the peasantry as a single hostile mass, is open to revision provided that an alternative account is provided of the structure of the peasant economy. Lenin's work in the 1890s went some way to effecting this, and at the end of 1899 he produced 'A Draft Programme of our Party' the bulk of which addressed itself to the peasant question and the draft produced by the Emancipation of Labour Group.

Lenin was to play a central role in the construction of a Social Democratic agrarian policy, for the Russian Social Democratic Labour Party did not in fact have a programme until its Second Congress in 1903. While the party had been formally constituted in 1898, it never discussed a programme and in fact gave the task of drawing up a statement to Struve, who some months later produced a Manifesto with a series of organisational points appended.[5] The arrest and dispersion of those who attended the First Congress within weeks of its meeting meant that further work in the Party devolved upon others, in particular the *Iskra* group, and it was in fact the editorial board of this newspaper that produced the only programme to be discussed at the Second Congress.

The Emancipation of Labour Group's draft thus remained the only basis for the construction of a programme until shortly before the Second Congress, and this can be seen from two of Lenin's early outlines of a programme for Social Democracy,[6] which substantially repeat and enlarge on the 1888 draft, although the hostile line on the peasantry is moderated. In the more detailed 'Draft Programme of our Party' (1899) he explicitly declares that this draft should be made the basis for a Russian Social Democratic programme, subject only to editorial changes, corrections and detailed amendments.[7] The promulgation of such a programme is vital to the development of the party, argues Lenin, for it is only on such a basis that the objectives of Social Democracy can be clarified, unity be given to agitational work, and the extent of the divisions within the party be assessed. In altering the Emancipation of Labour draft, he proposes that it should be brought closer to the Erfurt programme, since in Russia the same basic form of capitalist development, and the same basic tasks, face socialists in Russia and in Germany. There are however features specific to Russia which must find full expression in the programme: the political tasks and means of struggle, the struggle against pre-capitalist remnants 'and the specific posing of the *peasant* question arising out of that struggle'.[8] The bulk of Lenin's commentary on the earlier draft in fact takes the form of a re-examination of its agrarian components, and the development of an alternative which was to dominate the relation of Social Democracy to the peasant question until 1905.

The burden of the revisions that Lenin proposed with respect to the peasant question was to reject the conception of the peasantry as a reactionary mass which was the 'bulwark of absolutism', and identify feudal remnants as the objective of progressive agrarian agitation. Lenin's earlier economic studies had led him to view the 'peasantry' as a differentiated ensemble of relations, and he often used inverted commas in this way when forced to discuss the peasantry as a bloc, disassociating himself from both Narodnik tendencies and Plekhanov's approach.

But in the case we are discussing here, Lenin instead turned to Marx for justification of his rejection of peasantry-as-reactionary-mass, citing the comments on the duality of the peasantry from the *Eighteenth Brumaire*. On this basis, Lenin argued, the working class had to support the revolutionary side of the peasantry, while seeking to separate out elements as a political force against the reactionary side. The basis of the proposed alliance was formulated thus:

> the working-class party should inscribe on its banner *support* for the peasantry (*not by any means* as a class of small proprietors or small farmers), *insofar as the peasantry is capable of a revolutionary struggle against the survivals of serfdom in general and against the autocracy in particular*.[9]

The question that then arose, argued Lenin, was how to formulate proposals in such a fashion that they did not degenerate into a defence of petty proprietorship, and to establish if significant sections of the peasantry were in fact capable of revolutionary struggle against feudal remnants and absolutism.

The latter point was seen as confirmed by the constant unrest among the peasantry, which while of a restricted nature did indicate that some revolutionary elements existed.[10] However, Lenin then emphasised that the only thing that follows from such a consideration is that to make the peasantry the vehicle of a revolutionary movement, and to therefore make the revolutionary nature of this movement conditional upon the mood of the peasantry, would be utterly misguided. Demands had to be constructed that would enable a progressive movement to be formed among the peasantry that could ally itself with Social Democracy, and these demands, unlike those of liberals and others, did not seek to defend peasant property directly through various state measures. Instead, Social Democracy in Russia should make a series of demands aimed at the removal of the feudal burden from the countryside, demands that would find the widest possible reception without at the same time compromising the political principles of a workers' party. Accordingly it was proposed that the vague formula of the 1888 draft concerning a 'radical revision of agrarian relations' be replaced with a number of points, such as the abrogation of land redemption and quit rent payments, the return to the peasantry of redemption payments made to state and nobility, the abolition of collective liability and of laws hampering the free disposition of land, and the abolition of relations perpetuating the feudal dependence of the peasant on the landlord.[11]

The propositions put forward here had two main aims: the abolition of feudal relations in the countryside, and the promotion of a class character in the struggles proceeding in the countryside. This last point is of major importance in evaluating Lenin's proposals, and as we shall see represents the significant political difference between his proposals and those of objectors at the Second Congress. While this critique of the Emancipation of Labour draft was not published at the time, the principles that it embodies were contained in an article published in *Iskra* early in 1901 entitled 'The Workers Party and the Peasantry'.[12] Lenin's outline thus became the official *Iskra* proposal on the agrarian question, and while it was Plekhanov who drafted the theoretical part of the *Iskra* programme, the extensive comments that Lenin made in criticism of this led to major modifications in the light of his position.

Plekhanov did not produce his long-awaited draft until late 1901, and Lenin's reaction was to first of all criticise the piece in detail and then produce a draft of his own. The 'practical' part of the programme was drafted by the *Iskra* Board together, and these with one or two alterations embodied the proposals that Lenin had made in his criticism of the 1888 draft. Significantly, one of the few alterations that Lenin wished to be made was that the preamble to the proposals should have inserted into it the phrase 'for the purpose of facilitating the free development of the class struggle in the countryside' after 'With the object of eradicating the remnants of the old serf-owning system'.[13] This objective of attacking feudal remnants was conditioned for Lenin by the effects which such action would have on the development of class forces in the countryside, not by the social or economic requirements of the peasantry as a mass.

That the peasantry were no longer a mass was repeatedly argued by Lenin; but when confronted with the remnants of the serf-owning system and its consequences the peasantry became united as a class, since they were all oppressed by it in some way. Lined up in this way against the remnants of a feudal order, the aspirations of the peasantry as a class coincided with those of the emergent rural proletariat. The question of 'feudal remnants' became in the *Iskra* draft summarised in the demand for the return of the lands 'cut-off' from peasant holdings by the landlords under the settlement of 1861. This did not mean that a promotion of peasant property was being proposed, but that the physical existence of these pieces of land as symbols of a feudal order and of peasant poverty made them objects around which a united struggle could be formed. To go beyond this demand, to a demand for the expropriation of landlord's land *in general*, would result in a division of the peasantry into opposing fractions, and in particular would decisively introduce a division between landed and landless peasants. The return of the cut-offs, argued Lenin, represented the maximum demand for the peasantry as a class. To demand land nationalisation, as some critics of the draft later did, was to misunderstand the fundamentally *political* nature of the calculation embodied in the draft. Lenin admitted that if, after the smashing of the feudal order, democratic institutions were created within a constitutional democracy, then land nationalisation might be a possible demand for a Social Democratic programme, but in the absence of such institutions such a proposal was simply divisive.[14]

Maslov published in mid-1903 a pamphlet criticising the agrarian elements of the *Iskra* draft, shortly before the Second Congress later in the summer. He questioned the pertinence of a demand for the return of cut-off lands in the destruction of feudal relations, arguing that such a demand was transparently no solution to the problems faced by large sections of the peasantry. As we have noted above, Maslov identified over-population as the critical problem of the Russian economy, and since this can never be an absolute problem, what he actually meant was that a general shortage of land confronted the bulk of the population. This shortage of land was only in part a direct creation of the Emancipation settlement, and was ameliorated by the growth of forms of renting, which however only perpetuated feudal relations. This burden would be little affected by the return of the cut-offs, and he then proceeded on the basis of some dubious examples to demonstrate that no relation existed in general between labour renting on the one hand and the persistence of cut-offs on the other.[15] Not only was there no connection between the burdens on the peasantry and the cut-offs in the way that Lenin had suggested, argued Maslov: the return of the cut-offs would in fact worsen the situation, since the number of small peasants dependent on landlords would increase, promoting an intensification of feudal relations.

These criticisms were rejected by Lenin in his 'Reply to Criticism of Our Draft Programme', where he also indicated the contradictions in the pamphlet produced by Maslov. The political nature of the objective outlined in the *Iskra* were re-emphasised, objectives designed not to improve the welfare of peasant farmers but rather to facilitate political development in rural areas:

> The whole essence of our agrarian programme is that the rural proletariat must fight together with the rich peasantry for the abolition of the remnants of serfdom, for the cut-off lands. Anyone who examines this proposition closely will grasp the incorrectness, the *irrelevance* and illogicality of an objection such as: why *only* cut-off lands, if that is not enough. Because *together with the rich peasantry* the proletariat *will be unable* to go, and must not go, beyond the abolition of serfdom, beyond restitution of the cut-off lands, etc. *Beyond that*, that proletariat in general and the rural proletariat in particular will march alone; not together with the 'peasantry', not together with the rich peasant, but *against him*. The reason we do not go beyond the demand for the cut-off lands is not because we do not wish the peasant well or because we are afraid of scaring the bourgeoisie, but because we do not want the rural proletarian to help the rich peasant *more than is necessary*, more than is essential to the proletariat.[16]

Social Democratic politics are for Lenin based on the proletariat, or more precisely the most advanced sections of the proletariat. In Russia, as in all other instances, the proletariat cannot however rely on its own forces to achieve its objectives, and therefore it is necessary in political struggles to seek alliances which either increase the forces at its disposal or decrease the forces opposed to it. Russian Social Democracy conceived the immediate objective of its agitation the achievement of a constitutional democracy, which would in turn provide the basis for the further and open struggle of revolutionary forces. This immediate objective could however involve other political tendencies, such as progressive liberals, and other sections of the population, such as the peasantry. The development of an agrarian programme was therefore firmly situated in the principles of Social Democracy and in the analysis of the development of Russian capitalism that Lenin had undertaken in the 1890s. The fragmented nature of the Russian peasantry that Lenin had identified provided the basis for the identification of differentiated forces. But the simple existence of these different (economic) fractions did not provide Lenin with a simple index of class interests and political forces through the ascription to each fraction of an economic essence and a consequent political tendency. On the contrary, the basis of the calculation that led to the proposition that the return of cut-off lands should be the centre of Social Democratic politics with respect to the peasantry was an evaluation of the relation between the fractions identified and the forces that this relation gave rise to. It was consequently possible to establish a policy that was conditional on a particular balance of forces and a particular theoretical analysis. Just as the 'peasantry in general' did not exist for Lenin, so neither did the 'political future in general'.

This was reaffirmed during the Second Congress, where in particular Martynov made objections to the question of the cut-off lands contained in the *Iskra* programme, proposing that they represented a false historical approach to the problem of the feudal remnants, and that land supporting serf-bondage ought to be alienated no matter what its mode of acquisition.[17] This form of criticism in many ways recapitulated that made by Maslov, and was subjected in the debates to the same rebuttal: cut-off lands are the sign of the feudal economy, and the purpose of demanding their restoration of their former holders was to unite the peasantry against the landlords and to divide the rural proletariat from the rural bourgeoisie. To demand that other land be alienated was to confuse the question of the economic viability of peasant farming with the political problem of an alliance with sections of the peasantry.

While the RSDLP was preparing for its Second Congress another party, which was to challenge Social Democracy in the leadership of peasant action, was in the process of formation and it also proposed a different theoretical analysis, based on Marx's work, of the class forces in the countryside. Notwithstanding the abuse heaped on the Socialist Revolutionary Party by Lenin in articles published in *Iskra* during 1902 and 1903, the leadership of this avowedly neo-Narodnik organisation attempted to provide a coherent Marxist analysis of the peasantry and the tasks facing revolutionaries in the countryside. By the time of the Second Congress, the Socialist Revolutionaries were judged a serious enough threat to the work of the RSDLP to warrant a separate resolution, proposing that the 'Socialist Revolutionaries' are nothing more than a bourgeois-democratic faction and that the Social-Democrats can in principle have no different an attitude toward them than toward liberal representatives of the bourgeoisie generally.[18]

In the period before the 1905 revolution the SRs were conceived as one of the major adversaries of Social Democrat politics, and were viewed by Social Democracy as effectively seeking to realise in political organisation the peasantist deviations that had developed in German revisionism. However, a definite pro-peasant policy was only adopted by the currents that came together to form the SRs in 1902; previous to this one of their principal political characteristics was the advocacy of revolutionary terror. This remained a constant element in SR circles, and it was perhaps this that gave rise to Lenin's wrath more than anything else, and tended in his published criticism to overshadow the theoretical differences that also existed between the two parties.

Here we are concerned only with those points of difference that are relevant to a discussion of agrarian policy, although of course this was central to the SR party as an organisation that became identified with the aspirations of the masses of the peasantry. While in this way a certain link can be traced to the more traditional Populist traditions (hence the label 'neo-Narodnik'), it should not be thought that the SRs simply represented an organisational realisation of classical Populist ideology. In contrast to one of the leading principles of nineteenth-century Populist writers, the SR leader Chernov argued that since 1861 Russia had been treading a capitalist path; far from denying therefore the impact of capitalism on the peasantry, the capitalist transformation of the countryside was regarded as an established fact. From this view there followed a rejection of the emphasis placed by the Social Democrats on the possibility of an alliance of workers and peasants in a bourgeois revolution; according to the SR analysis, this revolution occurred in 1861.[19]

A more certain connection with the older tradition of Russian revolutionary thought was to be found in the SR view of the commune as an expression of the basically egalitarian nature of the Russian peasantry, a nature which was also demonstrated in the form assumed by rural unrest. The commune therefore became an institution whose defence was vital for the success of a socialist transformation, any threats to its existence necessarily undermining at the same time the basis of political advance. The Social Democrat demands for rights of free exit from the commune and free disposal of land were therefore regarded as hostile to the peasantry and the prospects of revolutionary change. The SRs proposed that the task of socialist organisation was to *conserve* and *direct* this already-existing peasant socialist consciousness, and two main tasks were identified for the SR party in particular: firstly, the preservation of this peasant consciousness through the dissemination of propaganda revealing the ulterior motives of any government reforms that might be introduced to forestall peasant unrest; and secondly, the provision of leadership to peasant risings which, while expressive of a socialist consciousness, were potentially anarchic in nature. The instrument of this work was a bi-partite programme, divided into maximum and minimum sections, the former demanding the socialisation of production, and the latter the socialisation of the land.

To whom were such demands addressed? While the 'broad masses of the peasantry' were described as the initial sphere of agitation, effective work among the peasantry was conceived as depending on the creation of a peasant intelligentsia, since there was a general hostility among the peasantry to the urban intelligentsia. In fact in the years before 1905 agitation was often carried out by figures such as village teachers or medical assistants who were from the SR point of view ideally placed to distribute literature without becoming identified with 'urban agitators'. At this time the party was primarily composed of small groups of intelligentsia and students, and it was only during 1905–6 that membership of the party expanded beyond this social basis. In such conditions, where peasant cadres emerged they were usually the more prosperous elements, and these adopted the demands for reform more enthusiastically then any other section. Perrie suggests that this was because such peasants encountered difficulties in attempting to develop their holdings without being overwhelmed by the 'collective' responsibility of taxes. Their position in the commune therefore brought them into conflict with local authorities, and they had most to gain in the short run from the elimination of the burdens of the Emancipation settlement. Such adherents were however treated with caution by the SRs, and this tacit recognition of actual differences within the mass of the peasantry was dealt with by the elaboration of a model of class distinction based on source of income.[20]

Chernov argued in a series of articles in the SR newspaper that class position was determined by the relation to the means of distribution, not by the relation to the means of production (as argued by the Social Democrats). This was justified by reference to the unfinished last chapter on classes in *Capital* Vol. III, where Marx had added the landlord class to those of capitalist and proletariat in constituting the 'three classes of capitalist society'. These three classes were distinguished primarily, argued Chernov, by their relation to a source of income: in this case, rent, profit and wages respectively. From this was deduced a fundamental distinction between *two* forms of revenue flow: that deriving from productive labour, and that deriving from unproductive labour. The working class was then defined as those agents who received their income from their own productive labour, either through wages or independent activity. The bourgeoisie were those who lived through the exploitation of others. This had two major consequences: first, the ownership of the means of production by a small producer did not automatically make him part of the bourgeoisie. Second, small peasant producers, the rural and the urban proletariat were all part of the exploited working class. As Haimson points out, this is a reversal of the traditional Narodnik argument: whereas for the Narodniks all workers were really peasants, the SRs developed a class analysis that involved the assumption that most peasants were really workers.[21]

Accordingly, the peasantry are divided into two main groups, the first of which consists of two sub-groups:

1. working peasantry, *exploiting their own labour*
    i. agricultural proletariat, living by the sale of their own labour and in general deprived of the means of production
    ii. independent producers, in general living from the application of their labour to their own means of production, whether possessed communally, individually or through renting
2. middle and petty rural bourgeoisie, *exploiting the labour of others.*[22]

In this schema the possession of means of production does not form the basis on which two groups are opposed, those with and those without means of production. Instead, the critical distinction on which class formation turns is held to be one which separates capital and labour (assuming that means of production do not necessarily take a commodity form and are thus not necessarily capital). The working peasantry are consequently aligned with an industrial proletariat as 'exploiters of their own labours', and on this basis share common interests with them. There is no need for socialists to wait until the working peasantry is proletarianised, which was an attitude the SRs ascribed to the Social Democrats; the potential for an alliance of workers and peasants is regarded as fully developed, remaining only to be politically exploited. Further, any delay in this would be fatal, since contrary to the Social Democrats, the SRs conceived the impact of capitalism on agricultural production as almost entirely destructive in its effects.[23] This appreciation of capitalism and the peasantry differed considerably from that espoused by Social Democracy, and this difference could not simply be attributed to their 'revision' of Marxian class analysis. For the SRs, capitalist development in the countryside was not a process which gave rise to social and political forces to which guidance had to be given if revolutionary change was to be a possibility; on the contrary, these social and political forces had to be *reversed* by the popular action of all but the rich peasantry. Social Democracy's conception of a conditional alliance between sections of the peasantry and the working class around specific issues vanishes entirely; instead, according to the SRs these groups belong to the same class, are therefore possessed of common interests, and therefore are to be treated as a unitary political agency. The politics of class alliance, central to Social Democracy, are displaced by an analysis that deposits all revolutionary forces willy-nilly into one united class opposed to the bourgeoisie. Chernov referred to the *Communist Manifesto* for his authority in creating this image of class polarisation, but in reality such an image is a parody of the *Manifesto*'s account of the lengthy process of class differentiation and fragmentation which leads to the confrontation of workers and bourgeoisie. For the SRs, this history of class struggles meets its counterpart in Russia in the form of the Emancipation settlement. Capitalism originates in Russia with the promulgation of a decree, and furthermore is at the moment of its birth already mature.

Lenin's article 'Revolutionary Adventurism' (1902) devoted most of its critique of the Socialist Revolutionaries to the reactionary nature of their espousal of revolutionary terrorism, and little attention was paid to the theoretical principles being developed by Chernov and others. Two major problems are highlighted in this article: firstly, the idea that the spontaneous demands of the peasants are 'semi-socialistic' is argued to misrepresent the actual nature of the confrontation between bourgeoisie and proletariat in the countryside, a confrontation which if simply left to run its course would eventuate in the establishment of a bourgeois order, not a socialist one. Secondly, and related to this error concerning the actual nature of the rural class struggle, it is suggested that the SR treatment of a future redistribution of landlords' land among the peasantry as involving essentially a transfer from 'capital to labour' fails to comprehend the reality of such a transfer as one that would take place between semi-feudal landlords on the one hand, and a rural bourgeoisie on the other.[24]

As we have seen, both these conceptions were based on a specific analysis of Russian relations, but for Lenin the important point is not simply to demonstrate the theoretical weakness of such positions, or their heretical nature with respect to a Marxism invoked as a final authority. What is important about such propositions for Lenin is that despite the 'peasantist' line followed by the SRs, the policies that they advocate would result in a strengthening of the bourgeoisie and the disorganisation of the rural proletariat. The policies adopted by the SRs would not promote socialist politics; despite their apparently revolutionary nature, they were in effect supportive of liberal reformist policies.[25]

Lenin therefore evaluated the politics of the SRs not through a consideration of the class composition of its membership, nor through a demonstration of the manner in which they had reorganised Marxism. While he did criticise them for Narodism and the adoption of a revisionist version of Marxism, the motivation of such polemics was his defence of a political line whose implementation would be hampered if SR conceptions gained wide acceptance. He accordingly evaluated their politics in terms of *the conditions necessary for the realisation of their political objectives, and the consequences that would follow from such realisation.* They were of course denounced for various political and theoretical sins, but these were treated only as indices of the basic error embodied in the policy that they followed. As can be seen from the resolution adopted at the Second Congress cited above, the problem as conceived by the RSDLP was not that the SRs had revised Marxism, but that the proposals that they made on the basis of this revision supported the formation of a rural economy no different in character to that dreamed of by right-wing liberals. The failure of the SRs to produce an adequate analysis of the impact of capitalist relations on the Russian countryside led them to advocate policies which were in principle unrealisable; any attempt to implement them would in fact lead to results far removed from those envisaged, results which would themselves be condemned by the SRs. The decisive distinction between the analysis of the SRs and that of the Social Democrats is therefore to be found here, and should not be conceived as a matter concerning the theoretical legitimacy (however established) of the Marxism embraced by each.

In retrospect, that is from the standpoint of the revolutionary movement that developed among the peasantry and workers in 1905, the principal limitations of the 1903 Social Democratic programme can be traced to its hesitancy concerning the actual potential for action by the peasantry. In the absence then of widespread peasant unrest, the demand for the return of the cut-off lands became the leading element in Social Democratic agrarian politics because of its materiality as sign of the feudal economy. The elevation of the demand as an agitational device was justified by the argument that it represented the maximum that could be achieved by the peasantry as a mass against the landlords. Once the peasantry were in motion, however, the possibility of a demand for some form of nationalisation was not ruled out by the Bolsheviks.

1905 saw the peasantry in motion, in most respects as a body, and immediately the actions of the participants in uprisings went far beyond the schema envisaged in the programme of the RSDLP. Perrie calculates that seventy-five per cent of recorded instances of unrest involved confrontations between peasants and landed gentry, and the most vigorous of these attacks occurred in the Black Earth region, against the estates of the landowners.[26] In these cases, where the action involved the seizure of estate land (i.e. going beyond the simple repossession of the cut-offs), the land was not taken over in the name of 'the people', but was simply absorbed into commune land. Since this was the only collective agency that could administer that which was collectively appropriated this was only to be expected – but it would be wrong to simply argue that this demonstrates the persistence of a collective consciousness on the part of the peasants. As we have seen above, it was in the commune that differences between households developed, and while communes participated *en masse* in seizures, the rich peasants had certain advantages in making use of land so acquired. Furthermore, the rich peasants had carts and labourers to engage in illicit woodcutting, or stock that could be grazed on seized land; action by the poor peasants was more likely to take the form of rent strikes or boycotts.[27]

The rapid development of this movement was considered at the Third Congress of the RSDLP which was called by the Bolsheviks in April 1905. Discussion of agrarian policy led to a reassessment of the 1903 programme, in which the central place ascribed to action against the cut-offs was abandoned, while emphasis was placed on the creation of peasant committees as the means for the translation of economic struggles into political ones. In the 1903 programme such committees had been conceived as the means of execution of progressive reforms, but now they were to be posed as the political organs for the implementation of democratic reform.[28] The question that then arose in the arguments that followed was how far this involved a modification of the 1903 programme, and whether any other alterations ought to be made to it. In the event the party adopted a proposal for municipalisation in the resolutions of the 1906 Unity Congress, which involved a defeat for the arguments put forward by Lenin. The events and problems that made up this period were examined in detail then by Lenin in his *Agrarian Programme of Social Democracy in the First Russian Revolution 1905–1907*, but before discussing this, it will perhaps be useful to outline some of the points raised through the Revolution of 1905.

Lenin's newspaper article 'The Proletariat and the Peasantry',[29] which was published in March 1905, notes the development of peasant risings in the countryside, and poses the question of the appropriate attitude of the working class to such action. Re-establishing the tenet of the 1903 programme – first with the peasant bourgeoisie against serfdom, then with the rural proletariat against the peasant bourgeoise – Lenin warns that unlike parties such as the SRs, the Social Democrat Party cannot indulge in utopian demands, since its analysis of the class differentiation in the countryside leads it to view the composition of forces in the present struggles as complex. Proposing a draft resolution for the coming Congress, it is urged that the RSDLP should support revolutionary action among the peasantry, and in particular call for the establishment of revolutionary peasant committees that will support democratic reforms. No reference is made to the previous programme of the RSDLP, and indeed the call for independent committees among workers and peasants is one of the major points that Lenin repeatedly makes in his writing during the early part of 1905.

In addition to this, no specific demands are ascribed to such committees for, as Lenin stresses, to do so would be to fall prey to the error of 'project-mongering'. This is the error committed by the SRs when supporting peasant action with calls for nationalisation, for such slogans simply express valueless political projects without specifying how they could be achieved. In the circumstances prevailing in 1905 before the Third Congress, Lenin argued that it would be incorrect to advocate a specific set of reforms, for all that is on the agenda are political reforms which if attained (with the aid of a peasantry organised through its committees) would only then provide the basis for the drafting of economic reform. The abandoning of the 'cut-offs' as the central element of Social Democratic demands is in line with such an argument, for not only have the peasantry already gone beyond this demand, but such a slogan also directs attention to specific reforms that will only be relevant after the attainment of democratic reforms.[30]

A further problem with the SRs demand for nationalisation was identified as its failure to come to terms with the outcome of the contemporary peasant movement. As we have seen, the transfer of land from the land-owners to the peasantry was conceived by the SRs as a transfer of land 'from capital to labour', erroneously identifying the peasant petty-bourgeoisie who were the recipients of the land with the peasantry as a whole. The achievement of democratic reforms under a constitutional order would not, as the SRs assumed, herald a period of socialist harmony, but on the contrary according to Lenin would be characterised by a new period of struggle under changed conditions.[31] As we shall see, these arguments against nationalisation as a general slogan were to be taken up by Plekhanov, who steadfastly opposed nationalisation of any sort on different grounds, and which enabled him on the other hand to advocate municipalisation.[32]

Clearly the developments of a comparatively unified movement among the peasantry in 1905 directed against landlord estates implied that some errors had been made in the assessment of the economic forces operating in the countryside. Lenin was nevertheless correct in identifying the remnants of the serfdom system as the target of peasant action, as the intensity of outbreaks in the Black Earth region showed. However, these 'feudal remnants' were not specifically the cut-off lands, but the gentry estates as a whole. In the *Development of Capitalism in Russia*, Lenin had argued that capitalist relations were rapidly coming to dominate large landed estates through their reliance on bonded wage labour. The contradictions involved in the retention of such relations of servitude led eventually, Lenin had argued, to the displacement of the feudal aspects of the estates and the evolution of such enterprises on a 'Junker' path to capitalism. The manner in which capitalist relations in *Development* were simply identified and then argued to be autonomous non-divertible forces led Lenin to discount large estates in general as promoters of feudalism, and identify the cut-off lands as such. The outbreaks of 1905 demonstrated that this ascription of autonomous power to capitalist relations in agriculture had led to a serious overestimation of the level of development of Russian capitalism.[33]

This was first openly admitted by Lenin in his pamphlet *Revision of the Agrarian Programme of the Worker's Party* published shortly before the Third Congress. He suggested here that the big landed estate in Russia rested not on a capitalist system, but rather on a system of feudal bondage.[34] To oppose confiscation and parcellisation of such estates (as some Social Democrats, among them Plekhanov, did) was to ignore this fact. As long as the estates were conceived as capitalist enterprises it could be argued that such action would be reactionary, an obstacle to the free development of Russian capitalism. If on the other hand such estates were treated as more feudal than capitalist, it would be quite legitimate for Social Democracy to support peasant action aimed at division or confiscation, for under the terms of the 1903 programme this would be in itself progressive.

In this way the general line of the 1903 programme was preserved, while its specific resolutions were altered. The cut-offs had been identified as the support of the feudal economy, and therefore a legitimate object of progressive peasant action as a mass. 1905 had demonstrated that the basis on which the cut-offs had been so identified was incorrect, but all that was necessary was to alter the description of the support of feudal economy. The landed estates thus replaced the cut-offs in Lenin's designation of the maximum limit of mass action by the peasantry:

> The only stand Social–Democrats can take on the agrarian question at the present time, when the issue is one of carrying the democratic revolution to its conclusion, is the following: against landlord ownership and for peasant ownership, if private ownership of land is to exist at all. Against private ownership of land and for nationalisation of the land *in definite political circumstances.*[35]

These 'definite political circumstances' were related to the successful achievement of democratic reforms and the destruction of the Russian police state. The failure to specify such conditions was the primary reason for Lenin's attack on Maslov's proposals for municipalisation in later sections of this pamphlet. Such proposals, seeking to bypass the reactionary nature of the central state form by vesting land in democratic local assemblies, succeeded neither in providing the present movement with a suitable slogan, nor effectively indicating the measures necessary once a democratic republic had been formed. The Bolsheviks as a whole rejected such proposals, but Lenin was defeated at the Unity Congress and saw the RSDLP adopt essentially Menshevik positions on the agrarian question.

What exactly was this position, if it differed from the letter of the 1903 programme? Like the Bolsheviks, Menshevik theoreticians had been quick to abandon the demand for the restitution of the cut-offs when faced with a movement that went far beyond such a demand, but they did not adopt the proposal advanced by the Bolsheviks (and included in the resolutions of the Third Congress) concerning the central role of peasant committees as a political device and adequate slogan. While expressing general support for the peasant movement at its own Conference following the Third Congress, the concrete proposals ran thus:

... social democracy supports any attempts by the peasantry at forcible seizure of the land, explaining to the peasantry that its conquests in the struggle with the landowners can be firmly secured only by a freely elected national constituent assembly which must be required to form, on a democratic basis, special committees (peasant committees) which will bring about the final elimination of the old rural regulations which are so oppressive for the peasantry.[36]

Note here that the peasant committees are bodies derivative of a national assembly, and are conditional on the formation of such a democratic body. The work of Social Democrats in the countryside is thus restricted to encouraging peasants to agitate for a constituent assembly to secure their appropriated land, but without indicating the necessity for local committees as vehicles for such agitation. As we have seen, Lenin conceived the peasant committees not as the simple executors of reform, but as the condition for the development of the peasantry as a political force. Without such democratic organisations the peasantry could not exist as a political force in the agitation for democratic reform of the state, and the Menshevik position consequently demobilised any possibility of a worker-peasant alliance. *Such an alliance does not exist between classes or their fractions, but only in specific agencies, such as parties, committees, assemblies, and policy formation together with its modes of execution.*

In addition to this, what the Menshevik programme also neglected was the importance of the *manner* in which a reform is carried out. Lenin in his criticism of the Liberal proposals had argued that while many of the basic reforms proposed by them resembled Social Democratic demands, basic differences existed at the level of the objective and means by which this objective was realised. The Liberals in general sought to re-establish order in the countryside through the introduction of a number of reforms that would split the peasantry and bring the rural bourgeoisie over to the support of the landlords. This was to be achieved through the introduction of a number of reforms enacted in a fashion after that proposed by the Mensheviks.[37] This *granting* of restricted reforms by a central authority, rather than the making and enactment of reforms by peasant organisations, had major implications for the character of the reform in general. The existence of peasant organisations, and the slogan to this end, was, Lenin argued, crucial for Social Democratic policies.

The importance of such considerations was recognised by the Unity Congress of the RSDLP, although the advocacy of peasant committees was confined to the resolution 'On the Attitude Toward the Peasant Movement'. The new Agrarian Programme was dominated by demands for municipalisation, tempered only by a 'Tactical Resolution on the Agrarian Question' that made provision for a policy of division of the estates should conditions be unfavourable for the transfer of confiscated lands to organs of local self-government.[38] Lenin's 'Speech in Reply to the Debate on the Agrarian Question' at the Unity Congress therefore concentrated on combating the trend toward the inclusion of municipalisation as a major element of the RSDLP programme which became manifest in the course of the Congress, a struggle which he was to lose. His argument was twofold: first, the peasants would never agree to municipalisation; and second, without the establishment of democratic institutions municipalisation would be politically retrograde.

The proponents of municipalisation rejected nationalisation of the land as a viable demand, Plekhanov declaring that Social Democracy could 'not in any circumstances' support such a measure.[39] Such an unconditional statement was indicative of the 'principled' nature of the Menshevik line, for in declaring principles in this manner Plekhanov necessarily ignored the nature of the conditions which led him to regard such a demand as unworkable, and treated them as immutable. As Lenin pointed out, if a democratic republic was formed, political conditions would radically alter and might make nationalisation workable. What Plekhanov sought was a guarantee that any reforms in landholding could be secured against all future circumstances; nationalisation of the land would make a restoration of Tsarist autocracy too easy, and he therefore opposed such a measure. Lenin argued that no guarantees could be given, the only guarantee that would fill the bill was a revolution in the West, and this was hardly under the control of the RSDLP. Such a guarantee could not therefore be supplied, although some security could be introduced against the possibility of a restoration by utilising peasant committees as 'levers of change', for without a political revolution agrarian reform would not be possible.

In this context, Lenin argued, the demand for municipalisation diverted and obscured the central issue, which was the removal of the serf-owning system and its political conditions of existence through the establishment of a democratic constitutional state. To concentrate on the transfer of land to local assemblies as the principal element of a Social Democratic agrarian programme, without there being any indication of the manner in which land would be distributed, diverted the attention of the peasantry from the fact that their aspirations could only be developed in a different kind of state political order. If the Congress rejected nationalisation, Lenin argued

> you will cause our practical workers, our propagandists and agitators, to make the same mistakes as we brought about by our mistaken demand for restoration of the cut-off lands in our programme of 1903. Just as our demand for the restitution of the cut-off lands was interpreted in a narrower sense than it was meant by its authors, so now rejection of nationalisation and its replacement by the demand for division, to say nothing of the utterly confused demand for municipalisation, will inevitably lead to so many mistakes by our practical workers, our propagandists and agitators, that very soon we shall regret having adopted the 'division' or the municipalisation programme.[40]

As we have noted above, the Congress finally resolved to adopt the last of these alternatives, advocating in its programme that estate, crown and monastic lands should be handed over to local authorities for their disposition. This was to remain RSDLP policy until 1917, when the further eruption of the peasant movement was to lead to its being set aside.

Lenin's response to this defeat was to write a review of the issues concerned late in 1907 under the title *The Agrarian Programme of Social-Democracy in the First Russian Revolution 1905-1907*, which by virtue of it's being a reflection on the problems of a politically turbulent period provides a rich source for the assessment of Lenin's form of argument and analysis. The first chapter is devoted to a résumé of the progress of differentiation in the countryside and as such forms a *re-assessment* of the economy based on the latest statistics.[41] Material concerning the distribution of allotment land, and of horses, is considered, in an

## THE DEVELOPMENT OF AN AGRARIAN PROGRAMME 231

attempt to arrive at an estimation of the conditions of the peasantry and thus replace the 'tendency' analysis of *Development of Capitalism in Russia*. Subsequent chapters examine the theoretical principles involved in the debate between proponents of nationalisation and municipalisation of land, a general review of positions adopted on the agrarian question by Social Democracy, and finally an investigation of the policies pursued by the various parties in the Second Duma which is notable for the manner in which it dispenses with the apparently 'orthodox' Marxist reduction of the policy of a party to the class interests of its members and supporters.

As we have shown, *Development of Capitalism in Russia* had identified two paths of capitalist evolution for Russian agriculture, that of the landlord economy and that of the peasant economy. These two alternatives are there held to exhaust the possibilities present in the Russian economy; any analysis that does not recognise this is, according to Lenin, necessarily condemned to utopianism. By 1907 however these broad alternatives have altered their character: unless the peasantry took action to break up the feudal estates and convert them into peasant property then the future of Russian farming would be dictated by the landlord economy. Lenin describes these respectively as the American and Prussian roads. In 1899 the possibility was identified of the peasant economy gradually ousting the landlord economy through the economic collapse of the landlord class. By 1907, this possibility has waned and only one reformist path is viable: that of the landlord economy.

Corresponding to these two paths, there are two sets of programmes. There is the Stolypin programme, which is supported by the Right landlords and the Octobrists and which can be described as a landlord's programme. The Liberals also support this line in calling for redemption payments and the preservation of landlords' estates. The spokesmen of the peasantry (Trudoviks, some SRs) on the other hand defend a line of the peasantry against the landlords.[42] The line between right and left policies runs between the Cadets and the Trudoviks, and the policy of the Cadets is to attempt to win the Trudoviks over to their side.

Having set out the alternatives in this manner, Lenin turns to an examination of the programmes put forward by Social Democracy, beginning with the programme of 1885. The principal problem with this, conditioned by its appearance as a manifesto rather than a programme of an existing party, is that the economic basis of the 'radical revision of agrarian relations' that it calls for remains unexplored. While this cannot be said of the 1903 version, the restraint engendered by the lack of development of the peasant movement encouraged a definition of the 'revision' that was quite artificial, distinguishing between lands serving for the reproduction of feudal relations (the lands cut-off in 1861) and land used for capitalist farming:

> Such a tentative distinction was quite fallacious, because, in practice, the peasant mass movement could not be directed against particular categories of landlord estates, but only against land-lordism in general. The programme of 1903 *raised* a question which had not yet been raised in 1885, namely, the question of the conflict of interests between the peasants and the landlords at the moment of the revision of agrarian relations, which all Social-Democrats regarded as inevitable. But the solution given to this question in the programme of 1903 is not correct, for, instead of contraposing the consistently peasant to the consistently Junker method of carrying out the bourgeois revolution, the programme artificially sets up something intermediate.[43]

Lenin proceeds to suggest that the result of this was a failure to deal properly with the types of agrarian evolution that were possible following the victory of one of the forces engaged in the class struggle, but the analysis provided above indicates that this was not really possible at the time. To have seriously engaged in the calculation of possible tendencies of development, beyond the two paths indicated already in 1899, would have led the RSDLP into the kind of 'project-mongering' typical of other groups. In addition, it can be seen that the very reason for the cut-offs being deployed as the sign of the feudal economy, the overestimation of the pace of rural capitalist development which is later noted by Lenin,[44] would have in any case led to politically over-optimistic conclusions.

Lenin had already in 1899 emphasised the importance of a programme in 'drawing lines' between Social Democrats and both allies and enemies.[45] The review of the agrarian programme that Lenin undertook in 1907 is a thorough analysis of the deviations within the Social Democrat camp, and also an identification of the divergences between other parties. The manner in which this consideration of the agrarian policies of all political tendencies in Russia at the time leads to an identification of their political differences only emphasises yet again the importance of the agrarian programme for Social Democrat politics, and the manner in which the RSDLP was able, on the basis of specific principles of analysis, to both differentiate effectively political groupings, and formulate its own approach to the peasantry. There is not space here to do any more than indicate the contours of the issues involved, but it has been shown in this chapter that Russian Social Democracy both developed a programme based on a Marxist analysis of capitalist development, and altered this programme in attempts to bring it into line with the development of the Russian peasantry. In doing so it found itself faced with a number of competing political organisations (especially in the Duma elections and debates), among whom it had to identify allies and also consistently maintain a coherent political position. As we have seen, this was not effectively done by the Menshevik fraction of the party, and indeed one of their primary deviations in the 1905 revolution was to seek an alliance with those Liberals who were attempting to create a rural bourgeoisie as a bulwark of landlordism. Eventually the RSDLP adopted an agrarian programme on a compromise basis which, despite Lenin's attempts to defend it,[46] cannot be seen as anything other than a serious impediment to a consistent approach to the peasantry. With the appearance of a revolutionary situation in 1917 this programme was cast to one side and instead Lenin's April theses became the basic foundation for revolutionary Social Democratic politics.

This chapter has attempted to elucidate aspects of the politics of Russian Social Democracy by considering the manner in which 'the peasantry' entered into calculations of tactics and strategy in the socialist movement. The manner in which the discussion has been conducted aims at the abolition of the customary opposition of 'theory' and 'practice', in which the latter is conceived as the arena of reality in which the abstract propositions of theory find their validation or annihilation. While the slogan 'without revolutionary theory, no revolutionary practice' has been taken in some cases to be an elevation of theory over practice, it can be treated also as the denial of such an opposition. The 'practice' of a political grouping presupposes that it has an organisation which can formulate and execute policy, and also means by which to monitor and alter the results of such policy. But this process, which takes the form of committee organisation, debate, agitation, the production of leaflets and newspapers, the assembly of militants, the provision of problems for discussion, and so on, itself forms part of the 'practice' of a party. To separate then the words that are spoken in debate, the material that is contained in newspapers and leaflets, and treat the discussion of these as 'theory' is quite unrealistic and artificial.

As we have shown in this chapter, the first agrarian programme of the RSDLP proved insufficient from the outbreak of the 1905 rural disturbances. But it would be wrong to consider this as a 'practical' refutation of a 'theoretical' error, as though the task of theory was to predict the future and be condemned when the forecasts turned out badly. The reason for the inadequacy of the Social Democrat appraisal of the potential for peasant unrest and its assessment of the forms that it would take have been shown to be a failure in political calculation. The programme adopted in 1903, by the manner of its construction, did not effectively assess the nature of the political conjuncture at that time, nor did it contain means for dealing with any alteration in the balance of forces in Russia. The rectification that was carried out did not take the form of adopting the immediate demands of the peasants; it quite properly took the form of a recalculation of forces and the development of programmatic alternatives.

# 9 The Russian Peasantry as Object of State Policy, 1906–1929

As has been argued in previous chapters, the Russian peasantry does not form a given and unproblematic object for the theoretical and political ruminations of Social Democracy. In this chapter the emphasis is shifted from the writings of leading Social Democrats to the 'Agrarian Question' as it was constituted in state policy from the Stolypin reforms to Collectivisation. It may seem curious to unite in this way a series of measures introduced by, on the one hand, Tsarist autocracy, and on the other the first workers' and peasants' state, without at the same time subscribing to the fallacious notion that there is some essential and intransigent unity to agriculture and the peasantry. The intention here however is to examine the policy objectives and instruments, the exercise of which constituted diverse categories of the rural population as objects of state administration.

While the nature of the Russian state changed dramatically in 1917, more important for our purposes is the effect this had on the various attempts to subordinate defined sectors of production to the political and economic objectives of a centralised administrative agency. As we shall see, these attempts were not necessarily very successful, and in particular the lack of coordination between the allegedly centralised agencies of the Soviet economy becomes very important for our analysis of the problems of the New Economic Policy (NEP) and collectivisation. The use of the term 'state' or 'state apparatus' in the following in no way implies that the collection of institutions and policies thereby referred to possess any inherent common objective or cohesion. Contrary to customary present usage of such terms, the argument presented here is intended to demonstrate that the failure to effectively coordinate contradictory objectives generates many of the 'economic problems' of the Soviet economy of the 1920s, which are in turn subjected to increasing administrative pressure in attempts to overcome them. This creates further contradictory policy injunctions for the supposedly centralised and planned economy.

By taking the period 1906–29 we are also able to survey a diversity of agrarian policies that in many ways provide models for programmes of agrarian reform today. Our objective then is not simply to provide a narrative of the confrontation of state and agriculture during a period of rapid economic and political change. Instead, a few specific issues will be examined with a view to their general implications for discussions of agrarian reform. In the course of the discussion it is hoped to provide in addition some criticism of the customary treatment of the Russian peasant and the Soviet state.

By considering first some aspects of the so-called 'Stolypin' reforms of 1905–6 it will be possible to evaluate an attempt by the Tsarist autocracy to legislatively encourage a particular kind of capitalist development in Russian agriculture. Some understanding of the issues involved is particularly important when it is remembered that the alternatives that confronted Soviet policymakers in the late 1920s appeared to be collectivisation, or the development of capitalist agriculture along the lines of the Stolypin reforms. While it will be argued below that this apparent option was in many ways one which was created by the operation of state economic policy itself, the strategy of the 'wager on the strong' adopted in the years before the First World War provided a model of rural capitalist development that underlaid the economic debates of the 1920s.

Following this discussion of aspects of the Stolypin reforms, the destruction of this path of development by the peasant land seizures of 1917 will be examined. The question that will be posed here is: what does it mean for the peasantry to 'seize the land'? Too often unitary conceptions of the peasantry suggest that this action was unproblematically equalitarian, each cultivator simply appropriating to himself the means for the support of his family, reverting to a primitive natural economy of subsistence and independence. It will on the contrary be shown that the manner in which land and implements were appropriated in 1917–18 by the villagers and distributed among themselves could not be egalitarian, and that the subsequent inhibition of capitalist differentiation among the peasantry rested not so much in the 'strength of the commune' as in the action of legal and economic forces external to the 'peasant economy'.

The nationalisation of land and its redistribution during the revolution developed first into a period called War Communism, which was then followed by a trial construction of a peacetime socialist economy, which in turn gave way to the New Economic Policy. Stalin was in 1928 to claim that the New Economic Policy was simply a resumption of the policies initiated in 1918,[1] but this was as much a convenient reconstruction as was the description of War Communism by others as a strategy forced on the Soviet state by the Civil War and intervention. The abandoning of policies of requisition and direct exchange between industry and agriculture typical of War Communism was a decision made in the face of the chaos such policies led to in agricultural production. Replacing requisitioning by a tax in kind heralded the re-introduction of market relations in the regulation of agricultural production which was the basis of the worker-peasant alliance that characterised NEP. During the 1920s, a series of economic measures were introduced which sought to give effect to this political alliance, although they were not always consistent in conception or implementation. By examining the problems that this gave rise to it will be possible to elucidate the significance of the slogan 'worker-peasant alliance'.

The development of the conditions for socialist advance under the terms of NEP was often conceived in terms of the relation of town and country. As in the apparently analogous opposition, industry and agriculture, it is necessary to consider the implications and conditions of such modes of demarcating sectors within a national economy. By examining some of the problems that arise from these and associated categories it will be possible to finally demonstrate the way in which economic policy in the late 1920s was guided by specific, if questionable, conceptions of economic organisation. In particular, it will be suggested that the decision to collectivise that was taken sometime in 1929 should not be treated, as it is by many writers, as the realisation of utopian Marxist dogma on agriculture. The collectivisation of Russian agriculture as it developed in the early 1930s is more closely related to attempts to reorganise agriculture in conformity with the demands of a centralised directorate than it is with the realisation of a socialised agriculture.

These points can naturally only be developed here in a rudimentary fashion, but their implications can be judged or elaborated by reference to the extensive literature on Russian political and economic policy during the period in question.[2]

### The 'Wager on the Strong'

At the turn of the century, it became apparent to the Tsarist government that certain features of rural economic organisation were developing in a fashion that could threaten the political stability of the regime. Three special commissions were set up, the first on 16 November 1901 under the title 'For the Investigation of the Question of the Change during the Years 1861–1900 in the Well-being of the Village Population of the Central Agricultural Gubernias as Compared with other Parts of European Russia'.[3] The rural disorders of 1902 that quickly followed confirmed the apprehensions of those, like Witte, who saw in the repartitional commune a potential source of disorder, since the unrest of that year was concentrated in areas dominated by this form of tenure. One response by the government was to extend legislation, adopted in 1899 in relation to land held in hereditary tenure, which abolished communal responsibility for taxation in the troubled repartitional communes.[4] The disturbances of 1905 however similarly centred on the Central Agricultural Region, where differentiation among the peasant population was least developed and which represented therefore the heartland of the collectivism so feared by Witte.[5] In late 1905 plans were developed for a thoroughgoing agrarian reform which would undermine the collectivism of the rural commune and which would at the same time establish for the Tsarist autocracy a secure body of political support in the countryside. The measures that were adopted in the following year have become known as the Stolypin reforms after the Minister who supervised their execution. The reforms were however enacted for the most part by Witte, Krivoshein and Gurko before Stolypin assumed office, and it was in fact Krivoshein as Minister of Agriculture who was responsible for the policy itself.[6] In many ways the programme of land reform adopted represents the first example of modern reconstructions of agrarian relations, intervention by a state apparatus seeking to re-order property relations for agricultural and political purposes.

The basis of the reform programme that developed until the outbreak of war was the so-called 'wager on the strong' – the promotion of an independent peasant bourgeoisie whose existence would undermine the commune. The existence of these 'strong peasants' would on the one hand therefore provide a source of political support, and on the other weaken the collectivist aspects of the commune that were identified as a threat to the autocracy. Stolypin argued that given twenty years' undisturbed operation the reform would have succeeded in transforming Russian agriculture, and Wolfe has subsequenly written of a 'race' between Stolypin and Lenin for the Russian peasantry which the latter won fractionally, largely because of the coming of the war.[7]

In fact as will be outlined below, such a race never took place for several reasons, not the least of which being that the problematic Central Agricultural Region was relatively untouched by the effects of the reform, although it was the area for which the measures had initially been conceived.[8] The principal measure which typified the spirit of the reform – the exit of a peasant household from communal tenure and its establishment on a unified and separate plot with the farmstead sited within its boundaries (the *khutor*) – was in reality overshadowed by partial alterations in tenure which then obstructed full implementation of the reform. But before assessing the implications and effects of the various measures that constituted the reform, it is perhaps best to summarise first their features.

The general intention of the measures adopted in 1905 and 1906 was both to remove certain disabilities borne by the peasantry and to create an economic environment in which certain sections of the peasantry could take advantage of the new conditions. The first main measure, the abolition of redemption payments and the redemption debt, was promulgated on 3 November 1905 and was aimed at one of the major sources of peasant grievance.[9] A further measure introduced at the same time relaxed the conditions under which the Peasants' Land Bank could lend money, and the Bank was later to become a central instrument for the implementation of the reform. In March 1906 the Land Organisation Commissions were established which were to organise the revision of rural relations, and then in October restrictions on the free movement of peasants outside the village were relaxed. Finally, a decree of 9 November 1906 laid down that 'a householder might demand and receive, with or without the consent of the communal assembly, a separate and permanent title to all or a certain part of the strips of plough-land held by his household'.[10] Restrictions on the same of house and garden plots were also lifted, weakening the power of the communal assembly and making it possible for individual households to effectively dispose of their plots without reference to a village assembly. Further decrees in 1910 and 1911 extended the provisions of this set of measures, and there are of course a series of subsidiary points, such as the expansion of agricultural education, which are also important; but by the end of 1906 a series of decrees had laid the basis for the destruction of the commune as the major feature of the Russian countryside, and provided for its replacement by the independent farmer. This last figure was referred to by Stolypin as the 'sound and strong' as opposed to the 'wretched and drunken', a kind of yeoman stock whose own efforts and hard work would transform the social and political configuration of the Russian rural scene.[11]

The 'hard work' of the 'strong' was of course to be assisted by the work of the Land Organisation Commission and the Peasant Land Bank, and Stolypin was not above describing this cooperation of the state and the peasantry in terms of socialism:

> The idea that all the force of the state must come to the aid of the weakest part of it may be termed the principle of socialism; but if this is the principle of socialism, it is state socialism, which has been applied more than once in Western Europe and has achieved real and substantial results . . .[12]

It would be wrong however to read into such propagandist statements the conception that the reform consisted of a clearly worked out central policy which was simply transmitted through an apparatus and which resulted in a preconceived reorganisation of the countryside. The decrees mentioned above were on the contrary too vague to provide any definite blueprint for the commissioners working in the rural areas, and the consequent changes largely resulted from the adaptation of central guidelines to varying situations.[13] This is demonstrated by the failure of the 'full reform' to take root in the majority of areas, some kind of half-way house being arranged instead. In fact after 1910 the establishment of individual property rights and possible individual consolidation began to impede the consolidation of villages as a whole, such that the implementation of private tenure under the reform prevented the carrying of the reform any further. Such a state of affairs was strongly opposed by those in charge of the reform, without it seems any effect.[14] The other main type of reform settlement, the *otrub*, where plots were consolidated but the farmstead remained in the village, also developed against the wishes of the reform organisation. In fact the 'ideal farm', the *khutor*, never represented more than 30 per cent of consolidation settlements.

The implications for tenure and the organisation of agricultural production that the Stolypin reforms brought with them were diverse, although physical adjustments of two main kinds were involved: the concentration of formerly-scattered holdings into unitary plots and the partition of land which had previously been undivided. Such juridical and physical alterations produced an individual plot which condensed the economic activity of the householder within a restricted space separate from that of the village, although some pasture and common might still be used communally. Village control over the cycle of crops and the rights of common pasture on the fallow necessarily also lapsed, and the way was open for the adoption of multi-course farming instead of the old three-year cycle which effectively had restricted agriculture to only two-thirds of available land at a time.

It should not be assumed however that the consolidation of individual plots and the assignation of rights of use to a householder, rather than a village commune, heralded the establishment of private property as opposed to communal property. Such an opposition has little meaning when compared with the complex of rights characteristic of economic organisation, and the apparent simplicity of private/communal holding has led to countless (and contradictory) misconceptions concerning types of agrarian reform. In this case, while the holder of an individualised plot of land could cultivate according to his own wishes, certain aspects of his tenure retained the characteristics of allotment land. Thus such plots could not be mortgaged to an individual or an institution, and while it could be sold, the prospective purchaser had to be another peasant. The purchase of land by peasants was further qualified by restrictions on the amount of land that could be held in one district by any one peasant. In no way therefore can it be thought that the establishment of individual property rights in unified plots of land automatically carries with it the rights of disposal which are necessary for the formation of a market in land.[15]

One of the early European writers on the land reform identified the major problem of Russian agriculture as the parcellisation of holdings, which prevented effective cultivation of all the land and also led to wastage due to the geographical dispersion of the holdings of the individual household.[16] This problem was to re-emerge forcibly in the 1920s, and it does seem that much of the effort of the Stolypin Commissioners concentrated itself on this problem. The 'success' of the reform in establishing the solid body of 'strong peasants' aimed at in the original legislation is however questionable. Applications for appropriation of communal land peaked in 1909 and subsequently declined, despite the introduction of a decree of 1910 which forcibly converted repartitional communes into hereditary ones even if only one application was received.[17] Of 9.5 million peasant households in communes in European Russia in 1905, 2.7 million applied for separation up until 1915, 2 million in fact being completed. During the period 1907–16, 1.3 million consolidated farms were established on allotment lands, and as we have seen the majority of these did not correspond to the full-reform type.[18]

Not only do the gross figures of consolidations indicate something less than a runaway success for the reform policy in its first ten years of operation, but consideration of the geographical distribution of such settlements casts further doubt on its effectivity. It is noteworthy that in Preyer's *Die russische Agrarreform*, a major prewar study of the Stolypin reform, the series of completed reform settlements laid out in the maps in the appendix includes only one example from the central region. By taking his cases from the northwest and southeast Preyer in fact concentrates on areas where either hereditary tenure already existed before 1905, or where communal landholding had never existed. Likewise Owen emphasises that the Stolypin measures were most effective in those areas where differentiation of the peasantry was already well-established in 1905, such as the southern steppes.[19] Aimed at the overpopulated and troubled centre of the country, the Stolypin reforms developed to their greatest extent in those provinces which were politically unproblematic. In addition, when the Bolshevik party found itself threatened by counter-revolutionary forces during the civil war, it drew on its support from the central regions to defeat the threat which came from the fringes. Wolfe's dramatic picture of a contest between the Bolsheviks and the Tsarist state for the Russian peasantry in the decade before the First World War is therefore very misleading: in fact both parties found their source of support among sections of the population that had been to some extent discounted.

Having briefly considered the nature of the Stolypin reforms as the expression of the political objectives of the Tsarist autocracy, some comments are in order at this point concerning the features of Russian agriculture during this period. During the 1920s, the condition of agricultural production was repeatedly compared with either output in 1913 (which was in fact a good year for cereals), or averages over the period 1909–13. Later on this chapter it will be shown that often such comparisons were quite misconceived, but it is nonetheless necessary to consider the rural economy apart from its purely tenurial aspects.

Oganowsky argued that in fact the Russian government did neglect agriculture for the sake of land reform in this period; he estimates that in 1912 total spending on agriculture by government agencies amounted to an average of 15 kopecks per head of the total population (excluding *khutors*).[20] The bulk of government spending on agriculture went not on promotion of better technique or training, but rather on the physical reorganisation of the rural economy. While the basis of these figures is unclear, and certainly underestimates a considerable growth in the number of state-employed agronomists in the period,[21] indices such as those supplied by Pavlovsky concerning the staggeringly low storage capacity for grain bear out the points made by Oganowsky.[22]

One of the policies promoted alongside the tenurial settlements associated with the Stolypin reform was an attempt to ease the population problem in the centre of European Russia through the settlement of emigrants in border areas. This of course was a continuation of previous settlement policies, aimed either at the Russification of the frontier regions or at the opening up of internal colonies. The completion of the Siberian railroad made eastern settlement easier, and it was thought that the sections of the population effectively dispossessed under the new order would find scope for the establishment of independent farms in the Russian interior. There was in fact a rise in emigration during 1907–9, but it soon decreased again, primarily because of the occupation of all suitable land in Siberia.[23] In any case, the total for emigration in this period accounted for only a quarter of the natural population growth for European Russia. Further, while the emigrants were in the main poorer peasants, the distribution of their places of origin was very uneven, and not related directly to rural overpopulation.[24]

Other attempts at colonisation in the Far East and in Turkestan met with even more questionable results. In the Amur region, the introduction of settlers after the Russo-Japanese war was followed rapidly by an exodus which was attributed to the unsuitable natural conditions. In Turkestan, attempts to develop cotton cultivation conflicted with the economy of the indigenous population, while in one area 5,100 pastoralists were driven out to make way for 3,000 colonists.[25] While a great deal of money was spent on these and associated projects by the Russian government, the benefit gained was of dubious value, either in terms of relocation of population or in terms of the opening-up of virgin lands.

One of the principal indices that are cited to emphasise the backwardness of Russian agriculture compared with that of Western Europe concerns the low rate of return characterised by low yields in a variety of crops. Measured in tonnes per hectare, for instance, the average Russian yield in 1910 for wheat was .72, compared with 1.08 in France, .96 in the United States, 1.95 in Germany and 2.19 in Belgium. The figures for rye, barley and oats are comparable.[26] When these figures are put together with the distribution by type of holding (peasant as against non-peasant) it is apparent that yields on peasant holdings were increasing at a slower rate than those on non-peasant holdings.[27] However, it was the peasant holdings that accounted for 90 per cent of marketed grain at the outbreak of war, small producers in the Black Earth region being forced to sell their wheat and consume potatoes as a result of the taxation system that brought such a situation about.[28] In such areas the pressure on the land led to leasing patterns that rapidly exhausted the soil, depressing yields still lower in the absence of manure or fertiliser to use on the land. It was the non-black soil areas that improved more rapidly in the early part of the century, areas where for instance the consolidation of holdings had gone the farthest.

To use figures on yields of various crops as a measure of the level of development of Russian agriculture can however be misleading. As von Dietze emphasised, low yields are not necessarily indicative of poor farming, and we will see below in dealing with the famine of 1921 that uncongenial natural conditions played a great role in the apparently poor performance of Russian agricultural production.[29] International comparisons perhaps give a general idea of the disabilities of Russian agriculture, but without further investigation of the combination of factors producing such a situation it is difficult to draw any definite conclusions. In particular, broad comparisons between the American prairies and the Russian steppes in the assessment of Russian agriculture since collectivisation have often neglected large differences in climatic and soil factors.

Despite low productivity, Russia was before the war a major exporter of grains. 75 per cent of the total wheat exports was taken by Holland, Britain, Italy and France, while 57 per cent of the exported barley went to Germany (chiefly as a result of a treaty of 1904).[30] The majority of the exported cereals moved through the Black Sea ports, thanks mainly to the structure of the rail network. The poor internal storage capacity mentioned above did however seriously affect the manner in which the movement of exports developed after the harvest; lacking internal storage capacity, crops moved rapidly to their port of embarkation, where in turn poor facilities for purifying existed. The low quality of grain and the need for merchants to clear the ports quickly weakened Russia's position with respect to the world market in grains, so that while Russia was by volume a large exporter, the price gained for the various grains was comparatively low. In absolute terms then, the weak structure of agricultural production and distribution in Russia before the war led both to the producers being heavily pressured by fiscal measures to yield a surplus over what was needed for rural consumption, and a poor price being gained for the exported portion of this hard-won surplus. These aspects of the Russian grain trade will be returned to below.

It might be thought that the impact of war on this fragile though extensive economy would of itself be devastating. In fact this was not so, and while 40 per cent of the able-bodied men were eventually called up, and 2.6 million horses requisitioned, the cessation of exports, the banning of distilling and other factors combined to mitigate what apparently was a shattering blow to the basis of the Russian economy. Aside from the long-term effects of the war and the occupation of strategic areas, it was the private estates which suffered most heavily, while the peasantry relapsed into a slow decline, marked by the increase of the proportion of cereals, particularly rye and oats, compared with other crops grown.[31] Labour intensive crops like roots declined, and this of course was a crop which was often part of an improved rotation. The absence of animals also led to a fall in the small amounts of manure available, and thus a number of factors combined to encourage a return to older systems of cultivation in places where more intensive rotations had been adopted.

It was the disruption of the system of distribution, more than the absolute decline in production, that led to problems in food supply. The massive requirements of the army for grain did not of themselves cause a crisis, but the control of the railway network by the military authorities in which military traffic had precedence resulted in an increasing interruption in the flow of supplies to the towns, while the supply to the army was not badly affected. The resulting uncertainty in the provisioning of the towns resulted in a rise in price unrelated to the actual conditions of production, and this situation promoted speculations in grains, driving the price yet higher. State regulation of prices and markets began in 1915, and during 1916 the decision was taken to supply a proportion of the requirements of consuming areas through government agencies. By late 1916 price regulation had been extended to all foodstuffs dealt with by the authorities.[32] Finally, a projected deficit in the army's requirement for grain was dealt with by a measure in November 1916 which introduced a national grain levy, contributions being calculated down through provincial level to the villages themselves.

The collapse of the grain trade and its marketing apparatus preceded the political upheavals of 1917, and was due not to an absolute decline in agricultural production, but rather was a result of the dislocation of the mechanisms, economic and physical, that distributed a portion of the annual crop through space and through time in the year following a harvest. In effect, central government and regional army authorities competed for the supplies of grain that had to move along the railway lines that the army controlled and which were themselves the major axes of military operations. In this struggle the military authorities had all the advantages, and the various attempts by central government to regulate trade through nationalisation of various sectors and the fixing of prices failed to bring the apparatus of distribution under the sway of the Tsar's government. In February 1917 this had fatal results.

## The Peasantry 'Take the Land'

While the collapse of the Tsar's rule in February 1917 was in large part immediately consequent on the inability of the government to supply the towns and cities, the political ramifications of this did not at first affect the rural population. This was not merely because the revolution itself was at this stage a matter for the workers, whose leading political representatives in Russia were ignoring the peasantry as a political force; the cycle of rural activity was such that preparations for cultivation carried out in the early months of the year tended to prevent general political action. It had been the same in 1905. Then an outbreak of strikes in January and February had met with little support in the countryside, the rural movement only gathering force in May and June.[33] It cannot be argued either that the occupational distinction between worker and peasant precluded such sympathetic action, for the occupational structure of Russia was at this time not clearly divided into such categories, many workers either having households in rural areas or retaining an involvement in farming operations.[34]

When rural unrest did begin to gather pace in April and May 1917, its nature was immediately distinct from that of 1905. Then the single most important incident was arson, followed by destruction of landlords' estates, illicit woodcutting and other depradatory and destructive actions. In 1917 the initial form of 'unrest' was the simple takeover of gentry arable land for peasant cultivation. At first this was for a reason unconnected with the rural politics of landlord-peasant relations. As outlined above, during the war years it had been the private landlords who had suffered most from the mobilisation of labour, the absence of wage-labour making it necessary to reduce the sown area. As the shortage of food became pronounced during the spring of 1917, peasant committees began to take over the unsown land from the landlords and sow it themselves. Rented land was dealt with in the same fashion, and grazing land taken over by the peasants.[35] The Provisional Government opposed such actions, and during July their incidence began to diminish, partly as a result of measures taken by the government, and partly because of the labour requirements of the harvest. While unrest in the non-Black Earth areas of European Russia continued the declining trend from a July peak, August saw an upturn and rapid rise in the Black Earth region, and it was in this region that the fiercest struggle was to take place. Faced with the opposition of the Provisional Government, and reinforced by deserters from the army home for the harvest, peasants in this region became convinced that they could not achieve their objectives peacefully and that it was necessary to take more decisive action. The overthrow of the Provisional Government in October did not seriously alter a trend that had become evident in August, and in most areas the institutions established by the Provisional Government remained in existence until early the following year. In many cases such organisations were not under the control of the Ministry of Agriculture and the Ministry of Supply anyway, and were devoting themselves to administering temporary reform arrangements without central authorisation.

The Provisional Government had been consistently hostile to the independent initiative of the peasantry, declaring from the first that any reform must be formulated and carried out by legal means. Its nationalisation of apanage and cabinet lands[36] in march had no bearing on the problems of the Russian peasantry, since the lands involved were mostly northern forests or in Asiatic Russia. It decreed that land left unsown was not to be appropriated by the peasants, but placed under the jurisdiction of the local supply committee, which was charged with leasing such land on behalf of the owner. The land reform agency that was set up in March and April suffered from unclear powers and poor legal standing, and when the apparatus for preparing the land reform fell to Chernov on his assumption of the post of Minister of Agriculture in May he failed to take advantage of his position.[37] While the central authority for the design of a land reform became the responsibility of the SRs, this authority became increasingly engaged in delaying tactics which sought to postpone any decision on the land question until the convocation of a Constituent Assembly. The result of this was that what control the Main Land Committee had over its local agencies quickly disappeared, despite the despatch of Commissioners to quell unrest in October, and the constitution of *zemstva* as sources of rural authority.

Local elections had been held to the *zemstva* in August, and while the turnout was low SRs had in the main been elected. Instead of these bodies absorbing the heterogeneous and unofficial organisations of peasant action however, the administrative structure that they represented rapidly disintegrated, despite belated attempts to extend the powers of the local land committees.[38] Nevertheless, it was not so much the failure of the central authorities to effectively control the rural unrest that hastened its downfall, but rather the failure to procure sufficient grain that was effectively a symptom of the same administrative problem. Its collapse was hastened by the adoption of tougher policies on procurements at the same time as it dismantled the apparatus for the enforcement of these policies.

A State Supply Committee had been established in March, and later that month a state monopoly had been established in which farmers were required to surrender their entire crop apart from seed, fodder and subsistence. The higher prices that were fixed failed to reflect the rise in the cost of living, and the arrangements for collection and storage were poorly specified. In addition, the provincial supply committees were heavily dominated by townspeople, while producers found themselves represented effectively only at the lowest levels of an apparatus that was itself poorly defined. Attempts by the State Supply Committee to supply fertiliser and machinery directly to the producers met with failure, encountering similar problems to comparable efforts in 1919–21. Failure to coordinate the procurement apparatus led to competition among its various agencies, partly attributable to the absence of geographical demarcation for the supply-zones of the respective regions.[39] Shortages increasingly occurred through the summer of 1917, and even when the harvest of that year was completed it proved difficult to extract more than a proportion of the usual grain balance from the peasantry. The increasingly draconian but nonetheless ineffective measures for the procurement of grain taken by the Provisional Government, combined with their failure to decisively establish a programme of agrarian reform, stimulated the peasantry in specific regions to large-scale unrest, creating the backdrop for the demise of liberal democracy in Russia.

As Keep emphasises, all the authorities on the subject agree that the disturbances were most acute in the Central Agricultural and Middle Volga regions. Here the object of disturbances focussed on privately held land, and in particular arable land. In 1917 the richer peasants and the *khutors* did not figure prominently in the statistics,[40] for it was the estates which became the object of increasingly violent agitation. The forms of unrest were various, ranging from the withdrawal (or blocking) of labour to direct terror. Dubrowski estimates that the first accounted for 7.9 per cent of all outbreaks in 1917, while the most common incident involved the felling of timber (20.1 per cent of all cases).[41] This can be attributed partly to the growing shortages of fuel in the countryside, and also to the attempts at stockpiling on the part of some sections of the peasantry who anticipated direct exchanges for manufactured goods. Up until September it seems that most assaults were attributable to armed robbery and banditry, but at this time the sacking of estates began, and these incidents had by the end of the year accounted for 10.5 per cent of recorded cases of disturbance.

What is important about such direct attacks on the estates of the nobility is that they no longer took the form of agricultural appropriation, since those crops which were discovered were frequently destroyed along with the estate buildings. The sowing of the estate land by peasants was often at the cost of neglecting their own land, and most decisively, the implements and the inventory of the estates was in general not appropriated systematically. Over the winter and spring of 1917–18, the peasantry of Russia took part in a 'Black Repartition' which had been the dream of Russian radicals since the mid-nineteenth century. But what is notable is that this division of the assets of the rural economy was more likely to be egalitarian when the county authorities could impose their will on the eventual settlement.[42] A levelling tendency in the allocation of agricultural land could however be discerned, although as we shall see later in this chapter there were real problems in the manner in which it was distributed.

Apart from the consequences of the distribution that took place for the organisation of agricultural production in the 1920s, it is worth noting at this point the varying conceptions of what an 'egalitarian' land settlement would be. Lenin in his April Theses had called for the confiscation of landed estates and the nationalisation of all lands in the country, the regulation of land use to be subsequently in the charge of Soviets of Agricultural Labourers' Deputies.[43] While popular organs of control soon emerged in the rural areas, the ambiguous status of the call for nationalisation of the land made necessary some elucidation of this slogan. Given that some conception of a distribution of land to the peasantry was involved, the critical question was the basis on which confiscated land should be apportioned, and, perhaps even more important, whether confiscation should extend to affect the rich peasantry as well as the gentry.

It has often been suggested that the failure of the established Bolshevik agrarian programme to coincide with the popular movement as it developed in Russia between February and October 1917 led the Bolsheviks first to an appropriation of the SR policy, and then to its implementation. In this way the popular base of the SRs is supposed to have been undermined, and the Bolsheviks inherited a support that they ill-deserved. A necessary but unstated corollary of such a criticism, if it is to remain coherent, is that the SRs, while a 'peasant party', were constituted as such not through a mass peasant membership, but rather through electoral support (as in the *Zemstva* elections previously referred to). Only if SRs were made up of members whose class composition was broadly similar to that of the Bolsheviks could they have in this way taken over and gained support for a policy formerly espoused by a competing organisation. But as Perrie has shown, both these assumptions are correct: in the years before the First World War, there was a similarity in the social composition of the SR and Bolshevik rank and file, which furthermore promoted a degree of interchange between the two parties. The 'peasant' status of the SRs was given not in the nature of its membership but rather in terms of its policy and consequent electoral support.[44] If the SR leadership deviated from this policy, then the party as a whole ran the risk of forfeiting its political support. This was in fact what happened during 1917, the Bolsheviks moving in on the SRs and giving some direction to a movement that the SRs were unwilling or unable to lead. The common view alluded to above generally fails to follow through the implications of the version according to which the Bolsheviks steal SR clothes then accuse their owners of being badly dressed, and promotes instead a view of the SR party as having a mass peasant basis in terms of membership. As can be seen this position is necessarily contradictory, or alternatively imputes supernatural political powers to the leaders of the Bolsheviks, who are thereby conceived as political 'Pied Pipers'.

The agrarian programme of the SRs called not for nationalisation of the land but instead for its socialisation; the difference being that nationalisation was a measure that could be carried out by a variety of state forms and which did not necessarily therefore involve the possession of the land by the people. Land was to be distributed according to the labour of the household available to work it, and the number of consumers in each household. These were the so-called 'labour' and 'consumer' norms, which sought to provide for each locality a means of arriving at an egalitarian land settlement. The Bolsheviks however saw such efforts as nothing but vain attempts to stem the development of capitalist relations through the artificial regulation of land distribution, and they consequently always stressed the necessity for the state to take over large agricultural enterprises undivided. These would form the basis of a future socialist system of production that would only be a possibility in general after peasant agriculture had run the necessary course of capitalist evolution, providing working examples of the practicability of socialist agriculture to the peasantry as it was ground down gradually by capitalist forms.

The problem in 1917 was that the SRs failed to implement the policy that had been established after the 1905 Revolution, even when they had gained control of the apparatus charged with organising a land reform. The Bolsheviks on the other hand adapted their policy by supporting the land seizures conducted by poor peasants (seizures which the SRs from their official positions sought to prevent), while emphasising the unworkability of the SRs notions of redistribution according to specific norms. As far as the Bolsheviks were concerned, any land reform was bound to be temporary, and so the question of norms was really only a secondary concern when compared with the question of *the manner in which the reform was carried out*. For the SRs on the other hand it was vital that the norms established for each district should facilitate as egalitarian a partition as possible, since this represented the definitive agrarian reform which would end the exploitation of labour for ever. The objective of the Bolsheviks was an eventual transfer to some form of collective property in which individual plots would disappear, while for the SRs the individual plots were the basis of collective holding of land.

The 'Report on Land, October 26' which Lenin delivered to the Second All-Russian Congress of Soviets expressed the basic principle that land should pass into the control of those who used it, while abolishing private ownership of land at the same time –

implying that land could not be sold, purchased, leased, mortgaged or otherwise alienated.[45] While household land was to be reserved for the exclusive use of its present owners, items like the stock and implements of confiscated estates were to pass into either the hands of the commune or of the state, depending on the size and importance of the inventory involved. The employment of hired labour was to be banned, and provisions were made for the assistance of householders who were temporarily unable to cultivate the land assigned to them. Those who were too old to cultivate the land were to lose the rights they had enjoyed, and receive instead a state pension. Instead of reverting to the commune, as had previously happened, land was to revert to a land fund administered by local government which would periodically carry out re-allocations of agricultural land. The 'Report' finally declared that the land of 'ordinary peasants and ordinary Cossacks' would not be confiscated, leaving open the question of who was to be counted as an 'ordinary' peasant.[46]

While private property in land was abolished, it was not made entirely clear who then held the rights over land. Clearly certain of them rested in the 'local authorities', while these agencies were unspecified. The role of the state was not clarified, although the declaration that the final disposition of the land reform was a matter for the Constituent Assembly indicates perhaps that such details were to be left for later clarification. When the final text was promulgated on 19 February 1918 the distribution of agricultural land was entrusted to the various levels of the Soviets, while Article 11 defined the purpose of a socialist agrarian programme as the development of collective agriculture.[47] Accompanying this was the SR principle of 'land to the tiller' and the abolition of hired labour, while guidelines were laid down for the labour-consumer balance which was to form the basis of the allocation of land. The assumption here was that any deficiency could be made up from the fund represented by the confiscated estates, and where this was not possible migration was held to be the only solution.

During the early months of 1918 the land was reallocated in all those areas which were secure, but what immediately became apparent was that the schema laid down in the Decree on Land, however contradictory it was in its embracing of the aim of collectivisation at the same time as it declared in favour of aspects of SR policy, was not in any case being carried out in the manner envisaged. Apart from the ultimate small size of those sections of agricultural production retained in state hands as model farms, the reallocation of land did not take place on the district level, but rather took place within individual villages. This not only indicates the weakness of the local authorities which were supposedly to oversee the settlement, it also had the consequence that the distribution of land was not ideal for each household. Carr points out that the prewar problem of the dispersal of holdings was if anything aggravated, and the neglect of distant plots of land by individual households was in the 1920s to be a contributory factor in the slow recovery of agricultural production, and the promotion of rural differentiation.[48] For the time being, while the Bolsheviks supported the distribution of all land (fostering the antagonism between large and small peasant holders), the SRs sought to contain redistribution to the old estate land. The result of this was that the poorer peasants did relatively less well than those who had already reasonable plots of land and stock.

The question of the seizure of land by the peasants in 1917 is sometimes dealt with as if it involved a reversion to the values of the pre-revolutionary commune, and that this very movement demonstrated the resilience of the Russian countryside to the corrosion of capitalist values.[49] What this fails to consider is the basis on which local peasant organisation could have emerged. It has been shown in earlier chapters that the village settlement was not congruent necessarily with the commune, and it is noteworthy that local communal action in 1917 based on specific villages becomes automatically labelled a 'reversion' to the commune. If the commune did re-emerge as a powerful force in 1917, it can be suggested that it had less to do with the heritage of the Russian peasant than with the adoption of the only suitable form for the task in hand. As has been suggested above, the allocation of land that was subsequently undertaken by such institutions had no inherent principle of equality, and the distribution of holdings during 1917–18 was made in such a fashion as to positively encourage differentiation in some cases.

Apart from the actual possession of plots of land, the distribution of implements and stock was also decisive. Draught animals were not subjected to a general redistribution, and would in any case be of little use to poor peasants without carts or ploughs. The inventory of confiscated estates was often destroyed as a symbol of the power of the landlord, and where it survived it was natural that it should fall to those who could use it. The commune functioned as a collective agency only with respect to the distribution of land, while live-stock and implements remained the property of individual households. Thus the apparently even distribution of land which is alleged to represent the egalitarian nature of the land settlement and the basis of peasant resistance to the Soviet state until 1929 conceals the very uneven distribution of the means to work the land won in the struggles of 1917-18. In some cases indeed local differences were in this way aggravated by the settlement.

While the statistics on landholding for this period show a levelling tendency, there was between 1917 and 1920 only a slight fall (from 29 per cent to 27.6 per cent) of holdings without horses, while those with only one rose from around half to almost two-thirds.[50] The distribution of implements was especially poor: Meyer estimates that between half and two-thirds of all peasant holdings did not possess a full inventory of equipment and had to lease implements to cultivate their land. In Kiev province 75 per cent of the peasants had no plough, and over 50 per cent no equipment at all.[51] During the early 1920s this situation generally worsened, as we shall see, and in the face of such factors the traditional indices of rural differentiation become inapplicable. 'Land to the Tiller' meant that the richer peasants could secure a distribution of land according to their ability to work it, so that an apparently egalitarian principle secured a result in the interest of the better-off. While the degrees which distinguished rich from poor might be hard to discern, even small differences were significant, and the famine in 1921 with the subsequent good harvests of 1922 and 1923 created conditions for the development of rural differentiation. This was not however manifested through the holding of land, but rather through complex leases of labour and implements, in which the rich peasant was frequently registered as the employee of the poor.

The abolition of private rights in land and the distribution of land more or less equally among the peasant population did not then of itself ensure the stability of the system of cultivation thereby created. While the requisitioning under War Communism seriously affected all rural producers, it did not interfere with the inherent inequality built into the settlement of 1918. To treat the commune, however defined, as an expression of peasant tradition revived in the struggles of 1917–18 and only extinguished by collectivisation is to misconceive the forces operating in the Russian countryside at this time. The relations built into the commune were in some cases divisive, despite the general failure of the Bolsheviks to engender a decisive struggle within it between rich and poor peasants. It was not the commune as a traditional institution that inhibited the development of differentiation, but rather a series of state decrees, such as the ban on the hire of labour and leasing of land, and the price policy related to the different procurement programmes, that ensured a degree of stability. During the period of War Communism, these same measures contributed to the breakdown of the system of supply, and some readjustment became necessary. The various measures that were to be united under the title of the New Economic Policy relaxed these inhibiting factors, while attempting to guard against a slide into peasant capitalism.

### NEP and the Conditions for a Worker-Peasant Alliance

The body of decrees and measures that were introduced in the course of 1921 and which have become known as the New Economic Policy were aimed specifically at a political objective: the formation and maintenance of a worker-peasant alliance. This amounted to the setting of a new course for the Soviet state, since the original conception of the politics of alliance had been that of a bloc of heavy industry and state agriculture against petty production, i.e. in this case virtually the whole of agriculture. The stagnation of agricultural production and the breakdown of industrial production in 1920 (in part consequent on the failure of the government to supply the industrial workers with food) led to a political crisis represented by the Kronstadt rising. The partial restoration of market conditions in the countryside, which had been limited or suppressed since the outbreak of the First World War in 1914, opened the way for a new form of relation between the urban workers and the rural peasantry within the new Soviet state. This alliance did not of course embrace the peasantry *en masse*, conceiving them either as a particular type of producer or simply a rural population: instead the distinction of small from middle, and middle from large peasants became inscribed within the policy instruments and objectives of NEP. The success of the

Policy hinged to a great extent on the manner in which these differences were formulated, and then acted upon within the general political goals of NEP.

It is generally assumed that NEP succeeded War Communism as the means of creating a breathing space while the economy recovered from the ravages of the Civil War and Intervention. The schema finds its confirmation even in the words of Lenin, who in 1921 declared that:

> It was the war and the ruin that forced us into War Communism. It was not, and could not be, a policy that corresponded to the economic tasks of the proletariat. It was a makeshift. The correct policy of the proletariat exercising its dictatorship in a small-peasant country is to obtain grain in exchange for the manufactured goods the peasant needs. That is the only kind of food policy that corresponds to the tasks of the proletariat, and can strengthen the foundations of socialism and lead to its complete victory.[52]

Others described the period of War Communism in terms of a besieged fortress forced to live off itself for the duration, and in the terms of Lenin's words cited above the change of course to NEP signalled a recognition of the need to develop agriculture as a condition of socialist development.

If then the orthodoxy is followed, we are presented with a period of Civil War in which the organisation of the economy is characterised by improvisation, the absence of the usual economic mechanisms leading to forced exchanges which gradually erode the ability of the economic system as a whole to reproduce itself: during this period the Soviet economy exhausts its resources for the sake of its political survival. In peacetime conditions this cannot be sustained, and so the New Economic Policy has to be introduced to restore the ravaged economy through capitalist mechanisms in order to lay the basis for a socialist economy. War Communism gives way in peacetime to NEP as soon as is practicable.

This version of Soviet economic historiography is a rationalisation, whether it is found in the writings of the political leadership of the time or in those of modern Western historians. If it is accepted that War Communism is primarily a series of improvisations (many of whose instruments were of course inherited from the Provisional Government and the Tsarist wartime economy) then a curious lag has to be explained between the cessation of hostilities and the adoption of NEP. It is not sufficient to argue that the form of economic management typical of 1919–20 simply persisted, since the cessation of hostilities and the lifting of the Allied blockade preceded the first measures of NEP by over a year.

This problem can be resolved in two different ways: either War Communism must be considered not as a series of *ad hoc* measures, but rather as a more or less coherent policy which, while necessarily implemented in an *ad hoc* fashion under the pressure of foreign invasion, does represent a particular kind of socialist construction; or alternatively the period between the cessation of hostilities and the introduction of NEP must be treated as a specific economic phase. These are the only two possibilities: in either case the version given by Lenin above must be rejected, since the only conclusions are that War Communism was either not a makeshift, or if it was then NEP was introduced as a response to something other than a 'makeshift' period of War Communism.

If the word of Lenin and his comrades was thought sufficient for the establishment of the directions of economic policy, then NEP could not be anything other than temporary a response to hastily formed policies directed not to the construction of socialism but to the prosecution of a war. But seen in this light NEP becomes a postwar recovery period which has resort to limited market relations for the purposes of economic reconstruction. This however would be to demote NEP from a major and novel form of socialist development, characterised by specific forms of political relations, to a temporary measure forced on the Soviet state by circumstances. It will be suggested below that NEP must not be viewed as either a political or economic expedient, but is rather the only progressive path open to the Soviet state in the absence of world revolution. The abandonment of NEP at the end of the 1920s marked the end of a period of socialist experimentation, and heralded the construction of a modern industrial state on lines that were neither capitalist nor socialist. NEP was introduced not as a response to War Communism, but as a response to the failures of the *first* programme of socialist construction. This programme, developed in 1920, was based on the expectation of a revolution in the West coming to the aid of the Soviet state, and can be characterised as 'Proletarian Natural Economy'.[53] As we shall see, the peasantry were to play a crucial part in the fate of NEP, and it is therefore necessary to outline some aspects of the economic systems which it replaced, so that the implications of the reforms characterised as a 'New Economic Policy' can be properly assessed.

It has been emphasised above that the use of the marketing apparatus to distribute agricultural produce had been steadily eroded since 1914, partly through interruption of transport and partly through government measures. The policy of requisitioning that characterised War Communism then simply made a virtue of policies that predated the 1917 revolution, adding to them the use of the government printing press to promote inflation and the erosion of monetary calculation. Divested of an apparatus of market exchange, however limited, the Soviet authorities were forced to rely increasingly on coercion for the distribution of supplies to the towns and the army. Compulsory requisitioning of the off-farm 'surplus' was resorted to, the attempt to introduce a tax in kind in October 1918 remaining a mere formality in the absence of means to assess and collect such a tax.[54] The Commissariat of Supply was responsible both for the collection of the produce and its distribution to consumers; the problem was that its inability to build good relations with the producers, and on the other hand deliver to consumers sufficient food, both drove a wedge between workers and peasants and represented the state as that wedge. As Dobb points out, to the degree that requisitioning replaced market relations peasant resistance grew, as the inability of the collection apparatus to identify a 'surplus' to subsistence requirements of the peasantry naturally developed into a system of arbitrary levies.[55]

Lenin identified the struggle that eventuated as one between capitalism and socialism:

> Collecting all grain surpluses in the hands of the Soviet central authorities and correctly distributing them means making our Red Army invincible, it means the final rout of Kolchak and Denikin, it means the rehabilitation of industry and guarantees proper socialist production and distribution, guarantees the complete victory of the socialist system.[56]

The problem with this vision was that the Commissariat of Supply did not possess the means of performing the task it is here given. Lenin notes that the urban worker only received half of his food from the state supply organisations, the other half coming from the black market, but instead of recognising that this state of affairs indicated the weakness of the supply organisation he proceeded in this article of August 1919 to denounce profiteers. In an earlier and more reasoned piece Lenin had recognised that socialist development in Soviet Russia resolved itself at the economic level into questions of accounting, organisation and cooperation, stressing the administrative problems of the emergent state.[57] In the heat of 1919 such reflections are abandoned in an attempt to abolish private trade by fiat, freedom to trade in grain being conceived as a slogan that in time would result in a total restoration of capitalism.

Kritsman described the main feature of the economic system that was developing as 'centralised but unplanned',[58] such that while certain aspects of capitalist economy were done away with, its more anarchistic elements persisted. During 1920 attempts were made however to introduce a more considered set of objectives into the organisation of the economy, rationalising and coordinating the various devices that had developed in the previous two years. While the use of 'Proletarian Natural Economy' deviates from Kritsman's original use to describe this period, it is necessary to sharply distinguish the conditions of economic organisation during the war and those that were established shortly after, but before NEP.

The economic conditions of 1920 were not at all favourable to the sometimes grandiose programmes of construction that were proposed. National Income for 1920 was 20 per cent of the 1913–14 level, and the destruction of the war had hit technically advanced sections of the economy particularly hard. Industrial concerns that had not been destroyed were engaged in war production, so that the goods required by the peasantry as an exchange for their crops simply did not exist. Taking the 1913 output as 100, production of cotton textiles in 1920 was 5.1; of cement 3.1; of ploughs 13.3; of agricultural machinery in general 3.2.[59] To some extent peasant requirements for industrial goods were met by a clandestine exchange of grain for the products of small industries, grain moving north from the producing areas in exchange for basic manufactured goods moving south. This arrangement was however disrupted by the procurements which stripped the countryside of the means to carry on this traffic.

The collapse of industry and the stagnation of agriculture was accelerated by the state of the transport system. Before the war, the average distance travelled by marketed grain between site of production and site of consumption was 556 kilometers demonstrating the dependence of the grain trade on the reliability of the railway network. Even before the war however some of the rolling stock and locomotives were obsolete. Meyer estimates for instance that 25 per cent of locomotives in 1913 were over forty years old. The destruction and breakdown of locomotives during the war was then exacerbated by the shortage of coal which led to use of wood as a fuel, corroding the boilers and leading to further breakdowns. Altogether 56.8 per cent of the existing locomotives in 1920 were defective and the rate of repair was very low,[60] as was the rate of building.

The breakup of the estates had also an effect on the production of 'technical' crops such as flax, sugar beet and cotton, which had before the war been principally grown by the landlords. Industry found itself lacking in the raw materials normally supplied to it by Russian agriculture, apart from having a labour force that periodically deserted *en masse* in search of food. The number of horses in agriculture was 20 per cent of the 1913 figure, and most of the cattle herds remaining were very aged. Not only had economic relations between sections of the national economy been disorganised by the war, but the material basis on which they could be reconstructed was in many cases absent.

The Ninth Party Congress in 1920 proposed that economic recovery could only be effected on the basis of a unified economic plan, and a set of priorities were established while at the same time it was recognised that the means for the construction of an effective plan did not exist. A series of measures through 1920 intensified the struggle against private ownership, with for example the nationalisation of middle and small enterprises. In agriculture, it was suggested that the road to socialist production was not through the collectives but rather was through increasing state control of production (the implementation of labour conscription, forced savings, regulation of field activity and so on).[61] This article became the basis of a draft law 'On Measures for the Strengthening and Development of Peasant Agriculture' of 1 December 1920, which was unanimously approved by the Eighth Congress of Soviets. Under this law, careful cultivation became a legal duty to the state, and an apparatus was planned for the direction of sowings and the determination of the share to be requisitioned.

The agricultural campaign for 1920 was conceived at the time as a step on the road to the abolition of the difference between town and country, and shortly a particular instrument was isolated as ideal for this task – electrification. Here was a source of power which, while it was produced by an industrial sector, could be used in dispersed sites remote from urban areas, with a whole range of applications in the improvement of farming processes. As an article of the time emphasised, electrification was the precondition for the socialisation of production and the realisation of the collective spirit of mankind.[62] It also could be viewed as the best means in the hands of the state against a possible rural counter-revolution, spreading the benefits of the revolution for the first time amongst the peasantry. Although it was not clear how far small producers could take advantage of such a power source when they lacked even the most basic implements, it was thought that the *sovkhozy* might be able to first make use of electrical power, subsequently transferring the benefits to neighbouring peasant producers.

Lenin presented the Plan for Electrification to the Eighth Congress of Soviets in December 1920 and called it the 'Second Party Programme'. A construction programme was planned on an ambitious scale, which was to be financed one-third through foreign concessions, and two-thirds by the export of agricultural produce. Within this plan there was no room for private entrepreneurs, and indeed the electrification programme was a key component in the construction of a marketless socialist economy. Associated with measures like the public canteens which fed millions, and the abolition of money, during 1920 there was a definite attempt to construct a marketless economy which would function in peace-time, but which was however predicated on the imminent World Revolution. Especially important was the possibility of a revolution in Germany which would solve, according to the Russians, the industrial problems of the Soviet economy with great rapidity.

This 'proletarian natural economy' was not supplied however with the material means for its own survival. Shortages of food led to successive cuts in the urban ration quotas during 1920, productivity in turn falling ever lower. During January 1921 only 15.8 days were worked in Moscow; the lack of fuel for the railways threatened to deprive the towns and cities of even the meagre supplies that they were receiving.[63] Unrest in rural areas over the requisitions developed to a dangerous intensity, Siberia being cut off from European Russia for three weeks early in 1921 by uprisings along the lines of communication.[64] Delegates to the Tenth Party Congress in 1921 had in many cases to negotiate areas on their route which were no longer under Soviet control, and arrived at the Congress armed. The Kronstadt rising was only the most visible aspect of a rapidly deteriorating national situation. A revised economic policy was clearly necessary, but more crucial was a reorganisation of the political basis of Soviet authority. The measures of the New Economic Policy, in responding to the collapse of the proletarian natural economy, sought to provide this.

In early February the Politburo, under pressure from the increasing number of peasant disturbances, abolished the requisition of grain in thirteen central provinces. A series of measures were to follow which had the effect of reversing the construction of a proletarian natural economy, and instead substituting a worker-peasant alliance as the means of political restabilisation. The first measure to be passed into law under this new course was the replacement of requisitioning by a tax in kind, calculated as a percentage of the crop harvested. This tax was designed to be progressive, falling more lightly on middle and poor peasants than on the rich. Tax rebates were offered to those who increased their sown area, and it was proposed that a state fund be established for direct exchange of manufactured goods against any surplus voluntarily delivered in excess of the tax.

The corollary of this was the restoration of limited rights to trade in grain, and in late March restrictions on 'local exchange' were abolished, as were regulations affecting the private transport of foodstuffs. According to the writings of Lenin in 1919, such a move was tantamount to the invitation of a capitalist restoration, and such an accusation was common at the time. Lenin characteristically dealt with this criticism by arguing that the capitalist aspects of the new course were a socialist virtue, and establishing the continuity of his argument by quoting at length from his 'Left Wing Childishness' of 1918, in which he had argued that the appropriate economic organisation for Russia was German state socialism without the hegemony of the Junkers and under the control of the Soviet state. The conception of 'state capitalism' that he developed here was one in which it could be argued that a common economic basis underlay socialism and capitalism, and that it was necessary to take over from the capitalist economies the conditions which were required for socialist construction:

> At present petty-bourgeois capitalism prevails in Russia, and it is *one and the same road* that leads from it to both large-scale state capitalism and to socialism, through one and the same intermediate station called 'national accounting and control of production and distribution.'[65]

The development of socialism in Russia required that the productive forces be improved and rebuilt, and to do this, in a predominantly agricultural country, it was necessary to start with the peasantry. This was to accept a much longer process of socialist development, but what was also implicit in this was the idea that such a process of development would have to be carried out independently of international revolutionary assistance in the form of successful revolutions. The tacit acceptance of the possibility of socialism in one country then involved a reassessment of the political significance of the peasantry, and in this new strategy emphasis was to be shifted from support for the poor peasantry to support for those peasants who could produce a surplus. As we shall see, there was to be a great deal of confusion on precisely this issue, *but in principle the objective of NEP was the construction of an alliance between the working class and the poor and middle peasantry.*

In the article 'The Tax in Kind' Lenin went on to argue that attempts to block trade by force would be disastrous; instead what should be done, he argued, was to encourage the development of capitalist relations while channelling it into state capitalism. The critical question was how to hedge capitalist development so that it would in the future grow into socialism. In answer to this problem, Lenin proposed two broad policies: the development of cooperatives, and the attraction of domestic and foreign concessionaires. Both of these were conceived as means of confronting petty capitalist production:

The concessions policy, if successful, will give us a few model – compared with our own – large enterprises built on the level of modern advanced capitalism. After a few decades these enterprises will revert to us in their entirety. The co-operative policy, if successful, will result in raising the small economy and in facilitating its transition, within an indefinite period, to large-scale production on the basis of voluntary association.[66]

As we shall see, these two prime conditions for the success of NEP did not in the following years develop in a satisfactory fashion, so that the emergence of petty capitalism was provided with no counter-weight other than administrative check. This problem was to contribute to the collapse of NEP in 1929, although the crisis which led to the dismantling of its policies in the countryside was one largely created by agencies and measures conceived and implemented within the framework of NEP.

As mentioned above, free trade was conceived in the legislation of March 1921 as strictly a local affair; the establishment of regional or national markets in specified products was not envisaged. At the national level, there was to be direct exchange between industry and agriculture in kind. A decree of 24 May 1921 proposed that the total product of state industry should be conceived as a 'commodity exchange fund' to be administered by the supply commissariat. Organised through the cooperatives, the exchange was to be conducted according to specified coefficients, and the role of the cooperatives was strengthened by involving them in the collection of the tax in kind. Accordingly a contract was drawn up between the Supply Commissariat and the Central Union of Consumer Cooperatives which immediately indicated that the shortage of industrial goods had tripled their prices since 1913.[67]

Things did not go smoothly during the summer and autumn of 1921; the trains loaded with goods for the villages took weeks to travel around, had their cargo stolen or confiscated, and in addition were found to be loaded with huge quantities of goods unsuitable for village consumption. Thus the Cooperative fund turned out to include 540,000 boxes of talc and 240,000 bottles of perfume. In addition, the agricultural crisis of 1921 had the effect of raising the purchasing power of agricultural produce within the period for which the supply contract had been established, introducing a serious rift between state prices and prices on the free market. The shortfall of the Cooperative collection (3276 tonnes collected by October instead of planned 524,160 tonnes) meant that the towns had necessarily to turn to private trade in order to obtain supplies of food, or make up the deficit. Eventually the Cooperative organisations were forced to alter their coefficients of exchange, breaking their contract with the Commissariat of Supply.

The objective of effecting the delivery of a surplus above the tax in kind to the towns through the operation of direct exchanges of products according to specific coefficients was therefore somewhat less than a success. More important, we can see here how the ineffectiveness of aspects of the apparatus of exchange itself first engendered a differential between state and market prices, and then promoted private trade through its inability to fulfil the function for which it was put into operation. One of the persistent problems of the 1920s in the Soviet Union was that the various agencies of the state either could not assess or implement various measures effectively, or alternatively found themselves in competition with each other pursuing divergent strategies. This is not to suggest that the Soviet state was at times powerless before the resistance of sections of the population to it: these 'sections of the population' were themselves constructed in the calculations of the agencies, the problem was however that the conditions did not always exist for the pursuit of a consistent policy with respect to these populations.

One condition that was beyond the control of the Soviet state was the climatic factors that affected Russian agriculture. Fluctuations in the pre-revolutionary harvest had always been greater than those in Western Europe partly because the low level of technique made agriculture more dependent on climatic variables, and partly as a result of taxation policy. The fluctuations were least in the northern and western provinces, but these were primarily grain consuming, rather than producing, areas. The south and south-east, that is to say the 'producing' areas, were prone to failure for a number of reasons: the summer corn mostly grown did not benefit from winter rainfall, poor weeding reduced yields, manuring in some areas was unknown, and the short hot summer left little time for work and threatened the crop. In this area the crop failed on average once in five years, but the failure that developed in 1921 was of catastrophic proportions, producing a yield per head of the population 12 per cent of the average.⁶⁸ The traditional grain surplus area of Russia was worst hit: an estimated four to five million people died as a result, and cases of cannibalism were reported daily. The centre of the area worst hit was 1500 km. from the Baltic ports, and over 1000 km. from the Black Sea ports, and the poor state of the road and rail network meant that great difficulty was encountered in transporting the massive grain shipments of the American Relief Administration.

With the 1921 famine the new programme for socialist construction got off to a poor start, particularly in the areas not seriously affected; here the administration which had barely been established found itself called upon to make up for the shortfall in the tax collections consequent on the famine. In the non-agricultural sphere however a number of measures established NEP and dismantled the proletarian natural economy: charges for services and amenities were reintroduced, rents were levied, heating fuels sold and not rationed, public feeding cut back heavily, small enterprises de-nationalised. More generally, commercial calculation was reintroduced to revive an almost complete collapse of state industry, and enterprises were supplied with wages according to production and not number of employees.

The reintroduction of commercial principles in the absence of over-all direction of the economy led some sections of industry into competition with each other, attempting to increase production and turn over their stock. In some cases this led to products being sold below their cost price, and Meyer argues that the real basis for the development of private traders in NEP can be found in this period, where private trade could take advantage of the uncoordinated competition of state enterprises. The figure of the NEP man was to be a familiar one in the 1920s, but he was an economic agent that resided in the gaps of economic policy. The failure to develop an adequate strategy during NEP and the ineffectiveness of legislative controls made it almost impossible for the figure to be banished; and as we shall see again, the failures of various state apparatuses to meet their objectives promoted the existence of private trade to rectify losses or shortfalls.

In May 1922 a decree was issued which completed the process that the introduction of the tax in kind had begun. The 'Fundamental Law on the Utilisation of Land by the Workers' recognised all forms of holding (*artel, otrub, khutor, mir*) equally, and in no way definitely supported the commune. More significant, the leasing of land and the hire of land was conditionally permitted; in the case of households temporarily weakened by natural events, leasing of part of the land for two rotations was permitted; and labour could be hired providing that members of the hiring household worked alongside the wage workers.[69] Coupled with the conversion optionally of the tax in kind to cash in 1923,[70] this implementation of NEP in the countryside gave an impetus to differentiation previously contained by the decrees which NEP revoked.

The success of NEP thus came to depend on the manner in which the relation between sections of the national economy were constructed, or on the political level, how the worker-peasant alliance was realised in economic policy. The reintroduction of market relations to coordinate different spheres of production and distribution, and the reversion to monetary calculation, necessitated effective coordination of state agencies if the programme of 'state capitalism' was to be prevented from collapsing into capitalist restoration, or the state and capitalist sectors of the economy from colliding. It was in fact in these terms during the mid-1920s that the progress of NEP was assessed.

## The 'Agrarian Question' as a Problem of Soviet Administration

We now turn to a consideration of the various factors that constituted the 'agrarian question' for the Soviet Government in the later 1920s. In 1929 a beginning was made on a new strategy that was to transform Soviet agriculture and indeed the structure of Russian society – the forced collectivisation of agricultural production. This has usually been dealt with as a hasty attempt to solve the problem of grain supply which during the 1920s was threatened by the weakness of socialist forces in the countryside. It is important to note however that the scope of collectivisation as it was carried out in the early 1930s went far beyond the grain producing sector and eventually included all significant areas of agricultural production. For example, meat production had recovered to the pre-war level by the later 1920s, and played an increasing part in the diet of the population. The forced collectivisation programme took in the meat producing sector and resulted in a slump in output that took until 1939 to recover.[71] Milk production shows the same trend.[72] Thus while the grain question is often located as the origin of collectivisation, the scope of the measures that were taken went far beyond the solution of difficulties in grain supply; and this raises problems that will be explored below.

It has been shown that the introduction of NEP was consequent in part on a breakdown of agricultural supply, and was conceived as a means of forging a bloc between peasants and workers that would make possible the joint development of agriculture and industry. The conversion of the tax in kind to money and other measures of 1924–5 placed greater emphasis on peasant prosperity as the basis of national economic development, providing at the same time the means for the development of socialism. For the grain surplus collected by the state or entering the extra-village market performed a double function in Soviet strategy: it subsisted the growing industrial population, and through exports earned the foreign exchange so desperately needed for the reconstruction and modernisation of the economy.

The very measures introduced to promote the recovery of agriculture had the effect however of promoting rural differentiation, based not on the simple possession of land, but rather on the private possession of draught animals and implements. While the extent of this process of differentiation was not clear, already in 1925 it was thought to be far enough gone to interfere with the state collections of that autumn. The shortfall from the planned collection that became marked in November was ascribed to a 'strike' by kulaks who sought to force the government to raise their collection price by withholding their grain. The situation recurred in 1927, and the growing problems in collections in the later 1920s was blamed on the development of petty capitalist enterprise that was conflicting with the objectives of the state sector.

The conception of the transfer of resources between agriculture and industry had been enshrined by Preobrazhensky as one in which socialist construction must needs have recourse to a process of 'primitive socialist accumulation', in which a surplus was extracted by the state (industrial) sector from a petty capitalist (agricultural) sector. While Bukharin heavily opposed this and correctly pointed out later the error of associating the 'village' with agricultural production in general,[73] it is clear that the major difference during the 1920s between the proponents of rapid industrialisation and those who questioned its viability rested in a difference over the *rate* at which a 'surplus' was 'pumped over'.[74] The difficulty of extracting this surplus led to the apparent dilemma faced by the Soviet administration by 1929: either permit capitalist development of agriculture to proceed and accept the persistence of a dualism between capitalist and socialist sectors of the economy; or compel agricultural producers to form collective agencies in a rapid socialist transformation of agriculture. This is the broad alternative that has been accepted by most Western historians among them Carr and Lewin, but there are in fact a number of problems in such a position. While some of these will be outlined below, we can at this point indicate schematically the deficiencies of this apparent alternative.

The first question is whether the difficulty of the state collections was really due to the resistance engendered by capitalist relations in agricultural production. In particular, it is quite erroneous to describe the events in 1925 as the result of a kulaks' strike for one very simple reason: the kulaks did not market their grain until the spring in any case—the autumn collections that formed the bulk of the State appropriation originated with small and middle peasants. Dobb pointed this out several years ago.[75]

More recently, the work of the Soviet historian Barsov has demonstrated that the apparent objective of collectivisation, the securing of a grain surplus through the control of a collectivised agriculture for the purpose of socialist development, failed dismally. Nevertheless, it cannot be questioned that the Russian economy made prodigious advances during the 1930s. Thus the actual industrialisation of the Russian economy took place independently of the agricultural surplus that was thought so vital in the 1920s.

The evidence offered by Barsov can in some ways be seen as a realisation of the theoretical deficiencies of the 'surplus' model itself. It has been shown above that classical Marxist analysis of capitalist economic organisation did not take the form of identifying regions of the economy and then uniting them on the basis of value terminology. Lenin for instance specifically rejected the suggestion that the analysis of Russian capitalism should be based on the identification of feudal and capitalist modes of production and the manner in which the formation of surplus value in the latter rested on an exploitation of the surplus product of the former. And yet it is this form of analysis that characterises the work of Preobrazhensky, where the economy is divided into state socialist and private capitalist sectors and the exchange between them conceived in terms of the exploitation of a surplus. The ascription to agriculture in the case of Preobrazhensky of the power to produce a surplus which is to be the basis of a 'primitive socialist accumulation' is given its Marxist credentials by his use of an analogy with Marx's account of primitive capitalist accumulation.

But as Millar points out, Marx was concerned with the constitution of the *institutions* of capitalist economy, not with the capital forms set to work through these institutions.[76] The demarcation between industry and agriculture, state and private, socialist and capitalist elements in a national economy is too often coupled with the conception that the formation of the one is parasitic on the productive powers of the other. The bases on which such divisions are constituted are rarely examined, and questions of economic development are resolved into a search for the origins of the money capital assumed to be necessary for growth. The search for the necessary surplus for industrial growth in Soviet Russia identified agriculture as the only possible origin, and collectivisation as the means of securing to the state control of this origin. The implications of Barsov's work for the analysis of Soviet industrialisation, and by extension many of the problems of economic development, have yet to be fully appreciated, for what it indicates is that conceptions of 'surpluses' or the 'transfer of resources' are quite irrelevant to the prospects of rapid economic development.

A final question that can be raised at this point concerns the 'socialist' nature of collectivisation. As with nationalisation, the transfer of rights of ownership in economic enterprises to the state in no way implies that those enterprises are 'socialised', even when the state in question is a socialist one. In the case of collectivisation, the enterprises concerned were largely a creation of the state – collective agencies underwritten by economic and legal measures which established them as a specific form of enterprise. It does not follow however that collectivisation is necessarily a socialist measure, either in its form of implementation or in terms of the conditions of existence of the enterprises so formed. This point also has implications for discussion of agrarian reform in developing countries today, where collective or cooperative enterprises are formed for the most diverse reasons unconnected with the tasks of socialist construction.

The terms on which the major histories of the agrarian problem in the USSR are constructed tend to obscure these points, subordinating such questions to a historiography that provides coherence and unity wherever division and dispersion appears. E. H. Carr's monumental history, all the more remarkable for its detail and consistency of argument more than three decades after its inception, nevertheless is modelled on political and administrative historiography, whereby the succession of edicts and records of meetings provides the framework from which all else flows. The solidity of its basis in the political record of the 1920s results in an image of the period that is essentially the one adopted by the political leadership. The heavy use by Bettelheim of Carr is thus not coincidental, for the account provided by Carr when combined with an uncritical use of the writings of Lenin does very much produce a political history of Bolshevism.[77] Within such a framework it is difficult to problematise effectively the bases on which political and economic calculation was made at the time, without of course severely disrupting the course of historical narrative.

Lewin's major work on the peasant problem during the 1920s – *Russian Peasants and Soviet Power*, avoids the problems of a political history, while retaining a reliance on an opposition between society and state which generates the conclusions that are developed. The general thesis of the book is that the Russian peasantry constituted a mass of population which represented a constant obstacle to Soviet administrators, the poor development of rural Soviet institutions and the centralised decision-making apparatus of the state combining to prevent either the gathering of reliable intelligence or the conclusion of appropriate decisions. The drive for collectivisation is thus treated as the forcible invasion of rural society by the state in which the state seeks to restructure agriculture in a manner amenable to its control. While there is much that is true in this view, the opposition of state-society relies on the support of a secondary opposition of homogeneity to heterogeneity; so that the state apparatus tends to be posed as a unity seeking to impose its will on diverse social forces. The actual diversity and lack of coordination between state agencies is thereby obscured, and the existence of such agencies as social forces themselves ruled out.

As Millar and Guntzel have pointed out in a review of this book, Lewin accepts the need for rapid industrialisation, at the same time also accepting that Bukharin's programme of long-term socialist construction (which he otherwise endorses) was not feasible in the late 1920s. While his book is devoted to a description of the impending social and economic disaster that was collectivisation, the last is seen as a brutal solution to a dilemma that Lewin himself fails to resolve.[78] E. H. Carr accepts the collectivisation solution with political equanimity, Lewin on the other hand heavily condemning it; both authors however share a conception of the problems facing the Soviet economy which fails to establish if any such dilemma was more than a creation of the state apparatus itself.

Karcz in his article 'Thoughts on the Grain Problem' does begin to describe how the 'grain crisis' was created by the organisation of collection agencies and pricing policy under conditions in which there were no special production problems for Russian cereals, but his overall perspective remains firmly within the 'surplus' problematic, since his conclusion is that with a better policy a surplus could have been extracted. Beginning with an assessment of the statistics used by Stalin in 1928 to argue that a serious deficiency in surplus grain existed with respect to that available before the First World War, Karcz first concludes that the figures cited are completely misleading, and then goes on to consider the actual structure of the market for grain and the influences affecting it. It is stressed that under the conditions of NEP the market determined the scale and mix of production, while government attempts to dominate the market through the re-organisation of the collection apparatus and the proliferation of its agencies simply dislocated it. His conclusion that the procurement crisis of 1927–8 was largely the result of inept price and fiscal policy combined with a hasty reorganisation of the procurement apparatus is justifiable, but it is implied that with a better policy the state could have after all extracted the surplus that was there, if only it were capable of gaining control of it.[79] R. W. Davies later demonstrated that the figures used by Stalin were on the whole accurate after all, questioning the existence therefore of the surplus that Karcz suggested was there simply awaiting the appropriate policy, and Karcz later accepted the criticisms in a reassessment of his arguments.[80]

As the work of Barsov demonstrates, the question of the

existence or non-existence of the surplus was in the long run beside the point, since the drive for collectivisation failed to solve the administrative problems of the later 1920s that Karcz stresses. This failure did not however prevent the development of Soviet industrialisation, as work based on the research of Barsov has shown.[81] Indeed, perhaps the major effect of collectivisation was to cause, through its sheer assault on agricultural production, a significant reduction of the contribution of agriculture to the gross national product, forcibly bringing an end to the domination hitherto exercised by agriculture in the Soviet national economy. The customary view of economic development does of course envisage the displacement of agriculture by industry in the economic balance of advanced societies, but this is generally achieved by the growth of industrial production simply overtaking the output attributable to agriculture. In Russia, the establishment of an 'advanced' relation between industry and agriculture was achieved by the partial destruction of the latter, inflicting on it a series of blows from which it has never properly recovered. While the 'agrarian question' was undeniably liquidated for the Soviet state – insofar as the question concerned class forces and not simply technical problems of production – this was of the nature of a 'final solution' which reverberated throughout the Soviet economy in the years to come.

In conclusion, we will now turn to consider three aspects of the 'peasant question', selecting these examples simply as means for the elaboration of some of the points made above. The scope of the problems raised in the 1920s, and the complexity of the literature now available, unfortunately precludes little more than a very brief treatment of these three points, which are: the 'kulak strike' of 1925; the identity of the 'kulak'; and the question of a grain-based export strategy.

In the autumn of 1925 the harvest in grain had been good, although there was a deficit in the central region because of August rains, which created a demand for grain in this nominally surplus area. The state prices for grain were low, and this had stimulated a turn away from cereal production in the consuming areas to an even greater concentration on industrial crops, increasing the overall demand for grain. In this situation, a booming demand rapidly developed, creating a discrepancy between state and market prices. The state collections proceeded very slowly, until by January 1926 only half of the planned amount to that date had been collected. This was perceived as a crisis by the government, and Kamenev described the situation as a 'strike' by the kulaks who were holding the state to ransom.[82] From this point on the kulaks were faced with increasingly rigid state policy measures designed to limit their influence in the village and increase the control of state agencies over their activities. The perception of the grain collection problem as one caused by the overweening power of the kulaks was however an error.

As was observed above, the deliveries of grain made in the autumn generally originated not with the richer peasants but with the poorer. The reason for this is that the need of the poorer sections of the peasantry for money and manufactured goods obliged them to offload their harvest before the winter, and this was reinforced by the bulk of the agricultural tax falling due soon after the harvest. The richer peasants on the other hand could usually finance cash requirements during the autumn and early winter out of their reserves; their grain was sold during the spring, generally to other peasants. In fact many of the sellers of the autumn were buyers in the spring, since they had sold more of their crop than the amount needed to subsist the household through to the following harvest; and many richer peasants competed on the market in the autumn for the grain that would then the following year be resold to the sellers. The state agencies profited from this situation, since they bought when the prices were lowest and the supply greatest, it being usual for the price to rise during the spring and early summer chiefly under the pressure of those who had 'oversold' in the previous year.

In 1925 this relation was disturbed, and the usual supply of grain was not forthcoming. Partly this was a result of the lowering of the agricultural tax in May 1925, and the extension of the period over which it could be paid. The government thus removed one of its principal means of control of the grain market. In addition, 400,000 workers entered heavy industry in the autumn of 1925, placing an increased demand on the capacity for consumer goods which in turn reduced the availability of such goods in the countryside. The 'dearth of goods' that resulted during 1925–6 was at the time attributed to the too rapid rise in purchasing power on the part of the peasantry, but this was the reverse of the truth. Preobrazhensky's calculations to this effect rested on the error of failing to take account of the large differential that existed between retail and wholesale prices, a differential that worked almost wholly against the agricultural producer.[83] The expansion of purchasing power in the urban areas meant that the available output of the consumer goods industry was concentrated in the industrial north and north east, while peasants in other areas were offered marginal or unsaleable goods. Consumption per head of industrial goods in rural areas was in almost every case a fraction of that in urban areas.[84]

Perhaps most decisive in the series of factors that produced the phenomenon of the 'kulak strike' was the failure of Russian industry to deliver the implements so desperately needed in agriculture. As has been noted, it was the uneven distribution of implements that was a major factor in the development of differentiation among the peasantry, and the failure of an adequate supply of agricultural manufactured goods seriously undermined the worker-peasant alliance that was in large part built on this. Budget studies of the time showed that poorer peasants were prepared to purchase such equipment when available, for example from local industry, but these small enterprises were in turn denied the raw materials to substitute for the shortfall in deliveries from state industry.

Deliveries of agricultural means of production had virtually ceased by 1915, the total of the years 1913–24 barely exceeding 1913 alone.[85] It was estimated that a plough only lasted five years, a drill fifteen, and a cart fifteen; the average life of all agricultural implements was a mere ten years. Since there had been almost no investment in agriculture since 1913, this implied that in accounting terms there was next to no equipment left with a working life by 1925. The increase in investment that year resulted only in a small net capital increase, 0.8 per cent according to Gosplan.[86] The apparently large inputs of agricultural equipment during the late 1920s resulted in a very slow real rate of growth of capital stock, since the situation had been allowed to deteriorate to a position far inferior, comparatively speaking, to that of heavy industry in 1921.

The neglect of agriculture can also be shown in terms of electrification. The policy that Lenin had called the 'Second Party Programme' yielded derisory results in the countryside, where applications existed in abundance for the improvement of the processing of crops. By 1927, when rural areas were receiving perhaps 1 per cent of electrical output, most of this was being used for lighting. 24.2 per cent of this small total amount was used for productive purposes, of which perhaps half was for rural industries and half for agriculture. Grosskopf concludes as follows:

> The orientation of the production programme of heavy industry, the import structure and the situation of metal-working small industry proves that no priority was given by the Soviet authorities, during 1922–25, to supplying agriculture with means of production, despite the possibilities that existed. The support accorded the consumer goods industry, which afforded the state a quick return in the form of taxes, proves conclusively that the Soviet authorities never believed, during the 'period of reconstruction', in the possibility of an industrialisation policy based on a technical alliance with agriculture.[87]

The problems that occurred in grain procurements in 1925 largely arose from the fact that while the poorer peasants wished to purchase industrial goods, in particular agricultural equipment often of the most elementary kind, there was no supply of the goods which were required. There was no reason then to sell their crops as rapidly as had been necessary in previous years, since there was nothing to buy. But it was situations like these that were to engender campaigns in later years aimed at the 'reluctant kulak'.

But who was the kulak? According to one definition, anyone with grain during a procurement campaign. According to another, anyone not qualified to vote in a local soviet election.[88] But the discrepancies in the definition of such class divisions go beyond a simple sociological problem. The question of 'who is a kulak' was vital under NEP, since the effects of the various measures and instruments were conceived according to a central imperative which sought to strengthen the poor peasants, win over the middle peasants, and neutralise the rich. The distinction between these groups rested not on the possession of land, but on a series of hiring and leasing relations which were conditioned by laws which, while limiting the conditions under which they could occur, could not effectively prevent the formation of differential relations owing to the uneven distribution of draught animals and implements.

Among those who sought to deal with this statistical problem in the 1920s was Kritsman, who proposed that research should focus on relations of subordination and superordination, however generated, to uncover the extent and incidence of rural capitalist relations. To do this he started from the notion of an 'independent peasant', defined as he who could farm the land allotted to him with his own livestock and inventory. Two deviations from this existed: he who relied on others for his means of cultivation, and he who was relied upon.[89] The problem with this approach was that the middle peasant, a vital figure of NEP agriculture, statistically almost disappeared under a polarisation of varying degrees of proletarianisation and capitalist development. Under the conditions obtaining in the mid-1920s, it was unlikely that the poor peasants could be shown as anything other than heavily dependent on their richer neighbours, since there was a failure on the part of the state to provide them with the means to escape such dependence. The promotion of relations of dependency thus to some extent flowed from the failures of state policy.

Kritsman was criticised by Sukhanov and Dubrowski, who suggested alternative ways of constituting the 'kulak', but which were so restrictive as to conceal the ways in which relations of exploitation evolved.[90] Further attempts followed the introduction of an individual tax in 1929, which left it to local authorities to determine those who were liable. A Commission was then appointed to study the incidence of the tax on the population, in this roundabout way arriving at a picture of Russian social structure. The Commissariat of Finance then constructed a set of indices on the basis of the guidelines established, which were then modified into 'Indices of Kulak Farms in which the Labour Code is to be Adopted'.[91] The criteria so formulated were then used in the de-kulakisation campaign.

The kulak was not constituted just by fiscal policy, or in the operation of state procurement agencies; he also emerged in the electoral law of the Soviet Union. Under Article 69 of the Constitution several categories of people were disfranchised, while under articles 18 and 19 some of those disqualified for using hired labour were re-admitted. This presented a situation where the franchise could be extended or restricted through the differential application of the articles of the Constitution.[92] It was possible under these conditions for 'kulaks' to become dominant in local administration, particularly when the Soviet administration gradually gained some authority independent of the village assembly, which for many years remained the pre-eminent popular political form.[93] The emergence of the more enterprising local peasants as political leaders in the Soviet apparatus was in many cases predictable, given the qualifications required of such positions. But this situation in turn could be represented as a demonstration of the manner in which the rural bourgeoisie were taking advantage of opportunities to increase their power, a power which was thought to threaten the continued development of the Soviet economy.

As we have seen, the conception that it was particular class forces, that is, the resurgence of a rural bourgeoisie, that contributed to the grain crisis is a misapprehension of the problems of Soviet agriculture in the late 1920s. Insofar as class forces existed that were a problem in the rural economy, these were in large part engendered by the failures and contradictions of the policies pursued by the various state agencies. We can finally turn to the motivation of the procurement of grain, related to a great extent to a grain-oriented export strategy.

Russia was before the war a major exporter of grain, to such an extent that the foreign exchange so earned was the major factor in the financing of development projects. The level of these exports depended however on a tax and price apparatus that maintained peasant producers in a state of undernourishment. Consequently any comparison of exports before and after the war must take into account the social cost of the high export figures in the years immediately before the First World War, years in which in any case the structure of the world market was favourable for Russian grain.

The reconstruction of Russian industry, and in particular the electrification programme, was predicated on a high level of agricultural exports and on the attraction of foreign concessionaries, and since 'agricultural exports' was seen as virtually synonymous with grain, particularly wheat and barley, this led to emphasis on the collection of sufficient grain each year to permit substantial exports. While this was the view of the Soviet leadership, it has also become the assumption of Western historians, few of whom question the importance of grain exports for Soviet Russia's recovery and reconstruction. The 'struggle for grain' is thus accounted for as a continuing problem faced by the state, its options being conditioned by the structure of Russian agriculture on the one hand, and the need for foreign exchange on the other.

It can be suggested that this conception of the problem is an error. While Lenin delineated in his article 'The Tax in Kind' a leading role for agricultural exports in the electrification programme, there is in fact no reason why the structure of Russian exports in the post-war period should take the form of a resumption of the pre-war deliveries. As we have seen, the operation of state policy itself altered the internal structure of production, making the production of high-grade grains relatively costly. But more important, what is always neglected in discussions of the grain problem is that the world market for cereals had changed by the 1920s. Russia was in any case at a disadvantage: the railway network which was so crucial in rapidly transferring the harvest from the interior to the Black Sea ports, where it was sold to European customers before other harvests were complete, had been extensively damaged during the Civil war. Whereas other countries directly affected by the war began their industrial recovery in 1919, Russia was delayed by two to three years and suffered further damage. By the time reconstruction began to show some results, and agriculture was recovering from the disaster of 1921, the world market in grains had restructured itself without Russia. The dominant suppliers were now the United States, Canada, Argentina and Australia, whose internal communications and marketing apparatus had if anything been stimulated by the war, and which also enjoyed the advantages of falling shipping costs. It is therefore erroneous to consider the 'grain problem' as simply one of production; even if Russia had rapidly and consistently rebuilt the previous levels of grain production, it would have been difficult for her to find a suitable buyer in a market dominated by higher quality producers.

Entry into a world market for any country is of course possible at times when shifts occur in demand or in supply, creating a foothold for new suppliers. Such an opportunity occurred for Russia in 1925, for the North American harvest was poor, Australia shifted its exports to Asia, and Argentina did not enter the market until February. But as we have seen, during the crucial months following the Russian harvest in that year state collections were very low, making it difficult for Russia to make any significant impact on the market. By the time deliveries had partially recovered in the early months of 1926, the Argentinian crop was being traded, placing Russia again at a disadvantage.[94]

Reliance on grain as a major source of foreign exchange during the 1920s rests on two major errors: a failure to take into account the inflation of pre-war exports at the cost of the Russian peasantry; and a failure to consider the market-situation of Russia as an exporter of agricultural produce. It must be stated however that the requirement for foreign exchange was a real one – to take but one example, the laughable attempts to develop a Soviet tractor during the mid-20s ended in dismal failure, even when direct copies were made of Fordsons. The mechanisation of agriculture depended heavily on the import of cheaper, more efficient American products, which only in the early 1930s were successfully imitated.[95] Large quantities of sheep and horses were also imported to build up stocks, reaching such a level in the case of Merino sheep that Australia placed an embargo on further exports in 1929.[96] These and other imports placed heavy demands on reserves of foreign exchanges, and while such a strategy was being pursued, significant exports from Russia were essential.

There was no reason however why this should take the form of grain. In fact of course in most years during the 1920s there was a shortfall in planned grain exports, but the deficit was quickly covered by the increasing trade in butter, eggs and timber. In addition, Russia possessed significant oil reserves, and while the massive exports of oil products in the years preceding the war to an extent resulted from the shortage of applications available domestically, during the 1920s oil exports came to represent 20 per cent of total Soviet exports by value.[97] Given the existence of an import-based reconstruction programme, there was no special reason during this period for a unique reliance on grain as the major source of foreign exchange.

This point must be stressed, for it renders irrelevant most accounts of collectivisation as a means of solving an economic and political problem. The customary Marxist view is that the structure of class forces in the countryside, arising from the petty commodity character of peasant production, was gradually strangling the Soviet economy through denying it the grain needed for the increasing urban population and for export. Collectivisation is treated in these accounts as unfortunate, but necessary for the re-establishment of Soviet control over the organisation of the economy. This version of events naturally closely resembles that adopted by the majority of the Soviet leadership in the later 1920s, and it would be wrong to attribute the policy to the figure of Stalin alone. If the problem is considered from the position outlined above however, it can be seen that what appeared to be an actual dilemma rooted in the Russian countryside was in fact little else but the creation of state policy. While not denying the fact that a political problem was faced and 'solved' during 1929–33, it is notable that few historians have since that time sought to examine the foundations of the problem as it appeared to the leadership, and have either reluctantly assented to the necessity for collectivisation at that time, or condemned the policy without however showing a socialist alternative.

Some recent writers, foremost among them Shanin, have contested the Marxist view of the peasantry, and suggested that far from the Russian peasantry becoming divided along class lines in the 1920s, the major problem faced by the Soviet apparatus was that the peasantry as a more or less homogeneous mass resisted attempts to incorporate it into a national economy via the grain trade and other mechanisms. Differences between peasant households that could be observed in this period are argued to be a result of demographic cycles, a process common to all peasant households. The possession of land thus only reflects the size and working capacity of a family, and does not represent a permanent trend in the disposition of land.

Shanin's views have been criticised elsewhere, and there is no need here to repeat such criticisms.[98] As we have seen, possession of land is not the main factor in the differentiation of the peasantry during the 1920s, the possession of livestock and implements being far more crucial in importance. Unlike land, these factors of productions were neither shared between households nor subject to distribution equally after the appropriation of the gentry estates in 1917–18. More important however is the view that the peasantry formed a self-sufficient rural society separate from, and in opposition to, the wider national economy. Use of such terms as 'the Russian peasantry' of course implies this, although where it is used here it has been made clear that the term is by no means unproblematic. Conceptions of the 'persistence' of peasant economy in the face of Soviet development must however be rejected, whether this takes the form of arguments concerning the strength of the village commune as an expression of peasant solidarity, or of the insensitivity of peasant farming to wider economic pressures. As was shown in chapter one, the existence of a self-sufficient and separate peasant society cannot even be located in the later nineteenth century, since the process of capitalist development and the pressures of state policy consistently fissured and differentiated 'the peasantry'. It cannot be said that this situation was reversed by the distribution of land to the peasants in 1917–18; if anything, the situation steadily worsened. 'Peasant institutions' survived for much of the 1920s not because of their inherent strength, but because certain aspects of Soviet legislation on the use of land and the hire of labour were enforced, if only partially. The 'agrarian question' cannot then be treated in this alternative view as the resistance of peasant society to the encroaching powers of the new Soviet government.

Soviet economic policy is usually associated with the idea of planning, but while collectivisation occured within the period covered by the First Five Year Plan, this plan itself contained no provision for such a radical change in policy, limiting its proposals to relatively modest increases in output. In fact, it is doubtful if the 'policy' of collectivisation was ever planned and discussed as such; Narkiewicz has suggested that while some writers have located the decision to collectivise in the April Plenum of 1929 (when the free market in grain was abolished), it is in fact very doubtful if the policy developed from there was conceived as aimed at the complete collectivisation of Russian agriculture.[99] As has been mentioned above, the motivation of collectivisation has usually been couched in terms of the supply of grain, while the effects of collectivisation on non-grain-producing enterprises is rarely dealt with.

One of the principal arguments of this chapter has been that 'the state' cannot be treated as a coherent totality, but must instead be dealt with as an ensemble of agencies, institutions, policies, instruments and spheres of action, none of which are necessarily coordinated or effective. Different levels of an economic apparatus might for example operate according to partially conflicting injunctions and demands on their resources, such that while policy directives might be apparently clearly formulated at a high level in a political and economic structure, the manner in which they are executed might, without any 'inefficiency' being involved, be entirely contradictory.

Narkiewicz supplies an example of this from the material in the Smolensk archive. In the autumn of 1926 a decline of technical crops was noted, and given the growing demand for such products, it was decided at the fifteenth Party Congress to designate certain areas 'technical crop producers'. Around Smolensk, this took the form of provincial authorities arranging contracts for cultivation, and collecting advances of payment for the grain which was to be supplied to the farmers by the central supply organisation. These down-payments were passed on by the provincial authorities to the central supply agency, and the flax was subsequently collected as planned. However, it soon became apparent that no grain (already paid for) was forthcoming from the centre; and in fact the central authorities repudiated the contract, refused to repay the money advanced, and sold the grain again to workers' organisations. The provincial authorities were then forced to supply grain to the farmers themselves out of their own resources, although they were forbidden to use the free market, which was in reality the only alternative that they had.[100]

This case, which could be endlessly multiplied with similar examples, should not be read as simply illustrative of 'inefficiency' or poor organisation. The problem here rather consists in a lack of congruence between the imperatives of local authorities and those of a centralised supply agency which works according to its own set of priorities. The decision to develop technical crops, while perhaps appearing to a provincial body as a major objective, would not enter into the calculations of the central agency in the same way, and in the event of a shortfall of grain it would automatically divert resources in the manner described. The 'mistakes' that arise are in the nature of discrepancies and appear in the operation of an apparatus that is not, in fact, in a position to simply execute orders received from government bodies, assuming that these themselves represent reasonable directives. 'Policy' cannot be treated as a set of directives laid down by government officials; the structure of the apparatus charged with executing policy, and the nature of the instruments through which this is done, are of decisive importance in evaluating the nature of economic and political policy. As has been shown in this chapter, it is not possible to deduce the 'agrarian policy' of the Soviet government from a record of meetings, debates, newspaper articles and pamphlets which apparently lay down policy directives which can then be evaluated in their own terms. While this has tended to dominate discussion of the Soviet economy, an attempt has been made in the above to escape the conflict of personalities and political factions which is so often employed to organise an account of this period.

Finally, some comments can be made about the function of planning in situations similar to those just outlined. It is sometimes thought that 'planning' is a means by which an economic directorate can ensure that conflicts between agencies and resources do not occur. Lewin's discussion of Soviet planning is an example of this. Conceiving planning as a qualitative exercise ensuring proportionality in the process of production at the level of the national economy, Bukharin's support for limited industrialisation and defence of NEP is treated as a defence of *proportionality*. This is the only way of ensuring efficient production, according to Lewin, and he is consequently committed to a form of rationalism which associates planning with the optimum efficiency of the economy.[101]

The nature of NEP as the economic realisation of a political alliance between workers and peasants is obscured in this account, and if Bukharin's writings of the mid-20s are examined (heavily drawn on by Lewin), this becomes quite clear. His attacks on Preobrazhensky were conditioned by his belief that the latter's proposals would seriously undermine NEP,[102] which was based on the viability of a peasant-worker bloc as the means of constructing a socialist economy.[103] The fabrication of 'Lenin's cooperative plan' from statements in writings such as 'The Tax in Kind' was similarly conceived as a means of establishing new economic forms in which a class alliance could be expressed.[104] As we have shown above, the actual economic policies necessary for the realisation of such a political alliance were either poorly carried out, or not implemented at all; and in the light of this, it would not be justifiable to promote an argument according to which the statements of Bukharin were ascribed a truth which transcended the actual conditions in which they would have had to be implemented. Reference is made to them here only to emphasise that the conception of planning as the realisation of economic rationality obscures the political conditions of planning, and indeed the fact that the process of planning cannot be reduced to pure technique.

During the 1920s, the Soviet state found itself increasingly confronted with agrarian problems that it falsely ascribed to the development of indigenous capitalist forces. Insofar as these forces existed and were of a capitalist nature (in the form of the growth of commodity relations after the war), they were in general engendered by the policies pursued by the various economic and political agencies of the Soviet government. The contradictoriness of these policies was not something that could have been resolved by the earlier, and more effective, adoption of planning techniques. Ultimately the contradictoriness of the policies pursued was an effect of a failure to properly realise NEP as a process of socialist construction based on, and conditioned by, a class alliance of workers and peasants. Such an alliance was permitted to remain a political slogan, the institutional and material means for its implementation remaining in general nonexistent.

# 10 Conclusion

This book was originally conceived as a project which would relate classical Marxist analyses of the agrarian question to present-day discussions of land reform and underdevelopment. Effective treatment of the classical Marxist works required that these be studied in greater depth than hitherto, and once our work commenced it immediately became clear that the maintenance of a balance between sections on the 1890s to 1930s and those on modern cases (initially India, Tanzania and Chile) would be virtually impossible. A secondary problem also emerged: the objects and concerns of German and Russian Marxist writings on the peasants at the turn of the century were not the same as those of modern Marxist writings. The original intention of critically assessing various modern Marxist contributions to the 'agrarian question was thus abandoned, emphasis being shifted to outlining the important aspects of German and Russian writings.

As it happened, even by limiting our concern to the SPD and RSDLP and discarding the projected second half of the book there are a number of important issues that we have been unable to deal with properly in these pages. The genesis of 'revisionism' in the SPD for example has been shown to be related to the *Landagitation* and its assessment following its failure, but it has not been possible to devote much space to a question that has until now been treated purely as a canonical matter. Likewise the agrarian policy of the Bolsheviks has only been dealt with briefly, whereas there is a great deal more that must be said about the issues raised in the various debates to which reference has been made. We hope in future work to begin to explore the possibilities that these issues present; and of course we hope that others will be stimulated by the material that we have presented to re-examine aspects of the foundations of Classical Marxism. Our decision to concentrate on the German and Russian cases was in fact governed by belief in the necessity of demonstrating that this work provided a far more fertile basis for Marxist research than that offered by many modern theorists.

Despite the apparent diversity of the issues dealt with in the preceding chapters, we have attempted to consistently develop a number of arguments which are in some cases interrelated. Our concern has not been to write a history of the agrarian question, although those readers interested in such a project have been directed now and again to texts which could perhaps lay the foundation for such a history. In denying historical ambitions, we are not simply trying to evade the rigours of historical evaluation, nor denigrating the work of historians whose work has in places been invaluable. The purpose of this book has been to explicate certain issues which are of importance for Marxist theoretical and political work: the fact that the form in which the arguments are presented involves an investigation of German and Russian Marxism at the turn of the century is largely coincidental. For Marxism, historical work has no necessary consequences or virtues: only if a transcendental belief in the forces of history is adhered to can the study of History be seen as an enterprise to be undertaken for its own sake. We do not adhere to such historiographic metaphysics; for us, there is no totality in the past which can be recovered through the labours of historical research; the 'past' cannot be an adequate object of study except insofar as it is constituted in the theoretical and technical practices of the historian.

The purpose of this book then has been to present a series of arguments, which can perhaps be usefully summarised here as a set of theses. While these will not be exhaustive, it is hoped that presentation of major points in this fashion will elucidate the general project which this book has tried to realise.

**There is no fundamental project embodied in Marx's 'Capital' which provides the origin of Marxism and which establishes a finite series of problems for Marxism to work on.**

As we saw in the introduction to this Part, it is sometimes argued today that *Development of Capitalism in Russia* and *The Agrarian Question* are applications of the theoretical propositions of *Capital* to specific regions of capitalist economy. Kautsky's book is sometimes referred to as 'Volume IV' of *Capital*, emphasising its continuity with the project developed in *Capital*. The status accorded such texts in the 'classics of Marxism' has however remained one that is merely gestural – no recent writers have seriously tried to employ these texts in the analysis of capitalist agrarian development. Instead, the Marxist credentials of such work are established by direct reference to the source which Lenin and Kautsky supposedly built upon, *Capital* Vols. I–III. In particular, it is the analysis of rent in Vol. III that is often selected as the pertinent source for Marxist analyses of agrarian questions, whether treated as a theory of distribution or as a theory of the articulation of modes of production.

This by-passing of the work of Lenin and Kautsky both confirms their position as 'heirs and executors of Marx' while seeking in the work of the dead master a direct line of filiation for modern work. Marxism is dealt with as if it were a unity; *Capital* becomes a totality whose defects are merely those of an incompletely realised project, the history of Marxism being a history of attempts to finish that which Marx began. The means for such a final integration are held to be already present in the writings of Marx: the task of Marxist theoreticians becomes one in which these means are to be located and then deployed as solutions to identified problems.

These problems are to some extent issues that arise in capitalist economies which require the application or reworking of the theory of *Capital*. The history of Marxism becomes characterised by a double movement: the emergence of cases not covered directly in the text, and the extension of the text to account for such cases in manner consistent with the basic propositions of the text. In such activity, it is necessarily assumed that there *are* a set of basic propositions, since it is the existence of these that provides the foundation of the project of Marxism. And in this way, another aspect of Marxist writing arises which is complementary to the one just outlined: the attempt to establish these basic propositions and their fundamental coherence through exegesis and reflection on the writings of Marx. This writing also provides a position of authority from which permitted modifications can be assessed, giving rise to doctrinal disputes which sustain academic Marxism, publishing houses, independent printers and Rank-Xerox.

This process of a return to Marx as the source of Marxism surreptitiously and continually reworks Marxism as an 'unchanging totality' founded on the project of *Capital*. By treating the 'classics of Marxism' as simply the realisations of this project the unity of Marxism is affirmed while at the same time the necessity for serious consideration of these texts independently of this alleged project never arises. This has had serious affects on the manner in which the work of Lenin has been understood, for example.

Our analysis of the agrarian question as formulated by German and Russian Social Democracy has shown that the development of theoretical and practical work in these movements did not take the form of the development of a unitary project, and that in particular *Capital* did not provide a unique basis for the major texts of Kautsky and Lenin. Contrary to contemporary supposition, Marxism does not consist of a unity, but has been characterised by a series of substantial rifts which fracture irretrievably the totality that has been created by later writing. This leads us to our second thesis, namely:

**Debates within Marxism are internally differentiated, and that differentiation cannot be reduced to adherence to or deviation from the scientific problematic of 'Capital'.**

The characterisation of the history of Marxism above deliberately left to one side consideration of the mode in which it progressed as a totality *in potentia*. As with any other unity, integration is periodically re-established through the purging of particular sets of ideas or groups of persons, or more occasionally through their rehabilitation. In the case of Marxism, revolutionary purity is maintained by the identification of reformism or revisionist tendencies. The most notable example in the discussion above is of course the development of a 'revisionist tendency' in German Marxism associated with the name of Bernstein as well as with the lesser known figures like Vollmar and David. As we have shown this tendency developed in response to the political problems facing the SPD, but the campaign against revisionism conducted by leading Marxists took the form of identifying theoretical and political deviations from which political positions were deduced or merely imputed. When substantive arguments were developed against such a position, as for instance in *Die Agrarfrage*, the target of criticism remained un-named, thus the *raison d'être* of Kautsky's book has been consistently misconstrued by readers unfamiliar with the debates in the SFPD during the 1890s.

The essential feature of the criticism of revisionism and reformism by modern as well as classical orthodox Marxists is the assumption that political differences are ultimately premised on theoretical errors. What this assumption does is to surreptitiously transform every problem concerning the conditions of existence of political differences into an epistemological problem of locating the deviations from the presumed correct scientific path and tracing their sources.

The direct criticisms of Bernstein made by Kautsky, Luxemburg and Plekhanov treated his revisionism as a matter concerning a deviation from the scientific problematic of Marxism, enshrined in *Capital*. The criticisms of Plekhanov in particular treated Bernstein as a theoretical amateur who did not understand that he was a neo-Kantian, and not a Marxist.[1]

In contemporary discussions this general tendency to ground all political differences in epistemology is promoted by the treatment of Marxism as a body of ideas, and the consequent possibility of employing epistemological criteria in the evaluation of propositions pretending to a Marxist status. Revisionism is conceived as a general, theoretical form of deviation, of which Bernstein is merely the major exemplar. Colletti's discussion of Bernstein is a good example of this: the theoretical deficiencies of Bernstein can be established from an examination of some of his writings, and this in turn used to throw light on the political deviations of the Second International.[2] In a different way the epistemologisation of political differences is also a characteristic of the manner in which Althusser and his associates have recovered *Capital* as an object of theoretical investigation.

What we are arguing for is not that one should be fair to Bernstein and other revisionists more closely associated with the controversies around the agrarian question, and recognise the correctness of at least some of their ideas, because that would amount to nothing more than a charge of sides within the epistemological terrain. What in our view needs to be accepted as well as recognised is that the search for the epistemological sources of political differences rests on a strange and unspoken assumption that all political differences are always already predetermined in the theoretical field and the political arena itself is incapable of generating such differences. The point that we want to emphasise is that whether or not Bernstein surreptitiously drew on the Kantian philosophy has little relevance to why revisionism and reformism broke out within the ranks of the German Social Democrats within the 1890s.

Not only does the epistemological stance consist in conceiving of political differences as theoretical errors but also in creating a mythical unity: the orthodoxy or the rectitude of the scientific problematic. What such a stance does is to paper over the cracks and unevennesses within what supposedly constitutes the orthodoxy. For instance, what such a stance would do would be to neglect the important differences that exist between Marx's writings and those of Lenin and also those of Kautsky, provided that one is now willing to treat him as orthodox.

In particular our argument is that the 'agrarian question' can neither be regarded as a single problem facing Marxism, nor do the means for its resolution exist within the discourse of *Capital*. The evaluation of political positions adopted with respect to the variety of issues denoted by this 'question' cannot therefore be based on the establishment of their adherence to or deviation from the scientific problematic of *Capital*, or any other writings for that matter. This leads to our third point, that:

**The 'agrarian question' was not a question posed within Marx's writings, but represents a number of political problems faced by Social Democrat organisations; the significance of the theoretical debates that it gave rise to cannot be understood in isolation from this political context.**

As has been noted, Kautsky's *Agrarian Question* was implicitly directed against certain theses advanced by writers such as David, Ernst and Bernstein concerning the tendencies of capitalist development in the countryside. Subsequent readers of the text cannot be blamed for failing to register this, since this is never directly indicated by Kautsky; he in fact even obscures the problem by referring to Sombart in the introductory passages. Translations of the work have omitted the second part which directed itself to the consideration of the possibility of an agrarian programme; the book in any case sold out within a few years of its publication and was never reprinted, since the alterations that Kautsky would have wished to make were too extensive compared with the usefulness of such revisions.[3] These factors have encouraged the subsequent treatment of the work as one concerned primarily with the extension of Marx's analysis of capitalist economy into the agrarian sphere.

In the case of *Development of Capitalism in Russia*, the theoretical objective was clearer and cannot so easily be ignored, but the relation of this text to the subsequent political debates in the RSDLP has been similarily neglected. Such examinations of these and related texts that have been undertaken have dealt with them in isolation from the political problems that condition them. We have tried to show in the chapters above that a prior examination of the political terrain into which such texts are interventions is crucial to any effective assessment of their significance and general arguments. In these concluding remarks, we can perhaps turn briefly again to the question of the tendencies of capitalist development and their status within the political calculations of German and Russian Marxism.

It is often suggested that the central role assigned to economic tendencies in the Erfurt programme on the assumption that economic changes themselves will produce conditions for transition to socialism is indicative of the mechanical distortion of Marxism by the SPD. We have argued in the previous chapters that Marxism consists of a heterogeneous variety of discourses, some abstract and theoretical like *Capital* and some more directly political, like the Erfurt programme itself. What needs recognising is that a political programme like the Erfurt programme imposes its own requirements on what appears in it, and as a result it cannot be assessed just in terms of how faithfully it represents the master text. We have drawn attention to the fact that the status of the tendencies in the Erfurt programme and *Capital* even when formally identical is not the same in the two documents. For instance the question of the time it might take the tendencies to realise themselves is not crucial in a text like *Capital*, but it is central to a political programme. In fact *Capital* neglects the question more or less completely, yet it was this question around which the controversy concerning revisionism was centred.

That there is a form of evolutionism and economistic dogma implicit in the preamble of the Erfurt programme which lists the tendencies of capitalism is indeed correct, but simply registering that is not enough. We have argued that evolutionism has no unique and unambiguous consequences for politics, the arguments of both the sides in the revisionist controversy were equally evolutionist.

The listing of the tendencies of evolution did not, as we showed, solve the problem of political calculation. The 'agrarian question' denoted a series of political problems which turned on the electoral strategy of the SPD. As has been argued this strategy represented the only option open to the SPD in the later nineteenth century, given the combination of universal suffrage with autocracy typical of Wilhelmine Germany. An essential feature of the circumstances in which the German Social Democracy operated was that the time it would take for the successful realisation of its programme was incalculable. The influence of the SPD at the political level became dependent on the accumulation of votes and the supposition that eventual pressure of numbers (coupled of course with the undermining of police and army as bastions of reaction) would compel some alteration in the political order. That supposition, however, was not grounded in any calculation.

The SPD could neither give a clear and specific answer to the question 'what is needed for the party to capture political power?' nor could it neglect the question altogether. The questions concerning political calculation were posed in relation to the rate of realisation of tendencies. The debate over the future of the small farmer was, for instance, implicitly a debate on the potential electoral support for the party in an economy which had since the 1870s changed from a rural and agrarian formation into an urban and industrial power.

The question of the tendencies of capitalist development was also important for the RSDLP, for as has been shown it was the failure to calculate the rate of development of capitalism that was the weakness of the first agrarian programme of Social Democracy. The schema borrowed from *Development of Capitalism in Russia* of the relations of feudal and capitalist relations in the countryside was adequate to a refutation of Narodnik analysis, but was not appropriate to political calculations since it did not involve an assessment of the time-scale in which this took place. For a political organisation, this question is fundamental: calculation of its strategy and activity must necessarily involve the space of time in which these are to be realised. Unlike German Social Democracy, the Russian Social Democrats had in this respect more room for manoeuvre, their political stance permitted a number of different openings, which however were related to calculations concerning the rate at which Tsarist autocracy was decaying and capitalism developing. The role of capitalist tendencies was therefore distinct from that typical of the SPD.

In the 1920s, the question of tendencies of capitalist concentration in relation to the agrarian question assumed yet another form. In his introductory essay to *Beiträge zur Agrarfrage*, Varga counterposed the Social Democratic line on the question of concentration in agriculture to that of David and the revisionists, in which the disagreement is located as concerning the *rate* of concentration. For communists, suggests Varga, there is here no problem – the Revolution is, in the perspective of the Comintern, an actual, not a future, prospect, and so the eventual course of capitalist concentration is not a matter of interest.[4] All that mattered was the identification of sympathetic elements in the countryside and the neutralisation of hostile ones in the approaching struggle. Varga was subsequently accused of revisionism by Miljutin, but in his reply the Comintern argument that conditions were ripe for revolutionary struggles is again deployed to suggest the political irrelevance of a consideration of the tendencies of capitalist development.[5]

Propositions concerning the tendencies of capitalist development cannot therefore be treated simply as economic doctrine. In the three examples just referred to, these propositions were intricately related to political calculations on the part of Social Democratic and Communist organisations, isolating in diverse ways the assessment of the appropriate measures for political struggles. In the examples discussed in the course of this book, this problem was one of the central issues linking political and economic considerations in the diverse 'agrarian questions'. These then arose out of a number of factors, and cannot be reduced to the existence of a 'peasantry' doggedly resistant to the aims of Social Democratic politics. This brings us to the fourth thesis that we have advanced.

**There is no pre-given and constant object called the 'peasantry' which awaits discovery and description.**

The 'agrarian question' is not a problem that is simply generated by the discourse of *Capital*, nor does it represent the confrontation of this discourse with a 'peasantry' who resist integration into the general theory of capitalist development that *Capital* allegedly proposes. The identification of political and economic problems in diverse circumstances makes the 'agrarian question' as much a false unity as 'the peasantry' who are sometimes thought to constitute this problem. The foregoing chapters have consistently argued that 'Marxism' is not an entity that can be evaluated by reference to the writings of Marx; so here, the question of Marxism and the 'peasantry' cannot be reduced to the collation of Marx's stated views on the peasantry, hunting the peasantry through the pages of *Eighteenth Brumaire*, *Capital* and other texts.[6] Since there is no fixed and identifiable social group called 'the peasantry', it makes little sense to create such a unity through the citation of Marx's sometimes casual linguistic usage.

The arguments presented above have also been directed against those writers who conceive the peasantry as in some way or another a really existing and coherent section of national populations, which by their existence pose problems to both Marxist parties and Marxism in general. Examples of such an approach can be found in the work of Mitrany and Shanin, both of whom suppose that the 'peasantry' is a definable category of population, existing in specific geographical regions and subsisting on a common basis. While this approach is one often encountered today, it can be seen from the arguments presented in the preceding chapters that it would make no sense to compare on this basis a 'German' or 'Russian' peasantry. In each country, the 'peasant problem' for Social Democracy was a product of political and economic conditions that were quite diverse, and in no way indicative of a 'lapse' in the fabric of Marxism. Accordingly, analysis of the 'peasantry' did not begin from the specification of a type of economy, but was rather conducted in terms of the political and economic conditions themselves constitutive of the problem.[7]

While the 'peasant problem' was then in no way a unitary and pre-existing problem for Marxism, it also existed for quite different political tendencies. Thus for instance in Britain during the later nineteenth century such a term denoted the Irish problem on the one hand, and the decline of English agriculture on the other. In classical terms of course the peasantry had been abolished as a significant factor in Britain by the early eighteenth century, but the impoverishment of rural labourers and smallholders in the 1880s and 1890s led to a series of investigations into the conditions of this 'new peasantry', and the development of a number of legislative proposals.[8] Bourgeois political organisations called for partial land nationalisation as a solution to this problem, while followers of Henry George demanded the introduction of a single tax on land to displace the revenue derived from rent. An 'agrarian question' was thus constituted in Britain on foundations, and for political organisations, quite distinct from those typical for Germany and Russia in the same period.

Another example of the manner in which 'the peasantry' is an ever-reconstituted social category is to be found in a pamphlet of Bukharin, *The Peasant Question*. Given as a speech to an enlarged plenum of the Executive Committee of the Comintern in April 1925, Bukharin suggests that it is quite wrong to conceive the 'peasant question' as one relating only to countries like Russia with a large peasant population. To hold to such a belief would be to subscribe to a Trotskyist thesis of permanent revolution in which aid from W. Europe was vital to prevent the revolutionary seizure of power by the workers being opposed by peasant counter-revolution. This distinction, suggested Bukharin, between national and international revolutions, was erroneous. World revolution would pose further problems, since the majority of the world's population was made up of *peasants*. This was formulated in the slogan 'the colonial question is the specific form of the agrarian and peasant question'.[9] The current stage of capitalism was characterised by a struggle between the bourgeoisie and the proletariat for the peasantry, a struggle which was better understood by bourgeois parties than by communists.

It would be possible to take other examples: for example, the manner in which the 'German peasantry', resistant to the urban workers of Social Democracy for so long, was recruited as a substantial supporter of the urban workers of the Nazi Party. Research on this problem shows that this is not illuminated by the prior constitution of a peasantry as an independent and self-sufficient population, and that any solution of the apparent paradox requires the dissolution of the notion of a unitary peasantry.[10] Piling example on example would however only serve to elucidate the proposition that the category 'peasantry' is constituted in quite diverse ways, and consequently cannot be treated as a definable entity with uniform or broadly similar effects on economies and political groupings. In particular, it has been shown above that treatment of 'peasantry' as pre-capitalist survival was not a form of analysis that characterised the 'agrarian question' for Social Democracy, this being a relatively recent trend among sociologists and development theorists—thus:

**The 'agrarian question' is not one which was characterised by Social Democrats as the outcome of the confrontation of capitalist and pre-capitalist modes of production.**

Much writing on the peasantry and development has in recent years come to be dominated by the practice of identifying peasants with pre-capitalist forms of production, the gradual elimination of these forms with the extension of capitalist relations eliminating the basis for the continued existence of a peasantry. Thus the 'peasant problem', conceived as a political, economic, social or even cultural crisis. Alternatively, this specific problem can be inflated (in a manner reminiscent of Bukharin) to a general characterisation of development and underdevelopment on a world scale. As peasantries become academically modish, large sections of the world's population are reclassified accordingly.

Part of the problem for Marxists has been that there is little to be found in Marx's writings on peasants which is directly useable. What can be found however are substantial passages on pre-capitalist forms of production – in the *Grundrisse*, in *Capital* Vol. I, and *Capital* Vol. III. Although such passages are generally directed towards quite specific ends, such as the identification of a genealogy for capitalist production, they do possess the virtue of demarcating diverse forms of pre-capitalist systems, enabling some escape to be made from an equation of pre-*capitalist* societies in general with pre-*industrial* societies. The elaboration of theories of modes of production on this basis provides a way of recreating a Marxist position on questions of development which is established and evaluated with criteria generally recognised as Marxist.

From such an approach it follows that the question of the situation of peasant producers is one which is to be dealt with in terms of the *articulation* of these modes of production, specifically the articulation of pre-capitalist and capitalist modes. But as we have seen, this is not an approach that was followed by the classical Marxist investigations that we have examined; insofar as it has Marxist filiations, it belongs to the line initiated by Preobrazhensky in which distinct sectors are identified, the crucial problem being the manner in which their relation is realised and fought out. Modern versions of this style of analysis are however the result of a sociologisation of political issues, in which the question of articulation becomes a means for the constitution of differentiated social totalities.[11] The sociological problem of the structure of specific societies takes the place of the political problems of organisations faced with particular objectives and means for their realisation, which in their different ways constitute 'the peasantry' as a political object of relevance with concepts and categories drawn from Marxism. It is for this reason that it was decided to exclude any detailed analysis of modern Marxist theories of development and the peasantry, because the approach that they adopt is one that is largely incommensurable with that typical of German and Russian Marxism. It is notable that where definite attempts are made to draw on such works, a transformation takes place according to which these texts are converted to analyses of social change, rather than of political issues.[12]

Where concepts drawn from Marx's work are deployed for less academic purposes, as for instance in the series of studies of Indian agrarian capitalism that can be found in *Economic and Political Weekly*,[13] analysis is hampered by the necessity of adhering closely to the letter of Marx and Lenin's writings perceived as relevant. As we have noted, not only are Marx's writings far from consistent, but those of Lenin in certain important respects deviate from the letter of Marx's authorised positions. The treatment of the economic analyses of Lenin for example as nothing more than economic analyses leads to the employment of his categories to simply *identify* capitalist relations; this exercise becomes an end in itself if the purpose for which such an approach was used by Lenin remains unexamined. A general failure to question the basis of the orthodoxy established by Lenin leads to the utilisation of *Development of Capitalism in Russia* as the Marxist's guide to agrarian capitalism. This brings us to a further point:

**Many of the themes and notions that are to be found in writings on the agrarian question are inconsistent with the analysis of 'Capital'.**

We have argued above that there is no unique project that is founded by *Capital*, and that if the writings of Lenin and Kautsky are examined, the orthodoxy of their positions cannot be established *via* reference to *Capital*. In important respects, deviations exist between these writings and those of Marx: Kautsky's 'failure' to use the theory of rent, and Lenin's account of proletarianisation are two which we can instance here. The variations which we can identify have however been demonstrated to be conditioned by the specific problems faced by Lenin and Kautsky, and should not be regarded as deviations from the writ. Marxism is not a unity derived from an original doctrine laid down by Marx before 1883.

While there is a chapter on value and rent in *The Agrarian Question*, as has been pointed out these categories play no positive role in the arguments advanced by Kautsky; rent is identified only as an obstacle to capital accumulation on the part of the capitalist farmer, and is not treated as a means for investigating rural capitalist economic structure. By contrast, the summary of the text presented by Banaji[14] devoted inordinate space to this question, reflecting the demands placed on *Agrarfrage* as a Marxist classic rather than the actual order of importance of problems dealt with in the text. For Banaji, Marx's analysis of rent as presented in *Capital* Vol. III represents the means for investigating the class structure of capitalist agriculture, offering the possibility of identifying the manner in which surplus value is distributed and transferred. While Kautsky gestured toward such an orthodoxy, it is clear that there was little to be gained from the construction of such an analysis, and so the genuflection to Marx's theory of rent and value is left as a chapter without any place in the structure of the argument. Insofar as Marx's theory has found application by later writers, it has mostly served to further the sociologisation of questions of articulation and transition as discussed above.

Lenin also neglected this major contribution by Marx to the analysis of capitalist agriculture, reserving his discussion of it for polemics with others in which it served to establish the Marxist credentials of Lenin's position. It has been argued elsewhere that the major significance of Marx's discussion of rent in Vol. III lies in the requirement to reconcile the existence of rent with his theory of value; it does not exist primarily as an extension of the analysis of capitalist production to the agricultural sphere.[15] The doctrinal *raison d'être* of Marx's analysis of rent was thus tacitly recognised in the manner in which it was deployed by Lenin, as a means of preserving Marxist orthodoxy.

In chapter twenty seven of *Capital* Vol. I Marx outlines the process by which an agricultural proletariat was formed with the gradual separation of producers from the land. The rate at which this proletariat was formed is indicated by the rate at which possession of the means of production is destroyed through various mechanisms. It must be emphasised that this discussion of expropriation can be distinguished from that of bourgeois radicals who conceived this process as one simply of loss, as indicative of Man's decline. Engels for instance in his Foreword to the American edition of *Condition of the English Working Class* opposed the followers of Henry George who treated the separation from land as a universal basis of oppression; he emphasised that in medieval times the mode of connection of man and land had been the basis of exploitation.[16] Possession of the means of production did not therefore automatically involve the freedom of the possessor; more important was the manner in which land was appropriated.

This form of argument can also be detected in *Capital*, for instance where Marx is discussing the Sutherland clearances as a recent phase of expropriation.[17] While at points Marx states that the Highlanders so cleared from the centre of the estate to crofts and villages on the coast were being separated from land they had possessed for centuries, it is also stated that what occurred was in reality an alteration in the mode of tenure. Tenants before, and tenants after, the Clearances involved an attempt to reorganise estates so that they would become paying propositions. This involved moving tenants and providing them with a different mode of subsistence (fishing and crofting). The connection of the Sutherland estates with the Bridgewater estate and the conditions placed on the use of the revenues from the latter in fact involved a massive programme of investment financed from canal dues. Despite this, the estate remained unprofitable.[18]

There are in this way qualifications that can be detected in Marx's account of the formation of an agricultural proletariat, but the general theses involve an association of separation from land with the creation of a proletariat, such that this becomes conceived as a condition of capitalist development. When taken up in later studies by Marxists, the degree of separation from land is treated as an index of the rate and extent of capitalist development: indeed, this is often treated as the primary sign of capitalism in the countryside. As we have seen, however, Lenin deviates from the letter of his doctrine established in *Capital*. Not only is the formation of a proletariat treated independently of the question of possession of land (absolutely), the process of differentiation which is identified as the mechanism creating this proletariat is not one which involves individual labourers. The subjects of capitalist differentiation are according to Lenin *peasant households*, not individual peasants. The formation of a proletariat is therefore related not to dispossession, but to the economic activity of household units. It might be argued that this distinction is merely an effect of the legal conditions of the Russian rural economy, but the point is raised here because it has usually been completely overlooked by writers who assume that the analysis of proletarianisation that is to be found in Marx is simply exemplified by Lenin.

The evaluation of different types of rural organisation, and discussion of their possible future course of development, does not simply rest on the isolation of certain key categories drawn from *Capital*. In some recent cases, a logic of capitalist development is derived from the structure of *Capital* which is then translated into a set of imperatives of the capitalist mode of production. Reforms for instance can be assessed according to the manner in which they correspond to or deviate from these imperatives. It is also customary in such an approach to treat the state form as a realisation of the requirements of capitalist production, such that investigation of the state is a necessary prerequisite to the determination of the nature of development in any particular national economy. This leads to another thesis;

**The state cannot be treated as a representation of the integrity of a mode of production, the 'state apparatus' corresponding to coherent means for the realisation of that integration.**

It might be possible to construct an account of the SPD and its various political problems in terms of its relation to the Wilhelminian State;[19] we do not believe that such an exercise would however be very fruitful, and have accordingly taken a very different course in the earlier chapters. There does on the other hand exist a considerable literature devoted to the nature of the Soviet state, in which the nature of this state is conceived as the key to the analysis of the Russian social formation since the October Revolution. Again, the chapter dealing with agrarian reform in Russia explicitly rejects conceptions of the state as a social totality, in which the various agents of the state apparatus are merely representations of a particular type of class state. Preoccupation with the class nature of any specific state is a sociological problem in the same way that preoccupation with the question of articulation is; indeed, the two are in some instances related, the nature of the state being derived as a resultant of the articulated forces. One of the central theses advanced in this chapter is that the deduction of the modality of elements of a state apparatus from the imperatives of a capitalist, or even socialist, mode of production, results in the ascription to the state of universal powers. Charged with specific tasks, that state deploys its forces and seeks to impose its will on the society at large. What is neglected in this broad approach is the social nature of the instruments through which this 'will' is supposedly transmitted; and the fact that this 'will' is either unrealised because of the absence of appropriate instruments, or is constructed in the agencies themselves. If this latter position is adhered to, it is no longer possible to place any weight on theories of state power in which economic policy is a simple realisation of this power; the state as totality disintegrates, and is replaced by a conception of differentiated agencies as social forces. Consequently, it is no longer possible to deduce the nature of certain reforms from the structure of the state.

An example of this problem can be found in much of the Marxist literature on Tanzanian development. Since independence, Tanzania has undergone a series of rapid changes in rural organisation as a result of government policy: first the development of Ujamaa villages, conceived as model communal settlements; then the forced villagisation of large sections of the population, excluding tobacco, coffee farmers and others; then the dismantling of this programme in the face of the economic and political pressures that it gave rise to. All the phases of this process were officially couched in the language of socialist doctrine, although radical socialists increasingly denounced the government as being representative not of a socialist state, but of a bourgeois one. Since the execution of rural policy appeared to be directly consequent on a centralised decision-making apparatus, it appeared quite natural to examine the complexion of this apparatus before establishing the class complexion of the various reforms. This commits the same error however as is characteristic of Marxist analyses of Soviet policy in the 1920s. By treating the state as a totality which is simply realised in its effects, the contradictory nature of the various state agencies and their effects goes unnoticed. The attribution of a particular class character to a state does not solve the problem of the nature of specific policies and reforms: the latter cannot be evaluated by a process of deduction from the former. The character of specific policies and their effects can only be assessed by an examination of the instruments and agencies that execute certain measures, requiring not a class analysis of the state, but careful and detailed examination of the functioning of economic and political agencies, their organisation, areas of competence, and objectives.[20]

The points raised in these concluding remarks do not of course exhaust the issues that we have raised in the preceding pages; they merely seek to give direction to a work which is organised as a study of what might apparently be the historical contexts of Marxist theory. The sometimes polemical tone of the discussion of the various theses advanced here should be related to the substantive arguments presented in the foregoing chapters. The purpose of this book has been to raise certain problems in the manner in which Marxist analysis is conducted by means of a detailed discussion of German and Russian Marxism. In so doing, we seek to free Marxist theory of much of the baggage which has for so long prevented significant development of contributions that it might make to socialist struggles of all kinds.

# Notes to Part 2

**Introduction**

1. While this is often dictated by the necessity of rapidly summarising the development of Marxist politics in Russia (as in the first volume of Carr's *History* for instance) the association of Marxism with 'Leninism' is fairly general. This goes also for those writers who through a comparison of Marx and Lenin seek to show the latter's Blanquist, rather than Marxist, heritage (Harding (1977), ch. 1 for an exposé of this approach). This approach conveniently ignores the fact that Marx's writings on Russia are distinctly Blanquist.
2. Anderson (1976), p. 9.
3. This elementary critical point is neglected by Pipes in his oft-cited discussion of Narodism (1964). He suggests that 'Populism' as criticised by Lenin did not exist during the 1890s, and that Lenin therefore erred in creating such an object of polemic. Pipes fails to take into account Lenin's own comments on the definition of Narodism in 'The Heritage We Renounce', Lenin CW 2, pp. 513ff.

**6 Russian Agriculture 1860–1900: Some effects of the Emancipation Settlement**

1. See Gerschenkron (1962a).
2. Crisp (1976), p. 44.
3. Ibid., pp. 46–7.
4. This ignores for the time being the situation of the state serfs, which was different.
5. For accounts of the eighteenth and nineteenth centuries, see Blum (1961) and Confino (1969). We do not intend to suggest here that the Emancipation was a 'capitalist' reform: rather that in later arguments it could be deployed *as if it were* the origin of capitalist development.
6. Blum (1961), pp. 616–17.
7. Emmons (1968a), p. 21; but he goes on to suggest that a figure nearer 55 per cent might be more acurate.
8. Lyaschenko (1970), pp. 365–6.
9. While these regions took shape in the early part of the nineteenth century, it was only the development of the railways that enables the more fertile regions to become 'surplus' areas.
10. Crisp (1976), pp. 73–6.
11. Ibid., p. 78.
12. Treadgold (1957), p. 29.
13. Emmons (1968a), p. 27.

14. While some military planes were initially drawn up to deal with unrest, actual preparations for the Promulgation only took the form of appointing a military commander-in-chief for each administrative district to coordinate any measures necessary. In the period March to May 1861, 47 battalions, 187 infantry companies, 38½ cavalry squadrons and 3000 Cossacks participated directly in pacification (Emmons, 1968b, pp. 53–5). For a general account of the reception of the Emancipation terms, see Venturi (1966), pp. 206ff.
15. The following account is based mainly on Robinson (1949).
16. Crisp (1976), p. 82.
17. Simms (1977), pp. 379ff. Crisp suggests that for the bulk of the peasantry items bearing tax were effectively luxury goods, and that at the worst the impact of taxation on the peasantry as a whole was neutral. Crisp (1976), pp. 27–8. See Gerschenkron (1965), pp. 776–80.
18. Maslov (1907).
19. Oganowsky (1913), pp. 702–4.
20. Treadgold (1957), p. 129.
21. Crisp (1976), p. 17.
22. Even in 1941 the railways were the only suitable means of heavy transport, as the invading Germans found to their cost. In July, shortly after the beginning of the Russian campaign, rains rendered most of the Russian roads in German hands impassable to wheeled transport; van Crefeld (1977), p. 155.
23. Pavlovsky (1930), pp. 30–1.
24. In Britain the production of butter and cheese had been eclipsed by the superior quality of European and American goods, fresh milk being perhaps the only product that could not be imported from overseas producers; Orwin and Whetham (1971), pp. 146ff.
25. Nicolai-on (1899), p. 16.
26. Ibid., p. 22.

## 7 Russian Marxism and the Agrarian Question

1. Starr (1972), p. xv.
2. Ibid., p. xxxiiiff. For a discussion of Chernyshevsky's economic views, see Lampert (1965), pp. 88–96.
3. Quoted in Gerschenkron (1962b), p. 172.
4. An account of the development of these ideas can be found in Kimball (1973).
5. Becker (1870), p. 13.
6. The Russian edition of *Capital*, published in 1872, was the first foreign-language edition of the work to appear. One of the reports made to the Censor on this work suggested that since it attacked a system, and not persons, it represented no threat to the Royal Family. See Resis (1970).
7. But not in fact published in Russian until 1886: Marx and Engels, *Werke*, vol. xix, p. 558, n. 69; for a translation see Blackstock and Hoselitz (1952), pp. 216–18.
8. *Selected Correspondence* 353.
9. Before 1861 both Marx and Engels viewed Russia as a reactionary bastion

which threatened the stability of Europe, finding expression in their writings on the Polish and Balkan questions. Polish liberation was for example conceived not as a desirable end in itself, but rather as promising to move the Russian frontier to the East and in this way promoting the chances of German democratisation. Russian conditions were thus evaluated above all in terms of their effects on European democratic movements, and Marx's writings especially drew heavily on a literature of Russophobia then current in England. *The Secret Diplomatic History of Lord Palmerston* can for example be seen to owe more to this literature than to any 'Marxist' analysis. See Krause (1958), pp. 49ff.
10. Mendel (1961), p. 39.
11. Nicolai-on (1899), p. 97.
12. Ibid., pp. 139–40.
13. Mendel (1961), pp. 44–5.
14. See Walicki (1969), pp. 115ff.
15. Struve (1894), p. 351.
16. Wortman (1967), pp. 45–58.
17. *Selected Correspondence*, p. 348.
18. Marx and Engels, *Werke*, vol. xix, p. 391. A composite version of the drafts and final letter can be found in Blackstock and Hoselitz (1952), pp. 218–26. See also Carr (1952) Note C which gives a brief summary of Marx and Engels' views on Russia. Another recent discussion of the commune and Marx's views on it can be found in Levine (1978), but the usefulness of this is reduced by the writer's treatment of Marx's position as primarily the expression of a philosophy of history.
19. Marx and Engels, *Werke*, vol. xix, p. 296. See translation in Blackstock and Hoselitz (1952), pp. 227–8.
20. *Selected Correspondence*, p. 437.
21. Ibid., p. 509.
22. Marx and Engels, *Werke*, vol. xviii, p. 539. See translation in Blackstock and Hoselitz (1952), pp. 203–15.
23. Ibid., pp. 563–4. At the end of the article Engels does mention the role of communes in a revolution supported by proletarian uprisings in Europe, the latter being described as 'delivering the material means to the Russian peasants'. The significance of this conception is however diminished by its placement at the end of the article.
24. Marx and Engels, *Werke*, vol. xvii, pp. 663–74. See translation in Blackstock and Hoselitz (1952), pp. 229–41.
25. See Walicki (1969), pp. 110–14 for an outline of Flerovsky's work.
26. For an outline of Plekhanov's early political development, see Baron (1963), chs. 1–6; (1967).
27. Marx and Engels, *Werke*, vol. xviii, p. 557.
28. Frankel (1969), p. 10.
29. Plekhanov (1961), p. 120.
30. Ibid., p. 183.
31. Ibid., pp. 250–6.
32. Ibid., p. 260.
33. Ibid., pp. 275ff.
34. Ibid., p. 308.
35. Ibid., p. 309.

36. While the question of party organisation and the working class is not directly relevant at this point, it is worth pointing out that it was after the adoption by Russian Social Democracy of the theses on agitation and propaganda embodied in Kremer and Martov's *On Agitation* (1894) that work was able to break out of the 'circlism' of the mid-1890s and engage with worker unrest, promoting a wave of industrial strikes. In many ways the militant working class that Plekhanov called for in the mid-1880s emerged first in the 1890s, but *as a creation of Social Democracy itself*. See Frankel (1969), pp. 18–27; Wildman (1967), pp. 59–82; Harding (1977), pp. 115ff.
37. Loizou (1976), p. 12.
38. Harding (1977), ch. 2 stresses that *Socialism and the Political Struggle* remained authoritative along with *Our Differences* until the end of the century, and that in his early work Lenin built directly on them.
39. Haimson (1955), p. 148.
40. The SRs are discussed in the following chapter.
41. For instance, Mikhailovsky sought refuge in this way as Lenin points out in *The Heritage we Renounce*.
42. Lenin *Collected Works*, vol. I, p. 24.
43. Ibid., p. 37.
44. Ibid., p. 45.
45. Ibid. pp. 54–5.
46. Ibid. vol. II, p. 435.
47. Ibid. vol. I, p. 206.
48. Ibid. vol. II, p. 521.
49. Ibid. vol. III, p. 25.
50. Ibid., p. 38.
51. Ibid., p. 32–3.
52. Ibid., p. 181.
53. Ibid., p. 166.
54. Ibid., pp. 191–2.
55. Ibid., pp. 194–5.
56. Ibid., p. 210.
57. Ibid., p. 32.
58. Ibid., pp. 267ff.
59. Ibid., pp. 311–12.
60. Ibid., pp. 427–8.
61. This suggestion has been made by de Crisenoy (1978), p. 93. See the discussion of this in Tribe (1979).
62. de Crisenoy (1978), p. 100.
63. Lenin, *Collected Works*, vol. III, p. 27.
64. Ibid., vol. IV, p. 94.
65. Ibid., vol. III, p. 612.
66. See ibid., vol. IV, pp. 105–59; vol. 5, pp. 103–222.

## 8 The Russian Social Democractic Labour Party and the Development of an Agrarian Programme

1. Plekhanov (1961) Works 1, p. 405.
2. Ibid., p. 404.

3. Ibid., p. 408.
4. Ibid.
5. Elwood (1974), pp. 34–7.
6. 'Draft and Explanation of a Programme for the Social-Democratic Party' Lenin (1895), *Collected Works*, vol. II, pp. 93–121; 'Our Programme' Lenin (1900), *Collected Works*, vol. IV, pp. 210–14.
7. Ibid., vol. IV, p. 232.
8. Ibid., p. 235.
9. Ibid., p. 242.
10. Ibid., p. 243.
11. Ibid., p. 245.
12. Ibid., pp. 420–28.
13. Ibid., vol. VI, p. 30.
14. Ibid., p. 138.
15. Loizou (1976), p. 76–7.
16. Lenin, *Collected Works*, vol. VI, pp. 442–3.
17. Loizou (1976), pp. 90–103.
18. Elwood (1974), p. 51.
19. Perrie (1976), p. 58.
20. Ibid., p. 9.
21. Haimson (1955), p. 150.
22. Perrie (1976), p. 81.
23. Ibid., p. 82.
24. Lenin, *Collected Works*, vol VI, p. 201.
25. See also 'Vulgar Socialism and Narodism as Resurrected by the Socialist Revolutionaries' (Lenin, *Collected Works*, vol. VI, pp. 261–8) for a more detailed critique. While Lenin never realised his plan for composing a more detailed and comprehensive rebuttal of SR theory, the outlines of his arguments can be judged from his lecture notes (Lenin, *Collected Works*, vol. XL, pp. 53–63) and also from a draft for a pamphlet (Lenin, ibid., vol. XLI, pp. 70–77).
26. Perrie (1976), p. 119.
27. Ibid., pp. 132–4.
28. Loizou (1976), 132. See pt II of the dissertation for a detailed discussion of the debates during 1905. It is unfortunate that this thesis does not exist in a form that is more generally available. See also Carr (1952), pp. 16–24.
29. Lenin, *Collected Works*, vol. VIII, pp. 231–6.
30. Cf. 'On Our Agrarian Programme' Lenin, Ibid., p. 248.
31. 'Social Democracy's Attitude towards the Peasant Movement' Lenin, *Collected Works*, vol. IX, p. 237.
32. The political distinctions between nationalisation (ownership of lands by the state) and muncipalisation (ownership of land by local corporate bodies) are discussed below.
33. This has been touched on in the previous chapter.
34. Lenin, *Collected Works*, vol. X, p. 177.
35. Ibid., p. 181.
36. Elwood (1974), pp. 77–8.
37. Ibid., vol. VIII, pp. 319–22.
38. Elwood (1974), pp. 95–6.
39. Lenin, *Collected Works*, vol. X, p. 279.

40. Ibid., p. 288. As mentioned above, 'division' is not here discussed.
41. Ibid., vol.xiii, p. 220.
42. Ibid., pp. 243–7.
43. Ibid., p. 257.
44. Ibid. vol. iv, pp. 234–5.
45. Ibid. vol. xiii, p. 259.
46. Ibid. vol. x, pp. 279–88.

## 9 The Russian Peasantry as Object of State Policy, 1906–1929

1. Stalin, *Works* vol. xi, p. 173: 'Industrialisation and the Grain Problem' (9 July 1928).
2. The most useful general source in English remains the history by Carr, which despite some problems has a clear exposition of central issues and an overwhelming grasp of detail.
3. Robinson (1949), p. 145.
4. This was in 1903; see ibid., p. 146.
5. Owen (1937), p. 56.
6. Yaney (1964), p. 275.
7. Mosse (1964), p. 257.
8. Owen (1937), p. 56.
9. Outlined in ch. 1.
10. Robinson (1949), p. 212.
11. Stolypin; speech to Third Duma, 5 December 1908, quoted at length in Treadgold (1955), p. 5.
12. Stolypin; speech to Second Duma, 10 May 1907; Treadgold (1955), p. 3.
13. Yaney (1964), pp. 276–7.
14. Ibid., pp. 289–90.
15. Robinson (1949), p. 221.
16. Wieth-Knudsen (1913), p. 77. For a summary of this book in English see Ely (1916).
17. Atkinson (1973), p. 776.
18. Ibid., p. 777. These figures correspond to those given by Robinson, despite Atkinson's argument that all previous sources overestimate the effects of the reform settlement.
19. Owen (1937), p. 144.
20. Oganowsky (1913), p. 734.
21. In the period 1907–12 the number of state employed agronomists rose from 141 to 1365, while there was a corresponding increase in local government activity. See Brutzkus (1925), p. 106.
22. In 1906, the capacity of 19 out of Chicago's 89 grain elevators nearly equalled the total storage capacity of the Russian railways' elevators and granaries taken together. A construction programme was only getting under way at the outbreak of war; see Pavlovsky (1930), pp. 259–60. This is an important point to remember, considering the slow rate of agricultural and related investment until the late 1920s.
23. Oganowsky (1913), p. 710.
24. Ibid., p. 709.
25. Ibid., pp. 713–17.

# NOTES

26. Figures from Pavlovsky (1930), p. 249.
27. Antsiferov (1930), p. 54. If the 1861–70 average is taken as 100, then the index figures for 1901–10 are 149 for peasant and 164 for non-peasant (all grains).
28. Pavlovsky (1930), p. 250.
29. von Dietze (1920), p. 3.
30. Antsiferov (1930), pp. 109–10.
31. Ibid., pp. 140ff. See also Sorlin (1964), pp. 254–5.
32. Keep (1976), p. 37.
33. Dubrowski (1929) has graphs for these movements, pp. 41, 87.
34. Robinson (1949), pp. 249–50. See also discussion in ch. 1 above.
35. Dubrowski (1929), p. 63.
36. 'Cabinet' and 'apanage' lands were areas previously the property of the Imperial Family.
37. Keep (1976), pp. 163–6.
38. Ibid., p. 169.
39. Ibid., pp. 176–8.
40. See the table of disturbances by class object in Dubrowski (1929), p. 99, for period 1900–17.
41. Ibid., p. 101.
42. Keep (1976), p. 404.
43. Lenin, *Collected Works*, vol. xxiv, p. 23; 'The Tasks of the Proletariat in the Present Revolution'.
44. Perrie (1972), p. 249. See also Linhart (1976) and Sorlin (1964) for a discussion of the relation of SR and Bolshevik policy.
45. Lenin, *Collected Works*, vol. xxvi, pp. 258–9.
46. Ibid., p. 260.
47. Carr (1952), pp. 43–4.
48. Ibid., p. 47. See also Male (1971), pp. 8–10 on this problem.
49. This is the theme of Shanin's writings for instance (1972).
50. Meyer (1974), p. 274.
51. Ibid., p. 276. Possession of livestock showed a similar pattern.
52. Lenin, *Collected Works*, vol. xxxii, p. 343; 'The Tax in Kind (The Significance of the New Policy and its Conditions)'.
53. The term 'proletarian natural economy' comes from Kritsman (1929) and is used in a slightly different sense by Meyer.
54. Carr (1952), p. 150.
55. Dobb (1966), p. 116.
56. Lenin, *Collected Works*, vol. xxix, p. 567; 'Freedom to Trade in Grain'.
57. Ibid. vol. xxvii, 'The Immediate Tasks of the Soviet Government'.
58. Kritsman (1929), p. 200.
59. Grosskopf (1976), p. 96.
60. Meyer (1974), pp. 16–19.
61. Osinskii, article in *Pravda*, January 1920, entitled 'Agricultural Crisis and Socialist Construction in the Village', cited in Meyer (1974), p. 44.
62. Krzizanowski (1920), p. 1203.
63. Meyer (1974), pp. 96–7. A national campaign had in December 1920 raised the number of days worked per month to 22.4.
64. Ibid., p. 86.
65. Lenin, *Collected Works*, vol. xxxii, p. 335.

66. Ibid., p. 349.
67. Meyer (1974), pp. 141ff.
68. Ibid., p. 170; figure for the drought provinces only.
69. Carr (1952), p. 289.
70. See Carr (1958), pp. 250–2 for details of the way the tax was computed.
71. Clarke (1972), p. 135; Table 71. Output in following years: 1913, 4.1 million tons; 1928, 4.9; 1929, 5.8; 1930, 4.3; 1931, 3.9; 1932, 2.8; 1933, 2.3; 1934, 2.0; 1935, 2.3; 1936, 3.7; 1937, 3.0; 1938, 4.5; 1939, 5.1.
72. Ibid., p. 137; Table 72.
73. Bukharin (1928), p. 1379. For a discussion of Preobrazhensky see Millar (1978) and also for a review of some of the different policy positions see Spulber (1965). For a general critique of the 'surplus' problematic, see Millar (1970).
74. Dobb (1967).
75. Dobb (1966), pp. 214–15.
76. Millar (1978).
77. We are referring here to Bettelheim's *Class Struggle in the USSR* in particular (1976 and 1978).
78. Millar and Guntzel (1970), p. 110.
79. Karcz (1967), pp. 427–9.
80. Davies (1970) and Karcz (1970).
81. Millar (1974) and Ellman (1975); see also Karcz (1971).
82. Grosskopf (1976), p. 138. The following account draws heavily on her work.
83. Ibid., p. 198.
84. Ibid., p. 208; Table.
85. Ibid., p. 238.
86. Ibid., p. 245.
87. Ibid., p. 261.
88. See Lewin (1966).
89. Solomon (1977), p. 77.
90. Lewin (1966), pp. 193–4.
91. Ibid., pp. 195–6.
92. Narkiewicz (1970), pp. 72–4.
93. Carr (1959), pp. 313–16.
94. Grosskopf (1976), pp. 124–5.
95. Sutton (1968), pp. 133–7, for accounts of early Soviet tractors. 20,000 Fords were imported during 1926–7, and by 1927 85 per cent of tractors and trucks in Russia were made by Fords in Detroit.
96. Ibid., p. 123.
97. Ibid., p. 16.
98. Littlejohn (1973).
99. Narkiewicz (1969), pp. 235–6.
100. Ibid., pp. 237–8.
101. Lewis (1975). These criticisms, and the ones above of *Russian Peasants and Soviet Power*, should not be construed as denying the great value and merit of Lewin's work.
102. Bukharin (1925a).
103. Bukharin (1925b), pp. 61–3.
104. Bukharin (1925c), p. 608. See also Miller (1975).

## 10 Conclusion

1. Plekhanov's views on Bernstein were outlined in a number of articles; 'Bernstein and Materialism' (1898); 'What Should We thank him for?' (1898); 'Cant against Kant, or Herr Bernstein's Will and Testament' (1901). *Neue Zeit* refused to publish this last contribution; it is an extremely abusive and professorial tirade which asserts that to ask Bernstein to return to his school books would be to overestimate his intellectual capacity (1976), pp. 343–5).
2. Colletti (1972).
3. The book has been reprinted since of course, but under the altered status of a 'classic of Marxism'; however it was unavailable in German from the early 1900s until 1966.
4. Varga (1924a).
5. Miljutin (1924), Varga (1924b).
6. For an example of this, see Duggett (1975).
7. A schematic outline of this position can be found in Ennew, Hirst and Tribe (1977).
8. For a review of English rural life at this time, see Bennett (1914); and also Collings (1906) for the Radical Liberal programme of reform. A general account of this period can be found in Douglas (1976). A number of academic studies of the English agrarian problem appeared at this time, among them Gonner (1912), Johnson (1909), and the Hammonds (1911). For a critique of the attempts to restore the rural or urban labourer to the land, see Orwin and Darke (1935).
9. Bukharin (1925d).
10. See Loomis and Beegle (1946), Farquharson (1976), and Tilton (1975).
11. The sociological nature of the problems posed by the question of articulation can be seen at work in a review of a number of recent writings by Foster-Carter (1978).
12. See for instance Banaji (1976a).
13. See Patnaik *et al.* (1978).
14. Banaji (1976b).
15. Tribe (1977).
16. Marx and Engels, *Werke* xxi, 338–9.
17. *Capital* vol. I.
18. See Richards (1973), chs. 12 and 13.
19. Roth (1963): his account of the SPD perhaps approaches this.
20. For the 'class' and 'state' analysis of the Tanzanian economy, see Shivji (1975) and von Freyhold (1977). Accounts of Ujamaa can be found in Boesen (1976) and Boesen, Madsen and Moody (1977). A sometimes graphic account of villagisation can be found in Mmapachu (1976), especially the description of the encouragement offered by government personnel in burning the old villages. More recently the papers by Raikes (1978) and Coulson (1978) have broken away from the dominance of 'statist' analysis, the latter having a useful and extensive bibliography. See also Raikes (forthcoming).

# Bibliography to Part 2

Abramsky, C. and Williams, B. J. (eds), *Essays in Honour of E. H. Carr* (London: Macmillan, 1974).
Anderson, P., *Considerations on Western Marxism* (London: NLB, 1976).
Althusser, L. and Balibar, E., *Reading Capital* (London: NLB, 1970).
Antsiferov, A. N., et al., *Russian Agriculture during the War* (New Haven: Yale University Press, 1930).
Atkinson, D., 'The Statistics on the Russian Land Commune, 1905-1917'. *Slavic Review*, vol. xxxiii (1973) pp. 773-87.
Banaji, J., 'Chayanov, Kautsky, Lenin: Considerations Towards a Synthesis', *Economic and Political Weekly*, vol. xi, no. 40 (1976 [a]) pp. 1594-1607.
——, 'Summary of Selected Parts of Kautsky's *The Agrarian Question*', *Economy and Society*, vol. v (1976[b]) pp. 2-49.
Baron, S. H., *Plekhanov* (London: Routledge and Kegan Paul, 1963).
——, 'Plekhanov and the Origins of Russian Marxism', in A. Simirenko (ed.) *Soviet Sociology* (London: Routledge and Kegan Paul, 1967) pp. 56-68.
Becker, J. P. et al., *Manifeste aux travailleurs des campagnes* (Geneva: Propaganda Committee of German Section of International Workers Association, 1870).
Bennett, E. N., *Problems of Village Life* (London: Williams and Norgate, 1914).
Bettelheim, C., *Les luttes de classes en URSS. 1ère période 1917-1923* (Paris: Seuil/Maspero, 1974).
——, *Les luttes de classes en URSS. 2ème periode 1923-1930* (Paris: Seuil/Maspero, 1977).
Blackstock, P. W. and Hoselitz, B. F., *The Russian Menace to Europe* (London: George Allen and Unwin, 1953).
Blum, J., *Lord and Peasant in Russia from the Ninth to the Nineteenth Century* (Princeton: Princeton University Press, 1961).
Boesen, J., 'Tanzania: From Ujamaa to Villagisation', Institute for Development Research, Copenhagen Papers A. 76.7 (1976).
Boesen, J., Madsen, B. S. and Moody, T. *Ujamaa – Socialism from above* (Uppsala: Scandinavian Institute of African Studies, 1977).
Brutzkus, B., *Agrarentwicklung und Agrarrevolution in Russland* (Berlin: Verlag Hermann Sack, 1925).
Bukharin, N., 'A New Revelation as to Soviet Economics, or How the Workers' and Peasants' Bloc can be Destroyed', *International Press Correspondence*, vol. v, no. 6 (20 Jan. 1925[a]) pp. 39-48.
——, *Le chemin du socialisme et le bloc ouvrier-paysan* (Paris: Libraire de l'Humanité, 1925[b]).
——, 'Speech of Comrade Bukharin in the Discussion on the New Economic Policy in the Village', *International Press Correspondence*, vol. v, no. 46 (30 May 1925[c]) pp. 608-10.

——, *La question paysanne*, (Paris: Libraire de l'Humanité, 1925[d]).
——, 'Before the Eleventh Anniversary of the October Revolution', *International Press Correspondence*, vol. VIII, nos. 73, 75, 77 (19 Oct., 26 Oct. and 2 Nov. 1928) pp. 1327–9, 1377–80, 1434–7.
Carr, E. H., *The Bolshevik Revolution 1917–1923*, vol. II (London: Macmillan, 1952).
——, *Socialism in One Country 1924–1926*, vol. I (London: Macmillan, 1958).
——, *Socialism in One Country 1924–1926*, vol. II (London: Macmillan, 1959).
Chayanov, A. V., *The Theory of Peasant Economy* (Homewood, Ill.: R. D. Irwin, 1966).
Clarke, R. A., *Soviet Economic Facts 1917–1970* (London: Macmillan, 1972).
Colletti, L., 'Bernstein and the Marxism of the Second International', in *From Rousseau to Lenin* (London: NLB, 1972) pp. 45–108.
Collings, J., *Land Reform. Occupying Ownership, Peasant Proprietory and Rural Education* (London: Longmans, Green and Co., 1906).
Confino, M., *Systèmes agraires et progrès agricoles* (Paris: Mouton, 1969).
Coulson, A., 'Agricultural Policies in Mainland Tanzania', *Review of African Political Economy*, no. 10 (1978) pp. 74–100.
van Crefeld, M., *Supplying War* (London: Cambridge University Press, 1977).
de Crisenoy, C., *Lénine face aux moujiks* (Paris: Editions du Seuil, 1978).
Crisp, O., *Studies in the Russian Economy before 1914* (London: Macmillan, 1976).
Davies, R. W., 'A Note on Grain Statistics', *Soviet Studies*, vol. XXI (1970) pp. 314–29.
von Dietze, C., *Stolypinische Agrarreform und Feldgemeinschaft* (Leipzig: Osteuropa Institut in Breslau, 1920).
Dobb, M. H., *Soviet Economic Development since 1917*, 6th ed. (London: Routledge and Kegan Paul, 1966).
——, 'The Discussion of the Twenties on Planning and Economic Growth', in *Papers on Capitalism, Development and Planning* (London: Routledge and Kegan Paul, 1967) pp. 126–39.
Douglas, R., *Land, People and Politics* (London: Allison and Busby, 1976).
Dubrowski, S., *Die Bauernbewegung in der russischen Revolution 1917* (Berlin: Paul Parey, 1929).
Duggett, M., 'Marx on Peasants', *Journal of Peasant Studies*, vol. II (1975) pp. 159–82.
Ellman, M., 'Did the Agricultural Surplus Provide the Resources for the Increase in Investment in the USSR during the First Five Year Plan?', *Economic Journal*, vol. LIIIV (1975) pp. 844–64.
Elwood, R. C. (ed.), *Resolutions and Decisions of the Communist Party of the Soviet Union*, vol. I: *The Russian Social Democratic Labour Party 1898–October 1917* (Toronto: University of Toronto Press, 1974).
Ely, R. T., 'Russian Land Reform', *American Economic Review*, vol. VI (1916) pp. 61–8.
Emmons, T., *The Russian Landed Gentry and the Peasant Emancipation of 1861* (London: Cambridge University Press, 1968[a]).
——, 'The Peasant and the Emancipation', in W. S. Vucinich (ed.), *The Peasant in Nineteenth Century Russia* (Stanford: Stanford University Press, 1968[b]) pp. 41–71.

Ennew, J., Hirst, P. Q. and Tribe, K., '"Peasantry" as an Economic Category', *Journal of Peasant Studies*, vol. IV (1977) pp. 295–322.

Farquharson, J. E., *The Plough and the Swastika* (London: Sage Publications, 1976).

Foster-Carter, A. (1978) 'The Modes of Production Controversy', *New Left Review*, no. 107 (1978) pp. 47–77.

Frankel, (ed.), *Vladimir Akimov on the Dilemmas of Russian Marxism 1895–1903* (London: Cambridge University Press, 1969).

von Freyhold, M., 'The Post-Colonial State and its Tanzanian Version', *Review of African Political Economy*, no. 8 (1977).

George, H., *Progress and Poverty* (condensed version) (London: Hogarth Press, 1953).

Gerschenkron, A., 'Economic Backwardness in Historical Perspective', in *Economic Backwardness in Historical Perspective* (Cambridge Mass.: Harvard University Press, 1962[a]) pp. 5–30.

——, Economic Development in Russian Intellectual History of the Nineteenth Century', in *Economic Development in Historical Perspective* (1962[b]) pp. 152–87.

——, 'Agrarian Policies and Industrialisation, Russia, 1861–1914', in H. J. Habakkuk and M. Postan (eds), *Cambridge Economic History of Europe*, vol. VI (London: Cambridge University Press, 1965) pp. 706–800.

Gonner, E. C. K., *Common Land and Inclosure* (London: Frank Cass, 1966).

Grosskopf, S., *L'alliance ouvrière et paysanne en URSS (1921–1928)* (Paris: Maspero, 1976).

Haimson, L. H., *The Russian Marxists and the Origins of Marxism* (Cambridge Mass.: Harvard University Press, 1955).

Hammonds, B. and J. L., *The Village Labourer 1760–1832* (London: Longmans, Green and Co., 1911).

Harding, N., *Lenin's Political Thought*, vol. I (London: Macmillan, 1977).

Hindess, B. and Hirst, P. Q., *Pre-Capitalist Modes of Production* (London: Routledge and Kegan Paul, 1975).

Johnson, A. H., *The Disappearance of the Small Landowner* (London: Oxford University Press, 1963).

Karcz, J., 'Thoughts on the Grain Problem', *Soviet Studies*, vol. XVIII (1967) pp. 399–434.

——, 'Back on the Grain Front', *Soviet Studies*, vol. XXII (1970) pp. 262–94.

——, 'From Stalin to Brezhnev: Soviet Agricultural Policy in Historical perspective', in J. R. Millar (ed.) *The Soviet Rural Community* (Urbana: University of Illinois Press, 1971).

Kautsky, K., *Die Agrarfrage* (Stuttgart: Dietz, 1899) French ed. (1900) rep. (Paris: Maspero, 1970).

Keep, J. L. H., *The Russian Revolution* (London: Weidenfeld and Nicolson, 1976).

Kimball, A., 'The First International and the Russian *Obschina*', *Slavic Review*, vol. XXXII (1973) pp. 491–514.

Krause, H., *Marx und Engels und das zeitgenössische Rußland* (Gießen: Kommissionsverlag Wilhelm Schmitz, 1958).

Kritsman, L. N., *Die heroische Periode der grossen russischen Revolution* (Frankfurt: Verlag Neue Kritik, 1971).

Krzizanovskij, G. M., 'Die Elektrifizierung als Voraussetzung einer Vergesellschaftung der Produktion', *Russische Korrespondenz* (1920) pp. 1200–3.
Lampert, E., *Sons Against Fathers* (London: Oxford University Press, 1965).
Lenin, V. I., *Collected Works*, 45 vols (Moscow, 1960–71).
Levine, N., 'Dialectical Materialism and the *Mir*', in D. McQuarie (ed.) *Marx: Sociology/Social Change/Capitalism* (London: Quartet, 1978) pp. 162–78.
Lewin, M., 'Who was the Soviet Kulak?' *Soviet Studies*, vol. xviii (1966) pp. 189–212.
——, *Russian Peasants and Soviet Power* (London: George Allen and Unwin, 1968).
——, *Political Undercurrents in Soviet Economic Debates* (London: Pluto Press, 1975).
Linhart, R., *Lénine, les paysans, Taylor* (Paris: Editions du Seuil, 1976).
Littlejohn, G., 'The Peasantry and the Russian Revolution', *Economy and Society*, vol. ii (1973) pp. 112–25.
Loizou, M., *The Development of the Agrarian Programme of the Russian Social Democratic Labour Party: 1900–1907* (University of Birmingham: Unpub. M.Soc.Sci. dissertation, 1976).
Loomis, C. P. and Beegle, J. A., 'The Spread of German Nazism in Rural Areas', *American Sociological Review*, vol. xi (1946) pp. 724–34.
Lyaschenko, P. I., *History of the National Economy of Russia to the 1917 Revolution* (New York: Octagon Books, 1970).
Male, D. J., *Russian Peasant Organisation before Collectivisation* (London: Cambridge University Press, 1971).
Marx, K., *Capital*, 3 vols (Moscow: Progress Publishers, 1954–9).
Marx and Engels, *Selected Works*, 3 vols (Moscow: Progress Publishers, 1970).
—— *Collected Works* (Moscow: Progress Publishers, 1970).
—— *Werke*, 39 vols (Berlin: Dietz Verlag, 1969).
Maslov, P., *Die Agrarfrage in Rußland* (Stuttgart: Dietz Verlag, 1907).
Mendel, A. P., *Dilemmas of Progress in Tsarist Russia: Legal Populism and Legal Marxism*, (Cambridge, Mass.: Harvard University Press, 1961).
Meyer, G., *Studien zur sozialökonomischen Entwicklung Sowjetrußlands 1921–1923* (Cologne: Pahl-Rugenstein Verlag, 1974).
Miljutin, W., 'Agrarrevisionismus', *Internationale Press Korrespondenz*, Jg. 4, Nr 159 (9 Dec. 1924), pp. 2179–81.
Millar, J. R., 'Soviet Rapid Development and the Agricultural Surplus Hypothesis', *Soviet Studies*, vol. xxii (1970) pp. 79–93.
——, 'Mass Collectivisation and the Contribution of Soviet Agriculture to the First Five-Year Plan', *Slavic Review*, vol. xxxiii (1974) pp. 750–66.
——, 'A Note on Primitive Accumulation in Marx and Preobrazhensky', *Soviet Studies*, vol. xxx (1978) pp. 384–93.
—— and Guntzel, C., 'The Economics and Politics of Mass Collectivisation Reconsidered: A Review Article', *Explorations in Economic History*, vol. viii (1970) pp. 103–16.
Miller, R. F., 'Soviet Agricultural Policy in the Twenties: The Failure of Cooperation', *Soviet Studies*, vol. xxvii (1975) pp. 220–44.
Mitrany, D., *Marx against the Peasant* (London: Weidenfeld and Nicolson, (1951).

Mmapachu, J. V., 'Operation Planned Villages in Rural Tanzania: A Revolutionary Strategy for Development', *Africa Review*, vol. VI (1976) pp. 1–16.
Mosse, W. E., 'Stolypin's Villages', *Slavonic and East European Review*, vol. XLIII (1964) pp. 257–74.
Narkiewicz, O. A., 'Soviet Administration and the Grain Crisis of 1927–28', *Soviet Studies* vol. XX (1969) pp. 235–41.
——, *The Making of the Soviet State Apparatus* (Manchester: Manchester University Press, 1970).
Nicolai-on, *Die Volkswirtschaft in Rußland nach der Bauern-Emancipation* (Munich: Verlag von Hermann Lukaschik, 1899).
Oganowsky, N. P., 'Die Agrarfrage in Rußland seit 1905', *Archiv für Sozialwissenschaft und Sozialpolitik,* Band 37 (1913) pp. 701–57.
Orwin, C. S. and Darke, W. F., *Back to the Land* (London: P. S. King and Son, 1935).
——, and Whetham, E. H., *History of British Agriculture 1846–1914*, 2nd ed. (Newton Abbot: David and Charles, 1971).
Owen, L. A., *The Russian Peasant Movement, 1906–1917* (New York: Russell and Russell, 1963).
Patnaik, H et al, *Studies in the development of Capitalism in India* (Lahore, Pakistan: Vanguard Publishers, 1978).
Pavlovsky, G., *Agricultural Russia on the Eve of Revolution* (London: George Routledge and Sons, 1930).
Perrie, M., 'The Social Composition and Structure of the Socialist-Revolutionary Party before 1917', *Soviet Studies*, vol. XXIV (1972) pp. 223–50.
——, *The Agrarian Policy of the Russian Socialist Revolutionary Party* (London: Cambridge University Press, 1976).
Pipes, R., 'Narodnichestvo: A Semantic Inquiry', *Slavic Review*, vol. XXIII (1964) pp. 441–58.
Plekhanov, G., *Selected Philosophical Works*, vol. I (Moscow: Progress Publishers, 1961).
——, *Selected Philosophical Works* vol. I 2nd rev. ed. (Moscow: Progress Publishers, 1976).
Preyer, W. D., *Die Russische Agrarreform* (Jena: Verlag von Gustav Fischer, 1914).
Preobrazhensky, E., *The New Economics* (London: Oxford University Press, 1965).
Raikes, P., 'Rural Differentiation and Class Formation in Tanzania', *Journal of Peasant Studies*, vol. V (1978) pp. 285–325.
——, *The State and Agriculture in Tanzania* (Hassocks: Harvester Press, forthcoming).
Resis, A., '*Das Kapital* Comes to Russia', *Slavic Review*, vol. XXIX (1970) pp. 219–37.
Richards, E., *The Leviathan of Wealth* (London: Routledge and Kegan Paul, 1973).
Robinson, G. T., *Rural Russia under the Old Regime* (New York: Macmillan, 1949).
Roth, G., *The Social Democrats in Imperial Germany* (Totowa (N.J.): Bedminster Press, 1963).
Shanin, T., *The Awkward Class* (London: Oxford University Press, 1972).

Shivji, I., *Class Struggles in Tanzania* (London: Heinemann, 1976).
Simms, J. Y., 'The Crisis in Russian Agriculture at the End of the Nineteenth Century: A Different View', *Slavic Review*, vol. XXXVI (1977) pp. 377–98.
Solomon, S. G., *The Soviet Agrarian Debate – A Controversy in Social Science, 1923–1929* (Boulder, Colorado: Westview Press, 1977).
Sorlin, P., 'Lénine et le problème paysan en 1917', *Annales*, vol. XIX (1964) pp. 250–80.
Spulber, N. (ed.), *Foundations of Soviet Strategy for Economic Growth* (Bloomington: Indiana University Press, 1964).
Stalin, J. V., 'Industrialisation and the Grain Problem', *Works*, vol. XI, pp. 165–96 (Moscow: 1928).
Starr, S. F. (1962) 'Introduction' to A. von Haxthausen, *Studies on the Interior of Russia* (Chicago: University of Chicago Press, 1962) pp. vii–xlii.
von Struve, P., Review of Nicolai-on, Russian ed. (1893) of (1899) above, *Archiv für soziale Gesetzgebung und Statistik*, Band 7 (1894) pp. 350–58.
Sutton, A. C., *Western Technology and Soviet Economic Development 1917–1930* (Stanford: Hoover Institute on War, Revolution and Peace, 1968).
Tilton, T. A., *Nazism, Neo-Nazism, and the Peasantry* (Bloomington: Indiana University Press, 1975).
Treadgold, D., 'Was Stolypin in Favour of Kulaks?', *Slavic Review*, vol. XIV (1955) pp. 1–14.
——, *The Great Siberian Migration* (Princeton: Princeton University Press, 1957).
Tribe, K., 'Economic Property and the Theorisation of Ground Rent', *Economy and Society*, vol. VI (1977) pp. 69–88.
—— 'Introduction to de Crisenoy', *Economy and Society*, vol. VIII (1979) pp. 1–8.
Varga, E., *Beiträge zur Agrarfrage* (Hamburg: Verlag Carl Hoym, 1924[a]).
——, 'Vorläufige Antwort an dem Genossen Miljutin', *Internationale Press Korrespondenz*, Jg. 4, Nr 169 (30 Dec. 1924[b]) pp. 2327–30.
Venturi, F. *Roots of Revolution* (New York: Grosset and Dunlap, 1966).
Walicki, A., *The Controversy over Capitalism* (London: Oxford University Press, 1969).
Wieth-Knudsen, K. A., *Bauernfragen und Agrarreform in Rußland* (Leipzig: Duncker und Humblot, 1913).
Wildman, A. K., *The Making of a Worker's Revolution* (Chicago: University of Chicago Press, 1967).
Wortman, R., *The Crisis of Russian Populism* (London: Cambridge University Press, 1967).
Yaney, G. L., 'The Concept of the Stolypin Land Reform', *Slavic Review*, vol. XXIII (1964) pp. 275–93.

# Index

Agricultural conditions, pre-1914 243–5; 1914–17 245–7
Agriculture, Danish 22–3, 25–6, 140(n)
European 24–5, 27
German 21ff., 60ff.
Agronomy 14, 23, 49–50, 116, 200
Althusser, L. 291
Anti-Socialist Law 4–5, 7

Bakunin, M. 12, 183
Banaji, J. 300
Barsov, A. A. 270–1, 273–4
Bebel, A. 3, 78, 82, 93, 100
Becker, J. P. 172
Bernstein, E. 4–5, 8, 19, 80–3, 105, 107, 290–292
Bettelheim, C. 272
Bismarck 3–4
Blanquism 177, 305(n)
Bohm-Bawerk, E. 203
von Bortkiewicz, L. 204
Bukharin, N. 269, 285, 297
Bulgakov, S. 204
Bund der Landwirte 20–1, 30, 34–40, 51, 58, 71, 74, 92, 98, 135–6

Capitalism, American road of development 199, 231
form of development in Russia 173–5, 183–5, 191–2, 194, 199, 226
Junker road of development 194, 199, 226, 231–2
organisation in rural areas 193ff., 201
tendencies of 80–2, 84f., 103–13 passim, 138, 189, 197

Capitalist agriculture 47, 49, 52, 69–70, 106f.
and market relations 115ff.
Carr, E. H. 208, 254, 270, 272–3
Centre Party 21, 30, 35, 58, 75, 83, 92, 95, 101, 140
Chayanov, A. V. 68
Chernov, V. 218, 220–22, 248
Chernyshevsky, N. G. 171, 183
Clausewitz 90
Civil War 257–8, 280
Collectivisation 235, 237, 268–71, 281–3
Commune, as peasant institution 162–3, 171–2, 175–9, 183–6, 218–9, 224, 238, 240, 254, 255–6, 267, 282–3
Engelhardt's 175–9
Conservative Party 37, 58, 75, 92, 100
Constituent Assembly 253
Cooperatives, discussion of 8–9, 119, 139(n.17), 145(n.25)
Crimean War 158
de Crisenoy, C. 201
Crisp, O. 160, 167
Cut-off lands, problem of 214–17, 225–7, 230

Danielson, see under Nicolai-on
David, E. 85, 102, 105, 112–13, 122, 201, 290, 292, 295
Davies, R. W. 273
Decree on Land, 1918 253
Democracy, parliamentary 2–3, 31
von Dietze, C. 244
Distribution of stock and implements among peasantry 254–5, 269–70, 282

320

# INDEX

Dobb, M. H. 259, 270

East Elbia 32, 40, 52ff., 65–6, 75, 90
Electrification, as programme of socialist construction 262, 276–7
Emancipation of Labour Group 178, 180, 183, 208
Programme 209ff.
Emancipation Settlement 158, 161–4, 197–9, 209, 215, 221
Emigration, *see under* Rural labour, migration
Engels, F. 4, 8, 16, 39, 76, 92
*Peasant Question in France and Germany* 1, 10, 17–18, 26–7, 68, 98
Erfurt Programme of SPD 4, 6–7, 72, 74, 77ff., 93, 110, 212, 293, and agrarian commission 86, 97ff., 130–1
Ernst, P. 292
Evolutionism 78–9, 110ff.

Famine of 1921 265–7
Farms, distribution by size 61ff.
family labour 68, 121
large 108
medium 25, 26f.
small 21, 25, 27, 62ff.
disappearance of 27, 121
size of 13, 60ff., 85–102 passim, 119ff., 188
Feudal production 115–16, 137
Feudalisation 36, 47–8
Fideikomiss 65–6, 127–8
First International 2, 12–13, 15–16, 139(n.13)
Free Trade, Marx on 38–9
French Revolution, and agrarian conditions 46–51
Fiscal system, and rural economy 165, 263, 275–6

German Social Democracy 196–7, 203
Gerschenkron, A. 32, 136, 165
von der Goltz, T. 25

Gotha Programme 3, 8, 72
Guesdistes *see under* Parti Ouvrier Français

Handicraft production 157, 184, 200–01
von Haxthausen, A. 171
Herzen, A. 171

Industrial production, German 53
Internal settlement and colonisation 243–4

Junkers, estate organisation 23, 25, 35, 41–45, 52–3, 54ff., 142(n.51) and politics 34–7

Karcz, J. 273–4
Kautsky, K. 192, 201–03, 288–9, 291
*Agrarfrage* viii–ix, 1, 9, 24, 27–8, 59, 89, 94, 103ff.
analysis of rural conditions 52ff., 62–71, 98–100
and SPD 8, 10, 17, 79, 82
and revisionism 86
Korsch, K. 79
Kritsman, L. N. 260, 278
Kronstadt rising 256, 263

Labour theory of value 203–04
Land, distribution between classes 198
Land municipalisation, as political objective 208, 229–30
Land nationalisation 10, 13–16, 59, 130, 139(n.21)
as political objective 208, 225–6, 251
and peasant seizure 252
Land reform 41–49
Land tenure, and mortgage 59, 95, 118–19
Landlords, and estate economy 197–9
Lassalle, F. 3, 6, 8–9, 11
Lehmann, H. G. 78

Lenin, V. I.  182, 211, 257, 262, 264, 280
  *Agrarian Programme of Social-Democracy*  208, 230f., 288
  agrarian writings  viii, 67, 69, 108–110
  critique of Liberal agrarian reform proposals  228
  critique of SRs  222–3, 224–5
  *Development of Capitalism in Russia*  viii, ix, 1, 40, 48, 102, 104, 125, 154, 186–7, 192ff., 226, 231, 288, 293–4
  comparison with *Agrarfrage*  203–4
  drafting of agrarian programme  211ff.
  and forms of political calculation  217, 234
  as representing Bolshevism  154
Lewin, M.  270, 273, 285
Liebknecht, W.  3, 78, 100
List, F.  29
Lukacs, G.  79
Luxemburg, R.  79–80, 82, 86, 114–15, 291
Lyaschenko, P. I.  159

Mao-Tse Tung  74
Market relations in agriculture  237, 256, 267
Martynov, A.  217
Marx, K.  3–4, 6, 8, 12–15, 38, 81, 86, 105, 108, 132, 135,
  *Capital*  172, 175–6, 192, 201–03, 211, 271, 289, 295–6, 300–02, 306(n.6)
  and Engels, on Russia  154, 169, 173, 176–180, 181, 205, 306–07
Marxism, Legal  186
Marxism, Russian  154, 171–2, 179–80, 205
Maslov, P.  167, 215, 217, 227
Matthias, E.  78
Menshevism and Mensheviks  180, 206, 227, 233
Meyer, G.  261
Mikhailovsky, N. K.  173

Mitrany, D.  viii, 13, 18, 211, 296

Narkiewicz, O.  284
Narodism and Narodniks  154, 182, 186–7, 191ff., 212, 220; *see also under* Populism
National Liberal Party  75, 83, 100
Natural economy  193–4, 197, 201
  as form of self-sufficiency  114–15
  Proletarian  259–63
NEP, agrarian policy  195, 235, 237, 256ff., 268f.
  class alliance as basis of  264, 268, 277
Nicolai-on  168–9, 173, 186

Octobrists  231
Owen, L. A.  242

Parti Ouvrier Français (Guesdistes)  1, 9, 16
Parvus  60
Peasantry, and economic development in Russia  157
  labour services and associated obligations  42–3, 46–7, 55ff.
  and land reform  41–2; *see also under* Land tenure, reform
  land tenure and Stolypin reform  241–2
  middle  21, 35, 37, 52, 89, 195–6, 277–8
  in 1905  223ff., 238
  in 1917  247ff.
  poor  224, 255, 277
  as pre-capitalist form  298ff.
  proletarianism, and differentiation  35. 42, 61, 66, 69–70, 107–109, 146–7
  rich  195–6, 216, 224, 240, 255–6, 269–70
  'kulak strike' of 1925  274ff.
  size of holding in later nineteenth century  163–4
  small  35, 37, 52, 89, 108, 125
  SR analysis  220–1
Peasants' Land Bank  164, 239–40

Plekhanov, G. 177, 180ff., 191, 205, 212, 214, 226, 229–30, 291
Political party, as socialist organisation 6, 10, 12
Population growth 166
Populism, Russian 172ff., 186, 218
Preobrazhensky, E. 269, 271, 275, 285, 299
Preyer, W. D. 242
Property, communal 14, 16, 95, 100
  peasant 10, 13, 16, 42–3, 94
  private 13–14, 16
Protectionism, socialist response to 38–9
Proudhon, P. J. 10–11
Provisional Government, agrarian policy 247–8
Prussia, constitutional structure 73f.

Railway network, role in economy 168–9, 246, 261, 280, 305–06
Rent, absolute and differential 14, 117–18
  Marx's theory of agricultural 204, 300
Revisionism 6, 18, 19, 74, 95, 102, 107, 111, 288, 290
Robinson, G. T. 163, 165
RSDLP
  Second Congress (1903) 206, 217
  Unity Congress (1906) 224, 227, 229
Rural indebtedness 58ff., 160–1
Rural labour 44–5, 68–70, 88ff.
  ban on hiring 253
  conditions 54ff., 74
  migration and emigration 45, 51–3, 55ff., 74, 122–3, 167
  Polish 52–3, 58
  services and obligations 198
  use of wage labour 166, 184, 190, 195–6, 198
Russian agriculture in nineteenth century 159

Saxony, constitutional structure 73
Schaeffle, 76
Schönlank, B. 96
Schulze-Delitsch 9
Second International 2, 79
Serfs, private and state 160
Shanin, T. 282, 296
Socialist agriculture, problem of transition to 113, 137
Socialist Revolutionary Party 187, 207, 217–19, 254
  agitational work 209–10
  proposals on land in 1917 252–4
  relation to the Bolsheviks 251
Sombart, W. 85, 292
SPD, attitude to Federal and state budgets 83
  Bavarian 83–4, 94, 134
  congresses
    Halle (1892) 72–4, 78, 87
    Cologne (1893) 83, 91–3
    Frankfurt (1894) 76, 95–7
    Breslau (1895) 86, 98–101, 103, 134
    Hamburg (1897) 83
    Mainz (1900) 83
    Lubeck, (1901) 83
    Jena (1905) 79
    Mannheim (1906) 79
  debate on General Strike 79
  insurrectionism and illegality 4–5, 8, 10–12
  as mass party 3–5, 72ff., 131
  in German political structure 73
  proposal of class alliance 84
  structure of electoral support 75, 82, 87, 92, 95, 101
Stalin, J. V. 237, 273, 282
State collection of grain 257ff., 274–6
State price regulation 246
State socialism 9–10, 57
Steinberg, H. 78
Stolypin Reform 231, 236, 238ff.
  progress of reform 240–3
  uneven impact 242–3
Struve, P. 159, 175, 194, 211

Tanzanian rural development 303

Tariffs 29ff., 60
  Caprivi treaties 33, 38, 53
  Kanitz motion 35, 51
  SPD attitude to 38–40
Tax in kind 263–4
Thaer, A. 49–50
Tkachev 178, 183
Trade in grains, consumption, exports 22, 245, 279–81
  international competition 20, 74
  price structure 23–4, 32, 51, 60, 140(n.), 164
  private 260
  transport 21–2
Trudoviks 231
Turkestan 244

Varga, E. 295
von Vollmar, G. 6, 76, 93–7, 290
Vorontsov, V. 173–7, 183–4, 186

Wagner, A. 10
War Communism 237, 255–7, 259–60
Weber, M. 36, 47, 51–2, 55ff.
Witte 166, 238
Wolfe, B. 239

Yields, grain 244

Zasulich, V. 177
Zemstva 248

The manufacturer's authorised representative in the EU is Springer
Nature Customer Service Centre GmbH, Europaplatz 3, 69115 Heidelberg,
Germany. If you have any concerns regarding our products, please
contact ProductSafety@springernature.com

Printed and bound by CPI Group (UK) Ltd, Croydon, CR0 4YY
23/03/2026
02076458-0017